Financial Management

6th Edition

Raymond Brockington, BCom, MSc(Econ), FCA

Lecturer in Finance and Accounting, University of Bath

DP Publications
Aldine Place
London W12 8AW

1993

Acknowledgements

The author wishes to record his thanks to the following professional bodies for their permission to use questions selected from their past examination papers:

Chartered Association of Certified Accountants

Chartered Institute of Management Accountants

ISBN 1 85805 025 1

First Edition 1978
Second Edition 1981
Third Edition 1983
Reprinted with corrections 1984
Fourth Edition 1987
Fifth Edition 1990
Sixth Edition 1993
Reprinted 1994
Reprinted 1996

Typeset by DP Publications

Printed in Great Britain by Progressive Printing (UK) Ltd.
Leigh-on-Sea, Essex

Preface

If you have bought, or are thinking of buying this book you will want to know what you can expect it to do for you and how you ought best to use it.

It is intended for students who are preparing to take an examination in Financial Management at final professional level and it will provide them with the knowledge and the skill in applying it which they will need to pass. If you aspire to excel, perhaps even to win a place or a prize, you cannot expect to rely on one book alone. The highest marks are given to those candidates who display evidence of the widest reading absorbed by a critical mind, a combination, that is, of extensive information and of a highly intelligent appraisal of it. No single book can provide either of these things. What it can do, however, is to provide an adequate amount of information and acceptable competence in handling it.

It should be stressed that this book is written to teach you and not merely to tell you. To benefit from its design you need to know how to use it. The subject is treated under broad topics which form the basis of the twenty-three chapters. Every chapter is broken down into sections and numbered paragraphs each of which gives some vital segment of knowledge. This is to aid note taking and stage-by-stage understanding. The first paragraph generally 'sets the scene' explaining the place of that topic in the context of the subject as a whole. At the end of the chapter is a brief summary of what it has said. This is followed by a set of review questions which enable a student to test his understanding of what has been read. These should be regarded as triggers to thought about the subject and detailed written answers should not be attempted. The exercises which follow the review questions require a more rigorous application of the knowledge acquired. Here it will be helpful to draft a full answer and then to compare it with the detailed solution and explanation which appears in Appendix 1. Many of the exercises seek to extend knowledge by requiring the application of principles to unfamiliar situations. The answers provided go beyond what the average student will produce for himself and so a careful reading of them will be valuable.

In the examination a student must be prepared to meet questions which draw on a number of areas of knowledge. It will not, therefore, necessarily be possible to identify an examination question with a specific chapter in this book. To give practice in answering these questions, a representative selection of them, drawn from actual past papers, is reproduced in Appendix 2. Detailed suggested solutions appear in Appendix 3. A feature of these solutions is that each is prefaced by an Analysis setting out the author's preliminary thoughts on the question and thus guiding the student on how to sort out his ideas before commencing work. Appendix 4 contains further past examination questions without answers which may be used as additional practice or set by the teacher as course work assignments.

For those using this book as their main teacher for the examination, the following procedure is recommended.

(a) Read the chapters in the order given.

(b) Read each chapter carefully, making notes on the main points and ensuring that these and the numerical examples illustrating them are fully understood. Reread until this is so.

(c) Test your understanding by answering the Review Questions which appear at the end of each chapter.

(d) When you are satisfied that the contents of a chapter have been mastered work the Exercises, preferably under examination conditions.

(e) Compare your answers with the ones in Appendix 1. Note carefully any points given there which you missed – you are bound to miss some – and be sure you understand clearly the reason for any error.

(f) After reading the whole book gain examination practice by working the questions in Appendix 2 under examination conditions.

(g) Mark your work by reference to the solutions in Appendix 3 and revise where weaknesses are revealed.

I should like to end this Preface by recording my thanks to Dick Chapman of DP Publications Limited for his painstaking editorial guidance through five editions of this book and to the reviewers whose helpful comments have led to many important improvements. I am also grateful to readers who have written to me pointing out minor ambiguities and errors which I have been able to put right for the new edition.

Note to the sixth edition

I have been greatly assisted in the preparation of the sixth edition by comments made by those using the book, in particular those lecturers who are closely in touch with current syllabus requirements and the needs of the student working for examinations. I am pleased that so many continue to find the book of value and appreciate the kind comments made. For the current edition I have replaced the chapter on statements of source and application of funds which has been made obsolete by the withdrawal of SSAP 10. It has been replaced by a chapter on cash flow statements. Chapter 23 on the international dimension to financial management has been completely rewritten and takes a broader view of the issues involved in this area than did its predecessor.

Lecturers' Supplement

A lecturers' supplement is available free of charge to lecturers recommending the book as a course text, on application to the publishers on college headed paper. The supplement contains suggested solutions to test exercises and examination questions in the book.

Contents

1: Introduction

1.1 The Function of the Financial Manager

1.1.1 The function of a financial manager is to manage finance. This apparent statement of the obvious begs, in fact, a lot of questions which we ought to consider before we begin our study of the set of theoretical constructs and techniques which make up the subject known as financial management.

1.1.2 First of all we should note that the financial manager is one member of an overall management team. His/her activity is not an individual one but is a contribution to the total management effort and must, therefore, be co-ordinated properly with other contributions.

Management has the implied function of planning and control. It must set up an objective and plan how this may be achieved. It must control the resources used and the situation in which they operate so as to implement its plan. In designing the techniques of financial management certain objectives are frequently assumed but it must not be forgotten that a technique cannot determine an objective and if the objective changes then different techniques may become appropriate.

1.1.3 An analogy may make this point clear. Both trout farming and river fishing for sport have superficially the objective of producing food. In the former case, however, the objective is the maximum value of food at the minimum cost. In the latter case recreation, through the development and use of a skill, is the primary objective. The techniques used are very clearly dependent on these objectives. A trout farmer would no more harvest his crop with a rod and line than would an angler take the catch with a trawl net!

1.2 Management Objectives

1.2.1 The most commonly presumed objective of management is the maximisation of the value of the firm (i.e. the maximisation of profit relative to investment). This may not be quite so simple as stated. The maximisation of profit in the long run, for example, may require unprofitable activity in the short run (e.g. to build up customer goodwill or to head off damaging industrial conflicts). Such far-sighted activity in the short run may, however, put survival in the long run into doubt. Then again the maximisation of profit requires that profit can be both defined and measured accurately and that all factors contributing to it are known and can be taken into account. It is very doubtful whether this requirement can be fully met.

1.2.2 The matter is further complicated by the fact that management may in practice have other objectives either instead of, or as well as, that of profit maximisation. A few possibilities are given below.

(a) **Growth**

The maximisation of profit does not necessarily require a firm of large size. Corporate power, however, is often a function of size and this may become a management objective. Non-profit making organisations, such as mutual assurance companies and building societies, where the profit motive cannot operate, often adopt pure growth as an objective.

(b) **Risk reduction**

Many potentially very profitable enterprises also carry a high risk of expensive failure. Prospecting for oil, for example, is very profitable if a rich strike is made but ruinous if the exploration proves abortive. It may, therefore, be a management objective to ensure survival by the avoidance of risk, profit becoming a secondary objective.

(c) **Personal aspirations**

People who obtain senior positions in management are likely to be highly motivated towards their own career objectives. Important objectives for a manager may therefore be the improvement of his own salary, career prospects or security. This may mean a desire for quick results which will stand to the immediate credit of the manager involved as against more solid but longer term profit making objectives.

(d) **Social objectives**

Some organisations adopt an altruistic social purpose as a management objective. Thus they may be concerned to improve working conditions for their employees, to provide a wholesome product for their customers or to avoid anti-social actions such as environmental pollution or undesirable promotional practices.

(e) **Efficiency**

Some enterprises, such as charities or public services, have as a fundamental objective the provision of a required service which is not supplied in the market place. A suitable management objective for them is the provision of the service at minimum cost.

(f) **Orderly liquidation**

A firm will sometimes reach a point where it is appropriate for it to go into liquidation. This may be forced on it by a financial crisis or a failure of its commercial viability or it maybe undertaken voluntarily because the purposes of its original foundation have ceased to exist. In either case, once the decision has been taken, the objective of management will be to operate the business until its demise so as to balance the conflicts of interests of employees, shareholders and customers, to fulfil contractual obligations, e.g. to pay creditors and debenture holders, and to bring a tidy conclusion to all outstanding matters.

1.2.3 Where a particular management action has implications for more than one objective a view must be taken as to the balance to be struck. For example, the objective of the maximisation of profit may be in conflict with the objective of minimising risk. The judgment to be made is subjective and, therefore, not susceptible to analysis although it is usually made by reference to some explicit or implicit overall corporate objective.

1.3 The Contribution of the Financial Manager

1.3.1 Although Financial Management is a subject in its own right with its own body of literature and an identifiable philosophy, a good financial manager will need a knowledge of other subjects in order to fulfil his or her duties properly. These other subjects include Financial and Management Accounting, Law, Economics, Quantitative Methods (including Mathematics and Statistics) and Taxation. They are not *part* of Financial Management but *support* it in that they provide useful information or give an understanding of the constraints within which the activity of financial management takes place. This book will assume that the student understands these other subjects to the level required by his or her previous professional studies.

1.3.2 Finance, i.e. the ability to purchase things, is used by a business in its operations just as much as are, say, labour and materials and it needs management in a closely analogous way. Purchasing power can be transferred from one person to another (by the lending of money) and can thus be supplied to a business, at a price (rate of interest) just as can physical goods or the services of labour. Like materials or labour, finance should be bought in the most favourable market and used in the most effective and economical way.

1.3.3 The specific functions of a financial manager are to ensure that funds are:

(a) made available at the right time,

(b) made available for the right length of time,

(c) obtained at the lowest cost and

(d) used in the most effective way.

These functions are inter-related. The correct timing of the raising of funds, for example, depends on the requirements of the proposed uses. Conversely, whether or not a particular use of funds is both feasible and attractive depends on the cost and availability of those funds.

1.3.4 The consequences of bad financial management can be very serious. As a simple example, let us suppose that a decision has been taken to set up a new plant and that this will require the expenditure of £100,000 in six months' time. It is then expected to give a return equivalent to 10% per annum on this investment over a period of five years.

In order to make this plan possible £100,000 must be made available at the required time. Owing to bad financial management the following occurred:

(a) the amount made available was £120,000. The result is that, after the project has been financed, there is £20,000 left over. This has to be paid for (interest charges) but there is no guarantee that there will be any profitable use for it. It may merely lie wastefully idle.

(b) the amount did not become available until after nine months. The start of the project was, therefore, delayed. Other plans following from this one, e.g. a planned increase in labour recruitment, may be disrupted, competitive advantages may be lost, profits which could have been earned during the period of the delay will not be earned.

(c) the amount was raised by means of a bank loan repayable in twelve months' time. As the project will still be running for long after this, new finance will have to be found when the bank loan runs out and this lays up a difficult problem for the future.

(d) the agreed rate of interest is 15% per annum. Since the project yields only 10% per annum we are bound to make a net loss. The project is not, in these circumstances, worthwhile.

1.3.5 In order to ensure that there is good financial management we must develop sensible objectives, useful concepts, techniques for analysing situations and principles for the guidance of action. These are the matters to which we shall be giving our attention in this book.

It should be stressed, however, that none of these things can replace sound judgment. Success in business depends more than anything else on that. The subject of Financial Management seeks to inform judgment and not to replace it.

1.3.6 A financial manager is rarely asked to make decisions either in a vacuum or in a wholly new situation. He will generally be operating within the context of an existing business. This means that his decisions will have impacts on other elements of the business's operations and will, in their turn, be influenced by those elements. It also means that he will need to have knowledge of, and regard to, the position reached by the business as determined by what has happened in the past. A careful examination of the balance sheet may thus be very valuable.

1.3.7 **Example.** Comment, from the point of view of the financial manager, on the life history of Longterm, plc, whose balance sheet at 31st December 19x1, appears below. Emphasise the areas in which decisions have to be made. The company is a manufacturer of small, precision made, metal components.

Longterm, plc
Balance sheet at 31st December 19x1

				£000s
Fixed assets				
Buildings				1,920
Plant and equipment				1,240
Fixtures and fittings				990
				4,150
Current assets				
Stocks: Raw materials	740			
Work in progress	1,050			
Finished goods	1,420	3,210		
Debtors		2,240		
Cash at bank		590		
		6,040		
Less Current liabilities				
Trade creditors	2,820			
Current taxation	470	3,290	2,750	
			6,900	

Financed by:	£000s
Share capital	
Ordinary shares of £1 each	4,000
8% preference shares of 50p each	1,000
Reserves	
Share premium account	500
Profit and loss account	900
Loan capital	
10% debentures 19x9 (secured on buildings)	500
	6,900

1.3.8 The general direction of Longterm's life was established when the company was formed with objects which set it up as operating in a particular field. As a manufacturer of precision metal components we shall not, for example, expect to find it printing books or supplying cinemas with ice cream. These objects will have been given legal formality in the company's Memorandum of Association and will have been the first constraint within which the judgment of the financial manager will have had to operate.

A number of actions have been taken concerning the projects undertaken by the company since it started. Some of these will have followed from quite independent decisions. For example, various items of plant and equipment may have been purchased with a particular product line and its market in mind. Others will have been actions which were consequential on other decisions and actions. The purchase of one machine to make a component may have required the purchase of another to finish and pack it. The setting up of any manufacturing capacity will have required the provisions of raw material stocks and also lead to additional debtors as customers for its product are found.

On the other side of the balance sheet decisions to issue preference shares and loan capital depend on the pre-existence of a sufficient level of ordinary share capital. We may note the existence of a share premium account which may imply that more than one issue of shares has taken place. A premium frequently represents an increase in the value of a company from its initial flotation to the time when further shares are issued for expansion. It should be noted, however, that sometimes an initial issue is at a premium. This may be done to allow more flexibility in the future pricing of issues (since shares cannot legally be issued at a discount) or in order to enable the original promoters of a business to invest in it on more favourable terms than members of the public.

The past decisions reflected in the present balance sheet are several. The constitution of the fixed assets results from a series of decisions relating to investment opportunities which have presented themselves in the past. The amounts appearing in the current assets follow from a combination of the general level and nature of activities and the skill exercised by management in keeping working capital at an optimum level.

The capital structure of the business will have engaged some attention and this has led, in Longterm's case, to the particular mix of equity and debt which we see. A certain proportion of its financing has come from the retention of profits (represented by the balance on profit and loss account).

1.4 Relationship with Other Subjects

1.4.1 It may, finally, be helpful to give some illustrations of the ways in which Financial Management draws on related subjects:

(a) **Financial Accounting**

The balance sheet, a major financial accounting statement, could be regarded as a statement of the results of financial management. It shows the sources from which finance has been obtained and how this finance is currently deployed. Successful financial management will result in a 'healthy' balance sheet, i.e. one revealing a strong and stable position from which future progress can be made. Financial accounts also provide, in the form of profit and loss statements and of accounting ratios, important information for judging past activities and for deciding on future action.

(b) **Management Accounting**

Information on the costs and profitability of projects, the projection of cash flows, the effect of departures from previously established plans, etc. is all part of the raw material of the financial manager. Management accounting provides techniques which help to give this kind of information.

(c) **Law**

The law governs almost everything which a financial manager does. If, for example, he obtains funds by means of a secured loan, the law will ensure that he observes the agreed terms of repayment of principal and interest and will restrict his freedom to deal in the assets on which the loan is secured. If he raises money by means of a share issue he must comply with company law in the way this is done and the rights which he then allows to shareholders. When he wishes to pay a dividend he must observe the restrictions of the law on how much this may be. He must pay taxes as determined by law. The business's ownership of the assets which it finances is itself ultimately established and maintained by the law.

(d) **Economics**

A knowledge of what goes on in the world outside the business is essential to the financial manager and a study of economics will often provide help. There will be no point in borrowing money now at 15% per annum, for example, if interest rates are about to fall sharply below this. Again, it will be a mistake to invest heavily in advance of a slump in trade.

(e) **Quantitative Methods**

Many statistical and mathematical techniques are drafted to the aid of the financial manager. The statistical measure of variance, for example, is useful in risk analysis. Regression analysis can lead to an understanding of the behaviour of costs. Linear programming has a part to play in resolving problems relating to capital rationing. Time series analysis is a valuable tool in the forecasting aspects of budgeting.

(f) **Taxation**

Businesses operate under a considerable burden of taxation. The tax implications of a financial manager's actions may be decisive to their success or otherwise. The operation of tax laws, for example, has a very considerable effect on the pattern of the flow of net returns from any business project. It also has a bearing on the cost of finance from various sources. A sufficient knowledge of taxation to consider these properly is therefore required.

Summary

(i) Financial management is that part of the total management function which is concerned with the effective and efficient raising and use of funds. It must be operated within a framework of clearly understood objectives and on the basis of logical concepts.

(ii) Although it has some special characteristics, finance can be regarded as being much like any physical resource, e.g. labour or materials. It has a large number of competing uses. It is scarce but can be obtained at a price. It is bought and sold in a regular market.

(iii) A financial manager's function can be analysed as being to ensure that finance is available at the right time and at least cost and that it is used in the most profitable ways.

(iv) The effective discharge of his/her function requires a financial manager to have a good knowledge of Financial Accounting, Management Accounting, Law, Economics, Quantitative Methods and Taxation. This knowledge will be assumed in the discussions which follow.

Review Questions

(i) *1. Makepeace is a wealthy philanthropist most of whose wealth derives from his substantial shareholding in Makepeace Industries, plc. Some years ago he donated a major part of his fortune to the establishment of a charity, Makepeace Educational Foundation. Both the company and the foundation employ a financial manager. Comment on the different frameworks within which each will operate.*

(ii) Some time ago your company entered into a long term contract whereby a major supplier would supply a fixed annual quantity of material at a fixed price. The contract has now become onerous and the company is seeking release from it. List the factors which you think would need to be considered in the negotiations.

(iii) A major development proposed by the Board of Directors of Selfish, plc, will be very profitable for the company but will grossly offend and inconvenience the local community. How can the financial manager advise the Board in these circumstances?

(iv) 'Money is a marketable commodity just like raw materials'. Discuss the extent and limitations of the similarity of finance and other inputs to production.

(v) Would a financial manager ever recommend that the business to which he is responsible should engage in a project which is bound to result in a loss?

(vi) 'Bank overdraft rates of interest are now lower than they have been for some time. This is now, therefore, the right time for us to take the biggest overdraft we can get in order to build and equip a major extension to our factory.'Discuss the implications of this statement.

(vii) The law both constrains and supports the efforts of the financial manager. Give examples of some constraints and some supports.

(viii) 'Every financial manager's objective is a healthy balance sheet'. Do you agree?

Exercises

1. There follows the balance sheet of Dodo, plc. Look at this through a financial manager's eyes and comment on what it reveals.

Dodo, plc
Balance sheet at 31st December, 19xx

Fixed assets	£	£
Building	70,000	
Plant and machinery	41,160	
Furniture and equipment	33,620	144,780

Current assets		
Stock	17,000	
Debtors	22,600	
Cash	200	
	39,800	

Less: **Current liabilities**			
Bank overdraft	8,200		
Creditors	12,900	21,100	18,700
			163,480

Financed by:

Share capital		
100,000 ordinary shares of £1 each, fully paid		100,000

Reserves		
General reserve	20,000	
Product and loss account	13,480	33,480
		133,480

Loan capital		
10% debentures		30,000
		163,480

2. Dodo, plc can raise an unlimited amount of further finance in the market at a cost of 15% per annum. Its current activities pay it an average return of 25% per annum on the funds invested. In seeking opportunities for expansion the only projects it finds appear to be much less profitable than this. They are:

Project	Prospective yield
A	18%
B	17%
C	15%
D	12%

What should the financial manager do? What is likely to complicate the situation in real life?

3. Describe briefly the likely consequences of the following errors in financial management:

(i)   bad timing for capital raising;

(ii) inefficient capital raising;

(iii) inefficient use of funds.

4. Each of the following situations illustrates a possibility of conflict between management objectives. Briefly analyse the conflict involved in each case and then write a note on how such conflicts are resolved.

(i)   A lengthy and expensive research programme has been proposed. If successful it will yield a product for which a strong market is assured. There is, however, no guarantee of such success.

(ii) The labour force threatens to strike if its wage demands are not met. The management does not feel that it can afford the wage demand as it is unlikely to be able to recover the increased cost through higher prices. A strike, however, will be very damaging in terms of lost customer goodwill and disrupted production.

(iii) A rare opportunity has arisen to buy a prestigious site in a city centre. Interest rates, however, are currently high and this will make the cost of financing the purchase high.

(iv) A certain product is selling well and stocks are high in anticipation of future demand. The company's scientists have, however, discovered a potential fault in the product which gives it a risk of sudden failure and which, if publicised, is bound to cut demand and leave the company with unsaleable stocks.

5. Albatross and Co. plc has a very refined system for evaluating proposals for investment in fixed assets. Its current assets are relatively uncontrolled and the factors which determine their level have not been analysed. Questioned on this the managing director has said, 'Investment in fixed assets is long term and we would therefore be committed to our mistakes for a lengthy period. Current assets are very short term and do not carry that risk. It would in any case be difficult to evaluate the investment in current assets because they offer no financial return as do fixed assets'. Do you agree with this argument?

6. Comment briefly on the relevance to the work of the financial manager of a knowledge of taxation, law, economics and quantitative methods.

2: Cash Flow Statements

2.1 Cash flow

2.1.1 We said in the first chapter that a balance sheet could be regarded as a statement of the results of financial management in the past and as a basis from which future progress must be made. This suggests that the balance sheet will be a good starting point for our exploration of the subject and we shall learn most if we draw comparisons between the balance sheets of a business as they appeared at different points in time. This will lead us on to the construction of cash flow statements. Although questions directly involving the preparation of such statements are rare in a Financial Management paper (they are more likely to appear under the heading of Financial Accounting), an understanding of what a balance sheet tells us about cash flows is very important and cash flow statements are a useful medium through which to gain this understanding.

2.1.2 Below appears the summarised balance sheet of Casablanca, plc as at 31 March 19x5, together with comparative figures relating to the previous year.

	31 March 19x4 £000s	31 March 19x5 £000s
Fixed assets		
Freehold land and buildings	2,640	2,724
Plant and machinery	5,910	7,674
	8,550	10,398
Investments		
Quoted(cost)	2,496	2,160
Net current assets	7,458	8,835
Total assets less		
current liabilities	18,504	21,393
10% debentures (secured)	1,860	2,160
	16,644	19,233
Share capital		
Ordinary shares of £1 each fully paid	12,000	13,500
8% preference shares of £1 each fully paid	1,500	1,500
Share premium	150	450
Profit and loss account	2,994	3,783
	16,644	19,233

Notes to the balance sheets

1. Fixed assets

	Net book value £000s
Freehold land and buildings	
At 31 March 19x4	2,640
Add Purchases and improvements	84
At 31 March 19x5	2,724
Plant and machinery	
At 31 March 19x4	5,910
Add Purchases	2,781
	8,691
Less Book value of sales	192
	8,499
Less Depreciation	825
At 31 March 19x5	7,674

2. Investments

	£000s
At 31 March 19x4	2,496
Less Disposals at cost	336
	2,160

3. Net current assets

		31 March 19x4 £000s		31 March 19x5 £000s
Stock		5,991		5,427
Debtors		2,082		2,964
Cash and bank		6,114		7,512
		14,187		15,903
Creditors	3,903		3,990	
Proposed dividend	750		900	
Taxation	2,076	6,729	2,178	7,068
		7,458		8,835

4. Capital raising operations

During the year ended 31 March 19x5 there was a rights issue of £1 ordinary shares on a 1 for 8 basis at a price of £1.20 per fully paid share.

There was also an issue of £300,000 10% debenture stock ranking pari passu with the existing stock.

Both of these issues were fully subscribed.

5. Profit and loss account

	£000s
At 31 March 19x4	2,994
Add Trading profit	4,368
Income from quoted investments	300
Profit on sale of plant and machinery	30
	7,692

Less Loss on disposal of investments	36	
Dividends in respect of year:		
Preference (paid)	120	
Ordinary (paid)	600	
(proposed)	900	
Taxation	2,253	3,909
At 31 March 19x5		3,783

Note: The trading profit is arrived at after charging £201,000 debenture interest. The income from quoted investments includes the related tax credit.

2.1.3 The balance sheets gives us the summarised position and further details are given in the notes which follow them. From the summaries we can observe the general financial structure of the business. We can see that (31 March 19x5 figures) £10.398 million is invested in productive assets and that associated with this is £8.835 million of working capital (i.e. net current assets). Decisions will have been made, within the purview of financial management, that the series of investments making up this total is worthwhile and that it provided an optimum use of the funds available. Omitting the quoted investments, the total amount invested in the productive processes of the business is £17.073 million. The analysis of the profit and loss account reveals that, in the year to which this relates, these assets have earned £4.368 million – a return before tax of 25.6% on the investment.

2.1.4 We can also see the ways in which the funds for investment have been provided. The sources are shareholders, both ordinary and preference, retained earnings and loan capital. It will have been as a consequence of financial management decisions that these sources will have been used and that their relative proportions will have been established. A particularly interesting proportion is that which debt bears to the total amount of financing. This is described as gearing and is fully discussed in Chapter 6 (see 6.2).

The gearing for Casablanca at 31 March 19x5 is

$$G = \frac{2,160 + 1,500}{21,393}$$

$$= 0.17$$

Note that, although preference capital is legally part of equity it is sufficiently insulated from risk (by the existence of a substantial amount of ordinary share capital) for it to be better regarded analytically as debt and this practice is generally followed.

2.1.5 The ways in which these decisions are made and their implications will all need to be considered in later parts of this book. For the moment, however, we must pursue our present theme of the balance sheet as revealing the outcome of decisions of the past. In doing this we shall make our first encounter with a basic characteristic of our subject. This is that 'profit' and 'value' as defined by the accountant, are not normally of particular interest to the financial manager. A cash flow will be much more relevant than a profit (i.e. after charging depreciation and allowing for all accruals) and a value based on future cash generating potential or a current realisable value will be more informative than the traditional net book value (i.e. cost less aggregate depreciation to date).

A very useful process, highlighting this exists where, as here, we have two balance sheets separated by a period of operations. It is that of tracing the flow of cash during the period to prepare a cash flow statement. All large companies now do this as a matter of course and publish it along with their annual accounts in compliance with Financial Reporting Standard 1 (FRS 1).

2.2 Cash Flow Statements

2.2.1 FRS 1 was issued in 1991. It is mandatory for all company reports relating to accounting periods ending on or after 23 March 1992. It defines cash flow as including both actual cash and cash equivalents (i.e. short term and highly liquid investments). It requires that cash inflows and outflows during the financial period should be stated under a number of specific headings.

The headings are;

(i)   operating activities;

(ii) returns on investments and servicing of finance;

(iii) taxation;

(iv) investing activities; and

(v)   financing.

Operating activities refers to the trading and associated activities of the business. The cash flow will differ from profit as it will not include depreciation and will take account of changes in creditors, debtors and stocks which cause the cash flows to and from these accounts to differ from the corresponding profit and loss account items.

Returns on investments and servicing of finance will include interest and dividends both received and paid.

Taxation will be amounts paid to the State directly arising from the company's own tax burden i.e. mainstream corporation tax and advance corporation tax. It will not include payments, such as PAYE and VAT, where the company is merely a collector of those amounts.

Investing activities include the purchase and realisation of fixed assets.

Financing includes the raising of extra finance through share and debenture issues and the redemption of old finance.

2.2.2 It will be instructive for us to prepare a cash flow statement for Casablanca, plc.

Since any balance sheet must, by definition, balance, a change in any figure from one year to the next must be reflected by compensating changes in other figures. This arises naturally from the double-entry system of record keeping and requires no further proof. When preparing a cash flow statement the figure we choose to reflect is cash as defined in FRS 1. By its nature this cash provides the medium through which all financial management decisions are implemented. We do not raise capital in the form of buildings or machinery. We raise in the form of cash and then use this cash to buy the fixed assets required. Cash is the raw material, we might say, of the financial management process.

2.2.3 Our balance sheet shows a change in cash during the yera ended 31 March 19x5 as follows:

	£000s
At 31 March 19x5	7,512
At 31 March 19x4	6,114
	1,398

2.2.4 We can now build up the figures we require for the cash flow statement using the information at our disposal. It will be clear how this has been done if the figures below are traced through carefully.

CASABLANCA PLC
Cash Flow Statement for the year ended 31 March 19x5
Operating activities:

		£000s
Net cash inflow from operating activities		5,163
Returns on investments and servicing of finance:		
Dividends received	225	
Interest paid	(201)	
Dividends paid:		
Preference	(120)	
Ordinary (current year)	(600)	
(previous year)	(750)	(1,446)
Taxation (in respect of previous year)		(2,076)
Investing activities		
Sales of quoted investments	300	
Purchases and improvements to freehold land and buildings	(84)	
Purchases of plant and machinery	(2,781)	
Sales of plant and machinery (book value plus profit	222	(2,343)
		(702)
Net cash flow before financing		
Issue of debentures	300	
Rights issue	1,800	2,100
		1,398

Reconciliation of operating profit to net cash inflow from operating activities:

	£000s
Trading profit	4,368
Debenture interest	201
Depreciation	825
Reduction in stock	564
Increase in debtors	(882)
Increase in creditors	87
	5,163

Summary

i) A single balance sheet may be regarded as a statement of the present consequences of the financial management decisions of the past. As such it provides information on the value of funds currently employed in the business and the sources of the finance.

ii) Two balance sheets relating to different dates provide an opportunity to prepare a statement showing the cash flows during

17

the interval between them. Conventionally this interval will be one financial year. This cash flow statement is an important report on one aspect of financial management activities during the period. It has now become accepted as a component of the annual report to shareholders and is the subject of an accounting standard (FRS 1).

iii) The elements in a cash flow statement can be determined by reference to the change in balance sheet items from the commencing date to the finishing date as amplified by further information. The elements are:

operating activities;

returns on investments and servicing of finance;

taxation;

investing activities; and

financing.

iv) The statement is built up by proceeding in a methodical way through all the balance sheet changes and applying a knowledge of basic accounting principles together with any given information to an identification of them.

Review questions

i) *Cashflow, plc has made a profit after taxation in the year just ended of £1,962,849. According to its cash flow statement the cash generated by operations was £2,347,473. Suggest possible explanations for the discrepancy.*

ii) *"Depreciation is one of our heaviest expenses". "As always we have found depreciation to be a very useful source of funds". Can you reconcile these quotations from the Chairman's Report of two different companies?*

iii) *What constitutes cash from the point of view of a cash flow statement?*

iv) *Give four examples of actions based on decisions taken by a financial manager and explain how they would be reflected in a cash flow statement.*

v) *For each of the following items on a cash flow statement say where the figures from which they are determined would appear in the balance sheet and profit and loss account:*

Net cash inflow from operating activities

Taxation

Returns on investments and servicing of finance.

vi) *Give two examples of important events reflected in the balance sheet of a business which would not appear in a cash flow statement.*

vii) *The purchase of a building costing £1,500,000 has been financed by the issue of debentures of the same amount. The directors wish to omit any reference to this from the cash flow statement on the grounds that the two transactions "cancel out". What do you think and why?*

viii) *The information contained in a cash flow statement is largely a rearrangement of that already given in the profit and loss account and balance sheet. How then would you justify the work involved in preparing it?*

Exercises

1. *There appear below the summarised balance sheets of Red Rum, plc as at 31 December 19x2 and 31 December 19x2. From these and the supporting notes given below them, construct a cash flow statement for the company for the year ended 31 December 19x2.*

Red Rum plc
Balance sheets as at 31 December

	19x1 £000s	19x2 £000s
Fixed assets		
Freehold land and buildings (1)	1,500	3,000
Plant and machinery (2)	3,720	4,380
	5,220	7,380
Goodwill Cost less amounts written off	120	90
Net current assets (3)	3,576	4,701
Assets less net current liabilities	8,916	12,171
12½% debentures	300	300
	8,616	11,871
Share capital		
Ordinary shares of £1 fully paid	4,500	6,000
Reserves		
General reserve	900	1,200
Profit and loss account (4)	3,216	4,671
	8,616	11,871

Notes

1) *The freehold land and buildings, which had cost £1,500,000 were independently valued during the year at*

> £3,000,000 and this value was incorporated into the balance sheet. The surplus on revaluation was applied in making a bonus issue of shares to the ordinary shareholders on a 1 for 3 basis. There were no sales of, nor additions to, freehold land and buildings.

2) The plant and machinery account is summarised as follows:

	Net book value £000s
Balance at 31 December 19x1	3,720
Add Purchases	1,560
	5,280
Less Net book value of sales	210
	5,070
Less Depreciation for the year	690
Balance at 31 December 19x2	4,380

3) Net current assets are made up as follows:

	31 December 19x1 £000s	£000s	31 December 19x2 £000s	£000s
Stock	2,673		5,556	
Debtors	7,383		7,395	
Cash	810	10,866	363	13,314
Less Creditors	5,826		6,567	
Proposed dividend	675		900	
Taxation	789	7,290	1,146	8,613
		3,576		4,701

4) A summary of the profit and loss account is as follows:

	£000s	
Trading profit, after charging depreciation		3,681
Add Surplus on sales of plant and machinery		420
		4,101
	£000s	
Less Taxation	1,146	
Dividends: paid	300	
proposed	900	
Transfer to general reserve	300	2,646
Amount retained		1,455

2. Wasp, plc presents the following summarised balance sheets at 31 December 19x3 and 31 December 19x4 together with addi-

tional information. Prepare a cash flow statement for the year between these two dates.

	31 Dec. 19x3 £000s	31 Dec. 19x4 £000s
Fixed assets		
Freehold land and buildings	8,400	11,700
Plant and machinery	10,380	14,460
Motor vehicles	1,251	1,194
	20,031	27,354
Investment in associated company	684	702
Net current assets	25,260	33,786
	45,975	61,842
Loan capital		
12% debentures (secured)	1,800	1,800
	44,175	60,042
Share capital		
Ordinary shares of £1 each fully paid	24,000	28,800
Capital redemption reserve	3,600	
Profit and loss account	16,575	31,242
	44,175	60,042

Note 1. Fixed assets

	£000s
Freehold land and buildings	
At 31 December 19x3	8,400
Add Improvements during year	6,000
	14,400
Less Book value of disposals	2,700
At 31 December 19x4	11,700
Plant and machinery	
At 31 December 19x3	10,380
Add Purchases	8,400
	18,780
Less Book value of sales	1,380
	17,400
Less Depreciation for year	2,940
	14,460

Note 1. Fixed assets (continued)

	£000s
Motor vehicles	
At 31 December 19x3	1,251
Add Purchases	795
	2,046
Less Book value of sales	369
	1,677
Less Depreciation for year	483
	1,194

Note 2. Net current assets

	31 December 19x3 £000s		31 December 19x4 £000s	
Stock		27,540		28,050
Debtors		12,930		14,636
Cash and bank		8,580		12,720
		49,050		55,406
Creditors	9,780		12,200	
Proposed dividend	3,000		3,600	
Taxation	11,010	23,790	5,820	21,620
		25,260		33,786

Note 4. Profit and loss account

		£000s
At 31 December 19x3		16,575
Add Trading profit		25,230
Share of income of associated company:		
Dividend received	9	
Retained profit	18	27
Profit on sale of plant and machinery		360
Profit on disposal of freehold land and buildings		1,500
		43,692
Less Loss on sale of motor vehicles	30	
Dividends for the year	5,400	
Taxation	5,820	
Transfer to bonus share account	1,200	12,450
At 31 December 19x4		31,242

Note 5. During the year there was a 1 for 5 bonus issue of ordinary shares made out of existing reserves.

3. Since the publication of FRS 1 all companies have been required to issue a cash flow statement as part of the annual company report. Explain what this shows and comment on its value as a source of information to shareholders.

4. There appear below the summarised balance sheets of Claverton, plc as at 31 December 19x6 and 31 December 19x7. From these and the information given below them you are required to construct a cash flow statement for the year ended 31 December 19x7.

	31 Dec. 19x3 £000s	31 Dec. 19x4 £000s
Fixed assets		
Freehold land and buildings (1)	1,000	1,400
Plant and machinery	2,420	2,680
Investments (current market value) (3)	540	490
Net current assets	3,160	3,310
	7,120	7,880

	£000s	£000s
Share capital		
Ordinary shares of £1 each fully paid	4,000	5,000
Reserves		
Share premium account	100	
Plant replacement reserve	1,800	2,000
Profit and loss account (6)	1,320	780
	7,120	7,880

Notes

1) There had been expenditure of £400,000 on improvements to the buildings during the year.

2) The plant and machinery account is summarised as follows:

	£000s
Balance at 31 December 19x6	2,420
Add Purchases	1,090
	3,510
Less Sales (book value)	290
	3,220
Less Depreciation for the year	540
Balance at 31 December 19x7	2,680

3) *Investments:*

	£000s
Market value at 31 December 19x6	540
Less Sales (market value at 31 December 19x6)	30
	510
Add Purchases	62
	572
Less Amount to reduce to market value at 31 December 19x7	82
Market value at 31 December 19x7	490

4) *Net current assets are made up as follows:*

	31 December 19x3		31 December 19x4	
	£000s		£000s	
Stock	3,900		4,200	
Debtors	2,300		2,250	
Cash	200	6,400	40	6,490
Less Creditors	1,890		2,010	
Proposed dividend	400	500		
Taxation	950	3,240	670	3,180
		3,160		3,310

5) *One million ordinary shares were issued during the year at a price of £1.10 each.*

6) *Profit and loss account:*

		£000s
Balance at 31 December 19x6		1,320
Add Trading profit		1,063
Profit on sale of plant and machinery		60
		2,443
Less Net loss on sales and revaluation of investments	93	
Taxation	670	
Dividends	700	
Transfers to plant replacement reserve	200	1,663
		780

3: Sources of Finance

3.1 Finance as a Marketable Resource

3.1.1 We have referred to finance as a resource which can be bought in a market in very much the same manner as the raw materials of a manufacturing process. The analogy can be continued further, for, just as there are different types and qualities of materials which may be bought at different prices in different markets, so there are several different sources of finance each with their individual characteristics.

3.1.2 Just as the manufacturer of a product will require a particular blend of materials of different types, so efficient financing will require an appropriate combination of capital from the available sources. A financial manager will need an expert knowledge of these if he is to use them to best advantage. In this chapter and the next we shall consider these sources and the institutional framework within which access to them may be obtained. This will be a largely factual explanation which will clear the way for a consideration of the theoretical issues underlying their selection and deployment.

3.2 Equity Finance

3.2.1 Ordinary share capital

Ordinary share capital is the foundation of any company's financial structure. Business requires that capital be placed at risk and the ultimate bearers of that risk are the ordinary shareholders. The main characteristics of ordinary share capital or equity, as it is generally termed, are as follows:

(a) By law shares must have a nominal value, e.g. they are described as '£1 shares' or as '50p shares'. This nominal value is often but not necessarily the price at which the shares were first issued but it may bear no relationship whatsoever to their current market value. Just as a 'penny black' stamp is now worth far more than one penny, it is quite common to find a '£1 share' selling for several pounds. Occasionally a company will issue 'stock' rather than 'shares'. This is purely a difference in packaging. The capital is offered in bulk so that one subscribes for a quantity of it measured in terms of nominal value. A stockholder in a company would own (say) £100 of stock while a shareholder would own 100 £1 shares.

(b) Shares issued subsequently to a company's founding issue may be offered at a price equal to their nominal value (at par) or at a price exceeding their nominal value (at a premium). It would be illegal to offer shares at a price below their nominal value (at a discount). Very often such issues are restricted to existing shareholders when they are known as rights issues.

(c) Sometimes a company will issue bonus shares. These are always issued to existing shareholders in proportion to their existing holdings and are free of charge to them. It is important, therefore, to note that a bonus issue is not a source of finance as are issues for cash. It is a book-keeping operation performed, usually, to give recognition to the fact that legally distributable reserves have become permanently tied up in the business and will not now be distributed. This process is more fully described in Chapter 6 (6.6.2).

(d) The shares of a quoted company change hands frequently in the stock market. This has no direct financial effect on the company, which is not involved in the transactions, except that it is required to maintain an up-to-date register of ownership. The implication of the market to the financial manager is that it constrains the terms on which any future issues may be made and thus bears on the cost of capital.

(e) The income of the ordinary shareholder is the residual (i.e. after prior claims have been met) profit of the company. This may be either paid to him or her as a dividend or retained in the business for his or her ultimate benefit through its expansion. The decision as to how much of the profit to distribute as a dividend, an important one which we shall need to discuss later, is made by the directors.

(f) In normal circumstances the company is barred by law from repaying capital to its ordinary shareholders. Thus the only way they can withdraw their capital as individuals is by selling their shares on the market. In the event of a winding up the ordinary shareholders are entitled to the proceeds of the whole of the residual assets of the business. This may be a very large amount or it may be nothing at all.

A change in the law in 1981 (now embodied in the Companies Act, 1985) made it legal for a company to redeem its shares or to purchase and cancel them. This is not an exception to the general principle of the sanctity of capital (for public companies), however, as the redemption or purchase must be either out of the proceeds of a fresh issue of shares made especially for the purpose or out of profits otherwise available for distribution. The total value of the capital fund is thus conserved.

3.2.2 Preference share capital

Preference shares are distinguished from ordinary shares by being given preferential rights over profits and, in the event of a winding up, over surplus assets. Technically they are part of the equity since, like the ordinary shares, they are risk bearing. In practice, however, it is necessary to make their preferential rights attractive in order to sell the shares and this is achieved by keeping the number issued low relative to that of ordinary shares. In consequence they become virtually risk free and for analysis purposes they are usually classified with loan capital. Preference shares are not nowadays a very popular source of finance owing to certain tax disadvantages which they have as compared with debt. We shall look at this in detail in Chapter 15.

The preferences are:

(a) **As to income.** The preference shareholder is entitled to a dividend of up to a stated maximum amount before any dividend is paid to the ordinary shareholder. E.g. 8% preference shares may receive a dividend of anywhere between 0 and 8% of nominal value, but not more, and *must* receive the full 8% if any ordinary dividend is to be paid. Dividend rights may be non-cumulative, i.e. if not paid in a given year the dividend lapses or, more usually, cumulative, i.e. any arrears of dividend are carried forward and are given preference against future years' profits. This is determined by the stated terms of the issue.

(b) **As to capital.** In the event of a winding up, any surplus assets after prior claims (e.g. creditors and lenders) have been met, must first be used to repay up to the full nominal value of the preference shares. Only after this may the ordinary shareholders participate.

Preference shares with special rights are sometimes issued. For example 'participating' preference shares may be entitled to a further participation in dividends over and above their basic preferential dividend once the dividend paid to ordinary shareholders exceeds a certain amount. 'Convertible' preference shares confer the option to convert into ordinary shares on prescribed terms in prescribed circumstances.

The rights of preference shareholders will not normally be varied after the shares have been issued. Thus an issue of bonus preference shares would not be made to preference shareholders (although it might to existing *ordinary* shareholders).

It should be noted that preference shares suffer from the hidden defect that inflation progressively reduces the real value of the money income from them. They are not therefore quite as risk free as they appear.

3.2.3 Reserves

Some reserves arise as the result of 'paper' transactions and are not, therefore, sources of finance. One example of this is the Capital Redemption Reserve created out of an existing revenue reserve on the redemption of redeemable shares. Similarly, a General Reserve created from existing revenue reserves or a Revaluation Reserve arising from a revaluation of assets would give rise to no cash inflow. Reserves arising, however, from a genuine inflow of cash are a source of finance. One example of a capital reserve in this category is the Share Premium Account. More importantly, revenue reserves representing retained profits are a vital regular source of finance to most companies. They have the advantage to the financial manager of being readily available to him, on demand, merely by restricting distributions. This informality means that the expenses of raising capital, which may for some sources be considerable, are also kept to a minimum. The disadvantage is that the amount available is restricted to that generated by the company's own operations and that, therefore, total reliance on retained profits as a source of funds may lead to a very slow rate of growth.

3.3 Loan capital

3.3.1 Superficially loan capital, normally represented by fixed interest debentures, has something of the appearance of share capital. Its holders can buy and sell it in the stock market and they receive their income in the form of regular payments by the company (described, however, as interest rather than dividend). The loan capital has a nominal value (though it is often in the form of stock rather than of discrete share units) and this may differ from the market price. Loan capital, however, is quite different in nature from equity.

The essential distinguishing features of loan capital are:

(a) The income received by the debenture holders is a charge against revenues and is not a share of ascertained profit. The implication of this is that a fixed rate of interest is payable in full whether profits are available or not. It also has taxation implications which we shall consider at the appropriate time.

(b) The capital value of the loan may be repaid (depending on the terms of issue) although irredeemable debentures are sometimes issued. A company is usually empowered (by its Articles) to reduce its indebtedness by purchasing its own debentures on the market. There is no limitation in company law on this activity as there is in the case of shares.

(c) There is security for the interest and capital. This arises primarily from the contract between the company and the lender.

The debenture holders may sue if there is any breach of the agreed terms. This may be reinforced by giving the debenture holders a legal charge (i.e. a mortgage) on the assets of the business.

Companies will sometimes issue so-called 'convertible' debentures. These are exactly like normal debentures in most respects but carry the additional right that they may be converted into ordinary shares at the option of the holder. The terms of the conversion and the dates on which it can be exercised are set out by the company. Convertible debentures give the holder all the security associated with debentures but with the valuable additional opportunity to get into the equity at a later date if the company's success seems to warrant that.

3.4 Other Sources of Finance

3.4.1 Current liabilities

Current liabilities i.e. short term bank overdrafts, creditors, unpaid tax liabilities, etc. provide a useful source of short term finance. They are sometimes free of interest, e.g. creditors and unpaid tax, but must usually be paid off by a specified date in the near future. They are often, however, renewable, i.e. one generation of creditors is replaced by another, and may therefore, in effect, become part of the long term finance of the business.

Very often current liabilities are associated with specific assets and must be regarded as financing those assets. For example, creditors help to finance stockholdings since they actually arise out of the acquisition of those stocks. For the purposes of analysis, therefore, it is often helpful to treat current liabilities as a reduction in the requirement for working capital rather than as a free-standing source of finance.

3.4.2 Off balance sheet financing

The term off balance sheet financing refers to sources of finance which do not show up as liabilities on the balance sheet. In a sense it is a misnomer because it refers to methods of avoiding the necessity to provide finance. We will mention two important examples.

(a) **Leasing.** This can apply to any fixed assets and is quite commonly used for plant and machinery, office equipment and motor vehicles. Instead of acquiring these assets for itself the company enters into an agreement with a leasing company whereby the latter purchases the assets in question and then leases them (i.e. rents or hires them) on a long term basis to the former. No initial funds are required but there is instead a regular charge for lease payments to be charged in the profit and loss account.

It should be noted that, since 1984, SSAP 21 has created a distinction between operating leases and finance leases. An operating lease is one where an asset is leased or hired for a period of time substantially less than that of its useful life. A finance lease is one which lasts for the whole of an asset's useful life and where the lessee effectively takes on all the risks and benefits associated with ownership. A finance lease is, therefore, in form a leasing arrangement but in substance the purchase of an asset financed by the lessor as a lender. A finance lease is now required by SSAP 21 to be shown on the balance sheet as an asset at fair value and as a liability for future lease payments.

(b) **Debt factoring.** This applies to an important current asset, debtors. A company may sell its book debts (at a discount to allow a profit to the buyer) in order to avoid tying up capital in the credit it allows to customers. In another form of this, the factoring company advances a proportion, say 80%, of the amount of credit sales as they are made, without itself actually acquiring the debts. This is then repaid out of the cash paid by customers as it is received. Again there is a discount to allow a profit to the provider of this service.

3.5 Comparison of the Relative Positions of Equity and Debt Holders

3.5.1   X, plc has long term finance as follows:

£100,000	10% debentures (secured on assets)
200,000	8% cumulative preference shares of £1 each
1,000,000	Ordinary shares of £1 each

The following statement shows the position in a period of three consecutive years.

	Year 1 £	Year 2 £	Year 3 £
Profit before interest or dividend	100,000	20,000	200,000
Less Interest on debentures (**must** be paid)	10,000	10,000	10,000
Leaving	90,000	10,000	190,000
Less Preference dividend (paid subject to availability of profit and directors' discretion)	16,000	10,000 [1]	22,000 [2]
Leaving available for ordinary shareholders	74,000	Nil	168,000
Making possible a maximum ordinary dividend of	7.4%	Nil	16.8%

[1] Leaving £6,000 to be carried forward as preference dividend in arrear.
[2] Included payment of arrears from previous year.

It should be noted that the debenture holders have a very safe investment. Even following the very poor results of Year 2 there is no danger that the company will be unable to meet its obligation to pay the interest. Preference shareholders also enjoy a high degree of security. The profits of normal years are ample to cover the maximum dividend which, taking one year with another, is almost certain to be achieved. Ordinary shareholders carry the risks, in this case amplified by the existence of the prior charges and have fortunes which fluctuate with the profits. This additional risk to equity holders, caused by prior charges, is called financial risk and is discussed fully in 6.2.

Summary

(i) The financial manager should be aware of the various sources of finance available to him and their respective characteristics.

(ii) The sources of long term finance are:

  (a) Ordinary shares, commonly termed equity. Ordinary shareholders are the ultimate bearers of business risk and the ultimate beneficiaries when the risk pays off.

  (b) Preference shares are technically equity given special preferential rights. These rights, however, so change the effective nature of this form of capital that is generally regarded, for the purposes of analysis, as the equivalent of loan capital.

  (c) Reserves are funds attributable to the equity holders. Their most important source is retained profit. As such they are available, though in relatively restricted amounts, to finance expansion.

  (d) Loan capital is fundamentally different in nature from equity. Its holders bear no significant risk and are entitled to receive in full interest at an agreed rate. Frequently they are also guaranteed the ultimate return in full of their principal.

(iii) Short term finance can be obtained from creditors, bank overdrafts, tax provisions, etc. It is sometimes associated with the financing of specific assets, e.g. of stocks by creditors. It cannot be relied on on a long term basis.

(iv) Off balance sheet financing is a term used to describe sources of finance not showing on the balance sheet. Examples are the leasing of fixed assets and the factoring of trade debts. This form of finance is always associated with specific assets and may be expensive.

Review Questions

(i) *What are the essential differences between loan capital and share capital?*

(ii) *Define the following terms:*

(a) *Convertible debenture*

(b) *Redeemable shares*

(c) *Share premium account*

(d) *Revenue reserve*

(e) *Dividend*

(iii) *What is meant by off balance sheet financing and why might it be used? Name examples of so-called off balance sheet financing.*

(iv) *Current liabilities are sometimes regarded as a 'free' source of finance. Accepting this view would lead to a policy of maximising the level of current liabilities. What are the limitations imposed on such a policy?*

(v) *What would be the advantages and disadvantages of financing a business entirely by use of equity capital?*

(vi) *Why could no business be financed entirely by debt?*

(vii) *Explain to a bewildered shareholder the difference between a 'rights' issue and a 'bonus' issue.*

(viii) *To what extent is the ploughing back of profit a good policy? How would it be done?*

Exercises

1. *Rex, plc has the following capital structure*

Ordinary share capital	£500,000
9% cumulative preference shares	£200,000
6% debenture stock	£100,000

The profits (before interest charges and dividends but after tax) over five years have been.

Year	1	2	3	4	5
Profit	£30,000	£40,000	£20,000	£50,000	£25,000

It is the practice of the directors to distribute half of the available amounts as dividend to the ordinary shareholders. Calcu-

late for each year the ordinary dividend, the amounts paid to other investors in the business and the amounts retained. Comment on the apparent riskiness or otherwise of their income to each class of investor. Comment on retained earnings as a source of finance.

2. *As financial manager of a medium sized company you foresee a shortage of funds over the next few months owing to an expansion of production. Thereafter this expansion will become self-financing. How would you finance this situation?*

3. *What is so-called 'off balance sheet' financing? What advantages has it?*

4. *A friend who has a legacy which she wishes to invest in shares has been recommended to buy preference shares 'because they are better than ordinary shares.' Do you agree with this advice?*

5. *A company is raising finance by offering £500,000 convertible debenture stock at par. This will be convertible as follows:*

After 5 years: one £1 ordinary share per £2 nominal debenture stock
After 6 years: one £1 ordinary share per £3 nominal debenture stock
After 7 years: one £1 ordinary share per £4 nominal debenture stock

The conversion rights lapse after 7 years and the debenture stock then becomes irredeemable. List the advantages and disadvantages of convertible debentures to the company and to the holder and comment on the terms of this issue.

6. *Whenever a company engages a source of finance it accepts a commitment to the provider of that finance. This commitment, to some extent, constrains future operations. Describe the nature of the commitment and comment on the constraints imposed in the cases of equity capital, debentures secured on a building and a bank overdraft.*

4: Financial Institutions

4.1 Access to Finance

4.1.1 Having looked at the merchandise we should consider how and where it might be purchased. Thus, having considered various types of finance, we shall now examine the institutional mechanisms by which they are made available.

4.2 The Stock Exchange

4.2.1 In connection with business finance the Stock Exchange is the institution likely to come first to mind and, although there are several others of great importance, this will be a suitable starting point for our survey. The Stock Exchange is an organisation which provides a market for companies' shares and debentures and for certain other securities. It thus allows the transfer of these investments from one owner to another. It does not of itself contribute any funds to the process and is not, therefore, directly the mechanism by which a business gains access to funds. It thus fulfils the same kind of function for shares as is performed for property by an estate agent or for secondhand cars by the classified advertising in a local newspaper.

4.2.2 If A owns 1,000 shares in X plc which he wishes to sell and B is seeking to acquire 1,000 shares in X a very simple transaction can satisfy both parties. B pays A for the shares and A advises the company, by means of a formal transfer document, to amend its Register of Members so that B's name is substituted for that of A. The Stock Exchange is not essential to this process and private transactions may easily be set up. What is difficult, however, is for A and B to identify and contact one another in the first place and then to determine an appropriate price for the sale. The Stock Exchange provides a way in which both of these things can be achieved.

4.2.3 Buyers and sellers do not meet directly through the Stock Exchange. Their business is conducted for them by professional intermediaries. These are of two kinds, stockbrokers and market makers. Prior to 27th October 1986 (the date of the so-called 'Big Bang') members of the Stock Exchange were required under its rules to act in either the one capacity or the other but not both. Since that date dual capacity firms have been allowed and are now the norm. Because of a possible conflict of interest between a broker (who should give his client impartial advice and deal for him in the most favourable market) and the market maker (who seeks to buy securities as cheaply and sell them as dearly as possible) the functions are still carried out in separate departments.

4.2.4 Let us look at an example of how the Stock Exchange works. A wishes to sell his 1,000 shares in X and gives an instruction to that effect to his broker. The broker approaches a market maker who deals in the shares of X (there is likely to be more than one) and asks for a price without indicating whether he is a buyer or a seller but stating the size of the deal, i.e. 1,000 shares. The market maker will quote a price in the form £1.60 – £1.65. This means 'I will give you £1.60 per share if you are selling and charge you £1.65 per share if you are buying.' The difference between the two prices is known as the market maker's 'turn' and provides him with his remuneration. The broker may approach another market maker, in the hope of finding a more favourable price at which to deal, before agreeing to trade. He will then, following settlement, pay to A £1,600 less his broker's commission (which is his source of income). Similarly a broker acting for B will have gone through a similar process, paying £1,650 for the shares and charging this to his client plus commission.

4.2.5 The market maker will always buy and sell shares at the prices he quotes. At any one time he may hold shares in 'stock' or may be short, i.e. have promised to deliver more than he has yet bought. This is known as the market maker's 'position'. In the long run he must equate shares bought with shares sold and this he does by raising his price to encourage sellers and put off buyers or lowering it to achieve the converse. The market maker's turn is kept to modest proportions by competition from other market makers.

Prior to Big Bang Stock Exchange deals were conducted face to face on the trading floor of the Exchange. Now, increasingly, they are conducted electronically through a computer and communications network.

4.2.6 With the exception of transactions in certain Government Stocks, Stock Exchange transactions are not settled on a cash basis. The Stock Exchange divides its year into a series of 'accounts'. Each account is a period of time, normally of two weeks, but extending to three when it embraces a public holiday. The normal account is from Monday of the first week to Friday of the second. All transactions taking place in an account are to be settled on Settlement Day which is the Tuesday next but one after the end of the account.

4.2.7 Although obviously an administrative convenience, this method of working opens up interesting possibilities for the speculator (i.e. the gambler as opposed to investor). If he believes that share prices will rise substantially during an account he may buy far more shares at the beginning of the account than he can afford to pay for. Provided he sells before the end of the account he will not have to find any money but will receive a cheque representing his profit (or a bill for his loss) on Settlement Day. Such a speculator, gambling on a rise in prices, is called, in Stock Exchange terminology, a 'bull'. Even more interestingly, a speculator expecting a fall in share prices may sell at the beginning of the account shares which he does not own! He then buys them (more cheaply if he has been correct) at the end of the account and, again, receives his profit on Settlement Day. This type of speculator is known as a 'bear'.

4.2.8 Some would argue that the speculator is an irrelevant nuisance on a financial market since he has no intention of making any long term investment. He does, however, pay the full costs of his operations, which do not therefore fall on anyone else, and he is of considerable assistance in contributing to a free market in securities of all kinds.

4.2.9 The relevance of the Stock Exchange to a company's access to funds, as will have been seen, is a secondary one. A company does not obtain funds from the Stock Exchange but the existence of a free market in securities makes it easier to obtain them from investors and means that it can do so on more favourable terms. An investor is more easily persuaded to purchase new shares in a company if he knows that the Stock Exchange gives him an opportunity to re-assess his investment on a continuous basis than he might be if his investment decision were irrevocable and permanent.

4.2.10 The activity of the Stock Exchange leads, amongst other things, to a great deal of investor interest in share prices. The prices of all securities dealt in are given daily in the Stock Exchange Official List. These are in two forms. One is a list of the prices at which bargains have been struck during the day and the other is the official closing price. This is regarded as authoritative by other agencies (e.g. the Inland Revenue) requiring share valuations for any purpose. Certain financial newspapers and journals publish regularly an index of share prices. The most famous of these is the Financial Times Index of Ordinary Share Prices which has been computed daily since the 1930's. A more representative index of fairly recent origin is the FTSE 100 (Financial Times–Stock Exchange) index.

4.3 Merchant Bankers

4.3.1 The merchant bankers, some of whom have a history going back deep into Britain's past as an international trading nation, have a very important role in giving companies access to long term finance. They are not bankers in the normally understood sense of the term and their role is perhaps best seen as that of professional experts in the area of raising finance. Just as a sick person will visit a doctor and one in dispute with his neighbour may call on his solicitor, so as a company seeking to raise money may consult a merchant bank.

4.3.2 A number of important factors need to be settled and arranged in connection with a new issue of shares and in all of those experienced advice is likely to lead to a more satisfactory outcome than could be achieved by the company acting alone. Having determined these matters the merchant bank can also handle the administration of the issue. This will include the preparation of a prospectus, advertising the issue and the receipt and processing of cash and applications. A useful service, normally provided in the case of large public issues, is that the merchant bank will, for a special commission, underwrite the issue. This means that they guarantee its success by undertaking to take up themselves any shares not applied for by the public. This is extremely valuable to a company in need of finance which it can thus be assured will definitely be forthcoming.

4.4 Share Issues

4.4.1 There are three main categories of share issue which should be noted. These are:

(a) A Public Issue – in which any person or institution is publicly invited to subscribe. This is an appropriate form to use where the amount of capital to be raised is large, the company is new to the market but likely to be attractive to investors and it is desired to have a wide spread of ownership in the shares. A public issue, however, is relatively expensive in terms of the incidental costs of mounting it.

The mechanism of a public issue of shares is as follows. The company prepares a prospectus setting out the merits of the investment and giving detailed information (much of it required by law) about the company. It is a criminal offence to make deliberate mis-statements in a prospectus. The availability of the prospectus is advertised or, in some cases, the full prospectus is reproduced as an advertisement in the press. Applications for the shares may be made by any interested person subject only to stipulations made by the company about the minimum number of shares which may be applied for and the multiples in which the applications may be made. Commonly a company may also require a declaration that the applicant has not submitted more than one application.

When all the applications are in (which must be by a stated deadline) the company will allot the available shares as it deems fit. In the event of an oversubscription this may be done by allotting all applicants fewer than the number of shares they applied for or by drawing lots to determine which applicants should be successful. Some combination of these two methods may be used. Unsuccessful or partially unsuccessful applicants will receive a refund of surplus money sent with the application.

A public issue of shares may be made at a fixed price either payable in full on application or in instalments or it may be an offer by tender. The latter is rather less usual but, where it applies, an applicant must state the maximum price which he or she is willing to pay (subject to a stipulated minimum) and send that amount of cash with the application. When all the applications are in and the weight of demand can be seen the company will determine a price for the shares, known as the 'striking price'. The striking price will be at a level such that sufficient investors tendering that amount or more exist at least to absorb the full issue. Applicants offering less than the striking price will be rejected (and will receive repayment of their application money). Successful applicants tendering more than the eventual striking price will receive a part refund to bring their net payment down to the level of the striking price.

(b) A Rights Issue – This is an issue on a pro rata basis to existing shareholders. They are an obvious source of new funds as they can be presumed already to have an interest in the company. A rights issue is normally used for relatively small issues of shares and because of the relief from the necessity of preparing a prospectus and the reduction in administrative costs, expenses of this method are relatively low. The shareholders are usually offered the right to subscribe to the new issue on favourable terms (i.e. below the current market price of the existing shares). The rights are negotiable so that any shareholder not wishing to subscribe can sell his right to do so through the Stock Exchange. This offers a considerable guarantee of the success of the issue.

(c) A Placing – This is an issue of shares to a specific investor or investors directly introduced to the company, usually by a merchant bank. A placing is the least expensive method of issuing shares but obviously requires the existence of substantial interested investors. These are likely to be institutional, e.g. insurance companies, pension funds or other companies. Those receiving shares through a placing may release them to the market over a period (so as to avoid depressing the price by a sudden large sale) or may retain them permanently.

4.5 Commercial Banks

4.5.1 The ordinary 'High Street' bank, where most of us hold our current accounts, provide important financial services to industry and commerce. It is a normal banking principle that prudence requires that they lend 'short' i.e. on terms that require a fairly rapid repayment (the lending of money for house purchase is a very recent departure from this principle). It is uncommon, therefore, for a bank to provide a business with long term finance but it is invaluable in its provision of short or medium term funds either in the form of loans or as bank overdrafts.

4.5.2 It may be instructive to see, in simple terms, how a banking business operates. As an illustration we will suppose that a brand new bank opens its doors for business and that customers open current accounts and deposit with it a total of £10,000. Its balance sheet will appear like this:

Newbank, plc

Customers' accounts	£10,000	Cash	£10,000

As a simplification we have assumed that the bank has no capital of its own and no assets such as premises or equipment.

4.5.3 If the bank saw itself as a mere custodian of the deposited cash it would retain this in its vaults and could derive an income only from any charge which it made for this service. Experience would show, however, that it was very unlikely that all customers would ask for all their money back simultaneously and that most of it would, therefore, lie idle for most of the time. This gives the opportunity for the bank to lend that amount out at interest.

4.5.4 Let us say that it is decided to retain 10% of the deposited cash to meet customers' demand for it and to lend 90%. The balance sheet becomes:

Newbank, plc

Customers' accounts	£10,000	Cash	£1,000
		Loans to customers	9,000
	£10,000		£10,000

The money lent to customers will be spent by them and most of it will be deposited in the recipients' bank accounts. Some of them will bank with Newbank as will some of the recipients of cash lent by other banks. The amount deposited might be expected to give rise to a revised balance sheet such as the one shown below:

Newbank, plc

Customers' accounts	£15,000	Cash	£6,000
		Loans to customers	9,000
	£15,000		£15,000

4.5.5 Once again 90% of the new deposits can be lent and the balance sheet is altered again:

Newbank, plc

Customers' accounts	£15,000	Cash	£1,500
		Loans to customers	13,500
	£15,000		£15,000

It can thus be seen that much of the money lent by banks is recirculated and its amount is not, therefore, limited to their own cash resources. Money created by banks in this way is far more significant to the money supply within the economy than is actual currency.

4.5.6 The success of this method of banking, which requires long term stability, depends on:

(a) the maintenance of a prudent cash reserve;

(b) the lending of money on terms which make the loan as free from risk to the bank as possible and as readily realisable as possible;

(c) the undisturbed confidence of the business community in the banking system.

Commercial banks pay careful attention to all these matters. Failure to do so in the historical past has led to banking collapses due to uncontrolled runs on a bank's limited resources.

4.6 Private Investors

4.6.1 Traditionally the company investor is pictured either as a wealthy (and perhaps wicked) capitalist holding a large portfolio of shares in a variety of companies or as an elderly widow left a few shares in a company by her late husband and relying on the dividend for her Christmas spending money. Neither exists in sufficient numbers to provide the kind of financial support needed by a capital intensive industry. Nevertheless private individuals do hold shares in many companies in surprisingly large numbers. They range in temperament from a person taking an active interest in stock market affairs and regularly reviewing his or her investments to one who holds small numbers of shares indefinitely and takes no particular interest in the progress of the companies. A private individual can easily acquire shares. This is done either by applying for new shares in response to a newspaper advertisement or by instructing his or her bank or stockbroker to obtain them through the market.

The number of people in the U.K holding shares in a company has increased very dramatically in recent years as a consequence of government policies directed at that end. The biggest stimulus has been the privatisation of previously state-owned concerns like British Telecom, British Gas and the water industry. In all cases the government has favoured the small investor by giving small applications preference in the allotment of shares and by allowing payment for them by instalments spread over a year or more. The offers have been at attractive prices and successful applicants have made substantial profits either realised or unrealised. Longer term ownership has been encouraged by the offer of free shares equal to 10% of the number held issued to original investors who hold their shares for an unbroken period of three years.

More recently the introduction of Personal Equity Plans (PEP), which enable direct investment in quoted companies with freedom from capital gains tax on dealing profits and income tax on dividends has given further stimulus to the enthusiasm of the small investor.

4.7 Unit Trusts

4.7.1 The unit trust movement has become a very important medium whereby the savings of small investors can be channelled into investment in shares. By its operation a person with, say, £500 to invest can obtain an interest in several hundreds of companies where a direct investment would have to be limited to one or, at the most, two. Very small transactions are relatively expensive to process and this is reflected in the high dealing costs charged on them.

4.7.2 A unit trust is managed by a management company which for its services receives fees and commissions. It is often owned by a merchant bank or commercial bank. The basic object of the trust is to invest the money of the unit holders in a wide spread of investments. Sometimes these may be selected on a criterion reflecting an overall policy of the trust (e.g. investment in a special market sector like electronics or food retailing or investment in a particular geographical area like America or Australia). The total value of the fund and the number of units is flexible and continuously variable. It depends on the number of investors who can be persuaded to participate.

4.7.3 Each day the portfolio of investments is revalued by reference to stock market prices and divided by the number of units in issue to determine the value of a single unit. This is quoted in the form of a double price (as with shares) to allow a 'turn' to cover dealing costs. There will be a 'bid' price at which the trust will repurchase units offered back to it and a higher 'offer' price at which the trust will sell units. The income earned from the dividends on shares held by the trust is either distributed rateably to the unit holders or used to acquire extra units for them and re-invested.

It can be seen that the price of units does not depend on the supply of and demand for units but on the supply of and demand for the shares underlying them. As a consequence of this the managers must maintain a balance by realising investments whenever the number of units redeemed exceeds the number sold and investing more when the reverse is the case. They will hold some cash and moderate stocks of unsold units to facilitate the process.

4.7.4 Example. The Widespread Unit Trust is set up and subscriptions invited to buy units at 25p each. 800,000 units are sold initially bringing in £200,000. This is invested in a mixed selection of shares in accordance with the stated policy of the trust. On a certain future date the investments are valued at £250,000 and the number of units held is unchanged at 800,000. The underlying value of a unit is

$$\frac{£250,000}{800,000} = 31.25p$$

The managers quote a bid price of, say, 2.5% less than this and an offer price of 2.5% more. Thus they quote 30.5p bid and 32.0p offer (rounded off to one decimal place). Holders of 150,000 units decided to cash in their investment but applications are received for the supply of 200,000 new units. This is a net increase in the number of units outstanding of 50,000 and new units must be created to meet this. Thus:

Cash received for 200,000 units sold (32.0p each)	£64,000
In respect of 150,000 existing units to be reissued	48,000
Hence in respect of 50,000 new units	£16,000
Proceeds of resale of existing units (as above)	£48,000
Amount paid on repurchase by managers (30.5p each)	45,750
Managers' 'turn' on reissued units	£2,250
Proceeds of sale of new units as above	£16,000
Amount for investment in market (31.25p each)	15,625
Managers' 'turn' on new units	£375

The new value of the fund is £250,000 + £15,625. The value of units is unchanged at 31.25p. Only a change in the value of the underlying securities will affect this.

4.8 Pension Funds and Life Assurance companies

4.8.1 Very large sums of money become regularly available from pension funds and from life assurance companies in endowment business. It is essential characteristic of both of these that members make regular payments over a very long period of time in order to obtain a benefit either as a lump sum or as an annuity upon the arrival of a specified date. It is the object of the management of the fund to invest these payments as they are received so that the ultimate benefit shall be maximised.

4.9 Investment Trusts

4.9.1 An investment trust is a limited company, with its own conventional financial structure, whose business is to invest in the shares of other companies. By buying shares in the investment trust, investors obtain an interest in a relatively wide spread of underlying investments as they would with a unit trust. Unlike a unit trust an investment trust is closed and a potential investor must find someone willing to sell shares to him. This sale will be at an agreed price (determined normally by the operation of market forces) not immediately related to the valuation of the trust's investments. Shares in investment trusts can be bought through the Stock Exchange in the same way as the shares of trading companies.

Summary

(i) There are several institutional mechanisms which contribute to giving access to capital to corporate businesses. The most important are discussed in this chapter.

(ii) The Stock Exchange is a market. It does not of itself contribute funds to business but provides the background of the free exchange of investments which encourages these funds to come forward.

(iii) Merchant banks provide a professional service to companies seeking to raise funds by means of a share issue. This includes advice, the administration of the issue and underwriting services.

(iv) A share issue may be:
   (a) an issue to the general public;
   (b) a rights issue, i.e. to existing shareholders or
   (c) a placing, i.e. to a limited number of specially introduced investors.

(v) Commercial banks are particularly useful for the provision of short and medium term finance. By judicious lending of funds entrusted to their care banks are able to create large sums of money which would not otherwise be available.

(vi) Private investors are an important, though not dominant, source of finance.

(vii) A unit trust is an open ended fund which enables the small investor to spread his capital over a large number of investments.

(viii) An investment trust is itself a company. Its function is to invest its money in other companies.

Review Questions

(i) *What is the difference between a unit trust and an investment trust?*

(ii) *What is a merchant bank?*

(iii) *Explain the stock market terms 'bull' and 'bear'.*

(iv) *What is the function of the Stock Exchange?*

(v) *Distinguish between a stockbroker and a market maker.*

(vi) *How do stockbrokers and market makers derive an income from their work?*

(vii) *What information is given by an index of share prices?*

(viii) *Mr X believes that the price of the shares in a certain company will shortly halve in value. How can he profit from this information? What risk will be involved if he seeks to do so?*

Exercises

1. *'The Stock Exchange is little more than a gambling casino. It serves no function in the process of channelling new finance to industry'. Discuss.*

2. *'The commercial banks manufacture more money by their lending policies than does the Royal Mint'. How can this be?*

3. *Outline the ways in which the savings of the ordinary person may find their way into industrial investment.*

4. *The Crazy Unit Trust is set up with the policy of buying shares in loss making companies. It is believed that these will recover and that their share prices will increase substantially. The following events occur:*

    (i) *1,000,000 units were subscribed for at £1 each;*

    (ii) *the whole fund was invested in the market;*

(iii) *the fund was, after an interval, valued at the equivalent of £1.20 per unit and offer and bid prices set at 2.5% on either side of this;*

(iv) *500,000 units were sold to the public and 350,000 bought back from holders;*

(v) *all available funds were reinvested;*

(vi) *the fund, after a further interval, was valued at the equivalent of 90p per unit and offer and bid prices set accordingly;*

(vii) *100,000 units were sold to the public and 600,000 bought back from holders.*

Calculate the effects of these transactions. How does the management derive an income from its services?

5. Describe the following methods whereby a company may raise extra finance:

(a) *a public issue of shares;*

(b) *a rights issue of shares and;*

(c) *a placing.*

What are the advantages and disadvantages of each?

6. Compare and contrast the function of the broker and the market maker in the operation of the Stock Exchange.

5: Cost of Capital

5.1 Cost of Finance

5.1.1 A very important element in decisions about the use of any resource is the cost of that resource. This is true of finance just as much as it is of anything else. The cost of finance is generally termed the cost of capital. Individual components of capital may have quite different costs, being obtained from different markets. We need to consider these individual components and also the way in which they combine to give an appropriate overall cost of capital. The cost of capital is normally expressed, like a rate of interest, as x% per annum.

5.2 Average and Marginal Cost

5.2.1 We shall need in later analysis to distinguish between two distinct concepts of the cost of capital. The average cost of capital is the cost of the capital currently employed; being the weighted average of the costs for the individual components. The marginal cost of capital is the cost of the next increment of capital to be employed. The former is important to measures of performance and to a current valuation of the business. The latter is to be used to determine whether or not proposed developments are likely to be profitable.

It is likely that, as a business grows, its marginal cost of capital will be below average cost. This represents its improving access to less expensive forms of finance as it is perceived by the market to be a better investment. At some point, however, marginal cost is likely to become equal to average cost and then to rise above it.

5.2.2 The distinction between a marginal and an average cost is one which is well understood and used by the economist. It is an important one which an example will make clear. John has financed the purchase of his house, furniture and car as follows:

Mortgage £10,000 at 10% per annum

Bank loan £5,000 at 15% per annum

Credit cards £2,000 at 20% per annum

John's average cost of capital is

$$\frac{(10,000 \times 10) + (5,000 \times 15) + (2,000 \times 20)}{17,000}$$

which is 12.65% per annum. If John wishes to borrow more money he can do so only by going to a moneylender and paying 40% per annum (this is because he has 'used up' all cheaper sources of funds). His marginal cost of capital is, therefore, 40% per annum. If marginal cost exceeds average cost, as here, note that average cost will rise as the marginal capital is taken up.

5.3 The Cost of Ordinary Share Capital

5.3.1 Since the dividend paid on ordinary shares depends on the availability of profits and is, in any case, paid only at the option of the directors, it might seem to be logical to argue that ordinary share capital (equity) has no cost. It is certainly true that we are under no obligation to pay anything to existing shareholders but no business can maintain a long term existence on that basis nor can it raise additional funds. The cost of equity capital is therefore taken to be the rate which has effectively to be paid in order to maintain the present market value of the equity. The special nature of equity means that part of the 'payment' may be in cash (dividends) and part in an accretion to the reserves attributable to equity (leading to capital appreciation).

5.3.2 Example. X, plc has an ordinary share capital of nominal value £1 million in shares of £1 each. It earns an annual profit of £100,000 and pays out the whole of this as a dividend (i.e. 10% on nominal value). The current market price of X's shares is £1.50 each. The cost of equity capital to X is the same as the yield on the equity to investors, i.e.

$$E = \frac{d}{m} \times 100$$

$$= \frac{10p}{150p} \times 100$$

$$= 6.67\%$$

where: E = cost of equity capital

d = dividend per share

m = market value of share

This is the cost of equity capital currently employed.

5.3.3 Where, as in practice is more probable, the dividend does not absorb the whole of the profit, the calculation of the cost of equity becomes a little more complicated. The dividend is not now the only return to the investor. There will also be the growth in the capital value of his investment which the retained earnings will bring about.

5.3.4 Example. X, plc distributes only 5p per share. The other 5p is ploughed back into the business and is expected to give rise to a future growth in earnings and dividend, and hence in capital value, of 5% per annum compound. This figure will, of course, relate not only to what is retained but to how profitably it can be used.

$$E = \frac{d}{m} \times 100 + g$$

$$= \frac{5p}{150p} \times 100 + 5\%$$

$$= 8.33\%$$

where g = expected growth consequent on retention of profit.

5.3.5 The marginal cost of equity capital is determined by the conditions surrounding a new issue of shares and these would need to be predicted before it could be calculated. It should be noted also that the amount received by the company when it issues the shares is less than the amount paid by the investor. This is because the issue of shares is a procedure which has costs associated with it. A few of these are advertising, stationery, underwriting premiums, financial and legal advice, clerical costs, etc.

5.3.6 Example. X wishes to raise additional capital by the issue of 200,000 new ordinary shares. It anticipates that profits will increase in proportion to the increase in capital, allowing the maintenance of the present rate of dividend and of growth, and judges that the issue price of the new shares will have to be set at £1.40 to ensure success. The costs of issue will be 2p per share.

5.3.7 The marginal cost of equity is given by:

$$E = \frac{d}{m - c} \times 100 + g$$

$$= \frac{5p}{(140 - 2)p} \times 100 + 5\%$$

$$= 8.62\%$$

where c = cost, per share, of issue.

5.3.8 It should be noted that, if the expansion to be financed by the increased capital changes the perception of the company's prospects held by existing shareholders, the calculation of the marginal cost of equity capital is more complicated. The actual cost of the new capital has then to be amended by the increase or decrease in the cost of the old. This complication is not likely to be encountered in examination questions.

5.4 Cost of Retained Earnings

5.4.1 It would once again be a fallacy to assume that the cost of retained earnings is nil. For a company to retain some of its earnings rather than distributing them is equivalent to the issue of fresh equity to existing shareholders. Collectively they are required to make a further investment in their company. The cost of existing retained earnings is therefore the same as the cost of existing equity. The cost of new retained earnings is the same as that of a new equity issue (m, however, being the existing market price) except that there are no issue costs and thus the term c in the above formula disappears. (It could be argued that c actually becomes negative since by retaining earnings the company not only avoids the costs of issuing equity but it also saves its shareholders the cost of reinvesting their dividends). There are also tax considerations which affect the argument but these are looked at in Chapter 15.

5.5 Cost of Preferred Capital

5.5.1 The determination of the cost of preference capital is exactly like the determination of the cost of equity. The present cost is the yield currently received by preference shareholders and the marginal cost is the yield which has to be offered in order to attract fresh preference funds. The formula used is the same as that for equity but is made simpler because the term g, growth, does not apply. Preference shares have a fixed maximum rate of dividend and a fixed maximum capital payout in a winding up. No growth is, therefore, possible for them.

5.5.2 Example. X, plc has in issue some 8% £1 preference shares. The dividend has always been paid and, since it is well covered, is always expected to be paid. The shares stand in the market at 90p each.

It is proposed to make a further issue of these shares at $87\frac{1}{2}$p each. Issue costs will amount to $1\frac{1}{2}$p per share. Determine both the present and marginal costs of preference capital.

(a)   Present cost $\qquad P = \dfrac{d}{m} \times 100$

$$= \frac{8}{90} \times 100$$

$$= 8.89\% \text{ per annum}$$

(a) Marginal cost $\qquad P = \dfrac{d}{m-c} \times 100$

$$= \dfrac{8}{87\frac{1}{2} - 1\frac{1}{2}} \times 100$$

$$= 9.30\% \text{ per annum}$$

where P = the cost of preference capital.

5.6 Cost of Long Term Debt

5.6.1 The cost of long term debt is the yield received by its holders at current market prices. The marginal cost is the yield which must be given to attract new investment, after allowing for issue costs. The calculations follow the lines of those we have already seen.

5.6.2 Example. X, plc has in issue some 10% debenture stock which stands in the market at 85. A new issue made at par would have to offer $12\frac{1}{2}\%$ and issue costs would be equal to 1% of nominal value. Determine the present and marginal costs of debt.

(a) Present cost $\qquad P = \dfrac{i}{m} \times 100$

$$= \dfrac{10}{85} \times 100$$

$$= 11.76\% \text{ per annum}$$

(a) Marginal cost $\qquad P = \dfrac{i}{m-c} \times 100$

$$= \dfrac{12\frac{1}{2}}{100 - 1} \times 100$$

$$= 12.63\% \text{ per annum}$$

where D = the cost of debt.
$\qquad$ i = the rate of interest.

5.7 Cost of Other Forms of Borrowing

5.7.1 Bank loans and overdrafts and similar types of loan have costs which are equal to their explicit cost. E.g. if bank borrowing interest rates are 15% per annum then this is the cost of that source of capital.

There are no significant costs involved in arranging a bank loan and, since the loan is not a marketable security, its value is fixed by contract.

5.7.2 Creditors and other current liabilities

The cost of trade credit is normally nil but it has the characteristic that it cannot usually be expanded to add to the general amount of finance available. It expands or contracts along with current purchases of supplies and becomes, therefore, a specific source of finance for stock holding. Since these supplies are obtained to support some particular part of the business's activities it is also specific to that part. For this reason the value of creditors is generally regarded as a reduction in the amount of working capital required by a project and thus of an overall reduction in the amount of finance required, rather than as, in itself, a source of finance.

It should be noted that some creditors will offer a cash discount for prompt payment and, therefore, this form of finance may have a cost if payment is delayed so that the discount cannot be claimed.

Certain other current liabilities, e.g. unpaid taxation, may be regarded as a genuinely 'free' source of finance. They may depend, however, on factors other than the level of finance required and cannot normally be called on at will.

5.8 Overall Cost of Capital

5.8.1 Let us now return to the question of average v. marginal cost of capital. We will suppose that we are contemplating an investment in a particular project. For this we shall have to raise extra capital. What will be of concern to us will be the cost of this new capital, i.e. the marginal cost of capital. If the amount concerned is substantial and if the raising of it fundamentally changes the nature and prospects of the business, then the marginal cost of capital may be quite different from the present cost. If we are discussing a fairly minimal extension to our activities, the marginal cost may be equal to the present cost. All this means is that new capital in relatively small amounts may be able to be raised on similar terms to the capital already employed. For this reason the present cost of capital (which is relatively easy to determine since it involves less speculation about the future) is often used in the evaluation of new investment opportunities.

5.8.2 Weighted Average Cost of Capital

There is another way in which an average comes in, even to a calculation of the marginal cost of capital and this sometimes causes confusion. Let us suppose that we have made the following estimates for a certain company:

Source of finance	Current market value	Present cost	Marginal cost
Equity	£1 million	12%	12%
Preference	£½ million	15%	16%
Long term debt	£½ million	18%	20%

We wish to establish the viability or otherwise of a new project and this is to be financed by the issue of new debentures (i.e. long term debt). We may be tempted to argue that therefore the cost of capital for this project is the marginal cost of debt, i.e. 20% per annum. Had we planned to finance the project by equity, a similar argument would have said that the appropriate rate would have been 12% per annum (the marginal cost of equity). In this we would have been incorrect. These sources of finance are not specific to projects and in the long run we shall have to maintain a proper balance between them. If we finance the current project by debt, this may commit us to financing the next one by equity in order to restore that balance. If we now use equity, we may similarly be committed in the future to more debt financing. We meet this by regarding the marginal cost of capital as a weighted average of the costs of the sources available to us regardless of which source we actually intend to use. The weighting used will be that appropriate to our desired capital structure which, in most cases, we shall take to be the existing capital structure. The marginal cost of capital in this case then becomes:

$$\frac{(12 \times 1) + (16 \times \frac{1}{2}) + (20 \times \frac{1}{2})}{(1 + \frac{1}{2} + \frac{1}{2})} = 15\% \text{ per annum}$$

Note that a company is in a quite different position from an individual such as John who we met in 5.2.2. Most of an individual's finance is project-specific. A mortgage is used for buying a house but not for buying a car. A bank loan is given for the purposes specified in the original application for the advance and cannot properly be used for any other purpose. Marginal borrowing, therefore, cannot be regarded as coming in a similar mix to what has already been raised. Moreover, whilst a company can theoretically be expanded without limit, an individual can not. If you move house and double your mortgage it does not double your capacity to take on a bank loan, on the contrary it means that you will be less eligible for one. If a company doubles its equity, however, it does, other things being equal, double its borrowing capacity because assets and earning capacity have also increased pro rata with the increased equity.

5.8.3 The way in which a company's cost of capital is related to the size of the business has important implications. Where the marginal cost of capital is below average cost and is thus falling this means that as the business grows it becomes profitable for it to undertake projects that were previously unprofitable even though in other respects they are unaltered. Some would argue that this is what happens in practice as the larger a company becomes and hence the more widely known, the more cheaply can it raise funds. Where the marginal cost of capital is rising the company will reach an optimum size once the cost of capital has risen to equal the return offered by the best projects available. There are good reasons for thinking that this latter situation will ultimately prevail even if not in the early stages of growth. If not, one would expect the typical company to expand explosively. By and large this is not a phenomenon that is observed.

5.8.4 Both inflation and taxation can have a profound effect on the cost of capital and these matters will be considered in later chapters (inflation in Chapter 14 and taxation in Chapter 15).

Summary

(i) The cost of capital is the rate (as a % per annum) which a company has to pay for its finance.

(ii) Since most companies are financed from a mixture of sources, the cost of capital will usually be made up of a number of components at different rates.

(iii) The cost of equity capital is equal to the yield, allowing for capital growth as well as cash dividends, receivable by the ordinary shareholders at the current market price of the shares. This is the yield which must be met if the total value of the equity is to be maintained.

(iv) The cost of preference capital and debt is similarly calculated but here only the dividend or interest yield on the current price need be considered. No element of growth accrues to the holders of these securities.

(v) Where there are costs of issue for securities, these should be taken into account by deducting them from the market price before making the calculation of yield. This recognises that the amount of finance received by business is less, by the amount of the costs, than the amount advanced by the investor.

(vi) There is an important distinction to be made between the average and the marginal costs of capital. The former is the cost of capital currently in use and the latter is the cost of the next increment to be raised. They may, in a real situation, be equal in value.

(vii) Whether we are computing the average cost of capital or the marginal cost the components (debt, equity, retained earnings) must be weighted in accordance with their respective weights in the company's preferred capital structure. This is often, in practice, taken to be the same as its existing structure.

Review Questions

(i) *Retained profits are sometimes regarded as a 'free' source of finance. Why is this erroneous?*

(ii) *Distinguish carefully between the average cost of capital and its marginal cost. Why is the distinction important?*

(iii) *It is suggested that a project yielding 18% per annum should be financed by an issue of debt costing 16% per annum. What other information would you want before supporting this suggestion?*

(iv) *What important difference is there between the computation of the cost of equity and preference capital respectively?*

(v) *What would you understand by the term 'Project-specific finance' and why might this concept be important?*

(vi) *A company's capital is shown in its balance sheet at its nominal value. Its market value may diverge considerably from this. Which of the two valuations is of most significance to the financial manager and why?*

(vii) *'A company's cost of capital is merely the rate of interest which it pays for its funds.' Do you agree?*

(viii) *A company finds that the cheapest source of funds available to it is a secured bank loan. Why should it not raise all its finance requirements from this source?*

Exercises

1. *The following data are available for Holmes, plc.*

   Share capital
   500,000 ordinary shares of £1 each fully paid
   150,000 6% preference shares of 50p each fully paid

   Reserves

Share premium account	£100,000
Profit and loss account	£240,000

   Loan capital
   £125,000 10% debentures

In the stock market Holmes' shares and debentures are currently quoted as follows:

Ordinary shares	£1.30 each
Preference shares	40p each
Debentures	£167%

Holmes distributes all of its profits, which have been constant for some time, and the current ordinary dividend is 20%. Calculate the average cost of capital. Ignore costs of issuing securities.

2. *The terms on which fresh capital of various kinds could be issued by Holmes are as follows:*

   Ordinary shares @ £1.20 each, cost of issue 2p per share
   Preference shares @ 35p each, cost of issue $1^1/_2$p per share
   Debentures at current market price, cost of issue 1% nominal value

   Calculate Holmes' marginal cost of capital. The other facts are as given in Exercise 1.

3. *The following information is available for Watson, plc.*

	Current	Marginal
Cost of equity	22%	25%
Cost of preference capital	12%	12%
Cost of debt	8%	10%
Overall cost of capital	16%	18%

   The Board of Directors is considering investing in a project which is expected to yield a return equivalent to 15% per annum to be financed either by debt or by an issue of preference capital. Some members of the Board argue that preference capital should be used because it can currently be raised on similar terms to that already in issue. Others argue that debt should be used because it is the cheapest form of capital available and will thus give maximum profitability to the project. All are agreed that the project is worthwhile. Give your views.

4. *Mycroft, plc has currently an average cost of capital of 15% per annum on the funds which it employs which total £1,000,000, 75% of which is equity and 25% debt. Marginal costs of debt and equity are:*

Debt:	Up to £100,000	16% per annum
	Next £100,000	18% per annum
Equity:	Up to £250,000	20% per annum
	Next £250,000	25% per annum
	Thereafter	30% per annum

   Calculate Mycroft's marginal and average costs of capital at all critical levels.

5. *Moriarty, plc, an established company, proposes to raise an extra £1,000,000 by a public issue of £1 ordinary shares. After the issue it expects to pay a dividend of 12p per share initially and this dividend will grow at the rate of 10% per annum. Issue costs will be 2p per share. The equity cost of capital is estimated at 18% per annum. At what price should the issue be made?*

What will be the consequence of setting the wrong price? Ignore taxation.

6. Lestrade, plc is financed as follows:

1,000,000 ordinary shares of £1	£1,000,000
Revenue reserve	250,000
10 % debentures	200,000
	£1,450,000

The current market price of the company's ordinary shares is £1.80 each. This has been increasing at an average annual rate of 5% for some years and this rate of increase is expected to continue for the foreseeable future. The annual rate of dividend, which has been stable and is expected to remain so, is 15p per share. The 10% debentures stand in the market at 90.91%. Any new issues of either shares or debentures would require a similar market rating to the existing issues.

An investment project has recently come to the attention of the Board of Lestrade which has a projected internal rate of return of 12% per annum. There is a proposal to finance this by an issue of 8% debentures and the argument has been put forward that this will give a margin of 4% in favour of going ahead. The obvious merits of the investment, it is contended, will assure the success of the issue. Comment.

6: Capital Structure

6.1 Optimum Mix of Sources of Finance

6.1.1 We have now learnt that a financial manager seeking funds can look to a number of sources. We have also seen that each of these sources has its own associated cost, which will be different from one source to another, and that the overall cost of capital must be an appropriately weighted average. In this chapter we shall consider the problem of the optimum mix of sources of capital.

6.1.2 We drew an analogy earlier between the use, by a company, of different sources of finance in assembling its capital fund and the bringing together of different materials in the manufacture of a product. It is worth exploring that analogy a little further. In the case of the materials there are two factors to consider and the relative importance of each will vary from one situation to another. One factor is that technical considerations may govern the precise proportions of materials which may be used. A particular food product, for example, must contain certain ingredients in precisely determined quantities. The other factor is that of cost. In a case where no technical considerations affect the mixture then it will be of concern to use the most economical mixture.

6.1.3 In the area of finance there are a few technical constraints which need to be considered. The issue of preference shares, for example, has the prerequisite that a sufficient number of ordinary shares is in issue (otherwise the 'preference' will be of little value). Similarly loan capital must bear a reasonable relationship to equity if it is to be possible to issue it on reasonable terms. The number and value of mortgageable assets sets a limit on the amount of secured borrowing and this is another example of a technical consideration. These constraints, however, are fairly loose and by far the most important concern is that of how to arrive at a cost-efficient mix or capital structure.

6.1.4 We need first to address the question of whether the concept of an optimum capital structure is, in fact, a meaningful one. In view of what has been said before this might appear to be a nonsensical question. If the cost of capital is to be the weighted average of a number of sources at different costs then one might suppose that different weights (which follow from a different structure) must, by the arithmetic of it, lead to a different cost. This is, however, to overlook the fact that the costs of the various components of capital depend on market prices and these, in their turn, depend on an overall assessment of the prospects of the firm. This might depend, amongst other things, on its capital structure. There is clearly a somewhat complex relationship between capital structure and the cost of capital and we need now to explore it in detail. Before we do so we must look at some implications of the relationship between one form of financing and another.

6.2 Gearing

6.2.1 In order to simplify the analysis we shall consider only two kinds of finance, debt and equity. Preference capital has so much of the nature of debt that it is not worth putting it in a separate category.

Let us consider a firm with the stream of profits before dividends or interest (and ignoring taxation) set out below:

	Year 1	Year 2	Year 3	Year 4	Year 5	Year 6
Profit	£50,000	£60,000	£40,000	£50,000	£75,000	£37,500
Change over previous year	–	+20%	-33.3%	+25%	+50%	-50%

We will assume that the variations in profit are completely unpredictable and that, therefore, they represent the degree of risk inherent in the trading situation. This is described as the commercial risk. If the firm is wholly equity financed then, obviously, the risk borne by the equity holder is equal to the commercial risk.

6.2.2 Let us now assume that the firm is financed partly by equity and partly by debt. The debt involves interest charges of £15,000 per annum and this would, of course, be constant. Now we look again at our figures.

	Year 1 £	Year 2 £	Year 3 £	Year 4 £	Year 5 £	Year 6 £
Profit (as before)	50,000	60,000	40,000	50,000	75,000	37,500
Interest on debt	15,000	15,000	15,000	15,000	15,000	15,000
Available to equity	£35,000	£45,000	£25,000	£35,000	£60,000	£22,500
Change over previous year	–	+28.6%	-44.4%	+40%	+71.4%	-62.5%

The percentage changes in the amount available to equity holders are much larger because of the presence of debt which imposes a requirement of a fixed annual interest payment. To the commercial risk noted above has been added a factor which amplifies this. Since this is due to the different method of financing the operation this is described as a financial risk.

6.2.3 Our figures have shown the effect of financial risk to the equity holder. Since equity holders cannot withdraw their funds this risk represents no threat to the survival of the company. This is true, however, only where the proportion of debt to equity is relatively small. If it became high, so that profit fluctuations threatened not merely dividends but also interest, then foreclosure by the debenture holders would be a real possibility and financial risk would affect the company as a whole.

The use of debt along with equity is known as gearing. Its effect is always to add financial risk to the existing level of commercial risk.

$$G = \frac{D}{D + E}$$

where G = degree of gearing
D = market value of debt
E = market value of equity

The higher the gearing, the higher the degree of financial risk. In American texts gearing is termed 'leverage'.

6.2.4 Example. Overdrive, plc is, according to its balance sheet, financed as follows:

200,000 ordinary shares of £1 each	£200,000
£50,000 8½% debenture stock, 1999	50,000
	£250,000

Its ordinary shares are currently quoted in the market at £1.50 each and its debenture stock at £95 per cent. Calculate the degree of gearing.

$$G = \frac{D}{D + E}$$

$$= \frac{(£50,000 \times .95)}{(£50,000 \times .95) + (200,000 \times £1.50)}$$

$$= \frac{£47,500}{£347,500}$$

$$= \underline{\underline{0.14}}$$

6.2.5 Gearing is sometimes expressed in a different way from that shown above. It may be stated as a debt/equity ratio. This is given by:

$$R = \frac{D}{E}$$

For Overdrive in the present example:

$$R = \frac{£47,500}{£300,000}$$

$$= \underline{\underline{0.16}}$$

6.3 Gearing and the Cost of Capital – Traditional Theory

6.3.1   This theory argues that the cost of equity finance and the cost of debt are independently determined. If the cost of equity is higher, as logically it should be because it is more risky, then the more highly geared a company becomes the lower its cost of capital. We must recognise a limit to this process which, stated as above, leads inexorably to the conclusion that all companies should be financed exclusively by debt. This limit is that, at some point on the scale, the proportion of debt will become sufficiently large for it to become significantly risky to lend more to the business, i.e. its solvency will come into question. At a point near to this the risk to the equity holder also rises making the cost of this too take a sharp upward turn. The rule we are left with is that the rational company will employ as much debt as it can without impairing the safety of the company's future.

6.3.2   Example. Leverage, plc faces a cost of equity capital of 20% per annum and a cost of debt of 12% per annum. These rates apply up to a level of gearing of .75, i.e. where the company is 75% debt financed. The costs of both equity and debt then rise as shown below

Proportion of debt finance	Cost of debt (% per annum)	Cost of equity (% per annum)
80%	14	22
85%	16	24
90%	18	26
95%	20	28
100%	22	30

Determine the overall cost of capital for various proportions of debt finance. Plot a graph illustrating your figures.

6.3.3   The table below shows the calculation of the overall cost of capital and the graph appears on the following page as Figure 6.1.

Proportion of debt finance	Cost of debt (% per annum)	Cost of equity (% per annum)	Overall cost (% per annum)
10%	12	20	19.2
20%	12	20	18.4
30%	12	20	17.6
40%	12	20	16.8
50%	12	20	16.0
60%	12	20	15.2
70%	12	20	14.4
75%	12	20	14.0
80%	14	22	15.6
85%	16	24	17.2
90%	18	26	18.8
95%	20	28	20.4
100%	22	30	22.0

The cost of capital, as is shown by both the table and the graph, is minimised when debt represents about 75% of total finance.

6.4 Modigliani and Miller Theory

6.4.1 Another school of thought says that capital structure has no effect on the overall cost of capital (except at extreme levels of gearing) and that it may thus be determined quite randomly. This is the argument associated with the names of Modigliani and Miller who first propounded it. It is known for short as the MM theory.

6.4.2 MM states that the total value of a firm depends on its expected performance and its commercial risk and is independent of the way in which it happens to be financed. Any other position is one of disequilibrium which will be eradicated by investors playing the market through the process known as arbitrage. The following example illustrates this process.

6.4.3 Example. Companies A and B are identical except that A is ungeared, i.e. financed entirely by equity and B is geared, i.e. financed partly by debt. Details of performance are:

	A (£)	B (£)
Profit before interest or dividends	100,000	100,000
Interest on debt (market rate)	–	25,000
Available to equity holders	£100,000	£75,000

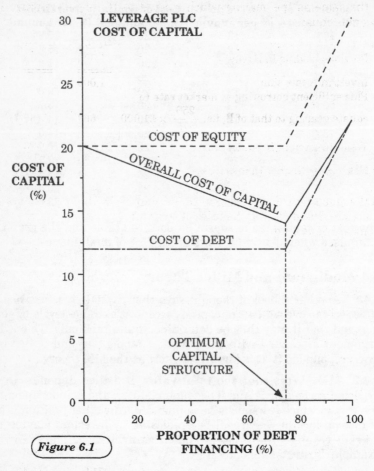

Figure 6.1

We will suppose that initially a disequilibrium condition exists where, for both companies, the equity stands at a price which gives it a yield of 20%. The market rate of interest for debt is 10%.

	A	B
	£	£
Value of equity	500,000	375,000
Value of debt	–	250,000
Total value of company	£500,000	£625,000
Cost of capital	20%	16%

MM would argue that, in this situation, B is overvalued and that arbitrage will take place. The reasoning behind this is that, if an investor in B sells his shares and purchases shares in A, borrowing part of the cost at the market rate of interest until his 'personal' gearing, and thus the degree of financial risk to which he is exposed, is the same as the gearing which existed in B, he will improve his income. Thus:

	Value	Income
Previous holding in B (say)	£1,000	£200
Invest in A this sum	1,000	
Plus sufficient borrowing at market rate to equate gearing to that of B, i.e. $\dfrac{250}{375} \times £1,000$	667	(66.7)
Total investment in equity of A	£1,667	333.3
Net income (higher than before)		£266.7

MM argue that this process continues, depressing the price of the shares in B and raising the price of those in A, until the firms' valuations are equal, e.g.:

	A £	B £
Value of equity (say)	600,000	350,000
Value of debt	–	250,000
Total value of company	£600,000	£600,000
Cost of capital	16.6%	16.6%

If our investor now practises arbitrage he is no better off for it.

	Value	Income
Previous holding B (say)	£1,000	£214.28[1]
Invest in A this sum	1,000	
Plus sufficient borrowing at market rate to equate gearing to that of B, i.e. $\dfrac{250}{350} \times £1,000$	714	(71.40)
	£1,714	285.68[2]
Net income (unchanged)		£214.28

Notes on previous calculations

1. $\dfrac{1,000}{350,000} \times £75,000 = £214.28$

2. $\dfrac{1,714}{600,000} \times £100,000 = £285.68$

Since there is no change in income following arbitrage there is no incentive to do it. This is, therefore, an equilibrium position and it has been demonstrated that the cost of capital does not depend on capital structure.

6.4.4 Critics of the MM theory point out that it relies on some important assumptions which are not valid in the real world. The main ones are that:

(a) Personal gearing carries precisely the same risk as corporate gearing. This is untrue. The limited liability which companies enjoy means that the investor is safer if his company borrows on his behalf than he is if he borrows on his own account.

(b) Personal borrowing is at the same rate of interest as corporate borrowing. This is unlikely to be true. In fixing rates of interest bankers have regard to the credit worthiness of the customer and the absolute size of the loan amongst many other factors.

(c) There is no taxation or else it is neutral as between debt and equity financing. This is not so. Taxation exists and we shall show elsewhere that, because debt interest is a tax deductible expense, whereas equity dividends are not, debt financing is relatively cheaper.

(d) There are no transaction costs in the arbitrage process. This is untrue. There are considerable costs involved in buying and selling investments and in monitoring the situation.

(e) There are no institutional factors against the arbitrage process. This is not so. Many large institutional investors, e.g. pension funds, life assurance companies, etc.would not wish or would be prohibited from borrowing to finance investment purchases. Many small investors may find their banks unwilling to lend to them for this purpose.

All this means that even if one accepts the logic of the MM theory one would have to anticipate that there would be considerable distortions arising from its translation to a real-life situation.

6.4.5 Example. Leverage, plc faces the cost of debt given in the previous example (paragraph 6.3.2). Its overall cost of capital up to the critical level of 75% debt financing is 15% per annum. What is the cost of equity corresponding to various capital structures?

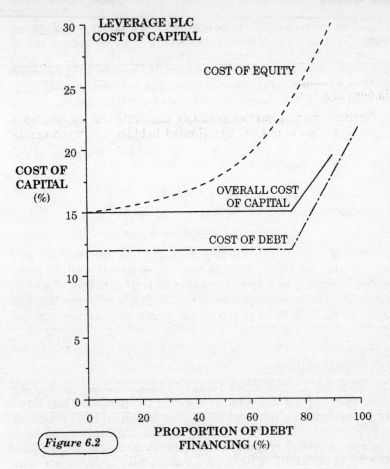

Figure 6.2

6.4.6 The table below shows the calculation of the equity cost of capital for debt financing up to 75%.

Proportion of debt finance	Cost of debt	Overall cost of capital	Cost of equity
	(% per annum)	(% per annum)	(% per annum)
10%	12	15	15.33
20%	12	15	15.75
30%	12	15	16.28
40%	12	15	17.00
50%	12	15	18.00
60%	12	15	19.50
70%	12	15	22.00
75%	12	15	24.00

Beyond this point the overall cost of capital would rise so that the cost of equity cannot be fully determined from the data available. The graph appears above as Figure 6.2.

6.4.7 There is a revised version of the MM theory which takes account of the effect of corporate taxation and thus removes one of the main objections to the original formulation. This concedes that, because the interest on debt is tax deductible, a geared firm is more valuable for a given total income stream than is an ungeared firm. This is another way of saying that its cost of capital is lower.

6.4.8 We can visualise the stream of income of the firm as divided into two portions. These are the return to equity, which bears corporation tax, and the return to debt, which does not. The value of the benefit of debt interest is:

$$interest \times tax\ rate$$

The increase in the value of the business is, therefore:

$$market\ value\ of\ debt \times tax\ rate.$$

6.4.9 The cost of capital, allowing for this tax effect, declines progressively as more debt is taken on until, as before, the critical point at which increased risk causes the cost of both debt and equity to rise sharply. The conclusion to be drawn is that a business ought to take on as much debt as it can at the prevailing market rate for debt.

6.5 A Compromise

6.5.1 We have set out above some of the main lines of thought relating to capital structure but it is a very complex issue and more could be said. Modigliani and Miller, for example, have conceded that differential tax effects vary their earlier conclusions and have produced a modified version of their theory to accommodate this. Similarly, traditionalists have partly accepted the MM view that capital structure is not an overriding determinant of the cost of capital.

6.5.2 Perhaps here we might settle for a view which largely reflects the way in which financial managers actually behave.

This is that extreme positions are to be avoided as being unlikely to give the minimum cost of capital. Thus if a company is wholly equity financed it is losing the opportunity of benefiting by use of some low cost debt. If, on the other hand, it becomes heavily debt financed, the financial risk thereby attracted is likely to push up the costs of both equity and loan finance. In between the extremes there is probably a very broad area where the precise debt/equity mix is relatively unimportant to the overall cost of capital. One therefore comes to rely on the historically tested, conventional mix. This is a satisfactory explanation of why we should take capital structure as given at the current proportions as we did in chapter 5 on the cost of capital.

6.6 Capital Reorganisations

6.6.1 Sometimes a company finds itself wishing to amend its existing capital structure. There are several situations in which this might occur and several ways in which it might be done. These are briefly described below:

6.6.2 Bonus issue of shares. A bonus issue of shares is always made to existing ordinary shareholders on a pro rata basis. The bonus shares may be of a different class from the existing shares (e.g. preference shares) but this is unusual and the common practice is to issue bonus shares which are identical to the existing shares. From the point of view of the shareholder his existing holding is increased by additional shares for which he is not required to pay. From the point of view of the company the issue is seen (more correctly) as the relabelling of reserves (either capital or revenue) as share capital. This has the practical effect of making the balance sheet more correctly represent the shareholders' permanent investment in the business. Where revenue reserves are used this will restrict the company's future right to pay dividends. Bonus issues of shares are a fairly common occurrence. They do not, other things being equal, affect the overall value of the business although they may indirectly do so if favourably interpreted by the market.

6.6.3 Example. Welldone, plc has the balance sheet shown below in summary form. The balance on the profit and loss account has been built up by a policy of conservative dividend payments followed over many years and the retained funds have been productively invested in expansions to the business. The directors now wish to rationalise the capital structure by making a bonus issue of shares on a one for one basis.

Welldone, plc
Summarised balance sheet at 31st December 19xx

Share capital:			
£1 ordinary shares	£1,000,000	Fixed assets	£1,729,200
Share premium account	100,000	Current assets	1,152,800
Profit and loss account	1,100,000		
Current liabilities	682,000		
	£2,882,000		£2,882,000

Show the balance sheet as it would appear immediately after the bonus issue.

6.6.4 Either capital reserves (here the share premium account) or revenue reserves (here the profit and loss account) are equally available to pay up a bonus issue of shares. Although the profit and loss account on its own is adequate in amount it is suggested that the share premium account should be used first. This will tidy up and simplify the balance sheet and will leave as big a distributable reserve as is possible. This preserves the directors' future freedom of movement.

Welldone, plc
Balance sheet after bonus issue
Share capital:

£1 ordinary shares	£2,000,000	Fixed assets	£1,729,200
Profit and loss account	200,000	Current assets	1,152,800
Current liabilities	682,000		
	£2,882,000		£2,882,000

6.6.5 Conversion of preference shares into debentures

From the point of view of both investors and company there is very little difference in practice between preference shares and debentures (there are, of course, important legal and thus accounting differences). The introduction of corporation tax in 1965, however, meant that debentures were a less costly form of capital, other things being equal, than preference shares and were therefore favoured by companies. This effect of taxation is explained in Chapter 15 (15.3). It led, after 1965, to a number of companies converting their preference shares into debentures. In accounting terms this is easily done and amounts to little more than a relabelling of the segments of capital affected. It should be noted, however, that certain legal formalities must be observed and that it may be necessary to make the conversion attractive to holders by varying their capital and/or income entitlements.

6.6.6 Reduction of capital

There are two sets of circumstances in which a reduction of capital may be desired. These are:

(a) to recognise a permanent loss of a substantial part of the company's financial resources:

(b) to return unwanted funds to shareholders after a diminution in the business opportunities available to the company.

Legal formalities surround both forms of reduction but the second is the more stringent because it involves an actual reduction in the fund available to meet the claims of creditors.

6.6.7 Example. Badluck, plc has traded at a loss for several years. Because of a shortage of profitable activities it has large amounts of surplus cash. The summarised balance sheet appears below:

Badluck, plc
Summarised balance sheet at 31st December 19xx

Share capital	£1,500,000	Fixed assets	£589,800
Profit and loss account	(500,000)	**Current assets**	
Current liabilities	246,000	Cash	263,000
		Other	393,200
	£1,246,000		£1,246,000

The directors have decided that future profitability depends on a reduced level of activities. They propose to reduce the ordinary share capital in the following ways:

(a) by writing one third off the nominal value of each ordinary share, thus extinguishing the debit balance on the profit and loss account, and

(b) by repaying in cash a further one sixth of the nominal value (which is thus reduced to 50p per existing £1 share).

Assume that all legal formalities have been observed and show the balance sheet after giving effect to the reduction.

6.6.8 The balance sheet appears as follows:

Badluck, plc
Balance sheet after reduction of capital

Share capital	£750,000	Fixed assets	£589,800
Current liabilities	246,000	**Current assets**	
		Cash	13,000
		Other	393,200
	£996,000		£996,000

6.6.9 Redemption or purchase of own shares

Since 1981 limited companies in the U.K. have been legally empowered to redeem equity or to purchase it for cancellation (which has the same effect as redemption). This power, now embodied in the Companies Act, 1985, existed only in respect of redeemable preference shares prior to 1981 and any purchase by a company of its own shares was illegal.

In the case of a public company shares may be redeemed or purchased only in a manner which conserves the fund available to protect creditors. The redemption or purchase must be either

(a) out of reserves otherwise available for payment of dividends or

(b) out of the proceeds of a fresh issue of shares made specially for the purpose or

(c) a combination of these two.

Where redemption is out of revenue reserves (i.e. qualifying under (a) above) an amount equivalent to the nominal value of the capital redeemed or purchased must be transferred to a capital redemption reserve to prevent its future use for the payment of dividends. The only purpose for which a capital redemption reserve may be used is to pay up an issue of bonus shares.

Where the purchase or redemption is at a premium this premium will normally be charged to revenue reserve. Where it is covered by the proceeds of a new issue (and certain other requirements are fulfilled) it may be charged to the share premium account, if there is one.

A company may wish to redeem or purchase its own shares for one of the following reasons:

(i)   to buy out a dissident minority of shareholders,

(ii)   to change the balance of control amongst the body of shareholders,

(iii) to enable investors to realise their holdings where no active market for the shares exists,

(iv)   to dispose of surplus funds.

6.6.10 Example. Bravo, plc has the balance sheet appearing below:

Summarised balance sheet at 31st December, 19xx

Share capital		Fixed assets	£1,400,000
£1 ordinary shares	£2,000,000	Current assets	950,000
Profit and loss account	250,000		
Current liabilities	100,000		
	£2,350,000		£2,350,000

Having obtained the appropriate authority from the shareholders the directors of Bravo purchased 100,000 of the company's own shares for £1.20 each and cancelled them. Show the balance sheet after the transaction.

6.6.11 Bravo, plc Balance sheet after purchase and cancellation of shares

Share capital		Fixed assets	£1,400,000
£1 ordinary shares	£1,900,000	Current assets (2)	830,000
Capital redemption reserve	100,000		
Profit and loss account (1)	130,000		
Current liabilities	100,000		
	£2,230,000		£2,230,000

(1)   Profit and loss account:

Original balance		£250,000
Less Premium on shares	£20,000	
Transfer to capital redemption reserve	100,000	120,000
New balance		£130,000

(2)   Current assets:

Original balance	£950,000
Less cash paid for share purchase	120,000
	£830,000

Summary

(i)   Our consideration of the cost of capital as an average from the components making it up might lead us to believe that capital structure was a crucial determining factor. The issue is, however, complicated by the fact that the cost of a given component of capital is not necessarily independent of the existence and size of other components.

(ii)   Gearing is an important concept in connection with capital structure. Gearing is said to exist wherever a company is financed partly by debt. The more debt there is, the more highly geared is the company. Debt creates a fixed annual charge against profits in the form of interest payments. This causes a magnification of any fluctuations in the residual profits available to equity holders, i.e. they become more risky. This increase in risk due to gearing is known as financial risk. It is to be distinguished from the commercial risk to which any business, however financed, is subject.

(iii)   There are two opposing theories of capital structure and its relationship to the cost of capital. The first of these, the traditional theory, says that, since debt is cheaper than equity, it will pay initially to increase the amount of debt financing used. At some critical point financial risk will begin to impinge on the cost of debt which will rise. When the cost of debt equals the cost of equity it will be disadvantageous to expand it further. There is thus a minimum cost combination of debt and equity which should be sought.

(iv)   The second theory is associated with the names of Modigliani and Miller and asserts that the cost of capital relates to the value of the business as an economic entity and is independent of the method of finance. This theory would imply that the financial manager had no important decision to make regarding capital structure.

(v) In default of a settlement of the issue by research – and it is not an easy proposition to test this in practice – the view may be taken that, within limits, the precise debt/equity ratio is not critical and the existing balance may be taken to be a desired structure which is to be maintained.

(vi) A company may sometimes find it desirable to reorganise its capital structure. The ways in which this may be done should be noted.

Review Questions

(i) Distinguish between commercial risk and financial risk.

(ii) 'Debt is cheaper than equity. The company should therefore borrow as much as possible in order to reduce the overall cost of capital .' Do you agree?

(iii) Why do different sources of finance have different costs?

(iv) What are the important assumptions underlying the Modigliani and Miller theory? Are they valid?

(v) Is the MM theory were fully accepted, what would be the main implications for a financial manager?

(vi) What is arbitrage? What is the effect of its operation?

(vii) What reason might a company have for retaining its present capital structure indefinitely?

(viii) What are the consequences to the ordinary shareholders in a company of a high level of gearing?

Exercises

1. Structure, plc is estimated to have a current cost of capital of 17.27% per annum which has been computed from the following figures:

	Market value	Cost
Equity	£10 million	18%
Debt	£1 million	10%
Weighted average		17.27%

The managing director argues that the overall cost of capital could be sharply reduced by increasing the amount of debt employed. Discuss using simple illustrations to clarify your argument.

2. The following particulars are available for two companies oper-
    ating identical businesses, Order plc and Chaos plc.

	Order £	Chaos £
Profits		
Profits before interest or dividends	250,000	250,000
Interest on debt (market rate 12% p.a.)	–	36,000
Available to equity	£250,000	£214,000
Capital structure		
Value of equity	1,000,000	600,000
Value of debt	–	300,000
	£1,000,000	£900,000

    Why would this, to a proponent of the MM theory, be seen as a
    position of disequilibrium? How would equilibrium be reached?
    Use imaginary figures for any information not supplied.

3. Your company has always operated on a gearing ratio of 0.2.
    What do you understand by this? What arguments would you
    use in its defence if its appropriateness were challenged?

4. Overdrive, plc has a long term gearing ratio of 0.25. The follow-
    ing represents its current position:

	Market value	Cost
Equity	£4,000,000	15% p.a.
Debt	£500,000	10% p.a.

    What cost of capital should be used in investment appraisal?
    How should future investment be financed, other things being
    equal?

5. Explain why one might expect the cost of capital to be high at
    extreme levels of gearing. Does this imply that there is an opti-
    mum gearing ratio?

6. Polonius, plc has always avoided borrowing believing that this
    makes it vulnerable to pressure from lenders. It is, therefore,
    wholly equity financed. Explain the consequences of this policy
    and comment.

7: Relevant Costs

7.1 Identifying Relevant Information

7.1.1 We have already commented that whilst a financial manager makes use of accounting information in aiding his decision making process he will not necessarily use it in the form in which it is conventionally presented. He must be selective in his choice of information and careful in the way he interprets it if he is not to be be misled. In this chapter we are to consider the relevance of accounting information and identify some of the pitfalls lying in the way of its uncritical use.

7.1.2 Example. Miss Pru Dent is a retired school mistress living alone. She manages her expenditure carefully so as to preserve her independence and to give herself as comfortable a life as possible. Recently she has become concerned at the cost of running her small car. For last year the costs were:

Fixed costs (licence, insurance, finance, etc.)	£500
Running costs (petrol, oil, servicing, etc.) for 10,000 miles	500
	£1,000

Although she has decided to keep the car for at least this year, she has also resolved to be careful in its use so as to keep the cost as low as she can. She wishes to visit her sister, Confey, a 100 mile round trip, and wonders whether to use the car or go by train. The return rail ticket would cost £8. Pru always takes the advice of her three cats on such matters but this time they do not agree. Claude says 'You must keep the total cost of the car to a minimum and therefore you should avoid using it whenever possible.' Maude says, 'The average cost of running a car is 10p per mile $\left(\dfrac{£1,000}{10,000} \right)$. If the rail fare is less than this you should go by train if not go by car.' Tom says 'The important thing is how your total costs, under whatever heading, are affected by the decision. Use the method which increases total expenditure by the least amount.' What is the decision to which each principle leads? Which is correct?

7.1.3 If we follow Claude's advice the car will not be used. In the extreme, however, this might lead to a situation in which Miss Dent was paying £500 per annum just to keep the car in the garage. If Maude's advice is taken the cost of the journey by car will be taken to be $100 \times 10p = £10$ and the train will seem cheaper at £8 and will be used. We must note, however, the paradox that if Miss Dent doubled her usage of the car the cost per mile would fall to $7\frac{1}{2}$p per mile, the more it is used therefore, the more it will seem it ought to be used. On Tom's rule we should reason that 100 miles would, if the car were used, add only its running cost,

$$100 \times \frac{£500}{10,000} = £5$$

to Miss Dent's total budget. To go by train would add £8 and so the car should be used.

It should be clear that Tom's rule leads to the best decision and is thus the one to use.

7.1.4 This emphasises that a decision should be based on relevant information only. Relevant information is information on matters which will be affected by the decision. In our example for a decision as to whether or not to use the car, running costs are relevant (because they are affected by the decision), fixed costs are not. Note that what is relevant depends on the nature of the decision. In a decision as to whether or not to *keep* the car the fixed costs become relevant because they can be avoided if the car is sold.

7.2 Fixed and Variable Cost

7.2.1 The concept of the relevance of costs and revenues is a very important one to financial management and is met in more than one form. A primary classification of costs is into fixed costs and variable costs. A fixed cost is one which does not change with output. A variable cost is one which does vary with the level of output. The relationship is normally presumed to be linear, i.e. doubling of output leads to a doubling of total variable cost. It should be noted that this classification is a simplification. In real life costs are not always easily categorised into either pure fixed or pure variable. There may sometimes be a very complex relationship between cost and output. The simple concept, however, usually serves us well enough.

7.2.2 To accommodate the situation where a fixed cost is attributable to a particular segment of production and either is or is not incurred according to whether the production is or is not undertaken (but does not thereafter depend on output) we sometimes use the secondary classification of cost into avoidable and unavoidable. All variable costs and some fixed costs (depending on the nature of the decision) are avoidable. Other fixed costs are unavoidable. To revert to our example of the running of a car petrol costs are variable (and avoidable). The cost of the licence and insurance is fixed (but avoidable by disposing of the car). Maintenance on a garage which is part of the structure of the house is fixed and unavoidable (because even if the car is sold the garage will remain).

7.3 Break Even Charts

7.3.1 A break even chart is a useful way of displaying the behaviour of costs and revenues. It should be noted that it is a schedule of possibilities and not a graph of events over time. The implication of this is that a firm can occupy only one position at a time on its break even chart. It may move to another position following some decision or other event but not merely by virtue of a lapse of time.

A break even chart has two axes. Along the horizontal axis is plotted the output of product on the basis that sales volume and production volume are equal. On the vertical axis are plotted money values representing, as appropriate, the revenues and the costs associated with the output. Two lines are drawn. One of these is sales against output. It is a line through the origin with a slope determined by the price of the product. The other is the total cost line. This is a line intersecting the vertical axis at the level of fixed cost and having a slope determined by variable cost. The sales line will cross the total cost line at a level of output termed the break even point. Below this level of output a loss will be incurred and above it a profit will be made.

7.3.2 Example. Lines, plc makes a single product selling for £5 per unit. Variable costs are £2 per unit and fixed cost £1,500. Planned production and sales for the forthcoming period is 1,000 units. The maximum capacity of the plant is 1,500 units. Show, by means of a break even chart, the alternatives of

(a) meeting the plan and

(b) reaching maximum possible output.

Assess the effect of the shortfall of the plan as against the maximum possible production.

7.3.3 The break even chart (Figure 7.1) is on the following page.

It can be read off from this chart that at the planned level of production profit will be £1,500. At the level achievable if the whole of the capacity is used it will be £3,000. There is thus a potential loss of profit of £1,500 in planning for less than maximum capacity usage.

It should be noted that we have also marked on the chart a quantity described as the 'margin of safety'. This is defined as the gap between the planned level of output and the break even level. Any shortfall of actual output below the planned level will still lead to a profit if it can be constrained within the margin of safety.

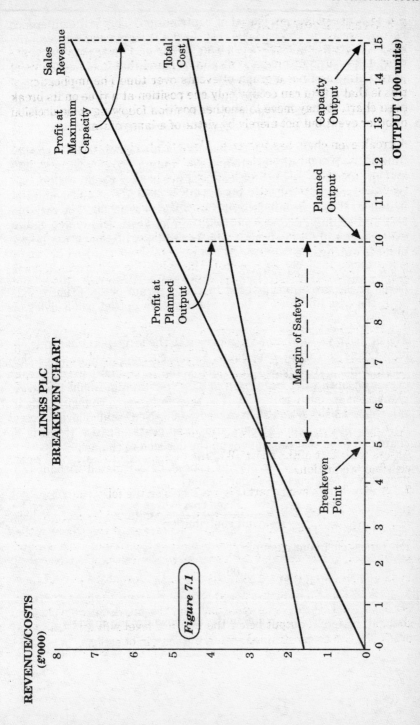

LINES PLC
BREAKEVEN CHART

Figure 7.1

REVENUE/COSTS
(£'000)

Sales Revenue

Total Cost

Profit at Maximum Capacity

Profit at Planned Output

Margin of Safety

Breakeven Point

Capacity Output

Planned Output

OUTPUT (100 units)

7.3.4 A useful concept is that of 'contribution'. This is the difference between revenue and variable cost. In the example above the contribution is £3 per unit (i.e. each unit sold would contribute £3 to the fund which will meet fixed costs and, eventually, give a profit.) Total contribution at sales of 1,000 units is £3,000 and at maximum capacity is £4,500. Note that the change in contribution is the same, in amount, as the change in profit. This is because fixed cost is irrelevant to an assessment of the effect of changes in sales.

7.3.5 Example. Squares, plc has its plant working to full capacity to produce 2,000 units of product per annum. Fixed cost is £1,000 and variable cost £1 per unit. Selling price is £2 per unit. Output can be increased only if larger plant with a capacity of 4,000 units is installed. If it is installed fixed cost will rise to £2,000 but variable cost and selling price per unit will be unaltered. Draw up a break even chart and decide from it whether the installation of the larger plant is worthwhile.

7.3.6 There are actually two break even charts to be considered here. These are superimposed in the diagram below (Figure 7.2) with the cost line for the large plant shown dotted below sales of 2,000 units as it would not then be used.

The decision as to whether to move on to the large plant depends on how far sales can be expanded. At the current level of sales the small plant gives a profit of £1,000 − the large plant would break even. Not until sales have risen to 3,000 per annum would the large plant earn as much as £1,000. It is, therefore, worth changing only if sales leap this gap and then exceed 3,000. Note that relevant costs here are both variable costs and fixed costs because there is a change in fixed cost consequent on the decision to change.

7.3.7 Break even points may, of course, be calculated without the necessity of constructing a chart. Thus

$$\text{B.E.P.} = \frac{\text{Fixed cost}}{\text{Unit contribution}} \text{ units}$$

For Lines, plc in our example

$$\text{B.E.P.} = \frac{£1,500}{£3}$$

$$= 500 \text{ units (as shown by the chart)}$$

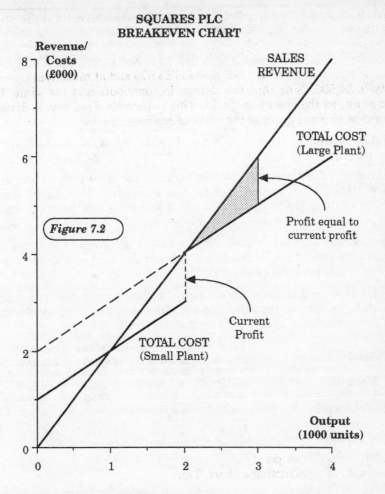

SQUARES PLC
BREAKEVEN CHART

Figure 7.2

7.4 Relevant Cost Statements

7.4.1 Example. Circles, plc makes three products, Aystacks, Beehives and Ceeshells. Each product makes use of fully variable labour and material. There are fixed costs attributable to each individual product and also general fixed costs which, for accounting purposes, are apportioned pro rata with sales. The results for an immediate past period are shown below:

	Total	Aystacks	Beehives	Ceeshells
Sales	£27,000	£10,000	£5,000	£12,000
Materials	£8,300	£2,000	£1,500	£4,800
Labour	6,650	3,000	1,250	2,400
Direct fixed costs	7,000	2,000	1,000	4,000
General fixed costs	4,500	1,667	833	2,000
Total costs	£26,450	£8,667	£4,583	£13,200
Profit/(Loss)	£550	£1,333	£417	(£1,200)

The direct fixed costs are specific to each individual product and are avoidable if production of that product is stopped. The general fixed costs relate to the business as a whole and have here been allocated to products on the basis of sales value.

A proposal is made to close the Ceeshells department in order to avoid its loss which is draining the profitable part of the business. Should this proposal be supported?

7.4.2 We need to draw up a statement showing the relevant information, i.e. containing sales and avoidable costs. General fixed costs will be unaffected by the decision and are irrelevant.

	Total	Aystacks	Beehives	Ceeshells
Sales	£27,000	£10,000	£5,000	£12,000
Materials	£8,300	£2,000	£1,500	£4,800
Labour	6,650	3,000	1,250	2,400
Direct fixed	7,000	2,000	1,000	4,000
	£21,950	£7,000	£3,750	£11,200
Contribution	£5,050	£3,000	£1,250	£800

From this statement it can be seen that Ceeshells department is, in fact, contributing £800. If it is closed profit (other things being equal) would decline by £800, to a loss of £250. Paradoxically it can be said that if it were not for the loss making department Circles could not make a profit! Of course if the capacity released by discontinuing production of Ceeshells were to be used for something else this might be worthwhile provided that the new product made a contribution greater than £800.

7.4.3 Example. Triangles, plc has an opportunity to purchase a machine for £28,000. The accountant has prepared the following statement showing the incremental profit which will arise from its use over each of the four years of its life.

Sales revenue		£20,000
Less Costs:		
Materials	£3,000	
Labour	2,500	
Supervisory wages	800	
Maintenance	1,000	
Fuel	2,200	
Insurance	500	
Apportionment of general fixed costs (machine hour rate)	2,500	
Depreciation 25%	7,000	19,500
Net incremental profit		£500

He draws the conclusion that the investment is not worth while as £500 represents an annual return of only $1^{3}/_{4}\%$ on the investment. Comment on this from the point of view of the financial manager.

7.4.4 Again this is a case where we should take into consideration what is relevant. The accountant is overlooking that in addition to the profit of £500 the project is contributing towards general fixed costs and is repaying, through the medium of depreciation charges, the amount invested in it. For our investment of £28,000 we shall receive an additional cash inflow of £10,000 (Revenue – avoidable costs) for four years. (This is actually a rate of return of 15% per annum although not until a later chapter shall we look as how this might be calculated.)

7.5 Contribution per Unit of Limiting Factor

7.5.1 Sometimes business expansion is constrained to that which is allowed by the availability of a particular factor of production, which may however be used in a variety of applications.

The limiting factors commonly encountered are special raw materials, trained labour and factory space. Where the scarce resource has only one use its effective deployment is not a problem. Where it has alternative uses it is likely to be more profitable to use it in one application rather than another. The contribution per unit of limiting factor made by each use is then a useful guide to decision making.

7.5.2 Example. Digger is a market gardener cultivating 10,000 square metres of land. His immediate past year's results appear, in summary form, below:

Crop	Carrots	Lettuces	Onions	Sprouts	Total
Sales	£24,500	£56,250	£16,750	£29,500	£127,000
Less Materials (1)	£7,000	£10,000	£5,000	£8,000	£30,000
Labour	6,000	25,000	3,000	6,000	40,000
Variable overhead (2)	1,500	6,250	750	1,500	10,000
Fixed overhead (3)	3,000	12,500	1,500	3,000	20,000
Total cost	£17,500	£53,750	£10,250	£18,500	£100,000
Profit	£7,000	£2,500	£6,500	£11,000	£27,000
Area allocated (square metres)	2,000	5,000	1,000	2,000	10,000

(1) Materials consist of seeds, fertilisers, insecticides, etc.

(2) Variable overhead varies directly with labour and is 25% of labour cost.

(3) Fixed overhead is £20,000 per annum for the business as a whole, charged for the purposes of this statement at the rate of 50% of labour.

Digger wishes to make a rational plan for production for the forthcoming year. There is no restriction on the amount of labour which he can use but the area of land cannot be increased. Any crop can be grown on any part of the land but sales cannot be increased by more than 20% for any individual crop. No other crops could be successfully cultivated on this land. What plan of production would lead to maximum profit?

7.5.3 Maximum profit will be made when the scarce factor, in this case land, is being used in its most profitable application. We must first, therefore, calculate what contribution per square metre is earned by land in each of the alternative uses. This is done below.

Crop	Carrots	Lettuces	Onions	Sprouts	Total
Sales	£24,500	£56,250	£16,750	£29,500	£127,000
Less Materials	£7,000	£10,000	£5,000	£8,000	£30,000
Labour	6,000	25,000	3,000	6,000	40,000
Variable overhead	1,500	6,250	750	1,500	10,000
Total Variable cost	£14,500	£41,250	£8,750	£15,500	£80,000
Contribution	£10,000	£15,000	£8,000	£14,000	£47,000
Contribution per square metre of land	£5	£3	£8	£7	

It can be seen from this that onion growing provides the most profitable use of land and lettuce growing the least profitable. If there were no other constraint the whole area should be devoted to onions.

As it is the maximum of 20% increase should be made to this crop. Similarly the maximum possible increases should be made to the area under sprouts (second best) and carrots (third best). This is shown below:

Crop	Area now cultivated (sq. metres)	Area to be cultivated (sq. metres)	Contribution per sq. metre	Total contribution
Onions	1,000	12,000	£8	£9,600
Sprouts	2,000	2,400	£7	16,800
Carrots	2,000	2,400	£5	12,000
Lettuces	5,000	4,000*	£3	12,000
				50,400
Less Fixed cost				20,000
Planned profit				£30,400

*Reduced to allow maximum increase on other crops.

7.6 Practical Problems

7.6.1 Useful though the concepts developed in this chapter are, we must not overlook certain difficulties that are commonly encountered in practice. Some of these are mentioned in the paragraphs which follow.

7.6.2 Variable costs. Although we have presumed that variable costs are variable proportionately with production this is not always the case. There may, for example, exist economies of scale which mean that variable costs rise less and less sharply as production rises. Another possibility is that variable costs rise in steps rather than smoothly. This would be the case where each level of variable cost held for a narrow range of different levels of production (e.g. because labour can be employed only as whole numbers of workers).

7.6.3 Fixed costs. Fixed cost is never, in practice, fixed for any or every level of production. Each level of fixed cost has associated with it a maximum productive capacity which it can provide. Beyond this a new level of fixed cost has to be accepted. The move from a lower level of fixed cost to a higher may be irreversible. Once a commitment to a bigger productive capacity is made it may not be possible, with decreased production, to revert to the previous state (e.g. a factory extension cannot readily be dismantled and its cost recovered).

7.6.4 Avoidable cost. In discussing the concept of avoidable cost we have assumed that certain costs can immediately be avoided if a certain segment of activity ceases. Contractual obligations or physical constraints may, however, mean that such costs are avoided only in the long run. Plant which has been leased, for example, would seem to give rise to an avoidable cost because the lease arrangement may be terminated and the payments saved. The terms of the lease may, however, require a minimum leasing period or an extended period of notice of termination so that this cannot be avoided immediately.

7.6.5 Multiple products. The break even chart we have constructed is based on a single product and thus there is a unique break even point related to the output of that product. Such a chart cannot be drawn if a number of products share the facilities represented by the fixed costs. In that case the precise position of the break even point depends on the mix of products contained in output,

Summary

(i)   In making his or her decisions the financial manager must identify the relevant information. This will not always be immediately available from existing accounting statements.

(ii)   Relevant information is that which will be affected by the decision. Costs and revenues unaffected by a decision cannot be relevant to it.

(iii) A useful distinction may be drawn between fixed cost and variable cost. For the purposes of analysis fixed cost is defined as that which is determined independently of the level of production. Variable cost varies proportionately with the level of production.

(iv) A break even chart is a useful graphical method of displaying the relationship between costs and revenue. It represents a schedule of possibilities rather than a history of events. The break even point is that level of production at which neither profit nor loss is made. The margin of safety is the gap which exists between the break even point and the planned level of output.

(v)   Accounting statements will often need to be redrafted to show the contribution made by products in order to facilitate a rational decision.

(vi) It will be useful to calculate contribution per unit of limiting factor where one scarce factor of production has alternative uses within the business.

Review Questions

(i) 'A fixed cost may change between one year and another whilst a variable cost may remain constant.' Is this true and, if so, what are the meanings of the terms fixed cost and variable cost?

(ii) 'To maximise contribution is a better objective than to maximise profit.' Do you agree?

(iii) Define the following terms:

    (a) break even point

    (b) margin of safety

    (c) capacity level of production

    (d) planned level of production

(iv) 'Our break even chart shows that we shall not start making a profit until the eighth month of the year.' What misapprehension is contained in this statement? How is a break even chart to be interpreted?

(v) Hens, plc manufacturers eggs (a prepacked food product). At the planned level of production of 50,000 eggs unit revenues and costs are:

Sales	£5.00
Variable cost	£2.50
Fixed cost	£1.50
	£4.00
Profit	£1.00

What is the break even point?

(vi) How does an avoidable cost differ from a variable cost?

(vii) 'Loss making products must be ruthlessly identified and rooted out.' Discuss this.

(viii) 'The bigger the margin of safety, the more likely is a company to make a good profit.' Is this true?

Exercises

1. Windermere, plc has a head office and a number of branches. The following is the profit and loss account for the Winchester branch for the year just ended:

Sales		£52,000
Cost of sales	£23,800	
Branch running costs	10,200	
Staff wages	12,500	
Manager's remuneration	4,520	
Central office charge (10% sales)	5,200	
Depreciation	3,000	59,220
Loss		£7,220

Windermere is considering a proposal to close this branch. The following facts are relevant:

(i) *If the branch were closed the manager would be employed elsewhere in the organisation to fill a post where the annual salary would normally be £3,000 per annum. He would continue to receive his present salary of £4,000 but would not continue to receive his commission of 1% sales.*

2. *Grasmere plc is proposing to manufacture a new product for which the following standard cost has been prepared on the assumption that 4,000 units would be made and sold in each year.*

Selling price		£5.00
Material	£1.00	
Labour	2.00	
Overhead*	1.50	4.50
Standard profit		£0.50

All overhead is fixed. 75p of this figure relates to overhead specific to the product and 75p is the general charge for fixed overhead included automatically in all standards. Calculate the break even point. Comment on the profit at the planned level of production.

3. *Derwent, plc manufactures a certain component which is later assembled into a final product. Costs of production are as follows:*

Per 100 components	
Material	£2.80
Labour	3.20
Variable overhead	
100% labour	3.20
Fixed overhead	
150% labour	4.80
	£14.00

An opportunity has occurred to purchase the components at a price of £10 per 100 instead of manufacturing them. The works manager has recommended this on the basis that £4 per 100 components would thus be saved. Comment on this and state what factors, other than those for which information is given, should be considered.

4. Waters, plc makes a product which goes through a finishing process. This process can either be performed manually or by means of a machine. Basing your answer on the following figures provide information which will help in the decision.

	Manual	**Machine**
Labour cost	£1.00 per unit	20p per unit
Fixed cost	£2,000 p.a.	£10,000 p.a.

5. Hills, plc has a stock of raw material which cost £10,000. Because of a change in market conditions the product for which it was purchased is no longer made. Proposals have been sought for its disposal and the following suggestions made:

(i) Sell it as waste. This would result in a loss calculated as follows:

Proceeds of disposal	£2,000
Cost of material	10,000
Loss	£8,000

(ii) Use up the stock in manufacturing a special line of product to be sold at an attractive price:

Sales		£12,500
Less Material	£10,000	
Additional material	2,000	
Labour	4,000	
Fixed overhead 150% labour	6,000	22,000
Loss		£9,500

(iii) Use it in substitution for a different material in another product. It is less effective but does not affect the quality of the final product. If used like this it would save about £6,000 in expenditure on the regular material but would lead to £3,500 conversion costs.

Show these figures in a comparable form so as to facilitate a rational decision and make a recommendation.

6. Dales, plc manufactures four different products which sell under the trade names Knights, Pawns, Bishops and Rooks. A summary of the company's profit and loss account for the past year appears below:

	Total	Knights	Pawns	Bishops	Rooks
Sales	£188,000	£73,000	£62,000	£39,000	£14,000
Material	£35,000	£10,000	£12,000	£9,000	£4,000
Labour	31,000	12,000	8,000	9,000	2,000
Variable overhead(1)	41,000	15,000	10,000	12,000	4,000
Fixed overhead(2)	46,500	18,056	15,335	9,646	3,463
Total cost	£153,500	£55,056	£45,335	£39,646	£13,463
Profit/(Loss)	£34,500	£17,944	£16,665	(£646)	£537

(1) All variable overhead is direct to the product.

(2) All fixed overhead is indirect and in this statement has been charged as a percentage of sales.

The management wishes to construct a plan of production for the next year which will lead to the maximum level of profit but subject to the following constraints:

(a) *No selling prices are to be increased. It is not anticipated that costs will increase either.*

(b) *It is considered necessary for the company to offer a complete range of products. No product, therefore, is to be produced in quantities less than 80% of the previous year's production nor more than 110% of that level.*

(c) *The size of the factory cannot be increased and hence the labour force is restricted to those currently employed. Labour can, however, be switched freely from one product to another.*

Draft a suitable production plan and show how the profit and loss account will appear if it is implemented.

8: Forecasting and Planning

8.1 An Important Distinction

8.1.1 Looking ahead in time is the essence of a financial manager's job and this has been implicit in almost every topic we have considered so far. In this chapter we shall look at techniques which are most explicitly concerned with future activities, those concerned with the preparation of budgets or financial plans.

8.1.2 We should draw first a very clear distinction between the activities of forecasting and of planning. These terms are sometimes confused and even used interchangeably but they are, in fact, differently defined and the difference is very important to our present discussion. Forecasting refers to the prediction of events or circumstances over which the forecaster has no control. Thus a financial manager may forecast the general level of incomes within the economy or the extent to which competitors may seek to invade his company's markets. Planning refers to the formulation of intentions concerning activities over which the planner does have control. A financial manager might plan for his company to set up new productive capacity or to mount an intensive sales campaign for certain of its products.

8.1.3 The important relationship between forecasting and planning is that planning must always take place within a context of constraints. Knowledge and expectations about that context are provided by forecasting. There will be no point in planning to manufacture and sell a product in certain quantities if a forecast of economic conditions indicates that such levels of sales are unlikely to be achieved.

8.1.4 Forecasts may be made with varying degrees of confidence. It can, for example, safely be predicted that the days in summer will be both longer and warmer than those in winter and this forecast could be very relevant to a business selling leisure goods. A forecast of the public taste for particular leisure activities might, however, be very uncertain depending, as this may, on fashion or unpredictable news events. Plans may respond to uncertain forecasts by being flexible so that they can be modified as events develop.

8.1.5 Example. Little Pigswill Villagers' Association is to hold their annual fund raising event. Indicate some of the forecasts and plans which might be made in order to help its success.

8.1.6 A combination of forecasting and planning will be required here. Forecasts which might be made are:

(a) the weather based on past experience, time of the year and long range forecasts;

(b)   the number of people who will attend based on local population and likely influx of holiday visitors;

(c)   the effect of similar competing events based on past experience and knowledge of other people's plans;

(d)   likely response to different types of events, e.g. displays, competitions, special attractions based on previous experience.

Plans which would be made are:

(a)   the date and time of the event:

(b)   the attractions to be provided;

(c)   the price to be charged for admission and for sideshows;

(d)   the scope and scale of refreshments;

(e)   the arrangements for bad weather provision;

(f)   the type and scale of advance publicity.

A consideration of the factors listed here will quickly show the nature of and relationship between forecasting and planning.

8.2 Sales Forecast

8.2.1   A business will formulate its forecasts and plans in financial form. A detailed financial plan is described as a budget. Every part of the process leading to this budget will contain elements of both forecasting and planning. The starting point will normally be the preparation of a sales forecast. This term would seem to imply that the level of forthcoming sales is taken as a given quantity beyond management control. To a considerable extent this is true as the level of sales depends on public taste, levels of income and major economic trends. It should be realised, however, that management has some control over this area, via the efforts of its sales force, and a so-called sales forecast may contain a large element of planning. Sales may be increased, for instance, by advertising and other forms of promotion, by improving the product or the quality of the service which goes with it or by increasing productive capacity to satisfy an existing demand. Sales may, conversely, be deliberately reduced (e.g. on unprofitable lines) by curtailing productive capacity. The whole process of sales forecasting and the construction of budgets is a highly complex one calling for the use of a number of skills and a considerable amount of intuition and inspiration. What follows should, therefore, be seen only as a basic outline of the methods used, illustrating the most important of the basic principles.

8.2.2   Example. Longterm, plc requires to prepare a detailed budget for the year 19–6. As a basis for this a sales forecast is required. Sales are seasonal and, it is believed, follow a consistent pattern year by year. It is also believed that the long term trend of sales is upwards. Quarterly figures (£000's) for the past five years are:

Year	1st Qtr	2nd Qtr	3rd Qtr	4th Qtr
19–1	20.1	23.2	28.0	25.3
19–2	22.5	25.5	30.5	27.1
19–3	24.3	27.2	32.8	29.4
19–4	27.0	29.1	34.3	32.0
19–5	29.2	31.3	36.2	33.8

8.2.3 These figures can be analysed by the technique known as the moving average. Most professional accountancy students will already be familiar with this technique from their studies in Statistics and questions requiring direct calculations of moving average are unlikely to appear on the Financial Management paper. It is useful, however, to describe the basic principles here although those finding the explanation difficult may safely omit it from their studies.

The sales figure for any quarter is regarded as having two main components. These are (a) the basic level of sales determined by the point of arrival on a line representing the long term trend of sales and (b) a seasonal variation which increases or decreases sales with respect to that basic level. The line representing the underlying trend may be plotted by averaging out seasonal variations. This is done by taking a succession of overlapping averages of four sales values.

The situation is illustrated graphically in Figure 8.1 where the figures of our example (trend and original sales values) are plotted.

The calculations that are necessary in order to determine the trend line are laid out in columns 1 to 6 of the table following Figure 8.1.

Column 7 of the table shows the amount by which actual sales either exceeds (+) or fall short of (–) the trend level. These variations may be averaged in order to determine the mean seasonal variation. This is done in the table on page 105.

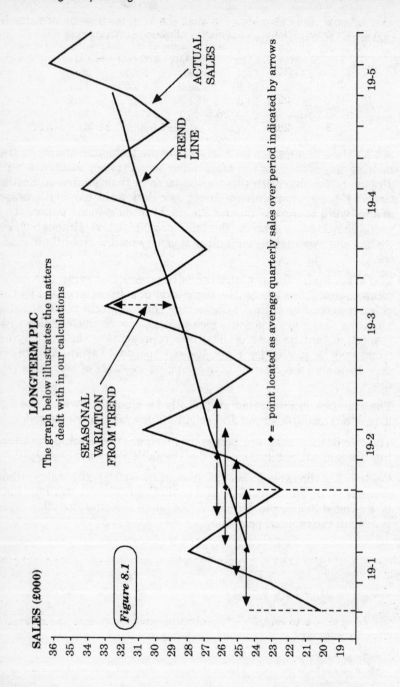

LONGTERM PLC

The graph below illustrates the matters dealt with in our calculations

Figure 8.1

SALES (£000)

ACTUAL SALES

TREND LINE

SEASONAL VARIATION FROM TREND

◆ = point located as average quarterly sales over period indicated by arrows

1 Year	2 Quarter	3 Sales	4 Sums of 4	5 Paired sums of 4*	6 Moving average (trend)	7 Seasonal variation (sales- trend)
19–1	1	20.1				
	2	23.2				
			96.6			
	3	28.0		195.6	24.45	+3.55
			99.0			
	4	25.3		200.3	25.04	+ .26
			101.3			
19–2	1	22.5		205.1	25.64	–3.14
			103.8			
	2	25.5		209.4	26.18	– .68
			105.6			
	3	30.5		213.0	26.63	+3.87
			107.4			
	4	27.1		216.5	27.06	+ .04
			109.1			
19–3	1	24.3		220.5	27.56	–3.26
			111.4			
	2	27.2		225.1	28.14	– .94
			113.7			
	3	32.8		230.1	28.76	+4.04
			116.4			
	4	29.4		234.7	29.34	+ .06
			118.3			
19–4	1	27.0		238.1	29.76	–2.76
			119.8			
	2	29.1		242.2	30.28	–1.18
			122.4			
	3	34.3		247.0	30.88	+3.42
			124.6			
	4	32.0		251.4	31.43	+ .57
			126.8			
19–5	1	29.2		255.5	31.94	–2.74
			128.7			
	2	31.3		259.2	32.40	–1.10
			130.5			
	3	36.2				
	4	33.8				

* This is a device to centre the trend values with respect to the original values for sales.

Summary of seasonal variations

	Q1	Q2	Q3	Q4
19–1			+3.55	+.26
19–2	–3.14	–.68	+3.87	+.04
19–3	–3.26	–.94	+4.04	+.06
19–4	–2.76	–1.18	+3.42	+.57
19–5	–2.74	–1.10		
Total	–11.90	–3.90	+ 14.88	+.93
Mean*	–2.98	.98	+3.72	+.24

* Logic demands that the mean seasonal variations sum to zero. This has been contrived here by appropriate rounding off.

8.2.4 We can now turn our attention to the forecasting of sales for the year 19-6. We have the information necessary to prepare this on a quarterly basis. The calculated trend line has risen from a value of 24.45 to a value of 32.40 in 15 quarterly steps. The average increase is therefore:

$$\frac{32.40 - 24.45}{15} = 0.53 \text{ per quarter}$$

The sales forecast for 19–6 is thus (£000's):

	Trend	Seasonal variation	Forecast
First quarter	33.99	–2.98	31.01
Second quarter	34.52	– .98	33.54
Third quarter	35.05	+3.72	38.77
Fourth quarter	35.58	+ .24	35.82
	139.14		139.14

It should be noted that we have prepared Longterm's sales forecast for 19-6 on the assumption that conditions in that year will be the same as they have been in the past and that the established trend will continue. Such assumptions should be used with great care and where good reasons exist for expecting any change in conditions the forecast should be modified accordingly.

8.3 Preparation of Budgets

8.3.1 When a sales forecast has been established, broken down as necessary over time, products and geographical areas, plans can then be formulated which will build up to a complete budget. A particular level of sales will directly dictate the level of production and hence the consumption of materials, labour and direct overhead. Indirectly it will lead to a plan for the general level of productive capacity (factory overheads) and of administrative and selling effort. Although in this chapter we shall consider only those areas, in the chapter on the management of the cash element of working capital

(Chapter 22) we shall see how the levels of finance for current assets as well as fixed assets also depends on the same budget. It should be recognised that the preparation of a detailed budget for a large business is a highly complex and lengthy process. Because of the interactions which occur between one part of the budget and another, great care has to be taken that the whole thing is fully integrated and that the working as well as the construction of the plan is carefully controlled. The examples which follow represent a considerable simplification of real-life processes but they will serve to illustrate the most important of the basic principles.

8.3.2 Example. Longterm now wishes to plan its activities for 19–6 and to formulate a budget. Its directors believe that although the sales forecast provides a useful point of departure for this budget, sales can be boosted to 35% above the forecast figure by a promotional campaign costing a total of £10,000. They wish this proposal to be built into the budget.

A summary of the company's profit and loss account for 19–5 is as follow:

Sales		£130,500
Less Variable costs:		
Material	£27,200	
Labour	19,500	
Overhead	19,500	66,200
Contribution		64,300
Less Fixed costs:		
Depreciation	20,000	
Overhead	28,500	48,500
Net profit		15,800
Less Dividends		10,000
Retained profit		£5,800

A summary of the company's balance sheet at the end of 19-5 is:

Share capital	£100,000	Fixed assets	£80,000
Retained profit	12,420	Net current assets	32,420
	£112,420		£112,420

The company plans to maintain its dividend. It has forecast that inflation will lead to a 10% increase in material and labour costs in 19-6 and a 12% increase in all overheads (both variable and fixed). No new investment in fixed assets is envisaged but £15,000 will be spent on a replacement for a machine which has reached the end of its useful life. The total depreciation charge will be unaffected by this acquisition. A management drive for greater efficiency is expected to lead a saving of 2% by volume of all items making up variable costs.

8.3.3 Again the mixture of forecasting and planning should be noted. The company is forecasting:

(a) the basic level of sales

(b) the effect of the promotional expenditure

(c) the impact of price increases on its costs.

It is planning:

(a) to undertake promotional expenditure

(b) to replace plant

(c) to improve its operating efficiency

(d) to maintain its dividend

(e) to manufacture sufficient product to meet expected demand.

8.3.4 The process of building up the outline budget is shown below:

Sales –	Original forecast	£139,140	
	Increase 35%	48,699	£187,839

Variable costs:

Material	$£27,200 \times \dfrac{187,839}{130,500} + 10\% - 2\%$	£42,205	
Labour	$£19,500 \times \dfrac{187,839}{130,500} + 10\% - 2\%$	30,257	
Overhead	$£19,500 \times \dfrac{187,839}{130,500} + 12\% - 2\%$	30,807	103,269
Contribution			84,570

Fixed costs:

Promotional expenditure	10,000	
Depreciation	20,000	
Overhead £28,500+ 12%	31,920	61,920
Net profit		22,650
Less Dividend		10,000
Retained profit		£12,650

This budget can be broken down by quarters as follows:

	Total	Q1	Q2	Q3	Q4
Sales	£187,839	£41,863	£45,279	£52,340	£48,357
Material	£42,205	£9,406	£10,174	£11,760	£10,865
Labour	30,257	6,743	7,294	8,431	7,789
Variable overhead	30,807	6,866	7,426	8,584	7,931
Promotional expenditure	10,000	2,500	2,500	2,500	2,500
Depreciation	20,000	5,000	5,000	5,000	5,000
Fixed overhead	31,920	7,980	7,980	7,980	7,980
Net profit	£22,650	£3,368	£4,905	£8,085	£6,292

The outline budgeted year end balance sheet is:

Share capital	£100,000	Fixed assets	£75,000
Retained profit	25,070	Net current assets*	50,070
			£50,070

*As last year		£32,420
Add Cash generated by trading		42,650
		75,070
Less Dividend	£10,000	
Machine	15,000	25,000
		£50,070

8.4 Flexible Budget

8.4.1 The budget which has formed the subject of our example is what is known as a fixed budget, that is to say it will remain the plan in force during the year to which it relates no matter what, in fact, occurs. Where the forecasts on which a budget is based are highly speculative so that quite large divergences from them must be expected it is often useful to prepare a flexible budget. Despite its name this is best thought of as a set of alternative budgets, each adapted to a particular set of actual circumstances. In the most common form of flexible budget a number of different levels of sales are separately planned and the budget used is the one which corresponds most nearly with the level of sales actually achieved. The big advantage of a flexible budget is that it can make a useful degree of planning possible in what might seem to be a chaotic situation. It avoids the disruptive effect of a fixed plan which goes so far awry that it no longer provides any useful guide to action.

8.5 Use of Budgets

8.5.1 Although our main concern here is with the preparation of budgets, it should not be overlooked that they have a use after preparation. As the year proceeds actual results must be compared with the plan and any departures subjected to careful scrutiny. This will allow timely corrective action to be taken where necessary or will enable management to make realistic changes to their original plan. Since responsibility for deviations from the budget can readily be fixed, the use of budgets can provide a strong motivating force within an organisation. No manager will wish to be a party to over optimistic planning if he knows that he will need to account personally for any failure to meet it. Those, however, responsible for putting forward proposals which have been incorporated into a budget will make every effort to ensure that the outcome is successful.

Summary

(i) A clear distinction must be drawn between forecasting and planning, both of which contribute to the preparation of a budget. Forecasts are made concerning matters outside management's control and plans are made regarding matters within its control.

(ii) A sales forecast is usually the foundation of any budget. The analysis of past records by moving average calculations is a useful way in which to prepare the basic sales forecast.

(iii) A budget is constructed around the level of activity presupposed by the sales forecast. Its parts should be carefully integrated and allowance made for forecast and planned changes in costs and conditions.

(iv) A key part of the budget process is the monitoring of actual results against budget as these occur and the taking of appropriate steps to restrain departures from plan.

(v) Flexible budgeting is the name given to that process whereby a series of budgets is prepared, each relating to a different set of conditions (e.g. levels of activity). The technique is useful when forecasts have to be made in a highly uncertain situation.

Review Questions

(i) Distinguish clearly between a plan and a forecast giving simple examples of each.

(ii) Why is it important for a business to plan its activities? What would be the result if it did not?

(iii) A certain company discovers a substantial shortfall in its planned profit after its first quarter year's operations. What action should it take?

(iv) *It has been argued that a business should always plan optimistically so as to aim for the very best achievement possible in the most favourable circumstances. This, it is claimed, will lead everyone concerned to aim for their best. Have you any comments on this interpretation of the motivational effects of such plans?*

(v) *The preparation of budgets normally depends heavily on information gained from records of the past. Since budgets, by definition, concern the future, how may such retrospection be justified?*

(vi) *It has been argued that the budgeting process leads to a stifling of a sense of adventure in business, encouraging the perpetuation of existing activities and discouraging the taking on of new ones. How important do you think this factor may be in the curtailment of business success and how would you counter it?*

(vii) *In what circumstances might it be appropriate to amend a budget during the period to which it relates?*

(viii) *What is a flexible budget and what are its advantages over a fixed budget?*

Exercises

1. *From the following information prepare a sales forecast for Arrowflight, plc for the year 19-9*

(Figures in £000's)

Year	1st quarter	2nd quarter	3rd quarter	4th quarter
		Sales		
19-4	53.1	49.2	52.4	54.9
19-5	52.3	48.3	51.8	53.5
19-6	51.4	47.6	50.2	52.8
19-7	50.9	46.1	49.5	51.6
19-8	49.2	45.3	48.7	50.3

The following matters should be taken into account:

(i) *Management believes that the generation of a better company image will shortly arrest and reverse the downward trend of sales experienced in recent years. Sales in the third and fourth quarters of 19-9 are expected to reflect this being 2% and 4% respectively above the levels which would otherwise have been predicted.*

(ii) *Selling prices have been constant for some years but will be raised by 5% from the beginning of 19-9.*

2. *The most recent accounts of Rifleshoot, plc are summarised below:*

Sales		£1,215,876
Less Materials		£228,721
	Labour	117,635
	Variable overhead	119,242
	Fixed overhead	183,478
	Depreciation	300,000
	Loan interest	120,000
		£1,069,076
Net profit		£146,800

Prepare a flexible profit plan (budget) for the forthcoming year on the alternative assumptions that sales volume will be 90%, 100% and 110% of the recent year's level. Take into account the following matters:

(a) Selling prices will be increased by 1%.

(b) Material costs are expected to increase by 5% due to increasing prices.

(c) Labour costs are expected to increase by 10% following wage negotiations.

(d) All overhead costs are expected to rise by 8%.

(e) Depreciation will amount to £350,000.

(f) Loan interest will reduce to £100,000 if the volume of sales is equal to that of last year. It will increase to £150,000 if the volume of sales increase by 10% and will reduce to £90,000 if the volume of sales is reduced by 10%. This is due to the effect of volume on the requirements for working capital.

3. *Your company currently prepares monthly management accounts which are carefully considered by the Board of Directors. Where they are thought to show unsatisfactory progress remedial action is proposed. You have been asked to prepare a report to the Board on the suggestion that the present system should be replaced by full budgetary control. Draft a list of the main points which you would wish to include in such a report.*

4. *The following figures show respectively the budgeted and actual results for Offcourse, plc for the immediate past year. Consider them imaginatively together with the additional information below and comment constructively on what has occurred:*

	Budgeted	**Actual**	**Variance**
Sales	£1,489,487	£1,432,198	(£57,289)*
Less Material	£536,214	£531,446	£4,768
Labour	327,687	314,187	13,500
Factory overheads	283,030	275,662	7,368
	£1,146,931	£1,121,295	£25,636
Operating profit	£342,556	£310,903	(£31,653)
Less Selling costs	£59,860	£68,948	(£9,088)
Administrative costs	86,290	86,300	(10)
Loan interest	30,000	32,180	(2,180)
Depreciation	52,186	52,298	(112)
	£228,336	£239,726	(£11,390)
Net profit	£114,220	£71,177	(£43,043)

* Figures in brackets indicate an adverse effect on profit.

(i) Selling prices were on average 2% above those which had been budgeted.

(ii) One month's sales (1/12 year) were lost owing to a transport strike although sales in other months ran at a higher level than forecast.

(iii) Material prices rose unexpectedly by an average of 5% half way through the year.

(iv) There was a national wage award of 15% half way through the year. The amount which had been anticipated and included in the budget was only 10%.

(v) Factory overheads are 50% fixed and 50% variable.

(vi) Following the transport strike selling costs were increased. This involved the company in unavoidable increased selling costs of £8,200 in total.

(vii) The wage award referred to in (iv) above also applied to some administrative staff. Their wages account for 60% of all administrative costs.

(viii) Interest rates charged by lenders were at the budgeted rate.

(ix) About 30% of selling costs and 20% of administrative costs are variable.

9: Capital Budgeting

9.1 The Decision to Invest

9.1.1 A very important part of a financial manager's job is to provide information which will assist the making of decisions concerning the investment of capital funds. This is the process known as capital budgeting. Examples of such decisions are:

(a) Shall we set up a new factory in another town?

(b) Shall we replace a manual process with a mechanised one?

(c) Should we set up plant to enable us to make and sell a proposed new product line?

The basic criterion for determining whether or not to undertake investment expenditure is the same as that for any business expenditure. The money will be spent when we believe that the resulting benefit will recover the cost and show an adequate profit. In this sense the purchase of a £1 million new factory is the same as the purchase of a £1 item of stock in trade.

9.1.2 The distinctive features of capital investment which make it worth while developing and applying a special set of techniques for appraising it are:

(a) The sums involved are relatively large so that bad decisions may have very serious consequences.

(b) The time scale over which the benefit will be received is relatively long so that a business has to live with any mistakes for a considerable period.

(c) The whole nature of a business and its direction and rate of progress is ultimately governed by its overall investment programme.

(d) Capital investment involves waiting for the recoupment of expenditure. Because money can be used to earn interest, waiting has a cost.

9.1.3 It is important to stress that calculations of costs and returns, however precisely they may be made and however clear cut an indication this may seem to give, are no guarantee of investment success. They inform judgment. They do not replace it. We will mention some of the reasons why this is so:

(a) **Uncertainty**. Our calculations, in the nature of the investment process, are based on predictions about the future. We may know what the project will cost but we cannot know for certain either what its future yield will be or over what period of time these yields will continue. An apparently correct decision may therefore sometimes turn out disastrously because of the intervention of unexpected factors.

(b) **Non-quantifiable factors**. We can build into our calculations only factors which can be measured in terms of money value. Important though these are, they may not be the only ones which ought to be considered. It might, for instance, be financially worthwhile to install machinery capable of performing more quickly and efficiently than an existing manual process. It may, nevertheless, be to our disadvantage to do this if the resulting redundancies lead to bad labour relations which will cause problems for years to come. Again, it might be financially unjustifiable to install plant for treating noxious waste products. We may, however, wish to do so in order to create for ourselves a better public image.

(c) **Unawareness of all available opportunities**. A truly optimum investment programme would require, amongst other things, complete knowledge of all the investment opportunities available. This we may not have. We may invest in a particular project quite unaware that a better one was available to us.

9.2 Methods of Investment Appraisal

9.2.1 In this technological age we are inclined to assume that we should aspire to the most sophisticated gadgetry that we can. Concorde, we are inclined to assume, is a better way of travelling than a Mini car. It is important, however, that we should see this in a context. Concorde is plainly not better than a Mini if we are talking about a shopping trip down the High Street. Similarly an elaborate means of investment appraisal requiring skilled staff, complex fact finding exercises and elaborate calculations will not be warranted when we are dealing with a large number of individually small routine investment decisions.

We shall consider, below, a number of techniques for informing the investment process. They require different kinds of information and lead to different conclusions. This raises the question of which method we should employ on any particular occasion.

9.2.2 Example. So as to compare and exemplify the various methods of investment appraisal let us set up a 'guinea pig' example.

A machine for producing a certain product is available at a total cost, including installation, of £10,000. It is expected to have a life of eight years and during that time will produce net cash inflows as follows:

Year	Net cash inflow
	£
1	500
2	1,000
3	3,000
4	4,000
5	4,000
6	2,500
7	2,000
8	2,500 (including £1,000 scrap value of the machine)

Note two important points:

(a) 'Net cash inflow' is not the same as 'profit' in a conventional accounting sense. It might be better described as 'contribution'. It is revenues directly attributable to the project less costs directly attributable to the project. Its calculation thus specifically excludes any element of fixed cost apportioned from elsewhere in the business (i.e. which would be incurred in any event) and depreciation, which is a restatement of the total cost of the investment.

(b) The scrap value of the plant, in this case £1,000, is added to the trading cash inflow of the final year. No distinction is made between trading receipts and receipts of a capital nature. This would be the case with any other cash receipts associated with the project, e.g. the sale of any existing machines made redundant by it.

We are attempting to resolve our investment decision into a simple question of the form: 'Our proposed investment promises us a series of cash inflows $£y_1$, $£y_2$, $£y_3$, etc. Are we willing to pay the price of £x for this benefit?'

9.3 Pay Back Method

9.3.1 The so-called pay back method of investment appraisal is fairly widely used in industry and is based on the following philosophy. The commitment of funds to any project involves two things. It involves forgoing the use of the funds in any other way so long as they are tied up, and it involves the risk that the money so committed will be permanently lost. Both factors are related to time. The longer the funds are tied up the longer before they can be re-used and, in general, the greater the risk of non-recovery. The pay-back method, then, is based on management's concern to be reimbursed the initial outlay as soon as possible. Overall profitability is left to take care of itself.

An arbitrary required pay back period is determined by management. Let us say that, for our example, this period is three years.

Management, that is, is saying that it is willing to invest in any project which repays its initial cost within three years but not if it takes longer than this.

How does our 'guinea pig' project fare under this criterion?

Year	Amount 'repaid' to date i.e. cumulative net cash inflow £
1	500
2	1,500
3	4,500
4	8,500
5	12,500

by which time the initial outlay is more than repaid.

By intrapolation we can see that pay back is achieved in about 4.375 years. This exceeds the required pay back period. We would not, therefore, invest in the project.

9.3.2 The pay back method has the advantage that:

(a) It is simple to understand and to apply.

(b) It promotes a policy of caution in investment.

(c) Empirically it can be shown to produce satisfactory results.

Its disadvantages are:

(a) It disregards total contribution and so could favour projects with a poor overall profitability just because they had a relatively large initial cash inflow.

(b) It could prevent investment in the very best projects of all which characteristically take years of development before they reach maximum profitability.

9.4 Average Rate of Return

9.4.1 This method recognises that the profitability of a project is an important factor in the investment decision and that this must be related to the amount of capital investment and to the period for which it is required. A required rate of return is determined, usually by reference to the cost of capital. Let us say, for our example, that this rate is 15% per annum, i.e. a project will be favoured if it appears to yield 15% per annum or better on the funds committed to it. The steps in the calculation are shown below.

Determine the total cash inflow given by the project.

In our example this gives	£19,500
Then deduct the amount of the initial investment	10,000
Giving	£9,500

105

This is the amount the project earns over the eight years of its life and is thus equivalent to

$$\frac{£9,500}{8} = £1,187.50 \text{ per annum}$$

The amount invested in the project initially was £10,000. The amount remaining invested at the end is nil (because the project has repaid the whole of its cost as well as yielded a profit). The *average* amount invested can reasonably be regarded as being half of the initial outlay, i.e. £5,000.

The rate of return is thus:

$$\frac{£1,187.50}{£5,000} \times 100 = 23.75\%$$

which comfortably exceeds the required rate of return. We should therefore invest in this project.

9.5 Time Value of Money

9.5.1 The average rate of return method has the advantage that it takes into account the overall profitability of the project. Its disadvantage is that it does not take into account the *pattern* of cash flows as opposed to their arithmetic total. Since we are, so to speak, 'waiting' for the return of our investment funds so that they can be invested profitably in other projects we ought to favour projects which, other things being equal, give us their cash flows the earliest.

9.5.2 This leads us to the idea that money has a time value. The whole notion of a rate of interest, or cost of capital, relies on this. What it means is that, in order to induce us to forgo the use of money for a period of time, an amount has to be paid in compensation for the waiting. It follows from this that money receivable at different points in time is of differing significance. The longer we have to wait for it the less valuable a given sum is. The extent of this is governed by the rate of interest.

9.5.3 Example. Let us suppose that we require a rate of return on invested funds of 10% per annum. A certain investment promises to pay us £1 in one year's time. The amount we would need to invest now to amount to £1 in one year's time is easily calculated. It is:

$$\frac{£1 \times 100}{110} = 90.9\text{p}$$

So 90.9p now and £1 in one year's time can be regarded as equivalent. 90.9p is the *present value* of £1 receivable in one year's time.

The calculation can be done for any amount and for any time. £10 receivable in three years' time has a present value of:

$$£10 \times \left(\frac{100}{110} \right)^3 = £7.51$$

Rather than calculate this afresh every time we can use what are known as present value tables (they are reproduced in Appendix 6) giving the present values of £1 receivable in n years' time given a rate of interest of x% per annum for a wide range of values of n and x.

This calculation of the present value of future returns is known as discounting and there are two methods of investment appraisal derived from it, both coming under the general heading of discounted cash flow (D.C.F.).

9.6 Present Value Method

9.6.1 We will return to our guinea pig example. We will determine the present value of each of the eight promised net cash inflows by reference to the table taking as our rate of interest (cost of capital) 15% per annum.

Year	Net cash inflow £	Discount factor* (from table)	Present value £
1	500	.870	435
2	1,000	.756	756
3	3,000	.658	1,974
4	4,000	.572	2,288
5	4,000	.497	1,988
6	2,500	.432	1,080
7	2,000	.376	752
8	2,500	.327	818
Total present value of project			£10,091

*Although these have been taken from tables they are very easily calculated if tables are unavailable. The factors are:

1. $\dfrac{100}{115} = \dfrac{1}{1.15} = .870$

2. $\dfrac{10,000}{115 \times 115} = \dfrac{1}{1.15^2} = .756$

3. $\dfrac{1,000,000}{115 \times 115 \times 115} = \dfrac{1}{1.15^3} = .658$ etc.

In general terms; where r is the rate of discount and n is the number of years, the nth discount factor is given by

$$\frac{1}{(1+r)^n}$$

The total present value of £10,091 means that, if we pay exactly that sum in order to invest in the project then we shall, on these figures, recover our investment with 'interest' on the amount outstanding of 15% per annum – just enough to cover our cost of capital. (The proof of this is given in paragraph 9.8.1). The investment would be marginal at that cost. In fact we are being asked to invest only £10,000. There is thus a margin in favour of the investment of £91. This quantity is referred to as the *net* present value:

Net present value = $\dfrac{\text{present value of}}{\text{net cash inflows}}$ – $\dfrac{\text{present value of}}{\text{cash outflows.}}$

An investment yielding less than the required rate of return would be signalled by a negative net present value.

Where an investment has a zero, or very small, net present value, the non-quantifiable factors referred to in 9.1.3(b) will be especially important and may tip the scales either way. Management judgment of the situation, not necessarily capable of being precisely evaluated, may thus be critical in these cases.

9.6.2 Discounted cash flow has the advantage that it takes into account return of capital, profitability and the timing of cash flows. Because of its conceptual superiority it is easier to allow in a satisfactory manner for other factors, e.g. uncertainty and inflation. We shall be looking at these things in later chapters.

9.7 Internal Rate of Return

9.7.1 The net present value method of applying discounted cash flow, described above, has as its criterion of acceptability for a project the existence of a non-negative net present value. Internal rate of return can be regarded as another way of applying the same D.C.F. principle. In practice it is rather less convenient to use but should normally lead to exactly the same result.

Use of this method requires the determination, by trial and error of a rate of discount which will equate the returns promised by an investment to its cost, i.e. which will create a net present value of nil.

9.7.2 In our example the internal rate of return is obviously a little in excess of 15% per annum. We could, therefore, 'try' 15.1%, 15 .2% and 15.3%. This is shown below:

Year	Net cash inflows	Discount factors* 15.1%	15.2%	15.3%	Present values 15.1%	15.2%	15.3%
1	£500	.869	.868	.867	£435	£434	£434
2	1,000	.755	.754	.752	755	754	752
3	3,000	.656	.654	.652	1,968	1,962	1,956
4	4,000	.570	.568	.566	2,280	2,272	2,264
5	4,000	.495	.493	.491	1,980	1,972	1,964
6	2,500	.430	.428	.426	1,075	1,070	1,065
7	2,000	.374	.371	.369	748	742	738
8	2,500	.325	.322	.320	813	805	800
					£10,054	£10,011	£9,973

*Not available from tables (must be calculated).

It can be seen that the nearest to the correct discount factor which we have tried is 15.2% and an almost exact figure of 15.23% may be established by interpolation.

Where a calculated internal rate of return exceeds the cost of capital the implication is that investment will be profitable and should take place.

9.7.3 An alternative 'trial and error' method for calculating the internal rate of return is to determine, from tables, two values known to be respectively too high and too low and then to interpolate between them. This is shown below:

Year	Net cash inflows	Discount factors 15%	16%	Present values 15%	16%
1	£500	.870	.862	£435	£431
2	1,000	.756	.743	756	743
3	3,000	.658	.641	1,974	1,923
4	4,000	.572	.552	2,288	2,208
5	4,000	.497	.476	1,988	1,904
6	2,500	.432	.410	1,080	1,025
7	2,000	.376	.354	752	708
8	2,500	.327	.305	818	762
				£10,091	£9,704

The difference in present value between 15% and 16% is £10,091 − £9,704 = £387.

The cost of the machine is £10,000.

This is £91 below the present value associated with a discount factor of 15%.

The internal rate of return is therefore

$$15 + \frac{91}{387} \times 1\% = 15.24\%$$

Note that this method gives (in this case) a slightly less accurate estimate of internal rate of return than our earlier calculation but with considerably less computational effort.

9.7.4 A technical problem may arise when using the internal rate of return. This is that, where there are large negative cashflows late in a project's life there may be no unique value for it (i.e. it may take two values).

9.7.5 Example. Development of a quarry requires initial expenditure of £64,000 and a further expenditure of £200,000 at the end of five years to restore the site to its original state. The annual cash flows generated during the five year life of the quarry are £50,000. What is the internal rate of return for the project?

9.7.6 The table below shows the relevant net cash flows:

Year	Cashflow £
0	(64,000)
1	50,000
2	50,000
3	50,000
4	50,000
5	(150,000)*

* This is the £200,000 restoration cost less the trading cash flow of £50,000.

Trial and error discounting will show that this project has a net present value of zero at discount rate of both 8.475% and 41.46%. These are, therefore, both equally valid internal rates of return.

9.7.7 Internal rate of return can also rank projects incorrectly. This is because its calculation presumes that funds released from the project are re-invested at the same rate of return. Net present value assumes that they are re-invested only at the cost of capital. This is a more realistic assumption. The point is exemplified in 9.9.4.

9.8 Verification of D.C.F. Result

9.8.1 It was stated above that if we had invested £10,091 in our guinea pig project (instead of the £10,000 actually required) which then proceeded to yield the anticipated returns, this would amount to a return on capital of exactly 15% per annum. The table below gives the proof of this.

	£
Amount invested beginning of year 1	10,091
Interest accrued after one year @ 15% per annum	1,513
	11,604
Amount 'repaid' by project at end of year 1	500
Amount remaining invested at beginning of year 2	11,104
Interest, year 2 (15% of £11,104)	1,665
	12,769
Repaid, end year 2	1,000
Remaining beginning of year 3	11,769
Interest, year 3	1,765
	13,534
Repaid, end year 3	3,000
Remaining beginning of year 4	10,534
Interest, year 4	1,579
	12,113
Repaid, end of year 4	4,000
Remaining beginning of year 5	8,113
Interest, year 5	1,216
	9,329
Repaid, end year 5	4,000
Remaining beginning of year 6	5,329
Interest, year 6	800
	6,129
Repaid, end year 6	2,500
Remaining, beginning of year 7	3,629
Interest, year 7	544
	4,173
Repaid, end of year 7	2,000
Remaining beginning of year 8	2,173
Interest, year 8	327
	2,500
Repaid, end year 8	2,500
	Nil

9.9   Investment over a Period of Time

9.9.1   Sometimes the investment required by a project will not take place in one initial lump sum but will be spread over a period as construction and other development takes place. An example of how this is treated appears below.

111

9.9.2 Example. Funlover, plc proposes to develop a leisure facility which will involve a considerable capital expenditure. It will, therefore, be opened in stages over a period of five years. The capital expenditure will be:

Year	Expenditure £000's
1	25,000
2	10,000
3	30,000
4	20,000
5	10,000

Trading cash flows will also build up over time reaching a steady state after seven years as follows:

Year	Cash flow £000's
1	10,000
2	10,000
3	12,000
4	12,000
5	14,000
6	14,000
7 and after	16,000

Funlover's cost of capital is 15% per annum. Evaluate the proposal ignoring taxation.

9.9.3 The value of the project at the end of the sixth year is the value of an indefinite stream of cash flows of £16 million each year. This is given by:

$$\text{Value} = \frac{£16 \text{ million}}{.15}$$

$$= £106.67 \text{ million}$$

This should be added to the cash flow of the sixth year in the DCF calculation.

Year	Net cash flow £000's	Discount factor	Present value £000's
1	(15,000)	.869	(13,035)
2	nil	.756	nil
3	(18,000)	.658	(11,844)
4	(8,000)	.572	(4,576)
5	4,000	.497	1,988
6	120,667	.432	52,128
			24,661

There is a positive net present value so the project is worthwhile. Note that, because the capital expenditure is built into the calculation, we do not have to make any deduction for initial investment.

9.10 Investment in Working Capital

9.10.1 It will often be the case that capital investment in a project will also require an associated investment in working capital. This is because stocks of material will need to be made available and debtors may have to increase to allow for the increased volume of trade. These outgoings may be partially offset by an increase in creditors. Analytically the increase in working capital should be treated as being as much part of the initial investment as is the capital expenditure. Usually, however, it has the characteristic that it will be released at the end of the life of the project. Where this is so the amount should be treated as an additional cash inflow at the end of the final year.

9.10.2 Example. Gofast, plc is considering the investment of £50,000 in plant to manufacture a new product. The product is expected to sell for five years after which time the plant will be uneconomic and will have no residual value. Manufacture of the product will also require Gofast to hold additional stocks of raw material costing £12,000 and to advance £6,000 in additional credit to customers. Creditors for supplies are expected to increase by £8,000. Working capital will be released at the end of the life of the project. Gofast's cost of capital is 12% per annum. The trading cash flows are expected to be as follows:

Year	Cash flow
	£
1	10,000
2	20,000
3	30,000
4	20,000
5	10,000

9.10.3 Calculation of working capital requirement:

	£
Stock	12,000
Debtors	6,000
	18,000
Less Creditors	8,000
	10,000

Initial investment is, therefore, £60,000 in total but the final year's cash flow will be augmented by the return of the working capital. The calculation is:

Year	Cash flow £	Discount factor	Present value £
1	10,000	.893	8,930
2	20,000	.797	15,940
3	30,000	.712	21,360
4	20,000	.636	12,720
5	20,000	.567	11,340
			70,290
Less Initial investment			60,000
Net present value			10,290

The investment would appear to be worthwhile.

9.11 Mutually Exclusive Projects

9.11.1 The analysis so far has been entirely in terms of the acceptability or otherwise of a proposed investment project where each is considered on its own merits alone. We have said that all projects should be accepted if they meet our required pay-back period or give a positive net present value or an internal rate of return higher than our cost of capital, according to which method we are using. It has not been necessary to compare one project with another because the question of their ranking has not been important. If projects A, B and C are all acceptable and we are going to undertake them all it is not further necessary to know which is the best and which the least good. There are two cases, however, in which ranking is important. These are the cases of capital rationing and of mutually exclusive projects. Capital rationing will be considered later (Chapter 12). Mutually exclusive projects we shall discuss now.

9.11.2 Projects are described as mutually exclusive when the acceptance of one precludes the acceptance of the other or others. If, for example, there is a good play on BBC television and a good film on ITV at the same time, the decision rule to watch all good programmes will let us down. The programmes are mutually exclusive and we have to decide which is the better of the two. Similarly, if two investment projects are available but cannot both be accepted, they must, in some way, be ranked. Ranking according to internal rate of return and ranking according to net present value may give different results. Ranking according to net present value is the appropriate method to use as an example will make clear.

9.11.3 Example. Fresh Pastures, plc wishes to purchase an automatic packing machine for its product. There are two alternative possibilities. One is the Smith Packing Machine which will cost £10,000 and will last for eight years. The other is the Jones Packer which will cost only £2,500 but will last for only four years and will be more expensive to run. In each case, however, there will be annual savings of £5,000 over the present manual method of packing. Annual running costs for the Smith machine are £3,000 and for the Jones £4,125. The company's cost of capital is 10% per annum.

9.11.4 We can discover (by trial and error) that the internal rate of return for the Smith machine is 12% per annum and that for the Jones is 15% per annum (approximately in each case). The Jones would appear, at first sight, to be the better investment. This disregards, however, that the Smith will produce its return for much longer and that this more than compensates for the lower rate. The net present value for the Smith machine is (£5,000 − £3,000) × (.909 + .826 + .751 + .683 + .621 + .564 + .513 + .467) − £10,000 which equals £668. The net present value for the Jones is (£5,000 − £4,125) × (.909 + .826 + .751 + .683) − £2,500 which equals £273. We should, therefore, choose to invest in the Smith machine.

9.12 Abandonment Value

9.12.1 A factor not always considered when investing in a project is the possibility of abandonment before the end of its economic life. Management often evaluates a project only on the basis that it is kept throughout its life and indeed this has been our assumption in the examples we have considered so far. Abandonment value is defined as the amount which could be realised by liquidating a project (i.e. selling the machine, etc.) while it is still useful. The abandonment value is used in calculations by including it with the other proceeds of the year in which it occurs and discounting appropriately. Obviously projected proceeds after the abandonment are then disregarded.

There are two uses for this technique. One is to aid a decision as to whether to withdraw from a project currently in progress. The other is to evaluate projects at the outset on alternative assumptions as to how long they will be pursued. The inclusion of abandonment values can have a dramatic effect on the evaluation of a project. Because the existence of abandonment values allows for early exit from a project which turns out to be disappointing this also has an important bearing on the degree of risk involved in the investment.

9.12.2 Example. Openair, plc is considering investing in a project having an initial capital cost of £17,500. The company's relevant cost of capital is 12% per annum. The project has an expected life of four years but could be abandoned with some recovery of the initial investment at the end of any one of the first three years. Figures are:

Year	Projected cash flow	Projected abandonment value
1	£5,000	£16,000
2	6,000	12,000
3	7,000	4,000
4	5,000	Nil

9.12.3 In a sense we have here four separate projects to look at. These are evaluated as follows.

If the project is maintained for the whole of its four year life:

Year	Projected cash flow	12% discount factor	Present value
1	£5,000	.893	£4,465
2	6,000	.797	4,782
3	7,000	.712	4,984
4	5,000	.636	3,180
			17,411
	Less initial investment		17,500
	Net present value		−£89

It is not worth while operating the project for the whole of its life. With abandonment after 3 years:

Year	Projected cash flow	12% discount factor	Present value
1	£5,000	.893	£4,465
2	6,000	.797	4,782
3	11,000*	.712	7,832
			17,079
	Less initial investment		17,500
	Net present value		−£421

The project is not worthwhile.

*£7,000 + £4,000

With abandonment after 2 years:

Year	Projected cash flow	12% discount factor	Present value
1	£5,000	.893	£4,465
2	18,000*	.797	14,346
			18,811
	Less initial investment		17,500
	Net present value		+£1,311

This investment is worthwhile.

*£6,000 + £12,000

116

With abandonment after a year:

Year	Projected cash flow	12% discount factor	Present value
1	£21,000*	.893	£18,753
	Less initial investment		17,500
	Net present value		+£1,253

*£5,000 + £16,000

This investment is also worthwhile.

The best course of action would appear to be to invest in the project and abandon it after two years. On a full life evaluation, however, the project would have been rejected.

9.12.4 Example. Wideworld, plc invested three years ago, at a cost of £100,000, in plant then believed to have an economic life of five years. The project appeared to offer a high net present value. The company's current cost of capital is 16% per annum and the plant is now expected to last for a further three years. An opportunity has arisen, which is unlikely to be repeated, to sell the plant now for £50,000 and this possibility is being considered.

The company's accountant has prepared the following projections for the next three years:

	Year 1	Year 2	Year 3
Revenue	£33,750	£41,250	£30,000
Less Variable costs	£11,250	£13,750	£10,000
Allocation of fixed cost	7,500	9,200	6,700
Depreciation	20,000	20,000	–
	£38,750	£42,950	£16,700
Profit/(Loss)	(£5,000)	(£1,700)	£13,300

If the plant is now sold this will give rise to an accounting profit as shown below:

Proceeds of sale	£50,000
Less Net book value	40,000
Profit on sale	10,000

The accountant argues from these figures that the plant should be sold. Results have been disappointing and losses are predicted for the next two years. Even over three years the overall profit expected to be earned by the plant is less than the profit which could be made by an immediate sale. Do you agree that the plant should be sold?

9.12.5 We need first to isolate the relevant figures from the statements which are presented to us. Allocated fixed cost and depreciation are not relevant. The former will be incurred even if the plant is sold and the latter is merely an accounting allocation of a cost already incurred when the plant was purchased.

The relevant cash flow is thus Revenue – Variable cost. The table below shows the calculation of this:

	Year 1	Year 2	Year 3
Revenue	£33,750	£41,250	£30,000
Less Variable cost	11,250	13,750	10,000
Cash flow	£22,500	£27,500	£20,000

The net present value of retaining the plant can then be determined:

Year	Cash flow	16% discount factor	Present value
1	£22,500	.862	£19,395
2	27,500	.743	20,433
3	20,000	.641	12,820
			52,648
Less Proceeds forgone if plant is kept			50,000
			+£2,648

There is thus a positive net present value of £2,648 to keeping the plant which should, therefore, be retained.

Summary

(i)   It is important that financial resources should be deployed to best advantage and so good investment decisions are vital to successful financial management.

(ii) There are several techniques available whereby investment proposals can be evaluated. Since, however, all require projections of future costs and returns they cannot be guaranteed to lead to successful decisions. It can, perhaps, be claimed that they increase the probability of success.

(iii) A highly sophisticated, apparently 'accurate', method of project appraisal with a sound theoretical basis will not necessarily give sufficient extra success to warrant the cost involved in using it. There is a place, therefore, for simple, rough and ready, techniques particularly for routine small investment decisions taken at a relatively low level of management.

(iv) All methods of investment appraisal use figures for the net returns expected from the project. This is not the same as accounting profit. It may best be seen as the contribution to be made by the project year by year, i.e. revenue less direct costs (but not including depreciation).

(v) The pay back method computes the length of time required for a project to recoup its capital outlay. The shorter the pay back period, the more favourably is the project regarded. It is generally used by prescribing a required pay back period, e.g. three years. The decision rule is then that a project with a shorter pay back period than this will be accepted and one with a longer pay back period will not.

(vi) The average rate of return method determines the overall projected profit of the project by subtracting the initial cost from the expected total returns. This is then expressed first as an annual absolute amount and then as an annual percentage of the amount invested. This is usually taken to average half of the initial capital committed to the project. The return computed by this means might be compared with the company's cost of capital.

(vii) The more theoretically sound methods of project appraisal are based on the discounting principle. This recognises that money receivable in the future has less present value than money receivable immediately because of the interest which the latter is capable of earning. Future returns are therefore discounted by a factor related to the rate of interest considered appropriate. There are two basic versions of discounted cash flow.

(viii) The net present value method discounts future returns by reference to the cost of capital. If this gives an aggregate value equal to or in excess of the initial investment (i.e. a positive or zero net present value) then the project is acceptable. A negative net present value would signify an unacceptable project.

(ix) The internal rate of return method determines (by trial and error) the rate of discount required to equate the present value of the projected future returns to the initial investment. This figure is known as the internal rate of return and the project is acceptable if it is not less than the cost of capital. Generally (there are some peculiar exceptions which need not concern us) the net present value and internal rate of return methods will lead to identical conclusions. The former is usually more convenient to use in practice as it avoids the tedious trial and error process.

(x) The normal decision rule is that all projects having a positive net present value (or an internal rate of return in excess of the cost of capital) will be undertaken. Their ranking is thus of no importance. Ranking is, however, important in two special cases, i.e. those of mutually exclusive projects and of capital rationing. In these cases ranking should be by net present value.

(xi) In order fully to consider all possibilities account should be taken, where feasible, of a project's abandonment value at points in time before the end of its economic life. It is sometimes more profitable to abandon a project at such an interim stage than it is to operate it for the whole of its theoretical life.

Review Questions

(i) *A certain project promises to yield an annual cash inflow of £10,000 for eight years. Calculate the present value of this flow using a cost of capital of 17½% per annum. (This cannot be obtained from tables and should be calculated).*

(ii) *Define carefully the following terms:*

   (a) *Abandonment value*

   (b) *Mutually exclusive projects*

   (c) *Pay back period*

   (d) *Discounted cashflow*

(iii) *Mr X is 70 years old and, statistically, has a life expectancy of 10 years. An annuity of £1,000 per annum starting one year after date would cost him £5,000. What rate of return does this offer him on the amount invested in the annuity? How can this example be related to the concept of an internal rate of return for an investment project?*

(iv) *Projects A and B are mutually exclusive. A outranks B on internal rate of return, B has a higher net present value than A but each has the same payback period. Which project would you favour and why? Explain how different methods of appraisal can rank projects differently.*

(v) *The term capital budgeting implies a plan relating to capital expenditure. To what extent is such a plan formulated by use of the techniques described in this chapter?*

(vi) *'Capital expenditure is more important than revenue expenditure.' Do you agree?*

(vii) *'This project has a net present value of nil. As there is nothing in it for us we should not invest.' Is this a rational point of view?*

(viii) 'If we embark on this project we shall have to see it through to its end.' Is this necessarily an appropriate attitude to take?

Exercises

1. A proposal has come before the Board of Directors of Greenfields, plc for the purchase of a machine to manufacture a new product. Anticipated results for the expected five year life of the machine are supplied by the company's accountant as follows:

	Year 1	Year 2	Year 3	Year 4	Year 5
Sales of product	£20,000	£22,000	£23,000	£16,000	£12,000
Direct costs	10,000	12,000	13,000	10,000	8,000
Depreciation	6,000	6,000	6,000	6,000	6,000
Total costs	£16,000	£18,000	£19,000	£16,000	£14,000
Profit/(/Loss	£4,000	£4,000	£4,000	Nil	(£2,000)

Greenfields, plc's cost of capital is 12% per annum. Would you advise the company to invest in this machine?

2. Compare and contrast the various methods of investment appraisal. To what extent would it be true to say that there is a place for each of them?

3. A certain project is expected to yield the returns given below over the next five years. It would require an initial investment of £13,500. Determine its internal rate of return. State how you would use this in deciding whether or not to invest in the project.

Year	Returns
	£
1	2,000
2	4,000
3	6,000
4	5,000
5	3,000

4. Tenacre, plc leases a piece of land which is not currently being used. The lease expires in five years' time and is unlikely to be renewable on acceptable terms. The company is considering three possible courses of action. These are (i) to sell the remainder of the lease for £20,000, (ii) to rent the land to a tenant at a rent of £5,000 p.a. or (iii) to take crops from the land which would have a net value of £15,000, £10,000, £8,000 and £2,000 respectively for the four years starting in the second year. If the last alternative is adopted the land will need to be cleared during the first year and this will involve expenditure of £5,000 payable at the

end of the year. Tenacre's cost of capital is 15% per annum. What should the company do?

5. Meadowland, plc plans to invest £25,000 in a project for which the following returns and abandonment values are predicted. Its cost of capital is 18% per annum. Advise the company.

Year	Returns if kept	Abandonment value
1	£4,000	£22,500
2	6,000	18,000
3	10,000	16,000
4	10,000	15,000
5	10,000	12,500
6	10,000	Nil

6. Wildflower, plc has to replace some factory equipment which has reached the end of its economic life. The selected replacement must have the capacity to process 100,000 units of product per annum. This yields an annual cash inflow, before charging the costs of operating the equipment, of 50p per unit. The choices have been narrowed down as follows:

Choice A
The Modmill machine
Capacity: 60,000 units per annum.
Required: 2 machines
Annual running cost for 100,000 units: £20,000 per machine
Cost of machine: £12,500 each
Economic life: 5 years

Choice B
The Finman machine
Capacity: 110,000 units per annum
Required: 1 machine
Annual running cost for 100,000 units: £30,000
Cost of machine: £75,000
Economic life: 7 years

Choice C
The Datproc machine
Capacity: 35,000 units per annum
Required: 3 machines
Annual running cost for 100,000 units: £12,500 per machine
Cost of machine: £17,500 each
Economic life: 10 years

The company's cost of capital is 15% per annum. Which choice should be made? Are there any factors not referred to here which you would wish to take into account?

10: Risk

10.1 The Risk Factor in Investment Decisions

10.1.1 In the discussion of the previous chapter there was one important matter which we did not consider and to which we must now give close attention. This is the factor of risk. Although we referred to the fact that the figures on which we were basing our calculations were estimates, we were not specific about how the possibility of error should be taken into account.

10.1.2 Risk may be defined as the probability that a prediction will turn out to be wrong. If there is a high probability that a prediction will prove to be considerably in error, then the risk is high. If the probability of substantial divergence is low, then the risk is small. Obviously, if a project guarantees us a rate of return of, say, 15% per annum, we shall favour this over a project which promises to achieve this rate of return but carries the risk that it will fall far short of it.

Risk may be reduced for a business by a policy of diversification. This, however, is a matter which we shall look at in the next chapter when we look at the risk associated with a portfolio or collection of projects. In this chapter we shall be concerned only with the individual risk attaching to a project.

10.1.3 The question may be raised as to why, if risk is seen as a problem, management should choose to invest in risky projects at all. The justification for doing so is that it is the most risky projects which, if they are successful, offer the greatest rewards. A useful analogy may be drawn from horse racing. If you stake £10 on a 5 to 4 on favourite you are very likely to win but the gain will be only £8. If you stake the money on a 100 to 1 outsider you will probably lose. If you win, however, the profit is £1,000. Similarly in business the prospect of great success is often bought at the risk of failure.

10.2 Reliance on Compensation

10.2.1 One method of dealing with risk in our calculations is to ignore it altogether. It may seem odd to regard this as a 'method' but it can be so regarded if the risk element has been specifically considered and it has been decided that it is random in its incidence and is as likely to cause better than expected results as it is to cause worse than expected. If, when we aim at a rate of return of, say, 12% per annum, we discover that, on average, this is what occurs, on the 'swings and roundabouts' principle, then risk can safely be ignored. We shall justify this technique further later.

10.2.2 Example. X, plc has invested in the following projects all of which were estimated exactly to meet the company's cost of capital of 15% per annum. Each project required the investment of an identical capital sum.

Project	Actual rate of return calculated after completion
1	17%
2	15%
3	13%
4	16%
5	19%
6	13%
7	14%
8	13%
Average	15%

Although projects 3, 6, 7 and 8 have yielded less than the cost of capital and, with hindsight, should have been avoided, this has been compensated for by the remaining projects which have done better than expected.

As we could not in advance distinguish between above average and below average projects, we may regard the end result as successful overall.

10.2.3 In practice this happy averaging out of projects does not usually happen. In most cases we are likely to find that the nature of the risk is such that we may find a project doing substantially worse than expected but rarely substantially better than expected. There are good reasons to anticipate this. One is that when people are putting up a case for capital expenditure on a project in which they are interested, they may tend to be optimistic in their expectations. Another is that estimates may be based on the assumption that an investment will be worked at or near to its full capacity. In that case there is little potential for improving on expected performance but plenty of scope for falling below it.

10.3 Risk Premium Discount Factor

10.3.1 A method commonly used for dealing with this situation is the use of what is known as a 'risk premium' discount factor. The idea is very simple. If the cost of capital is 15% per annum but experience shows that projects are frequently less successful than expected and yield on average, say, 2% per annum less than was envisaged, then all appraisal calculations are made at a discount rate of 17% per annum (i.e. 15% + 2%). What we are doing thereby is calculating on the basis of a required rate of return of 17% per annum so that when risk acts to reduce this the actual yield achieved should meet our genuine required rate of 15%.

10.3.2 Example. Y, plc has engaged in eight investment projects of equal size. Each was expected to yield precisely the company's cost of capital of 15% per annum.

Project	Actual rate of return calculated after completion
1	11%
2	12%
3	11%
4	13%
5	16%
6	15%
7	12%
8	14%
Average	13%

The management of Y, plc should from now on evaluate all its projects on the basis of a required rate of return of 17% per annum.

It should be pointed out that the use of a risk premium rate will cause the company to reject some projects which it should have accepted, i.e. they appeared profitable both in prospect and in retrospect. Provided that there is no shortage of available projects this may not be particularly important.

10.4 Expected Returns

10.4.1 A more sophisticated method of dealing with risk requires us to estimate for each project not only its life and returns for each year of that life but also the possible alternative returns together with their probabilities in the form of a probability distribution. Although not always easy to put into practice the theory of this is very simple and can be illustrated by means of an example.

10.4.2 Example. A certain project will require an investment of £18,000. It is expected to have a life of four years. The predicted positive cash flow in the first year is £8,000 but, because of risk, it is estimated that there is a .5 probability only that this will be the actual result (i.e. it has a 50:50 chance). All the other possibilities must now be assessed with their respective probabilities. There may in practice be a large number but we will assume, in order to simplify this example, that in this case there are only two. A return of £7,000 may occur with a probability of .4 and £9,000 with a probability of .1. The probabilities sum to 1 signifying that we have recorded all possible outcomes.

10.4.3 We can now set up a probability distribution for year 1.

Return	Probability	R × P
7,000	.4	2,800
8,000	.5	4,000
9,000	.1	900
'Expected' return		£7,700

A weighted average of the possible cash flows has been calculated and this gives what is known as the expected cash flow of the project for the first year. Note that it is 'expected' only in a particular sense as the precise figure is not listed amongst the possibilities and therefore cannot occur. It is expected in the average sense just as we might say that the average motor vehicle is expected to contain 1.3 people.

We can do similar calculations for all the years of the life of the project and the results are set out below. Note that in this example, as commonly in practice, risk increases as we move further into the future. This is shown by the increasingly wide spread of possible outcomes and arises because of the increased chance of unforeseen circumstances the further into the future we look.

Year 1		Year 2		Year 3		Year 4	
Returns £	Pr	Returns £	Pr	Returns £	Pr	Returns £	Pr
7,000	.4	6,000	.2	5,000	.2	4,000	.1
8,000	.5	7,000	.4	5,500	.3	5,000	.2
9,000	.1	8,000	.3	6,000	.3	6,000	.3
		8,500	.1	7,000	.2	7,000	.2
						8,000	.2

Expected return:
£7,700	£7,250	£5,850	£6,200

Our calculation is then completed by inserting our expected returns in a conventional D.C.F. calculation. We have taken as our cost of capital a rate of 15% per annum.

Year	Expected return £	Discount factor	Present value £
1	7,700	.870	6,699
2	7,250	.756	5,481
3	5,850	.658	3,849
4	6,200	.572	3,546
			19,575
Less Original investment required			18,000
Expected net present value			+£1,575

10.4.4 It might be argued that, although we are apparently introducing more precision into our analysis, the estimation of probabilities is a more difficult task even than was the estimation of future returns. This cannot be denied but it may be that by this means we are able to get closer to a realistic appraisal of a situation even if we cannot hit on it exactly.

10.4.5 In practice our probability distribution might not be discontinuous like the one in the example. We may, for instance, expect a normal distribution with a mean of £x and a standard deviation of £y. The expected return is thus £x and £y gives a measure of the degree of risk associated with the estimate. Interestingly the calculation of the expected net present value then proceeds exactly as in paragraph 10.2.1, a more scientific justification for our apparently careless policy mentioned there.

10.4.6 A very important feature of a risky situation is that a company must have regard to how much is being staked on a project. The concept of an expected return implies that a large number of projects is being undertaken so that the averages have an opportunity to 'work out'. Consider a simple analogy. You are offered the chance to bet on the outcome of the toss of a coin. The stake is 1p per toss. If you call correctly you will be awarded 5p. If you call incorrectly you lose your stake. Clearly, assuming a fair coin, this game is heavily biassed in your favour and you will be willing to play it indefinitely. In 1,000 tosses of the coin, for example, you would expect 500 wins, giving you £25 and 500 losses, losing you £5, net gain £20. If the stake is now raised to £10,000 per game, however, you will almost certainly be unwilling to play at all. The odds are still as favourable and the long term prospect of considerable gain is there but there is a high risk that you will not survive into the long term. If the first toss is a loser you are immediately bankrupted and out of the game with no chance of recovery.

Similarly a company may be unwilling to take even a small risk of failure on a project so large that it absorbs all or a very substantial part of its total resources.

10.4.7 Let us look again at the example set out in paragraph 10.4.3. This gave us an expected positive net present value of £1,575 and this indicated that we should accept the project. If, however, this project is the only one in which we are to engage we have to consider what would be the result of the worst possible outcome. This is shown below where we are taking the lowest possible return year by year rather than the expected value as before.

Year	Lowest return £	Discount factor	Present value £
1	7,000	.870	6,090
2	6,000	.756	4,536
3	5,000	.658	3,290
4	4,000	.572	2,288
			16,204
Less Original investment required			18,000
Net present value			−£1,796

Thus we see that the worst possible outcome is a negative net present value of £1,796 – an effective loss of nearly ten per cent of our total capital.

10.4.8 Computer simulation. Modern computer availability makes possible a particularly useful way of handling probability distributions in risk estimation. The distribution is put into the machine which can then generate a large number of predicted outcomes of the kind and in the proportions which might be expected to happen in practice. The computer's speed and capacity for dealing with highly complex distributions means that results may be obtained which would not be feasible by manual methods of calculation. It should, however, be noted that the ultimate result is no better than the data fed in and that the model used in the simulation still has to be set up on the basis of man-made predictions about the future. The quality of these remains the ultimate determinant of success.

10.5 Sensitivity Analysis

10.5.1 One of the difficulties of estimating future returns in a risky situation is the complexity of the influences which may work on them. Returns are not a simple uncomplicated quantity. They are the result of various factors, i.e. the revenues less all the relevant costs, and each of these may be subject to its own special risk unrelated to that affecting the others. In order to simplify the situation somewhat, use may be made of what is known as sensitivity analysis to isolate the more important factors from the less important. All that is meant by this is that we test the various factors to see how vulnerable the overall outcome of the project is to variations in each on its own.

10.5.2 Example. The following forecast exists for next year's results for one of our company's products:

		£
Sales		100,000
Less Direct costs:		
Material	25,000	
Labour	20,000	
Variable overhead	10,000	
Fixed overhead	20,000	75,000
Contribution		£25,000

We have included direct fixed costs but not indirect costs in calculating this figure. It is therefore the contribution which this product makes to the overall result of the business.

10.5.3 We will now test the sensitivity of the contribution to each of the factors making it up.

(a) **Sales volume:**

If sales volume varies from forecast by (say) 10% then contribution varies by 10% × £45,000 (final contribution + fixed overhead). This is

$$\frac{£4,500}{£25,000} \times 100 = 18\% \text{ of the contribution for the project.}$$

(b) **Selling price:**

If selling price varies by 10% then the final contribution varies by 10% × £100,000 = £10,000. This is:

$$\frac{£10,000}{£25,000} \times 100 = 40\% \text{ of the contribution.}$$

(c) **Material cost:**

If material cost varies by 10% (either because of greater usage or because of a higher unit buying price) then contribution varies by 10% × £25,000 = £2,500. This is

$$\frac{£2,500}{£25,000} \times 100 = 10\% \text{ of the contribution.}$$

(d) **Labour cost:**

If labour cost varies by 10% then contribution varies by 10% × £20,000. This is

$$\frac{£2,000}{£25,000} \times 100 = 8\% \text{ of the contribution.}$$

(e) **Variable overhead cost:**

If variable overhead cost varies by 10% then contribution varies by $10\% \times £10,000 = £1,000$. This is

$$\frac{£1,000}{£25,000} \times 100 = 4\% \text{ of the contribution.}$$

(f) **Fixed overhead cost:**

If fixed overhead cost varies by 10% then contribution varies by $10\% \times £20,000 = £2,000$. This is

$$\frac{£2,000}{£25,000} \times 100 = 8\% \text{ of the contribution.}$$

Thus we can see that the project is most vulnerable to changes in the selling price of the product. It is here that faulty estimating will have the greatest consequences and where, therefore, the greatest care needs to be taken in assessing the probable outcomes.

Summary

(i) Because the future cannot be precisely known, there is a risk associated with every investment of capital funds. The financial manager must respond to this by trying to evaluate risk, to take it into consideration in making his decisions, and to protect his investments from it so far as this is possible.

(ii) We may assume that management does not seek risk for its own sake. A risky project will only be undertaken if it is believed that the risk of loss is outweighed by the prospect of gain.

(iii) One method of dealing with risk is to ignore it. This will be appropriate where it is believed that projects are as likely to exceed expectation as they are to fall short of it and by a similar margin, so that on average, expectations are realised.

(iv) Where experience shows that the risk factor causes projects on average to do worse than expectation, this may be met by the incorporation in the discount rate of a risk premium. This merely means that expected returns from a project are discounted at a rate higher than that of the true cost of capital.

(v) Where all possible levels of return can be predicted and an appropriate probability attached to each we can calculate an expected return for each year of the project's life. This expected return is what is expected on average if a large number of projects of this type is undertaken. Having ascertained the expected return for each year these are then discounted in the ordinary way at the true cost of capital. It should be remembered that the theory of this method relies on there being a large number of investments undertaken to allow the averages to 'work out.'

(vi) Sometimes in a complex situation it will be helpful to concentrate attention on one part of it – that part most vulnerable to risk. Sensitivity analysis is a technique for determining which of the variables contributing to the final result will have most effect if it is incorrectly forecast. We might discover by sensitivity analysis, for example, that although the cost of a certain component of a product is subject to large and quite unpredictable variations in cost, that this has very little effect on the final contribution (because it represents a small element of total cost). In that case this risk, though great, may safely be disregarded.

Review Questions

(i) *What is meant by 'risk' and why is it important to the financial manager?*

(ii) *Distinguish carefully between the predicted returns from a project and the expected returns. What is the significance of the latter?*

(iii) *'The most profitable projects are often those which seem most risky. Management should, therefore, seek out rather than avoid risks.' Discuss.*

(iv) *Comment on some of the practical difficulties involved in allowing for risk in capital budgeting techniques.*

(v) *In order to allow for risk X plc uses a discount factor of 20% per annum in its capital budgeting calculations even though its true cost of capital is 15% per annum. Are there any disadvantages of this policy?*

(vi) *What is meant by sensitivity analysis and how might it be used?*

(vii) *What factors are likely to make a project risky?*

(viii) *What grounds might there be for believing that it is better to invest in a number of relatively small risky projects rather than in one larger one?*

Exercises

1. *Trafalgar, plc is contemplating the purchase of a machine at a total initial cost of £10,000 which it is estimated will last for at least four and not more than five years. The anticipated returns with their probability assessments are given below:*

Year 1		Year 2		Year 3		Year 4		Year 5	
Return	Prob.	Return	Prob.	Return	Prob.	Return	Prob.	Return	Prob.
£		£		£		£		£	
1,000	.2	2,000	.2	3,000	.6	2,000	.2	Nil*	.5
3,000	.5	3,000	.4	4,000	.3	3,000	.5	2,000	.3
4,000	.3	4,000	.3	5,000	.1	4,000	.2	3,000	.1
		5,000	.1			5,000	.1	4,000	.1

*'Returns' in year 5 if the machine lasts only 4 years.

Trafalgar's cost of capital is 14% per annum. Should it invest in the project? Comment on any recommendation which you make.

2. *'Risk taking is of the essence of entrepreneurship. If a business is unwilling to take a leap in the dark it can never be profitable.' Discuss.*

3. *Many businesses make no allowance for risk in their evaluation of capital projects. Are there circumstances in which this could be theoretically justified? Are these circumstances likely commonly to prevail?*

4. *Waterloo, plc allows for risk in its investment appraisal by adding a risk premium on top of its true cost of capital. Discuss this device drawing attention to any assumptions on which it is based and considering its likely consequences.*

5. *An insurance company is in business deliberately to take on risks, often risks which might lead to disaster. This might seem to be the recipe for spectacular failure but most insurance companies seem to thrive. Can you explain this paradox?*

6. *Alamein, plc is considering investment in three risky projects which it designates X, Y and Z. Details appear below.*

Project X

This will require an initial investment of £50,000 and will lead to annual net cash inflows over the next five years estimated as follows:

Most pessimistic (.25 probability)	£13,500
Most likely (.50 probability)	£18,000
Most optimistic (.25 probability)	£20,000

Some doubt has been expressed about the possibility that this project will infringe a competitor's patent. If this were so and he successfully pursued a claim for damages he may have to be paid as much as £100,000 in the third year. Lawyers estimate that there is only a 0.1 probability that this will happen.

Project Y

This will require an outlay of £50,000 spread in equal instalments over the next three years to finance a research project. If this is successful, and there is thought to be a 50/50 chance of this, it will lead to a patent having an estimated value at the end of the three years of £200,000. If not successful the whole of the expenditure would have to be written off.

Project Z

This will have an initial cost of £20,000 and is firmly expected to yield cash flows of £8,000 in each of its first two years. Thereafter the outcome is so uncertain that no estimate can be given.

The company's cost of capital is 14% per annum and it requires advice concerning its decisions on each of the above three projects.

11: Capital Asset Pricing Model

11.1 Diversification

11.1.1 It is axiomatic that an investor will spread his funds over a number of available investments and will not put 'all his eggs in one basket'. If asked why he does this he will reply that it reduces the risk of loss. If he invests in only one security and this fails he will lose money. It is unlikely that he will lose everything if he holds a number of investments.

11.1.2 Although the simple argument set out above sounds very plausible, there is, in fact, a serious flaw in its logic. This is that the risks to which investments are subject are often common to them all. A recession, for example, will cause all industrial and commercial activity to do less well and therefore no spread of investments could reduce vulnerability to this effect. Similarly substantial movements in the general level of stock market prices will affect all shares and a diversified portfolio will withstand this no better than an undiversified one. Clearly blind adherence to random diversification is not sensible and an analytical framework needs to be set up within which to devise a suitable policy.

11.1.3 The branch of financial management which deals with this is known as portfolio theory. The term 'portfolio' in this context simply means 'collection of investments'. For an investor through the Stock Exchange the portfolio will be a collection of shareholdings in different companies. For a property investor his portfolio will be a collection of buildings. To a financial manager within a industrial company his portfolio will be a collection of real capital projects. It will be seen that the actual nature of the components of a portfolio will depend on the population of opportunities from which the selection has to be made.

11.1.4 Portfolio theory was first developed in connection with investment in stock market securities. The extension to any situation where a collection of investments is made is quite straightforward and this leads on to the development of what is known as the capital asset pricing model for capital budgeting. There are several concepts which need to be understood. The most important of these are risk aversion, the efficient portfolio and the beta coefficient.

11.2 Risk Aversion

11.2.1 There is a presumption that an investor is risk averse, i.e. avoids risk where he can. It is obvious that a safe 10% return is preferable to a doubtful 10% return on an investment but risk aversion goes further than this. A simple example will illustrate the point. Investment X has a guaranteed pay back of £1,000 in one year's time. Investment Y will pay either £2,000 or nil in one year's time, each having an equal probability. Each investment has, mathematically, an expected value of £1,000 in one year's time and an investor with a neutral attitude to risk would not distinguish between them. A risk averse investor would favour investment X. For a given expected return, that is, he prefers the one having the least risk. Only an investor who positively relished risk (if such could be found) would prefer investment Y.

11.2.2 If an investor wishes to avoid risk he must be able to assess and measure it. Let us extend our example. Investment Z will pay either £1,500 or £500 in one year's time, each outcome having equal probability. Again the investment has an expected value of £1,000 in one year's time and again it is exposed to risk. It is, however, less risky than investment Y and will be preferred to it. Risk is seen here as measured by the variability of possible returns about their arithmetic mean (or the expected value). A useful statistical measure of variability is the variance (square of the standard deviation) and we shall use this in what follows. The measure will already be familiar to students of Statistics.

11.2.3 Risk aversion can be explained using the economic concept of diminishing utility. This merely states that the more a person has of a particular commodity (here money) the less desirable becomes the next increment. If an investor has £10,000, an increase in his wealth of £100 is less desirable to him than it would have been if he had started with only £1,000. It follows from this that, at any given level of wealth, the loss of £100 is regarded as being of more consequence than a gain of a similar amount. The average of the *utility* of predicted returns is thus lower than the weighted average of their *cash* values.

11.2.4 Let us suppose that money can be valued either in terms of cash or in terms of the satisfaction which it is capable of giving to its recipient. The former is independently determined and, for a given amount of money, fixed whilst the latter depends on the recipient's marginal utility for money. Although this is a highly subjective concept and no practical measure of utility exists, it is firmly based on accepted economic theory and plenty of evidence exists for its validity. The figures in the following example do not need to be regarded as precise quantifications for the principle of risk aversion to be demonstrated.

11.2.5 Example. Mr I.N. Vestor has the marginal utility for money shown in the following table:

Amount of money received	Units of satisfaction derived for each £1
£700 – £799	1.3
£800 – £899	1.2
£900 – £999	1.1
£1,000 – £1,099	1.0
£1,100 – £1,199	.8
£1,200 – £1,299	.7
£1,300 – £1,399	.6

The investment opportunities available to Vestor are:

Project X – with a certain net present value of £1,000

Project Y – with a net present value of either £800 or £1,200, each possible outcome having equal probability

Project Z – with a net present value of either £700 or £1,300, each possible outcome having equal probability

11.2.6 The expected net present values of the three projects X Y and Z are equal at £1,000 and so there would appear to be no reason to favour one as against another. Using Vestor's satisfaction schedule, however, gives a different indication.

Project X : £1,000 = 1,000 × 1 = 1,000 units of satisfaction

Project Y : £800 = 800 × 1.2 = 960 units of satisfaction
£1,200 = 1,200 × .7 = 840 units of satisfaction
Expected satisfaction is   960 × .5 =   480
840 × .5 =   420
        900 units

Project Z : £700 = 700 × 1.3 = 910 units of satisfaction
£1,300 = 1,300 × .6 = 780 units of satisfaction
Expected satisfaction is   910 × .5 =   455
780 × .5 =   390
        845 units

Vestor should choose project X which gives the highest level of expected satisfaction. The figures for projects Y and Z show that as risk increases projects of equal expected value become progressively less attractive. This is a demonstration of Vestor's risk aversion.

We come to the conclusion that, for a given expected return, the least risky investment will be selected. It also follows that, for a given level of risk, the investment giving the highest expected return will be favoured. Thus there is a trade-off in the investor's mind between risk and return. A risk averse investor will not necessarily avoid risk (indeed he may not be able to) but will need an inducement to take risk in the form of a higher expected rate of return.

11.3 Indifference Curves

11.3.1 A useful way of displaying the characteristic of risk aversion
is by means of a system of indifference curves. An indifference curve
(analogous to an isobar on a weather map) plots all points representing combinations of risk and return amongst which the investor is
indifferent. In the diagram below (Figure 11.1) the axes represent
the risks and returns respectively which may exist. Each of the
curves I_1, I_2, I_3, etc. represents a given level of utility to be obtained
from a portfolio. The investor will be indifferent as to any move
along an indifference curve, e.g. from point X to point Y on curve I_2.
He will be better off if he moves from a lower curve to a higher, e.g.
from point X to point W. He will be worse off if he moves from a
higher curve to a lower, e.g. from point X to point Z. Our set of indifference curves represents the investor's attitude to investment. It
has still to be faced with the investment opportunities available.

11.4 Efficient Portfolio

11.4.1 Investment opportunities will be represented by portfolios of
investments. These will vary according to the types and quantities of
investments combined. There may be an infinitely large number of
them but they must all exist within the spectrum of opportunities
available which is itself set by the type of investment under consideration. The diagram below (Figure 11.2) represents all the investment opportunities available at a particular time to an investment
fund of a particular size. The chosen portfolio may feasibly lie anywhere within the shaded area. We presume, however, that our
investor is rational. For any given level of risk, therefore, he must
choose that portfolio which gives him the highest return. Similarly
for any given level of return he must choose the portfolio giving the
minimum risk. Such portfolios, which are known as efficient portfolios, represent a small proportion of all those actually available and
in our diagram all lie on the line A – B.

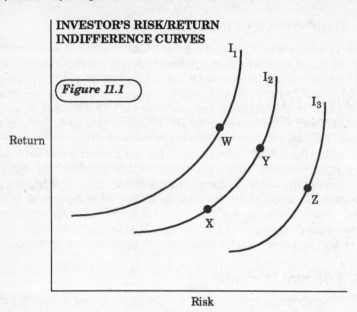

INVESTOR'S RISK/RETURN INDIFFERENCE CURVES

Figure 11.1

Return

Risk

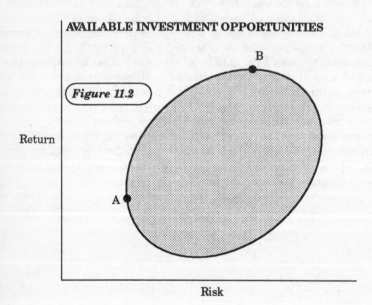

AVAILABLE INVESTMENT OPPORTUNITIES

Figure 11.2

Return

Risk

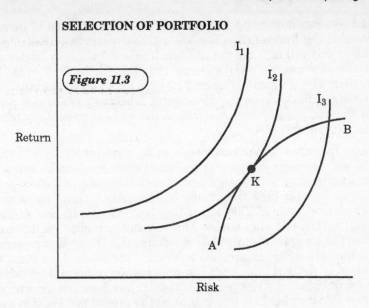

SELECTION OF PORTFOLIO

Figure 11.3

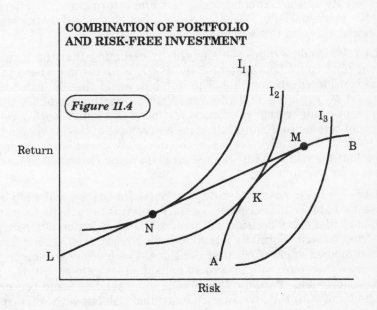

COMBINATION OF PORTFOLIO AND RISK-FREE INVESTMENT

Figure 11.4

11.4.2 We can now bring together our investor's attitude to investment and the line representing the efficient portfolios available to him and this will indicate the portfolio which will actually be chosen. For the moment we shall assume that the whole fund must be invested. The diagram (Figure 11.3) shows what will occur. The selected portfolio will be the one at point K because it is at this point that the opportunity line A–B meets the highest possible indifference curve, in this case I_2.

11.4.3 One other factor now needs to be considered. This is that there will normally exist a risk free market for funds to be lent and that such lending will be an alternative to investing in a risky portfolio. An investor may thus dilute his portfolio with an element of this risk free lending. This will reduce both his overall risk and his overall return but may enable him to reach a higher indifference curve. The diagram (figure 11.4) illustrates this. Point K represents, as before, the efficient portfolio selected if the whole fund must be invested in the portfolio. Point L represents the position if the whole fund is invested on a risk free loan basis. A line from L is drawn tangential to AB at M. This line is termed the capital market line as it represents all the combinations of risk and return currently offered by the market. The indifference curve I_1 can be reached by the combination at N and this will be selected.

11.4.4 We could extend the analysis by assuming that the investment fund could be augmented by risk free borrowing where this was considered appropriate. The line LM would then be extended beyond M. In figure 11.4 this would not be worthwhile but with a different configuration of efficient portfolios and indifference curves it could become so. Figure 11.5 gives an example of this. It should be noted that this analysis relies on the (probably unrealistic) assumption that the risk free rate of interest is the same for borrowed funds as it is for lent funds.

11.4.5 We need now to decide how portfolio theory will help an investor to make his decisions. To start with it is unrealistic for us to suppose that every decision will require the construction of a portfolio from scratch. Normally a portfolio will already exist arising from the combined effect of all past decisions. The investor's immediate decision, therefore, will concern an individual investment which it is proposed to add. Portfolio theory tells him that he should concern himself not with the investment's individual risk but with what contribution it makes to the overall risk of the portfolio. This contribution we shall describe as the investment's portfolio effect.

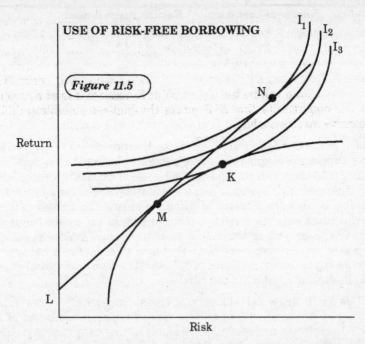

USE OF RISK-FREE BORROWING

Figure 11.5

Return

Risk

11.4.6 Here are a few simple examples of the operation of the portfolio effect. Project A has uncertain annual returns whose probability distribution can be represented by the results of throwing a die as follows:

Number thrown	Return represented %
1	10
2	11
3	12
4	13
5	14
6	15

Each possible outcome is equally probable. The expected return is the arithmetic mean of 12.5% and risk is represented by the variance of 2.92. Project A may be regarded as making up a simple initial 'portfolio'.

Under consideration are projects B, C and D. The results of project B are determined by the same die as project A (i.e. both projects are subject to exactly the same influences) and thus the table for Project A serves also to represent it. The results of project C are also determined by the same die but with reversed values attaching to each throw. Thus:

Numbers thrown	Return represented
1	15
2	14
3	13
4	12
5	11
6	10

Finally the results of project D are determined by a different die and are therefore completely unrelated.

Let us suppose that our investor is currently invested in a portfolio yielding 10% per annum and having a level of risk given by the value 5. A new investment is being evaluated which has a promised yield also of 10% (so that its addition will leave the overall rate of return unchanged) but having a level of risk given by the value 6. Whether the project is acceptable or not depends, however, on its portfolio effect. If this is, say, such that overall risk is reduced to $4\frac{1}{2}$ then the investment, in spite of its unattractive individual risk, would be a good addition to the portfolio.

11.4.7 We can draw certain very obvious conclusions. A portfolio made up of A and B will be no less risky than that composed of A alone. Diversification does, not, therefore, in this case reduce risk at all. The table below simulates the events of five years (by the throwing of a die) to illustrate this:

	Year 1	Year 2	Year 3	Year 4	Year 5
Number thrown	6	5	3	4	4
Project A return	15	14	12	13	13
Project B return	15	14	12	13	13
Portfolio average	15	14	12	13	13

If A is combined with C the returns year by year are constant and equal to the expected individual returns. Because the results achieved by C are inversely correlated to those achieved by A risk is completely eliminated.

	Year 1	Year 2	Year 3	Year 4	Year 5
Project A return	15	14	12	13	13
Project C return	10	11	13	12	12
Portfolio average	$12\frac{1}{2}$	$12\frac{1}{2}$	$12\frac{1}{2}$	$12\frac{1}{2}$	$12\frac{1}{2}$

Finally it can be seen that when D is combined with A (independent projects) risk is substantially reduced but not eliminated.

	Year 1	Year 2	Year 3	Year 4	Year 5
Number thrown die 1	6	5	3	4	4
Number thrown die 2	1	5	4	4	2
Project A return	15	14	12	13	13
Project D return	10	14	13	13	11
Portfolio average	12 $\frac{1}{2}$	14	12 $\frac{1}{2}$	13	12

11.4.8 The conclusion which we have reached is an important one for the financial manager. When evaluating a new risky project what is important is not the intrinsic risk attaching to the expected returns but the extent to which this is correlated with the risk attaching to the existing portfolio. Thus a project which is inherently highly risky but whose returns are known to be inversely correlated to the returns on the existing portfolio becomes, in that context, a method whereby risk can be reduced and is to be evaluated accordingly. Risk which can be eliminated by diversification because it is peculiar to the investment under consideration is known as unsystematic risk. Risk which is inherent in the market as a whole and which cannot, therefore, be eliminated is known as systematic risk.

11.5 Capital Asset Pricing Model

11.5.1 The model we have built up has important applications in the field of capital budgeting where it is known as the capital asset pricing model. It is operated by determining for each project an appropriate discount rate for use in calculating its net present value. This rate is the risk free cost of capital plus a risk premium where the premium is determined according to the degree of risk attaching to the project in the context of its addition to an existing portfolio. The existing portfolio has a rate of return which is regarded as being a risk free rate of return plus a risk premium appropriate to that portfolio. We could write this as $R_f + R_p$. The risk premium appropriate to a new project to be evaluated is determined by the application of a factor known as the β (beta) factor. Thus the rate of discount for the individual project is $R_f + \beta R_p$.

11.5.2 The β factor is (in theory) very easily determined and is given by:

$$\beta = \frac{\text{Covar.}_{pi}}{\text{Var.}_p}$$

Where: Covar.$_{pi}$ is covariance of expected returns of the existing portfolio and those of the new project;

Var.$_p$ is the variance of the returns of the existing portfolio.

Another way of expressing β which might seem more meaningful is:

$$\beta = \text{Corr}_{pi} \times \frac{\sigma_i}{\sigma_p}$$

When Corr_{pi} is the correlation coefficient between portfolio returns and individual investment returns (a correlation coefficient always takes a value within the range –1 to +1) and

σ_p is the standard deviation of portfolio returns

σ_i is the standard deviation of the individual investment returns.

Thus β depends on the correlation coefficient between the portfolio returns and the investment returns and the respective risks attaching to the portfolio and to the investment.

11.5.3 Example. Bull and Cow plc has a portfolio of capital projects yielding an expected 15% per annum with a standard deviation for the probability distribution of the returns of 3% per annum. The risk free market rate of interest is 6% per annum. A new project is being considered. Its promised yield is 13% per annum. The standard deviation of the probability distribution of its returns is 2% per annum. The coefficient of correlation between the returns on the existing portfolio and those on the project under consideration is +.7. Should the project be accepted?

11.5.4 Conventional project appraisal would merely apply an appropriate cost of capital as a discount rate to the expected returns of the project. This rate would probably be at least 15% per annum and the project would be rejected. Use of the capital asset pricing model leads to a different conclusion. First we calculate the risk premium on the current portfolio:

$$\begin{aligned} R_f + R_p &= 15 \\ R_p &= 15 - R_f \\ &= \underline{9\%} \end{aligned}$$

Then we calculate β for the new project:

$$\beta = \text{Corr}_{pi} \times \frac{\sigma_i}{\sigma_p}$$

$$= .7 \times \frac{2}{3}$$

$$= .47$$

Required rate of return is:

$$\begin{aligned} R_f + \beta R_p &= 6 + (.47 \times 9) \\ &= \underline{10.23\%} \end{aligned}$$

The project is therefore acceptable (because it yields in excess of this required rate of return).

11.5.5 Use of the capital asset pricing model can lead to curiously paradoxical results as in the following case. A certain company faced with a risk free market rate of interest of 5% per annum holds a portfolio yielding an expected $12\frac{1}{2}\%$ with a risk expressed by a standard deviation of 4%. A project becomes available with returns which are perfectly negatively correlated with those of the existing portfolio but with a high individual risk expressed by a standard deviation of 5%.

$$\beta = -1 \times \frac{5}{4}$$

$$\text{Required rate of return Rf} + \beta\text{Rp} = 5 - (1\frac{1}{4} \times 7\frac{1}{2})$$

$$= \underline{-4.375\%} \,!\,!\,!$$

Thus the project is acceptable even if earning a negative rate of return. This is because of its very high value in reducing the overall risk of the portfolio. If this is found difficult to accept, note that whenever a business pays an insurance premium it is, in effect, entering into a project with a negative net present value in order to obtain the benefit of a reduction in risk. In the same way the risk averse financial manager will be willing to make what is in effect a payment to reduce risk.

11.5.6 It should be noted that the situation described in the example is rarely likely to be encountered in practice. Most projects are subject to the same influences for good or ill as are existing portfolios and therefore the coefficient of correlation of the returns is highly positive. The portfolio effect is, in most individual cases, quite small. The best which a financial manager will generally find are projects which are relatively weakly correlated with the existing portfolio.

11.5.7 Example. (N.B. An understanding of the statistical measures of variance and covariance are required to follow the workings given below. Readers without that understanding may safely omit this example.)

The financial manager of Bow-wow plc is considering the investment of £50,000 in a capital project which will be added to the company's existing portfolio. He envisages the possibility, during the forthcoming period, of five possible states of the economy to which he has attached probabilities and predicted returns on both the existing portfolio and the proposed new investment. These figures appear below:

State of economy	Probability existing	Return on portfolio	Return on proposed investment
1	.2	16%	12%
2	.4	18%	11%
3	.2	20%	10%
4	.1	22%	9%
5	.1	24%	8%

The risk free market rate of interest is 5% per annum. Is the proposed project acceptable?

11.5.8 Calculate the variance of returns for the existing portfolio and the covariance of returns between the portfolio and the proposed new investment:

Probability (p)	R^{pf}	R^i	$(R^{pf}-R^{pf})$	(R^i-R^i) (a)	$(a)^2 p$ (b)	$(a)(b)p$
.2	16	10	−3	+.1	1.8	−.06
.4	18	9	−1	−.9	.4	+.36
.2	20	12	+1	+2.1	.2	+.42
.1	22	11	+3	−1.1	.9	−.33
.1	24	8	+5	−1.9	2.5	−.95
Average	19	9.9			5.8	−.56

$$\beta = \frac{\text{Covar}}{\text{var}}$$

$$= \frac{-0.5}{6}$$

$$= -0.097$$

Required rate of return is:
$$R_f + \beta R_p = 5 + (19 \times -0.097)$$
$$= 3.16\%$$

The project is acceptable since it has an expected rate of return exceeding this figure.

11.5.9 It was explained earlier that portfolio theory had been developed in connection with investment in stock market securities and only more lately extended to the field of capital budgeting. Investment in real projects has a number of characteristics which distinguishes it from investment in securities. These affect the way in which portfolio theory might operate in practice and should be noted. They are:

(a) They are often available only as large indivisible projects, e.g. the adoption of half a project is not possible.

(b) Disinvestment is not so readily achieved as investment so it is less easy to adjust the portfolio.

(c) Expected returns and probabilities may be less easy to estimate than for stock market securities.

Summary

(i) Instinct tells us that diversification will reduce the risks attaching to the process of investment. Portfolio theory provides a framework within which effective diversification can take place.

(ii) The investor is presumed to be risk averse and this presumption can be justified in terms of the diminishing marginal utility of money. Without it risk reduction would not be a desired objective. The theory of risk aversion can be explained by the use of indifference curve analysis.

(iii) Of all feasible portfolios there is a limited number of efficient portfolios. An efficient portfolio is one which, given the level of risk, maximises the expected return or which, given the expected return, minimises the risk. The selected portfolio must be an efficient one and must enable the attainment of the highest indifference curve possible.

(iv) Portfolio theory shows that in evaluating a proposed addition to a portfolio the financial manager should consider the portfolio effect of that addition, i.e. what it does to overall risk and overall return. However intrinsically risky an investment might be, it is particularly useful if its returns are expected to be inversely correlated to existing portfolio returns.

(v) The capital asset pricing model is based on portfolio theory. It involves the calculation of so-called β factors which enable an appropriate risk premium to be determined for each proposed investment. Risk premium is the excess of required rate of return over the risk free rate of interest. It may be negative i.e. a risk discount, if the proposed investment has a highly favourable portfolio effect. A β factor depends on the degree of correlation between portfolio returns and proposed investment returns.

Review Questions

(i) *What is meant by an efficient portfolio?*

(ii) *A certain firm diversifies on a random basis in order to reduce risk. Will this policy succeed?*

(iii) *Describe how β factors are determined and how they are used.*

(iv) *What are the portfolio effects of investments having projected returns which, relative to existing portfolio returns, are:*

    (a) *strongly inversely correlated;*

    (b) *not correlated;*

    (c) *strongly positively correlated?*

(v) *Why is strong positive correlation so commonly found in practice?*

(vi) *What is meant by a risk free rate of interest and why is it so important?*

(vii) *What is meant by the statement that managers are risk averse?*

(viii) *What is shown by a set of indifference curves?*

Exercises

1. *Alphabet, plc has a portfolio of capital projects which yield an average expected rate of return of 15% per annum. This return is subject to risk and this is estimated as a standard deviation of the probabilities of expected returns of $2\frac{1}{2}\%$. The risk free rate of interest is 6% per annum. Three projects have come up for consideration by the Board of Directors and these are designated X, Y and Z. Details of the estimates made for them appear below:*

	X	Y	Z
Expected return	10%	8%	6%
Risk (standard deviation of the probability distribution)	1%	1.2%	2.4%
Coefficient of correlation of project returns with portfolio returns	+.58	+.89	−.1

Determine in each case whether you would recommend acceptance of the project. Since all three projects promise a yield of well below that expected on the current portfolio, one member of the Board asks why they should be considered at all. How would you answer him?

2. *What is meant by risk aversion? Why is it crucial to the formulation of a theory of portfolio selection?*

Dr. Cleverdick, a psychologist, has discovered an accurate way of determining the utility, to different people, of money. He measures this in special units which he has devised for the purpose known as 'utils'. For two of his subjects his measurements reveal the following.

Change from present level of wealth	Subject A utils	Subject B utils
+500	+375	+550
+400	+320	+432
+300	+255	+318
+200	+180	+208
+100	+ 95	+102
−100	−105	−98
−200	−220	−192
−300	−345	−282
−400	−480	−368
−500	−625	−450

Sketch indifference curves to indicate each subject's attitude to risk (Do not attempt to plot the data given direct). Comment on the way you would expect each subject to behave as an investor.

3. *Gunwales, plc is considering investing in a risky project which would be added to an existing portfolio of investment projects also subject to risk. It envisages six possible states of the economy for which it has estimated probabilities and outcomes as follows:*

State of economy	Probability	Return on existing portfolio	Return on proposed project
1	.1	12%	8%
2	.2	14%	10%
3	.2	15%	12%
4	.3	16%	10%
5	.1	18%	14%
6	.1	20%	6%

Determine whether the project should be accepted. The risk free rate of return is 5%.

4. *'We spent £25,000 last year on insuring our property against fire although no fire actually occurred and the probability that it would was infinitesimal. It would be equally prudent to invest in loss making projects if they gave us the benefit of protection from the risks of economic variation to which we are subject.' (Statement by a financial manager to the Board of Directors of a large company).*

Amplify this statement showing in detail the circumstances in which investment in a loss making project could be justified. Explain why, in spite of sound theoretical justification, examples of such investment in the real world are hard to find.

5. *Portfolio theory was originally developed to explain the behaviour of an investor in stock market securities. The development into the capital asset pricing model for evaluating real investment projects has been criticised as relying on assumptions*

which, whilst valid for stock market securities, are not valid for real investments. Comment on the important distinctions between the capital asset pricing model and pure portfolio theory and argue for or against the underlying assumptions.

6. The publicity material for a unit trust includes the following words:

'Because their investment is spread over a wide range of shares unit holders will have the benefit of avoiding the risk that so often attaches to investment in a single company.'

Comment on this statement.

12: Capital Rationing

12.1 The Nature of Capital Rationing

12.1.1 Capital rationing is a large topic. It raises a number of very important problems at both the practical and theoretical levels and techniques have not yet been perfected for resolving these. All that we need to do here is to give a general indication of the nature of the problems and the extent of the theory as it is so far developed.

12.1.2 It is first of all essential to be quite clear as to what we mean by capital rationing. It is defined as an absolute constraint on the amount of finance available regardless of cost. We sometimes speak loosely of a 'scarcity of funds' when we merely mean that funds are so expensive that we cannot afford to make lavish use of them. This is not capital rationing. It is just that the marginal cost of capital is high and that consequently there are few attractive investment opportunities. This situation is dealt with quite adequately by the analysis presented so far.

12.1.3 Here are some situations which give examples of genuine cases of capital rationing.

(a)   A small family business has decided not to expand beyond its present size because it is believed that this will destroy its 'happy atmosphere'.

(b)   A company has decided, as a matter of policy, to restrict expansion to that which can be financed from internally generated funds, i.e. retained profits.

(c)   The shareholder-directors of a small company do not wish to raise any additional equity capital (nor, hence, given a desired gearing ratio, any additional debt) because this would involve the loss of a controlling interest.

(d)   As a matter of caution, a business decides to restrict the amount it borrows to a certain ceiling. Again, given a desired capital structure this also automatically limits the amount of equity financing.

12.1.4 Note the important point that capital rationing almost always arises from an artificial restraint on fund raising imposed by a business upon itself. Given different attitudes or desires on the part of those making the decisions the constraint could be lifted. It follows that, in conditions of capital rationing, an optimum position from the financial point of view will not usually be attained. Taking both financial and non financial factors into consideration, however, it is presumably perceived as an optimum situation by those who are in it. Thus freedom from anxiety or from interference from strangers may rank higher as goals than a maximisation of wealth.

12.1.5 It is important to our analysis to know how long capital rationing is to persist. It may be a permanent state of affairs or it maybe imposed temporarily to help a company through a bad patch or to enable it to consolidate past expansion. If it is short term the analysis is much easier.

12.2 One-Period Rationing

12.2.1 Let us first look at the case of one-period capital rationing. The situation is that there is a constraint on the total amount of investment during the forthcoming period but not thereafter. Our decision rule must be, as we have seen elsewhere, that we shall maximise our net present value. We must accept that capital rationing will mean that we have to forgo some apparently profitable opportunities, making use only of the very best ones.

12.2.2 In order to maximise total net present value it will be helpful to rank projects in the order of their individual net present values starting with the highest. This will sometimes lead to the simple result that we shall maximise total net present value by working down the list until the available capital is exhausted.

12.2.3 Example. L, plc has a cost of capital of 10% per annum and has imposed a one-period ceiling on investment of £300,000. The following projects, ranked in order of their internal rate of return would show a positive net present value, i.e. internal rate of return in excess of the cost of capital. Each project has a five year life with equal annual cash inflows for each year. What is the optimum investment policy?

Project	Investment required	Internal rate of return per annum	Net present value at 10%	Annual cash flow
	£		£	£
A	100,000	22%	32,367	34,916
B	100,000	20%	26,747	33,434
C	100,000	18%	21,234	31,980
D	100,000	16%	15,791	30,544
E	100,000	14%	10,428	29,129
F	100,000	12%	5,160	27,739

12.2.4 The £300,000 will be invested in sufficient projects starting at the top of the list, to exhaust it. In this case projects A, B and C will be undertaken. The net present value of this policy is £80,348 (£32,367 + £26,747 + £21,234).

12.2.5 The previous example has assumed that the investments available fit well to the finance available. This may not be the case and the indivisibility of projects may cause some difficulties.

12.2.6 Example. L, plc is in the same financial position as before but it is faced now with the following set of investment opportunities. Again the annual cash flow for any given project is constant and the project life is uniform at five years. The amount of the initial investment required, however, is variable. That is, of course, commonly the case in practice.

Project	Investment required £	Internal rate of return per annum	Net present value at 10% £	Annual cash flow £
A	500,000	22%	161,837	174,581
B	400,000	16%	63,164	122,174
C	300,000	14%	31,285	87,387
D	250,000	12%	25,797	76,508
E	80,000	18%	16,988	25,584
F	50,000	20%	13,373	16,717

12.2.7 On this occasion we cannot start at the top of the list because project A requires a greater investment than the amount we have available and is, therefore, ruled out. The first project which is within our investment constraint is C with a net present value of £31,285. This can , however, be exceeded by investing in both D and F and this is the correct policy. Note that these do not give the highest internal rates of return. An increase in the ration by 50% from £300,000 to £450,000 changes the situation entirely. Then B and F would be the accepted investment package. If the ration increased again to £500,000, project A would be selected.

12.3 Multi-Period Rationing

12.3.1 Where capital rationing is expected to persist, another factor comes into the reckoning. The total of funds available for investment during a second and subsequent period will consist of the new funds then made available plus those released through realisation of projects commenced in earlier periods. If it is therefore believed that highly profitable projects will become available in the second period which were not available in the first, this may be good reason for favouring currently investments with a rapid payback even though their internal rate of return is relatively low.

12.3.2 It is beyond the scope of your examination syllabus to go into detail of how the best decisions should be made in these more complex circumstances and, indeed, this area of the subject has not yet been fully developed. It might, however, be mentioned that linear programming may sometimes be applied to an analysis of the problem.

Summary

(i) Conventional analysis, such as we have employed so far, assumes that capital is available on the market in unlimited quantities so long as its price can be met. A business is thus limited in the total amount of finance it employs only by the availability of projects which are sufficiently remunerative to allow its marginal cost of capital to be met.

(ii) Capital rationing is a term used to describe a situation where remunerative projects do exist but are not taken up because of an artificial constraint placed upon the amount of finance employed. This constraint is almost always imposed on a business from within. It is inconsistent with a policy of value maximisation and it implies that other management goals have become dominant. Goals which might lead to capital rationing are, for example, a desire to retain control of a family business or a desire to remain small.

(iii) Capital rationing may be a short term phenomenon (restraint will be lifted at the end of a particular crisis), or persistent (representing a permanent management attitude). Short term, single period, capital rationing is more readily susceptible to analysis.

(iv) Where there is single period capital rationing, the available finance should be deployed so as to maximise net present value. As a working guide this will involve seeking the projects with the highest internal rate of return. Because of indivisibility, however, more profitable combinations may be found amongst projects which individually have lower internal rates of return.

(v) Multi-period capital rationing can become somewhat involved and fully developed analytical tools are not available. Linear programming has been used to resolve some of the problems. The complicating factor is that the rate at which a project releases funds considered alongside the future availability of profitable projects becomes highly relevant to an optimum decision.

Review Questions

(i) *'Capital rationing should never exist.' Do you agree?*

(ii) *Explain why net present value is a better guide to investment decisions when there is capital rationing than would be the internal rate of return.*

(iii) *Explain why multi-period capital rationing poses an immensely greater analytical problem than does single-period rationing.*

(iv) *'Capital is a scarce resource.' 'Capital is rationed.' What is the important difference in meaning between these two expressions?*

(v) *List the more important considerations which may lead to a policy of capital rationing.*

(vi) *In what circumstances might the best available project in terms of its net present value be rejected?*

(vii) *'If we are going to limit the amount we invest in new projects we must ensure that what we do invest is at the highest rate of return possible.' Is this valid?*

(viii) *Why might a business which imposes capital rationing on itself find it impossible to invest the full ration even where there is an ample number of profitable projects available?*

Exercises

1. *'Capital rationing is inconsistent with the maximisation of wealth. It should never, therefore, voluntarily be imposed.' Discuss.*

2. *The following schedule is a list of the projects which are available to Tiger, plc, together with the relevant data.*

Project	Investment required £	Internal rate of return (% p.a.)	Life	Annual cash flow £
A	600,000	25%	8 years	180,234
B	100,000	22%	5 years	34,916
C	20,000	20%	6 years	6,013
D	80,000	18%	4 years	29,740
E	300,000	16%	5 years	91,631
F	400,000	14%	3 years	172,265
G	200,000	12%	5 years	55,479
H	100,000	10%	2 years	57,604

Tiger's marginal cost of capital is 14% per annum. Plan a capital investment programme on the following alternative assumptions:

(i) *There is no capital rationing;*

(ii) *Capital is rationed to £400,000 for one period only;*

(iii) *Capital is rationed to £500,000 for one period only;*

(iv) *Capital is rationed to £600,000 for one period only.*

3. *Write brief notes on the additional analytical problems raised by multi-period capital rationing. Illustrate your answer by reference to the data of question 2.*

4. Lion, plc believes it to be unwise to invest more than £100,000 in new projects each year. More than this would overstretch management resources to an unacceptable extent. In order to ensure the acceptance of the best projects available Lion evaluates them on the basis of a cost of capital of 20% per annum. Its actual cost of capital is 15% per annum. The following is the list of projects available in a particular year. Advise on the cost to Lion of applying capital rationing and the wisdom of applying it in the fashion which it does.

Project	Investment required £	Internal rate of return (% p.a.)	Life	Annual cash flow £
A	20,000	23	3	9,945
B	10,000	22	2	6,702
C	15,000	22	4	6,014
D	25,000	21	2	16,567
E	30,000	20	2	19,646
F	20,000	19	4	7,582
G	10,000	18	5	3,198
H	20,000	16	4	7,148
I	25,000	15	2	15,375

5. The chairman of the board of directors of a small company has said, 'The cost of capital is so high now that we must ration our use of it.' Comment on this statement.

6. Panther, plc has a cost of capital of 18% per annum. It has a rigid Board policy of expansion from internal resources only and will not have recourse to the market. The retention of profit has generated an investment fund of £250,000 and the following projects are under consideration:

Project	Investment required £	Internal rate of return (% p.a.)	Life	Annual cash flow £
R	90,000	26	5	34,143
S	50,000	24	4	20,808
T	120,000	22	4	48,115
U	200,000	20	3	94,967
V	80,000	19	5	26,169
W	50,000	18	4	18,587
X	100,000	17	3	45,249
Y	75,000	15	5	22,368
Z	125,000	12	6	30,399

How should the £250,000 be invested? What investments would be made if the Board policy did not exist?

13: Inflation and Financial Reporting

13.1 The Problem of Inflation

13.1.1 In this and the next chapter we shall consider the problem presented to the financial manager by inflation. This has the effects, firstly, of distorting the information base provided for him by conventional accounting and, secondly, of introducing a new dimension to the forecasts on which so many financial management decisions depend.

13.1.2 We should be quite clear as to what we mean by the term inflation. In any economy there will be movements of prices from time to time reflecting the ebb and flow of the demand for and supply of goods and services. These movements will be in either direction and, in broad terms, will tend to cancel one another out in their impact on the overall cost of living. Where inflation exists there will be, superimposed on these market fluctuations, a steady general increase in prices such that it costs more and more as time progresses to maintain a given standard of living or to support a given level of economic activity.

13.1.3 It is often more useful to regard inflation as being a long term decline in the value of the currency unit than to see it as changes in prices. Thus we might observe, for example, that the value of the £ has halved in the last five years, although this is evidenced by a doubling of the general price level in the same period.

13.1.4 Although inflation is easily observed it is less easy to measure. This must be done by means of an index number (a type of average of prices). The view which is formed of the extent of inflation at any one time will thus depend in part on which index is selected. The one normally favoured for this purpose is the General Index of Retail Prices which is prepared under Government auspices and published monthly.

13.1.5 We shall now summarise the current position of the debate on the reflection of inflation in financial reporting. There are two main schools of thought associated with price level adjustments in accounts. One advocates current purchasing power (CPP) which uses the concept embodied in the shortlived provisional Statement of Standard Accounting Practice No. 7. The other supports current cost accounting (CCA) which was the method used under the later, but now also defunct, SSAP 16. Each has some relevance to our present discussion.

13.2 Current Purchasing Power

13.2.1 Proponents of CPP argue that money represents purchasing power. Because of inflation a given fixed sum declines in purchasing power as time passes. It is argued that the decline in purchasing power can be quantified by the construction and application of the General Index of Retail Prices. The decline in the purchasing power of money is taken to be the inverse of the general rise in prices. All figures in a set of accounts are then adjusted by reference to the extent of inflation between the date of the transactions on which they are based and the date of the accounts.

13.2.2 Example. Balloon, plc was set up on 1st January with an issued share capital of £10,000. It immediately purchased stock in trade, 8,000 units, at £1 each. On 30th June the company sold 6,000 units of stock for £2 each and purchased 8,000 more at £1.20 each. At 31st December 5,000 more units were sold for £2.50. No dividend was paid during the year. A suitable general index of prices stood at 100 at 1st January, 110 on 30th June and 121 on 31st December. Prepare a profit and loss account for the year ended 31st December and a balance sheet at the date (a) on a conventional historical cost basis and (b) adjusted for inflation using CCP.

13.2.3 (a) Historical cost accounts

Profit and loss account for the year ended 31st December

Sales (1)	£24,500
Less Cost of sales (2)	11,600
Net profit	£12,900

Balance sheet at 31st December

Share capital	£10,000	Stock (3)	£6,000
Profit and loss account	12,900	Cash (4)	16,900
	£22,900		£22,900

(1)	6,000 × £2	=	£12,000
	5,000 × £2.5	=	12,500
			£24,500

(2)	FIFO 8,000 × £1	=	£8,000
	3,000 × £1.20	=	3,600
			£11,600

(3) FIFO 5,000 × £1.20 = £6,000

(4) Proceeds of share issue   £10,000
      Sales   24,500

                                         34,500

     Less Cash purchases   8,000 × £1
                         8,000 × £1.20   17,600

                                       £16,900

(b)   CPP adjusted accounts

Balloon, plc
Profit and loss account for the year ended 31st December

Sales (1)	£25,700
Less Cost of sales (2)	13,640
Net trading profit	£12,060
Less Loss due to holding cash (3)	660
Net profit	11,400

Balance sheet at 31st December

Share capital	£10,000	Stock (5)	£6,600
Inflation reserve (4)	2,100	Cash	16,900
Profit and loss account	11,400		
	£23,500		£23,500

(1) $6,000 \times £2.00 \times \dfrac{121}{110} =$ £13,200

     $5,000 \times £2.50$ 12,500

                                £25,700

(2) $8,000 \times £1.00 \times \dfrac{121}{100} =$ £9,680

     $3,000 \times £1.20 \times \dfrac{121}{110} =$ 3,960

                                £13,640

(3)   Note this very interesting item. Since we are now accounting for general inflation we shall expect to show the losses due to holding depreciating cash. Conversely, where appropriate, we would show the inflationary profit due to incurring debt (creditors, bank overdraft, etc.)

     The loss due to holding cash is calculated as follows:

Cash generated 1st January £10,000 – £2,000 loses 21% i.e.	£420
Cash generated 30th June £12,000 – £9,600 = £2,400 loses 10% i.e.	240
Cash generated 31 st December £12,500 loses nothing	–
	£660

(4)   £10,000 × 21%

Technically this would have to be achieved by creating an 'inflation reserve' out of profits otherwise available for distribution and out of stock revaluation.

(5) $5,000 \times £1.20 \times \dfrac{121}{110} = £6,600$

13.3 Current Cost Accounting

13.3.1 The principle underlying current cost accounting is that current costs should be used in place of historical costs in valuing all resources either charged in the profit and loss account or shown on the balance sheet. Current cost is defined as value to the business or deprival value, i.e. the loss which would be suffered if the resource were lost to the business.

Adjustments have continuously to be made for all changes in current cost which occur from the time of the acquisition of a resource until the time it is written off against revenues or appears in a balance sheet. The adjustments are taken to a revaluation reserve.

If this remains undistributed it has the effect of augmenting the capital fund of the business so that its level of activities can in real terms be maintained.

13.3.2 Example. Curcost, plc purchased an asset on 1st January for £30,000 at which amount it was recorded in the books. On 30th June 5% of the service potential of the asset was consumed in the profit making process. The gross replacement cost of the asset at that date was £35,000, its net realisable value was £32,000 and its present value in its existing use was £38,000. Determine the amount of depreciation, the residual value of the asset and the amount of the transfer to revaluation reserve.

13.3.3 Value to the business or current cost is the lower of two quantities. These are:

(a)   replacement cost and

(b)   the higher of

    (i)   net realisable value and

    (ii) present value.

This can be tested against the definition given in 13.3.1 by looking at different combinations of replacement cost, net realisable value and present value. Here current cost is £35,000. The figures required are:

Revaluation credited to revaluation reserve	£5,000
Depreciation	£1,750 (5% of £35,000)
Residual book value	£33,250 (95% of £35,000).

13.3.4 Example. Prepare accounts for Balloon, plc on a CCA basis. The replacement cost of stock at 31st December was £1.50 per unit.

Profit and loss account for the year ended 31st December

Sales (1)	£24,500
Less Cost of sales (2)	14,700
Net profit	£9,800

Balance sheet at 31st December

Share capital	£10,000	Stock (3)	£7,500
Revaluation reserve (4)	4,600	Cash	16,900
	14,600		
Profit and loss account	9,800		
	£24,400		£24,400

(1) Sales as for historical cost accounts – no adjustment.

(2) Valued at replacement cost at the time of consumption

6,000 × £1.20	£7,200
5,000 × £1.50	7,500
	£14,700

(3) 5,000 × £1.50=£7,500

(4) Revaluation of stock consumed £14,700 – £11,600 = £3,100
Revaluation of stock held at 31/12: £7,500 – £6,000 =   1,500

£4,600

Note that shareholders' equity has been increased in money terms from £10,000 to £14,600. It can be inferred that this is the increase in money capital required to enable the business to conserve its real investment in the resources which it uses.

For the sake of simplicity our example omitted any reference to fixed assets. They are dealt with, however, in a way very similar to stock.

13.3.5 Example. A certain machine cost £10,000 and had a useful life of four years after which it was valueless. It was depreciated on a straight line basis. Additional information regarding price levels is given below:

	Start of year 1	End of year 1	End of year 2	End of year 3	End of year 4
General index of prices	100	110	120	130	140
Cost of new replacement for machine	£10,000	£12,000	£15,000	£16,000	£20,000

13.3.6 Depreciation schedule

Year	HC = 25% cost £	CPP = 25% cost × index £	CCA = 25% current cost £
1	2,500	2,750	3,000
2	2,500	3,000	3,750
3	2,500	3,250	4,000
4	2,500	3,500	5,000

Machine account

	HC £	CPP £	CCA £		HC £	CPP £	CCA £
Cost	10,000	10,000	10,000	Depreciation	2,500	2,750	3,000
Indexing		1,000		Balance	7,500	8,250	9,000
Revaluation			2,000				
	10,000	11,000	12,000		10,000	11,000	12,000
Balance	7,500	8,250	9,000	Depreciation	2,500	3,000	3,750
Indexing		750		Balance	5,000	6,000	7,500
Revaluation			2,250				
	7,500	9,000	11,250		7,500	9,000	11,250

	HC £	CPP £	CCA £		HC £	CPP £	CCA £
Balance	5,000	6,000	7,500	Depreciation	2,500	3,250	4,000
Indexing		500		Balance	2,500	3,250	4,000
Revaluation			500				
	5,000	6,500	8,000		5,000	6,500	8,000
Balance	2,500	3,250	4,000	Depreciation	2,500	3,500	5,000
Indexing		250					
Revaluation			1,000				
	2,500	3,500	5,000		2,500	3,500	5,000

13.4 Inflation Accounting in Practice

13.4.1 Since the abandonment of SSAP 16 there has been no formal obligation on companies to make any adjustment for inflation in their reported figures. It should be noted, however, that the Companies Act, 1985 permits, without requiring, current cost valuations and allows for a revaluation reserve in the standard balance sheet formats. All companies are subject to an overall requirement that their profit and loss account and balance sheet give a true and fair view and it could be argued that this is not done unless at least some reference to the effects of inflation is made. Although there is a temporary lull it would appear that further developments in the techniques of accounting for inflation will emerge in time.

Summary

(i) Two main methods have been advocated for adjusting the figures in financial reports so as to allow for inflation. One of these is based on current purchasing power (CPP) and the other on current costs (CCA).

(ii) Current purchasing power adjustment seeks to maintain the real value of the investor's equity in terms of its general purchasing power. It shows asset values at restated historical cost.

(iii) Current cost accounting seeks to maintain the real value of the invested capital in terms of its existing use. Balance sheet valuations are based on current market prices.

(iv) CPP and CCA are not incompatible. Full adjustment requires the use of both. In this case current valuations are shown in the balance sheet and inflationary gains and losses to the equity holders are also shown.

(v) Because of the impossibility of obtaining long term agreement there is currently in place no legislation or accounting standard which requires companies to make adjustments for inflation in their annual accounts.

Review Questions

(i) *'Current cost accounts do not allow for inflation any better than historical cost accounts.' Is there anything in this statement?*

(ii) *'Current cost depreciation is a better measure of the cost of resources consumed in using an asset than is historical cost depreciation'. Do you agree?*

(iii) *In what circumstances would:*

    (a) *HC, CPP and CCA give identical results,*

(b) CCA show a lower profit than CPP,

(c) CPP show a higher profit than HC,

(d) CPP and CCA give identical results to one another but both higher than HC?

(iv) In a series of CCA accounts (i.e. covering a number of years) the arithmetical total of depreciation will match neither the original cost of the asset nor its ultimate replacement cost. Attempt to sort out the book keeping problem which this creates.

(v) Is the current cost revaluation reserve a revenue reserve or a capital reserve?

(vi) What would happen in current cost accounts in a period of falling prices? Can you foresee any accounting difficulties?

(vii) Discuss the problem of selecting an appropriate index for use in CPP adjusted accounts.

(viii) 'Current cost accounts convey a better appreciation of the situation.' 'Current cost accounts are complicated and difficult to understand.' Can these two views be reconciled?

Exercises

1. The following is a record of stock purchases, usage and other relevant information for Dirigible, plc for one financial year. Calculate the value of cost of sales for the year on historical cost, CPP and CCA bases stating any assumption you have made.

Date	Purchase (units)	Unit price	Usage (units)	Retail price index
1st Jan.	10,000	£1.00	–	100
31st Mar.	20,000	£1.10	15,000	105
30th June	15,000	£1.20	20,000	110
31st Dec.	20,000	£1.30	25,000	115

2. Dirigible bought a machine on 1st January for £50,000. By 31st December the price of a similar machine (new) had risen to £60,000. Calculate depreciation on the same three bases as in (1). The life of the machine is 5 years.

3. Pneumatic, plc was set up on 1st January with an issued share capital of £50,000. It immediately purchased 25,000 units of stock at a cost of £1.80 per unit. On 30th June the company sold 20,000 units of stock for £4 each and purchased 15,000 more at £2.50 each. On 31st December 10,000 further units were sold for £5 per unit and 10,000 more were bought at £3 per unit. There were no other receipts or payments during the year. Prepare accounts for the year adjusted for inflation on the CPP basis.

The general price level rose by 5% in the period from 1st January to 30th June and by a further 8% in the period from 1st July to 31st December.

4. *Using information from the previous question prepare final accounts for Pneumatic on the CCA basis.*

5. *Hot Air, plc was set up on 1st January with a share capital of £100,000 and loan capital of £25,000. It purchased fixed assets, having a life of eight years, for £80,000 and commenced trading. Its final accounts produced at the end of the first year and prepared on the historical cost basis appeared as follows:*

Profit and loss account for the year ended 31st December

Sales		£180,000
Less Cost of sales	£80,000	
Other expenses	40,000	
Depreciation	10,000	
Interest on loan capital	2,500	132,500
		47,500
Deduct Dividend paid (12½%)		12,500
Retained profit		£35,000

Balance Sheet at 31st December

Share capital	£100,000	**Fixed assets**		£70,000
Retained profit	35,000	**Current assets**		
	135 000	Stock	£50,000	
Loan capital	25 000	Debtors	30,000	
	160,000	Cash	30,000	110,000
Current liabilities				
Creditors	20,000			
	£180,000			£180,000

The following further information is available:

(a) *Stock prices rose evenly by 15% during the year. Average stock turnover is three times per annum.*

(b) *Replacement fixed assets of the type purchased on 1st January would have cost £96,000 on 31st December.*

Prepare accounts for Hot Air on a current cost basis.

6. *Deadloss set up in business on 1st January, investing £10,000. He bought a machine for £6,000. This was to be depreciated at the end of each half year at the rate of 12½% cost per half year. Information about the first year's trading appears below:*

	Unit cost price of materials	Purchases of materials units of product	Unit selling price	Sales units of product
January 1	£5	500	–	–
June 30	£8	1,000	£15	1,000
December 31	£10	1,000	£20	1,000

Expenses totalling £5,000 on each occasion were paid on 30th June and 31st December and drawings of £2,500 were made on each of the same dates. The new price of the machine rose to £6,500 on 30th June and £8,000 on 31st December. A general index of prices stood at 100 on 1st January, 110 on 30th June and 121 on 31st December.

Prepare for Deadloss accounts for the year on the three bases historical cost, current purchasing power and current cost. Comment on the differences between them.

14: Inflation and investment appraisal

14.1 D.C.F. under inflation

14.1.1 The last chapter was concerned with how the effects of inflation should be reflected in financial reports. We must now see how it is taken account of in the decisions to be taken by the financial manager.

14.1.2 There is, of course, no particular novelty in the idea that changing prices should be incorporated into the projections used in investment appraisal. It is implicit in the forecasting of cash flows that these should embody any expectations about changing conditions, including the prices of inputs and outputs. It is obvious that, where prices are subject to large and unpredictable changes, this will make forecasting difficult but the basic principle is unaffected. Here is an example to illustrate a routine adjustment for expected price changes where there is, however, no general inflation.

14.1.3 Example. Company X is proposing to purchase a machine for £10,000. This will produce 1,000 units of product for each of the next five years. The selling price of the product will be held (by contract) at £10 per unit but the avoidable production cost, which will be £5 per unit in the first year, will escalate by 10% per annum owing to the increasing scarcity of raw materials. X's cost of capital is 18% per annum and there is no general inflation. Comment on the viability of the project.

14.1.4

Year	Sales £	Costs £	Net cash inflow £	Discount factor	Present value £
1	10,000	5,000	5,000	.847	4,235
2	10,000	5,500	4,500	.718	3,231
3	10,000	6,050	3,950	.609	2,406
4	10,000	6,655	3,345	.516	1,726
5	10,000	7,320	2,680	.437	1,171
					12,769
Initial investment					10,000
Net present value					+2,769

There is a positive net present value of £2,769 and the indications are, therefore, that X should invest in the project.

14.1.5 Our interpretation of the situation in the above example is that the cash flow generated by the project is declining over the years because of increasing costs. An essential feature of this interpretation is that we are regarding the £ as a stable currency unit, i.e. at whatever time it is received it has then a constant exchange value in terms of the generality of goods and services available.

14.1.6 If general inflation exists discounting based on current cash flow predictions may let us down. This is because of the basic presumption that future cash flows, at the time they are received, are all equally valuable, £ for £, in terms of their purchasing power. This presumption is plainly false. A future cash flow is thus doubly less valuable to us than a present cash flow – once because of the time lapse and again because of the decline in purchasing power. We can allow for this by double discounting to allow both for inflation and for the cost of capital.

14.1.7 Example. Company X is in the same position as in our previous example except that there is expected to be general inflation during the life of the project, superimposed on the other conditions, at the rate of 12% per annum. Again we are to comment on the viability of the project.

14.1.8 We may start with the net cash inflows calculated before. These must then be translated into currency units of constant real value (most conveniently equal to the real purchasing power of currency at the commencement of the project). We can use the 12% discount factors from tables to achieve this although we are not, on this occasion, 'discounting' but are 'deflating' our projected cash flows. These adjusted cash flows are then discounted in the usual way. This is illustrated in the table below.

14.1.9

Year	Net cash inflow £	Deflator	Adjusted net cash inflow £	Discount factor	Present value* £
1	5,000	.893	4,465	.847	3,782
2	4,500	.797	3,587	.718	2,575
3	3,950	.712	2,812	.609	1,713
4	3,345	.636	2,127	.516	1,098
5	2,680	.567	1,520	.437	664
					9,832
Initial investment					10,000
Net present value					-168

* **Note** Mathematically the same result could have been achieved by using a single factor which combined the deflator and the discount factor. The equivalent discount rate would have been 32.16% (18% + 12% compounded). Its terms could not, however, have been obtained from tables and would have had to have been specially calculated.

It will be seen that the effect of inflation has been to convert a positive net present valued into a negative one. Our calculation shows that the project would not now be an acceptable one.

14.1.10 Example. Company Y is considering the purchase of a machine for £30,000. It will produce 2,000 units of product for each of five years. At current prices the selling price will be £10 per unit and the avoidable cost will be £5 per unit. There is general inflation of 10% per annum and this will affect sales revenue and costs equally. Y's cost of capital is 18% per annum. There are no price changes other than those caused by inflation.

14.1.11 In the table below the cash flows have been set out in terms of the £'s of the years in which they occur. They are then converted to £'s of a standardised purchasing power equal to those of £'s at the commencement of the project. This is done by applying a deflator which can be obtained from the same tables as are used for the discount factors. The discount factor is then applied to the adjusted cash flows and a net present value determined in the usual way.

Year	Sales	Costs	Net cash inflow	Deflator	Net cash* inflows standard	Discount factor	Present value
	£	£	£		£		£
1	22,000	11,000	11,000	.909	10,000	.847	8,470
2	24,200	12,100	12,100	.826	10,000	.718	7,180
3	26,620	13,310	13,310	.751	10,000	.609	6.090
4	29,282	14,641	14,641	.683	10,000	.516	5,160
5	32,210	16,105	16,105	.621	10,000	.437	4,370
							31,270
Initial investment							30,000
Net present value							+1,270

* Slight discrepancies in these calculations are caused by rounding differences.

14.1.12 Because, in this case, inflation affects all money amounts to the same extent, an opportunity exists here to shorten the computation by recording all figures in terms of current £'s. We must be quite clear, however, when we do this that we are not calculating actual cash flows but cash flows as they would be if the price changes did not take place.

14.1.13

Year	Sales	Costs	Net cash inflow	Discount factor	Present value
	£	£	£		£
1	20,000	10,000	10,000	.847	8,470
2	20,000	10,000	10,000	.718	7,180
3	20,000	10,000	10,000	.609	6,090
4	20,000	10,000	10,000	.516	5,160
5	20,000	10,000	10,000	.437	4,370

					31,270
Initial investment					30,000
Net present value					+1,270

14.1.14 Most of the problems involved in investment appraisal under inflation arise where there are differential rates of price change. In practice this is the most common situation. It arises because normal market fluctuations in prices are superimposed on those attributable to general inflation. Thus some prices will rise faster than others.

14.1.15 Example. Company Z is considering the purchase of a machine for £40,000. It will produce 3,000 units of product for each of five years. Although there is expected to be a general inflation rate of 10% per annum over the five years, the selling price of the product is expected, because of competitive constraints, to rise by only 5% per annum while costs will rise by 12% per annum. At the beginning of year 1 these are £10 and £5 respectively. Z's cost of capital is 18% per annum. Evaluate the project.

14.1.16

Year	Sales	Costs	Net cash inflow	Deflator	Adjusted net cash inflow in £s of year 1	Discount factor	Present value
	£	£	£		£		£
1	30,000	15,000	15,000	.909	13,365	.847	11,549
2	31,500	16,800	14,700	.826	12,142	.718	8,718
3	33,075	18,816	14,259	.751	10,709	.609	6,521
4	34,729	21,074	13,655	.683	9,326	.516	4,812
5	36,465	23,603	12,862	.621	7,987	.437	3,490

							35,090
Initial investment							40,000
Net present value							-4,910

Note that we have assessed the money value of sales and costs using the information available on how these will move. We have deflated the net cash inflow by the general inflation rate to give this in terms of current purchasing power. It declines considerably and shows clearly the squeeze on margins caused by the different movement of selling prices and costs.

14.2 Inflation and the Cost of Capital

14.2.1   We have considered the effects of inflation on the returns given by an investment project. It has also, however, an effect on the cost of loan capital. In inflationary times this may make this form of financing very attractive. An illustration will make this clear.

14.2.2   A company borrows £10,000 for one year at a rate of interest of 10% per annum. General inflation during that year was at a rate of 8% per annum. The following table shows the effect:

	In money terms £	In real terms £'s at beginning
Amount paid back at end of year	$11,000 \times \dfrac{100}{108}$	10,185
Less Amount borrowed	10,000	10,000
Interest	1,000	185
Rate	10%	1.85%

Thus the real cost of loan capital is substantially less than the money cost. Where the rate of inflation exceeds the rate of interest charged loan capital would have a negative cost. This might imply that it was worthwhile raising capital to invest in a project which, on ordinary criteria, appeared to be loss making.

14.2.3   Example. Carrot, plc has been offered an item of equipment on a finance leasing arrangement (see 3.4.2). The useful life of the equipment is four years. Its cash price is £10,000 and the lessor will require four equal annual payments of £3,155, the first being paid one year after the delivery of the equipment. Possession of the equipment will confer on the company a benefit (in terms of cost savings) valued at current prices at £3,100 per annum. These benefits will also last for four years during which time inflation is expected to run at 15% per annum.

14.2.4   On the face of it this investment is not worthwhile. The internal rate of return is approximately 9% per annum and the cost of capital for the project-specific loan 10% per annum. On a year by year basis it can be seen that the cash outflow exceeds the benefit. If we take into account inflation, however, the picture is quite different. The adjusted discounted cash flow calculation is shown below:

Year	Payment £	Deflator (15%)	Cost at current prices £	Benefit at current prices £	Net cash inflow £	Discount factor (10%)	Present value £
1	3,155	.869	2,742	3,100	358	.909	325
2	3,155	.756	2,385	3,100	715	.826	591
3	3,155	.658	2,076	3,100	1,024	.751	769
4	3,155	.572	1,805	3,100	1,295	.683	884
							2,569

This shows clearly that the investment should be made.

14.2.5 If finance really can be obtained at negative cost then this, of course, has considerable implications for financial management. It is not a matter that has until now received much attention. This is partly because inflation has reached significant levels only in very recent years and partly because of what is known as the 'money illusion'. This merely means that, despite all evidence to the contrary, money still appears to many people to be a stable measure of value because they have been conditioned to see it as such. It requires considerable effort to accept fully that it is not and to act accordingly.

Summary

(i)   Inflation is that condition which exists within an economy where the currency unit is declining in its real value. It is seen as a pervasive and general rise in all prices. It is to be distinguished from sectional price rises caused by ordinary market forces.

(ii) Price changes not associated with inflation must be incorporated, to the extent that they can be foreseen, in our evaluation of the future returns and costs associated with a project.

(iii) General inflation may be dealt with by making calculations in terms of present £'s, i.e. disregarding price rises, or alternatively by using actually anticipated money figures and applying a deflator to the final returns. A deflator is drawn from the same tables as conventional discount factors but its purpose is to allow for the decline in the purchasing power of money as opposed to its time value. Either of these methods will lead to the same ultimate result.

(iv) A more usual and more troublesome situation is where there is differential inflation, i.e. the general decline in the value of the purchasing power of the currency unit has a different impact on different components of the figures. This may be caused by such things as lags in the operation of the market mechanism or government action designed to have this effect, e.g. price curbs, wages policy.

(v) The more complex situations are best analysed by making calculations in terms of actual money amounts expected to be received or paid in the future and then applying the deflator as described above to the final figure for net cash inflow. The action of inflation may easily render unprofitable a project which seemed to be very favourable.

(vi) Inflation may also have an effect on the cost of loan capital. Because a loan is conventionally made in money terms, the loan is repaid at the end of its term in £'s which have depreciated relative to their value at the beginning. The real cost of the capital is thus lower than its apparent cost and may indeed be a negative quantity. This would carry the implication that it may sometimes pay to invest in projects yielding less than the apparent cost of capital.

Review questions

(i) *What distinguishes the phenomenon known as inflation from market induced fluctuations in price?*

(ii) *'It is harder to make a profit in inflationary times.' Explain this point of view and comment on its validity.*

(iii) *Explain the use of a deflator in investment appraisal calculations.*

(iv) *A certain project will require an investment of £5,000 and will give rise to favourable cash flows of £2,000 each year for three years. The cost of capital is 10% per annum and the rate of inflation is also 10% per annum. Show how the project would be evaluated (a) disregarding inflation and (b) taking inflation into account.*

(v) *Inflation often has a differential effect on individual prices, i.e. some rise faster than others. How can this be dealt with in investment appraisal calculations.*

(vi) *Explain the effect of inflation on the cost of loan capital.*

(vii) *What would be the implication to the financial manager of a negative real cost of capital?*

(viii) *What is meant by the 'money illusion'. Give some examples of it.*

Exercises

1. *The management of Anycomp, plc is considering a proposal to invest in capacity to produce a new product. The facility will cost £35,000 and will last for five years. In that time annual sales are expected to be 5,000 units. The selling price in the first year will be £5 and avoidable costs of production will be £2 per unit variable and £2,000 per annum fixed. The company's cost of capital, to be assumed unaffected by inflation, is 20% per annum. Present calculations showing the viability or otherwise of the project on the alternative assumptions of (i) no inflation, (ii) general inflation of 15% per annum affecting all figures equally, (iii) general inflation of 15% per annum but selling prices increasing by 12% per annum, variable costs by 14% per annum and fixed costs by 20% per annum.*

2. *John Smith borrowed £10,000 from his bank to enable him to reequip his business premises. The terms of the loan were that interest should be calculated at 12% per annum and that five equal repayments should be made commencing one year after the loan was made. During the five years there was a constant annual inflation rate of 18% per annum. Calculate:*

   (i) *the amount of the annual repayment;*

   (ii) *the effective real cost of the loan capital expressed in current £;*

   (iii) *the net present value of the loan to the bank assuming its cost of capital to be 6% per annum taking inflation into account.*

3. *Careful, plc has been offered a contract to supply a large retailer with 100,000 units of its product each year for the next five years. This is to be at a fixed price of £1.55 per unit. Cost of production are estimated as follows:*

	pence per unit
Material	40
Labour	60
Other direct costs	30
Indirect costs	20
	150

   Production can take place largely within existing capacity but an additional investment (mainly in working capital) of £30,000 would be required if it were undertaken. Careful requires a real rate of return on its capital of 10% per annum. Make calculations which will guide the company in deciding whether or not to sign the contract. Make alternative assumptions about the general level of inflation (which will affect costs but not revenues) showing how vulnerable the project is to price changes.

4. *It has been argued that home buyers are financed by the building societies at a negative real rate of interest. This is based on the observation that gross building society interest rates (further reduced by tax concessions to the borrower) have often been below the going rate of inflation. Explain the argument and identify the effects which flow from the situation.*

5. *The following figures have been presented to you in support of a proposal to invest in an extension to manufacturing capacity.*

Investment required: £200,000
Anticipated annual cash flows:

Revenue		£150,000
Less Direct cost		
Material	£37,500	
Labour	25,000	
Overhead	37,500	100,000
		£50,000

Expected life: 8 years
Cost of capital: 15% per annum

The effect of inflation is expected to be that selling prices will rise by 8% per annum, material costs by 5% per annum, labour costs by 10% per annum and overheads by 2% per annum. The cost of capital, on the other hand, will, in real terms be only 12% per annum. General inflation is expected to run at the rate of 5% per annum.

Evaluate the project (a) ignoring inflation and (b) taking inflation fully into account. Comment on the difference between the two sets of figures.

6. *List and comment on those areas of financial management where inflation will have an impact on decisions and actions.*

15: Taxation in financial decisions

15.1 The importance of taxation

15.1.1 So far, for simplicity, we have carefully avoided, in our analysis, all mention of taxation. Unfortunately, in the real world we cannot disregard it as it is an important factor in our decision making. At first sight the matter might appear to be quite simple. The incidence of taxation, we might suppose, merely renders every project less profitable than it would otherwise have been and we have to accept, as a fact of life, that all our income is to be shared with the government. The tax rules, however, ensure that it is more complex than this. Taxation affects the cost of capital differentially and it also distorts the cash flows associated with a project. It is quite possible, therefore, that both the relative ranking of projects and their basic acceptability will be affected once we take taxation into consideration.

15.1.2 Before we can begin to understand all of this we need some knowledge of how direct taxation in the United Kingdom operates. The student will appreciate that taxation is a very large and complex subject in its own right. Here we shall be concerned only with the most basic of its principles. The illustrative figures we shall use will not necessarily be the current rates of tax, which change frequently, but will allow straightforward calculations to aid the explanations.

15.1.3 Corporate taxpayers in this country (i.e. companies) are subject to corporation tax on their profits. Private taxpayers (i.e. salary and wage earners, shareholders, etc.) are subject to income tax on their calculated income. Corporation tax and income tax are the subjects of separate legislation and different rules govern their calculation and collection. To complicate the issue further one taxpayer is often required by law to act as a collector for the taxes due by another. A very good example of this occurs where a limited company employs staff. It will have to pay them their salaries after deducting the income tax due on them. This income tax it will then hand over to the Inland Revenue. It will also hand over to the Inland Revenue any corporation tax which becomes due on its own profits. These amounts are quite separate and have different implications. The income tax forms no part of the company's own tax liability. The fact that the company actually pays it, therefore, is not to be seen as part of any additional cash outflow as the amount would otherwise have gone to the salary earners. The corporation tax, on the other hand is fully the company's liability and does represent a drain on its financial resources. We must thus be very careful to distinguish between tax actually borne by a company and that borne by another but transmitted via the company. Other examples of the latter are the income tax borne by debenture holders and, also, value added tax.

15.2 The tax rules – cash flow

15.2.1 Here now is a brief summary of the tax rules with which we are going to be concerned. We shall confine our attentions to corporation tax as most financial managers will be operating in the corporate sector. The important points come under three headings which are:

(a) The calculation of taxable profits.

(b) The effect of capital allowances.

(c) The timing of the payment of the tax.

15.2.2 Calculation of taxable profit

Apart from the matter of depreciation and capital allowances, discussed separately below, taxable profits are calculated on conventional accounting principles. There are, however, certain points which should be noted.

(1) Some expenses commonly charged in arriving at accounting profit are disallowed for tax purposes. Examples are charitable and political donations, fines for illegal acts and entertaining expenses (unless in connection with overseas customers).

(2) Debenture interest paid is an allowable deduction in calculating taxable profit but dividends (including preference dividends) are not.

(3) In the calculation of the cost of sales the FIFO method must be used. LIFO is not acceptable to the Inland Revenue.

(4) Provisions or reserves made for anticipated losses (e.g. a general bad debts provision or a provision for anticipated future repairs of equipment) are not allowed.

15.2.3 Effect of capital allowances

Depreciation, as such, is not an allowable expense in calculating taxable profit. In its place is substituted capital allowances which, in effect, are statutorily determined amounts of depreciation. Capital allowances have always been used as an instrument of government policy. At various times they have been used to encourage investment in capital assets, to discourage it, to encourage differentially investment in new as opposed to secondhand assets and to give special encouragement to investment in development areas.

15.2.4 The basic rule for capital allowances is that a first year allowance is given for each asset in the year in which it is purchased and a writing down allowance is given against the net book value for each year subsequently. The first year allowance is a percentage of cost and the writing down allowance is a percentage of the reducing residual balance. Different rates apply for motor vehicles and for plant and machinery. All our examples will concern the latter as this will invariably be the subject of any examination question.

15.2.5 From 1972 until 1984 the first year allowance on plant and machinery was 100% of cost. This led to the consequence that subsequent writing down allowances were nil. This policy encouraged investment in plant and machinery as it meant that, for tax purposes, the company could write off such assets when bought. This reduced the tax payment at that time and assisted the cash flow when the purchase had reduced it. It should be noted that this device did not affect the tax burden in the long run but merely redistributed it.

Capital allowances now comprise a writing down allowance of 25% on the reducing balance starting with the year of purchase of the asset. The first year allowance is nil. The rate of corporation tax has been reduced to 33%. It should be noted that where plant and machinery is disposed of for more or less than its tax book value this may give rise to a balancing allowance or balancing charge to equate total capital allowances to total net expenditure. The tax effects of these balancing allowances and charges are normally deferred by 'pooling' which merely means that, after the first year allowance has been given, items of plant and machinery cease to be separately identified.

15.2.6 The timing of the payment of the tax

Corporation tax is paid nine months after the end of the year in which the profit to which it relates was earned. We shall deal with this in our calculations by showing all cash flows relating to tax as being lagged by one year from the date on which the liability arose. This is a good enough approximation and will normally be expected in answers to examination questions in financial management.

15.2.7 Example. Accounts prepared by the directors of White, plc showed that, in the year ended 31st December 19-1, the company made a trading profit of £295,000 before deducting debenture interest, dividends or taxation. Depreciation charged in the accounts had totalled £52,000 and there had also been charged expenses totalling

£1,000 not allowable for tax purposes. Debenture interest paid or payable in respect of the year amounted to £40,000 gross and it was intended to pay net dividends totalling £100,000. The rate of corporation tax for the year in question was 33% and the company was entitled to capital allowances totalling £60,000. Calculate the amount of corporation tax due from White and comment on its date of payment. Calculate also the retained profit for the year.

15.2.8 Calculation of taxable profit

	£	£
As per accounts		295,000
Add		
Disallowed expenses	1,000	
Depreciation	52,000	53,000
		348,000
Deduct		
Debenture interest	40,000	
Capital allowances	60,000	100,000
Taxable profit		£248,000
Tax at 33%		£81,840

The tax would be payable on 30th September 19-2.

Calculation of retained profit

	£
As per accounts	295,000
Less Debenture interest	40,000
Profit before taxation	255,000
Deduct Taxation	81,840
Profit after taxation	173,160
Deduct Dividends	100,000
Retained profit	£73,160

15.3 The Tax Rules – Cost of Capital

15.3.1   Because debenture and other loan interest is regarded as a charge against revenues but dividends are regarded as appropriations of profit, these receive different tax treatment and this has implications for the cost of capital. We need now to see what these are. In what follows we will assume a Corporation Tax rate of 35% and will assume an Income Tax rate of 25%.

15.3.2   Example. A certain company is due to pay £10,000 in debenture interest. Calculate the cost to the company of this payment.

15.3.3   The company is obliged by law to deduct income tax at source from payments of debenture interest. Thus:

	£
Debenture interest due	10,000
Deduct Income Tax @ 25%	2,500
Amount paid to debenture holders	7,500
Amount paid to Inland Revenue	2,500
Total payments	10,000

But since debenture interest paid is charged in the profit and loss account, profits will be reduced by the gross amount and the corporation tax bill will be reduced by 35% of this.

Hence **Deduct** Corporation Tax saving	3,500
Net cost of debenture interest	6,500

15.3.4   Example. A dividend of £7,500 (after tax) is to be paid to ordinary shareholders. The company is not required to deduct *income tax* from this as it is paid out of profits which have already borne corporation tax. Under the imputation system, however, the £7,500 is regarded in the hands of the shareholders as income taxed at the basic rate of income tax and this amount of notional income tax, here £2,500, is imputed to them. For the personal taxpayer this might be important if he were subject to rates of tax higher than the basic rate or if he had no tax liability at all. In these cases a cash adjustment one way or the other would be made between him and the Revenue. For the company its only implication is that the law requires the company to make an advance payment of corporation tax equivalent to the amount of the imputed income tax. Thus the cost of paying £10,000 gross equivalent to shareholders is £7,500 plus the time value of the advance corporation tax (i.e. interest on the amount from the date it is paid until the date it would otherwise have been due). This latter amount is likely to be small and we will ignore it in our analysis.

15.3.5   If the gross cost of debt or equity capital is 10% per annum we can now see that the net cost, if it is debt, is $6\frac{1}{2}\%$ per annum and, if it is equity, is 7.5% per annum. There is thus a clear cost advantage in debt as opposed to equity brought about by the operation of the tax rules. Offsetting advantages of equity financing will ensure that debt financing will not be carried too far but we see here a clear explanation of the relative unpopularity of preference share issues under the imputation system. Preference capital is more akin to debt in its investment characteristics but from a taxation point of view it is treated exactly like equity. An important effect of taxation to be noted, then, is its effect on the cost of capital.

15.4 Appraisal of project

15.4.1 In the example which follows we shall put together the strands we have so far discussed. The effect of taxation on the pattern and size of cash flows and on the cost of capital will clearly be illustrated.

15.4.2 Example. Taxat, plc has the capital structure and costs of capital shown in the table below:

	Market value (proportion)	Gross cost	After tax cost
Debt	20%	12%	7.8% (gross – 35%)
Equity	80%	15%	11.25% (gross – 25%)*

*the small additional cost imposed by the necessity to pay advance corporation tax is, here, disregarded.

15.4.3 A weighted average cost of capital is calculated as:

Gross cost 14.4% $((12\% \times .2) + (15\% \times .8))$
After tax cost 10.56% $((7.8\% \times .2) + (11.25\% + .8))$

15.4.4 Taxat is considering an investment of £20,000 in a project which would give the positive cash flows (before tax) shown below:

Year	Cash flow (before tax) £
1	10,000
2	8,000
3	6,000
4	4,000
5	2,500

The company will be entitled to a nil first year allowance and annual writing down allowances of 25%. The project will have a residual value of £4,746 at the end of its life when this amount is expected to be realised. (Note: this residual value is deliberately selected to avoid, for this first example, a particular difficulty which will be discussed afterwards). All tax payments are made exactly one year after the end of the year in which the relevant profits were earned. The rate of corporation tax may be taken as 35% throughout the life of the project.

15.4.5 Our first task is to compute the net (i.e. after tax) cash flows associated with the project. This is done year by year below.

Year 1

		£
Tax calculation		
	Cash flow	10,000
	Less WDA* @ 25% of £20,000	5,000
	Taxable profit	5,000
	Tax @ 35% (payable in year 2)	1,750
Cash flow		
	Gross amount	10,000
	Less tax payment	nil
	Net cash flow	10,000

*Writing down allowance

Written down value of plant after year 1 is:

$$£20,000 - £5,000 = £15,000$$

Year 2

		£
Tax calculation		
	Cash flow	8,000
	Less WDA @ 25% of £15,000	3,750
	Taxable profit	4,250
	Tax @ 35% (payable in year 3)	1,487
Cash flow		
	Gross amount	8,000
	Less tax payment (from year 1)	1,750
	Net cash flow	6,250

Written down value of plant after year 2 is:

$$£15,000 - £3,750 = £11,250$$

Year 3

		£
Tax calculation		
	Cash flow	6,000
	Less WDA @ 25% of £11,250	2,812
	Taxable profit	3,188
		£
	Tax @ 35% (payable in year 4)	1,116

Cash flow

Gross amount	6,000
Less tax payment (from year 2)	1,487
Net cash flow	4,513

Written down value of plant after year 3 is:

$$£11,250 - £2,812 = £8,438$$

Year 4

Tax calculation	£
Cash flow	4,000
Less WDA @ 25% of £8,438	2,110
Taxable profit	1,890
Tax @ 35% (payable in year 5)	662

Cash flow

Gross amount	4,000
Less tax payment (from year 3)	1,116
	2,884

Written down value of plant after year 4 is:

$$£8,438 - £2,110 = £6,328.$$

Year 5

Tax calculation	£
Cash flow	3,000
Less WDA @ 25% of £6,328	1,582
Taxable profit	1,418
Tax @ 35% (payable in year 6)	496

Cash flow

Gross amount	3,000
Less tax payment (from year 4)	662
Net cash flow	2,338

Written down value of plant after year 5 is £6,328 – £1,582 = £4,746

Year 6

There is no further cash inflow from the project but the tax arising from the activities of year 5 still remains to be paid:

Cash flow   **£**

Tax payment (from year 5)   (662)

15.4.6 The net returns should now be summarised and discounted at the after tax cost of capital of 10.56%. This has been done in the table below.

It should be noted that discount factors have had to be specially calculated as they are not available in tables.

Year	Cash flow	Discount factor	Present value £
1	10,000	.904	9,040
2	6,250	.818	5,113
3	4,513	.740	3,340
4	2,884	.669	1,929
5	2,338	.605	1,414
6	4,084	.548	2,238
			23,074
Less Initial investment			20,000
Net present value			+3,074

15.4.7 It will be interesting to note the result of an appraisal which ignores taxation.

Year	Cash flow	Discount factor (14.4%)	Present value £
1	10,000	.874	8,740
2	8,000	.764	6,112
3	6,000	.668	4,008
4	4,000	.584	2,336
5	7,246	.510	3,695
			24,891
Initial investment			20,000
Net present value			+4,891

The 'cost' of taxation to the company is the loss of net present value between the tax free computation and that taking tax into account. It is £5,954 − £3,074 = £1,817, probably a much smaller sum than might have been supposed.

15.4.8 We must now deal with the case where the realisation of a project does not tally with its written down value for tax purposes. Where this occurs, provided that other items of plant and equipment are owned by the business, the residual balance remains in the pool of asset valuations and continues to modify tax payments through capital allowances until it is reduced to negligible proportions. This can be illustrated by determining the effect on the overall net present value of the previous example of there being no scrap value to the project.

Total net present value would, first of all be reduced by the present value of the disposal proceeds not now received. This is:

$$£4,746 \times .548 = £2,600$$

It would then be increased by the present value of the tax relief to be obtained by the writing down allowances which continue into the future. This is, in fact, an infinite series but its terms will, after a few years, decline to negligible levels.

The benefit in year 7 is:

$$£4,746 \times 25\% \times 35\% \times .495 = £205 \text{ (call this } x_1)$$

(These figures are respectively: the written down value of the plant at end of year 5, the rate of writing down allowance, the rate of corporation tax and the discount factor for the seventh year).

The benefit in year 8 is x_2 where

$$x_2 = x_1 \times 75\%^* \times .904†$$

* The proportion which a year's writing down allowance bears to the previous year's.

† The proportion which a year's discount factor bears to the previous year's.

We then determine $x_1 + x_2 + x_3 + \ldots$ to infinity (easily done with a pocket calculator). The figure is £636. Hence the revised net present value is £3,074 − £2,600 + £636= £1,110

15.4.9 Example. Tegdub, plc has an after tax cost of capital of 8% per annum. It is considering the investment of £50,000 in a project having an expected life of four years after which £5,000 of the capital expenditure can be recovered. Tegdub will be entitled to an annual writing down allowance of 25%. The rate of corporation tax will be 35%. The expected gross returns from the project are:

Year	Returns
	£
1	30,000
2	20,000
3	10,000
4	5,000

15.4.10 Again we will calculate cash flows and tax charges year by year.

Year 1

Tax calculation:	£
Cash flow	30,000
Less WDA @ 25% of £50,000	12,500
Taxable profit	17,500
Tax @ 35%	6,125

Cash flow:	
Gross amount	30,000

Written down value of plant after year 1 is:

$$£50,000 - £12,500 = £37,500$$

Year 2

Tax calculation:	£
Cash flow	20,000
Less WDA @ 25% of £37,500	9,375
Taxable profit	10,625
Tax @ 35%	3,719

Cash flow:	
Gross amount	20,000
Less Tax payment	6,125
Net cash flow	13,875

Written down value of plant after year 2 is:

$$£37,500 - £9,375 = £28,125$$

Year 3

Tax calculation:	£
Cash flow	10,000
Less WDA @ 25% of £28,125	7,031
Taxable profit	2,969
Tax @ 35%	1,039

Cash flow:	
Gross amount	10,000
Less Tax payment	3,719
	6,281

Written down value of plant after year 3 is:

$$£28,125 - £7,031 = £21,094$$

Year 4

Tax calculation:	£
Cash flow	5,000
Less WDA of 25% of £21,094	5,274
Tax relievable loss	(274)
Tax @ 35%	(96)

Cash flow:	£
Gross amount	5,000
Tax payment	1,039
	3,961
Add Realisation proceeds	5,000
	8,961

Written down value of plant after year 4 is:

$$£21,094 - £5,274 - £5,000 = £10,820$$

Year 5

Cash flow:	£
Tax relieved	96

Calculating the net present value:

Year	Net cash flow	Discount factor	Present value
	£		£
1	30,000	.926	27,780
2	13,875	.857	11,891
3	6,281	.794	4,987
4	8,961	.735	6,586
5	96	.681	65
Present value of residual capital allowances*			1,955
			53,264
Less Initial investment			50,000
Net present value			+3,264

* Calculated as follows:

$$x_1 = £10,820 \times 25\% \times 35\% \times .631 = £597$$

$$x_2 = x1 \times 75\% \times .926 = £415$$

$$x_1 + x_2 + x_3 + \ldots = £1,955$$

Summary

(i) Taxation has important effects on:

(a) the cost of capital and

(b) the pattern of cash flows,

and hence is of great relevance to the decision of the financial manager.

(ii) The U.K. system of collection of tax at source means that a company will be making payments of tax on behalf of others (e.g. employees, debenture holders) as well as on its own account. Only the latter payments are of real significance to the financial manager.

(iii) Loan interest is regarded as a charge to be made in determining profit. Dividends, whether preference of ordinary, are regarded as distributions out of profits already ascertained and taxed. Because of differential rates of income tax and corporation tax this means that loan capital becomes relatively cheaper than it would otherwise have been.

(iv) The pattern of cash flows is influenced by:

(a) capital allowances.

(b) the postponement of the payment of tax due to the operation of the rules on the date of payment.

(v) When tax has been taken into account in determining net cash flows these must be discounted at an after tax cost of capital rate in order to establish the net present value of the project.

Review questions

(i) Explain, in terms of their tax implications, the relative unpopularity of preference share issues.

(ii) One of the benefits to a company of being a taxpayer is that this reduces the cost of borrowing. Explain this statement and indicate the extent to which this can be regarded as a benefit.

(iii) Demonstrate how a project, unacceptable in a tax free situation, could become acceptable when taxation is imposed.

(iv) 'The crushing burden of taxation makes it very difficult for a company to find profitable investment opportunities.' To what extent is this likely to be true?

(v) Explain, briefly, the imputation system of taxation. What are its implications for the financial manager?

(vi)   *What is meant by the term capital allowance. What is the significance of capital allowances to the financial manager?*

(vii) *A company both bears tax in its own right and also acts as a collector of tax on behalf of the Inland Revenue. Give examples of each kind of tax and indicate the significance of the distinction.*

(viii) *'The tax considerations surrounding a decision are often more important than any others.' Comment.*

Exercises

1. *Itemise the important effects which the incidence of taxation has on investment project appraisal and write brief notes on each.*

2. *Kangaroo, plc is contemplating investment in a certain project. This would require the initial expenditure of £50,000 which could be raised at a net-of-tax cost of capital of 8% per annum. The project is expected to yield the following returns over the next six years and will have no scrap value:*

Year	Returns
	£
1	15,000
2	12,000
3	12,000
4	10,000
5	8,000
6	8,000

The rate of corporation tax is 35%, writing down allowance on capital expenditure of 25% per annum is given. Tax is payable one year after the profits on which it is based have been earned. Calculate the net present value of the project and hence advise the company.

3. *Suppose that the Chancellor of the Exchequer wished, by means of taxation provisions, to discourage corporate investment. What might he do?*

4. *Emu, plc has the following capital structure and costs:*

	Market value	Gross cost
Ordinary shares	£2,000,000	20% per annum
Preference shares	£800,000	18% per annum
Debt	£500,000	12% per annum

Assuming a corporation tax rate of 35% and an income tax rate of 30%, calculate Emu's net cost of capital for project appraisal purposes.

5. A manager working for Platypus, plc has produced figures to make a case for investing £25,000 in a new project. The project is expected to produce cash flows over the next five years as follows:

Year 1	£10,000
2	8,000
3	6,000
4	6,000
5	5,000

In the calculation produced by the manager, which uses the company's gross of capital of 12% per annum, taxation has been ignored. When this is pointed out the manager fears that the inclusion of tax will destroy his case. The company's after tax cost of capital is 8% per annum and the corporation tax rate is 35%.

Produce figures which duplicate the manager's original calculation and then produce a second set which show fully the effect of taxation. A writing down allowance of 25% per annum is available.

6. Downunder, plc is contemplating extending its existing highly profitable activities into a new venture which has a somewhat speculative outcome. This will require development expenditure over three years of £75,000 paid in equal instalments at the end of each year. This expenditure is fully allowable for tax purposes in the year in which it is incurred. The venture is then expected to yield the following positive cashflows:

Year	Cash
	£
4	10,000
5	30,000
6	40,000
7	50,000
8	60,000

No further cash flows are expected after the eighth year. The company's after tax cost of capital is 10% per annum. The three years' initial expenditure can all be set off for tax purposes against other income of the year in which it occurs. Corporation tax is at the rate of 50%.

Prepare figures which will enable an appraisal of the project.

16: Distribution policy

16.1 The dividend decision

16.1.1   One of the decisions which falls to be made by a company's Board of Directors is that concerning the amount of dividend which is to be paid to equity holders. We have already made reference to this matter obliquely in more than one context.

16.1.2   From the point of view of the shareholder dividends will be seen as a part only of his return from his investment in the company. The capital growth which occurs will also be important. In assessing the company's success he will have a particular interest in the figure for earnings per share which will include all profit whether distributed or not.

16.1.3   From the point of view of the company retained earnings may be an important source of investment funds but it has to be recognised that they have a cost, just as does finance from other sources, and must, therefore, be deployed in profitable uses. The dividend decision is thus one in which the financial manager is greatly concerned. The considerations involved may usefully be looked at under four headings, legal, liquidity, conventional and financial.

16.2 The legal position

16.2.1   A basic principle of company law is that a company's revenue profits may be distributed to shareholders but its permanent capital fund may not. This is in order to protect creditors otherwise vulnerable to loss through the operation of limited liability. There have in the past been many legal arguments as to what should be regarded as distributable profits and what should not. The law has now been considerably clarified and is contained in the Companies Act, 1985.

16.2.2   The present position is that a company may make a distribution out of 'profits available for that purpose'. These are accumulated realised profits less accumulated realised losses. In the case of public companies, it must also be ensured that after any proposed distribution there will still remain net assets equal (at least) in value to called up share capital and undistributable reserves. The effect of this is that *unrealised* losses (but not unrealised profits) must also be taken into account in determining the legal capacity to pay a dividend.

This does, of course, follow the normal accounting convention that only realised profits should appear in a profit and loss account but that all foreseeable losses should be provided for.

16.2.3 Example. The summarised balance sheet of Denominator, plc at 31st December 19-1 appears below:

Share capital	£500,000	Fixed assets	£400,000
Retained profit	200,000	Current assets	300,000
	£700,000		£700,000

In the year ended 31st December 19-2, the company's profit and loss account showed that a profit (after taxation) of £50,000 had been made. Certain fixed assets had become redundant during the year and it was known that the total realisable value of fixed assets was £20,000 less than the book value which appeared in the balance sheet. No provision for this loss had been made in the accounts. What is the maximum amount which Denominator may distribute by way of dividend in 19-2?

16.2.4 The maximum legal distribution is:

Accumulated realised profits at 31st December 19-1	£200,000
Add Current year's profit	50,000
	250,000
Deduct Unrealised loss on fixed assets*	20,000
Maximum legal distribution	£230,000

*Note that, since this is based on an overall net realisable valuation of the fixed assets, it is possible, and quite legitimate, for the unrealised losses on redundant assets to be offset by unrealised gains on other assets.

16.2.5 Example. The summarised balance sheet of Numerator, plc at 31st December 19-1 appears below:

Share capital	£800,000	Fixed assets	£500,000
		Current assets	250,000
		Profit and loss account	50,000
	£800,000		£800,000

Numerator's profit and loss account for the year ended 31st December 19-2 showed a profit of £100,000. The net realisable value of fixed assets was £750,000 and of current assets £400,000 at 31st December 19-2. These values were not incorporated in the balance sheet which continued to be based on historical cost. What is the maximum legal distribution?

16.2.6   The maximum legal distribution is:

Current year's profit	£100,000
Deduct Past realised losses (1)	50,000
Maximum legal distribution (2)	£50,000

Notes:

(1)   Although, because of the protection of limited liability, there is no obligation on the shareholders to make up losses (debit balances on the profit and loss account) by any fresh introductions of capital funds, the deficiency does become a first call on future profits and must be made good before dividend payments can be resumed.

(2)   The unrealised profits on holdings of assets are not available to support a dividend payment.

16.2.7   It should be noted that company law is not the only source of legal restraint on company distributions. Some of the Government's past income policies have limited dividend payments below the levels which would have been allowed under company legislation.

16.2.8   Within the legal constraints the amount of a dividend is at the discretion of the directors. The discretion will be governed by provisions in the company's Articles of Association. The usual position can, however, be described here. A decision as to the total amount of the dividend for the year will be taken after the accounts have been prepared and will be put as a proposal to the Annual General Meeting. At that meeting the members will vote on the proposal. It will normally be carried but members have the power to amend the proposal to some *lower* amount of dividend. Part of the dividend for the year will frequently already have been paid, at the instance of the directors, as an *interim dividend* part way through the year. (There may, indeed, have been more than one interim dividend, though this is relatively rare.) The remainder, the *final dividend*, is the only amount effectively at issue. Since the directors will wish to be assured of the adequacy of profits, interim dividends are normally at a relatively low rate and the final dividend represents the major payment of the year.

16.3 Liquidity considerations

16.3.1   The fact that legally a company may be entitled to pay a dividend does not in any way guarantee that it has available the liquid funds necessary to enable this to be done. If profits have been 'ploughed back' into the business they will be represented by fixed assets and stocks rather than by cash.

16.3.2 Example. Frozen, plc has the summarised balance sheet at 31st December 19-1 which appears below:

Share capital	£1,000,000	**Fixed assets**		£1,180,000
Retained profit	400,000	**Current assets**		
Current liabilities	200,000	Stocks	£250,000	
		Debtors	120,000	
		Cash	50,000	420,000
	£1,600,000			£1,600,000

All assets are valued at cost or net realisable value, whichever be the lower. Assess the company's ability to pay a dividend.

16.3.3 The basis of valuation of assets ensures that any unrealised losses have been fully provided for in the profit and loss account. The company is therefore legally able to pay a dividend of up to £400,000. It can, however, easily be seen from the balance sheet that this would be a difficult thing to do as the available cash would cover only a small part of such a payment. The present level of current assets bears a reasonable relationship to current liabilities and it is probably necessary, therefore, to maintain that level. It would appear that, on liquidity considerations, Frozen should pay no dividend.

16.3.4 It should be pointed out that it is not completely impossible for Frozen to distribute its retained profits. It could, for example, realise some fixed assets although this would have the consequence of reducing its level of activity. Another option open to it is to borrow money for the purposes of paying the dividend. Although this might seem to be a reckless course of action, akin to living beyond one's means by the use of credit facilities, it may in some circumstances be quite sensible. It could properly be seen as a change in the company's capital structure, substituting debt finance for equity finance. There is no reason to expect that this will have any adverse effect on the company's cost of capital. Under one view of the relationship between capital structure and the cost of capital, it may actually reduce it.

16.4 Conventions

16.4.1 It is generally accepted that it is desirable for dividends to remain relatively stable with, if possible, a gently rising trend over the years. Very little research has been done to provide evidence in support of this contention but it is often justified as follows:

(i) shareholders favour a reliable income from their investments as this facilitates personal financial planning;

(ii) a steady dividend trend seems to indicate a stable and well-managed company;

(iii) in an information-hungry situation, as the stock market is, any announcement is likely to be seen as conveying implicit information beyond what it actually states. Thus the announcement of a dividend substantially below that of the previous year may be taken to be an expression of deep pessimism about the future. Conversely a greatly increased dividend may be read as an assurance that profits are expected to reach higher levels.

16.4.2　If dividends are to be insulated from fluctuations in profit then clearly a cautious policy is required. If a company distributes the whole of its profit then even a temporary setback must mean that dividends are cut. If it distributes only part of its profit there is much more room to maintain the dividend over the bad years.

Most Boards of Directors would regard consistency of dividend policy as important. This is so that investors may know, as part of their investment strategy, whether a share should be regarded as an 'income' share, i.e. distributing the maximum amount of its earnings, or a 'growth' share i.e. retaining the maximum amount for expansion.

16.5 Financial considerations

16.5.1　We come now to the theoretical basis for determining the amount of the dividend. The simple rule is that if a company can invest its profit within the business more profitably than its shareholders could invest it elsewhere, then it should retain the profit. If not it should distribute it. This amounts to saying that the company should retain its profits if the available investment opportunities yield more than its cost of capital.

16.5.2　Example. The best alternative investment available to the shareholders of Tortoiseshell, plc (in a similar risk category) would give a yield of 12% per annum. Market forces have ensured that this is exactly the yield on the shares of Tortoiseshell so that there is no incentive for existing shareholders to move out of the company or for new ones to move in. The company is wholly equity financed and regards this as the most appropriate for its situation. Its legal maximum distribution (i.e. the aggregate of current profit and past revenue reserves) is £500,000. The following investment projects are available:

Investment	Finance required £	Internal rate of return % per annum
A	100,000	13
B	120,000	$12\frac{1}{2}$
C	200,000	11
D	180,000	10

What dividend should be paid?

16.5.3 The company's cost of capital is 12% per annum and therefore projects A and B should be accepted and C and D should not. Of the £500,000 available for distribution the company should retain and invest £220,000 (A and B) and distribute the remaining £280,000 as a dividend. The recipients are in a position to invest this on more favourable terms than can the company.

16.5.4 It will be seen from this example that, logically, distribution policy is merely an extension to the normal capital budgeting process. Investment should be made where this can be profitably done, using available funds together with additional finance where many good opportunities exist and distributing funds where these opportunities do not exist. It should be noted, however, that this logic may lead to some paradoxical results so that a company might seek to raise funds at a time when it is paying no dividend and might pay large dividends at a time when its future seems most bleak.

16.5.5 Example. In 19-5 Turnturtle, plc had net earnings of £500,000 (after interest and taxation). The cost of its various components of capital were:

Retained earnings	15% per annum
New equity	16% per annum*
New debt	13% per annum

*New equity has a higher cost than retained earnings because of the expenses of issuing new capital (see Chapter 5).

Turnturtle's desired gearing is .5, i.e. it is to be financed 50% by debt and 50% by equity. The investment projects available to it are as follows:

Investment	Finance required £	Internal rate of return % per annum
A	80,000	17.0
B	130,000	16.5
C	90,000	14.8
D	140,000	13.5
E	120,000	12.2
F	75,000	11.1
G	42,000	10.0

How much should Turnturtle pay in dividend?

16.5.6 The marginal cost of capital is 14% per annum (the average of equal parts of retained earnings and debt) for all increments up to £1,000,000 (composed of the full £500,000 of earnings plus, to preserve the desired gearing, an equal amount of new debt). Thereafter it is 14.5% (the average of new equity and debt). Taking these rates we shall run out of attractive investment opportunities before we reach the stage of raising new equity. At the 14% per annum cost of capital projects A, B and C would be accepted and the rest rejected. This would absorb £300,000 of funds of which, again given our desired gearing, £150,000 would come from retained earnings. The residue of £350,000 (£500,000-£150,000) would be distributed as dividend.

16.6 Concluding observations

16.6.1 It may be observed that there are a number of important points:

(i) In deciding whether or not to pay a dividend we should, strictly, have regard to each individual shareholder's opportunity cost of capital. This is unknown and unknowable and so we have to assume that market forces have brought this into equilibrium with the equity cost of capital.

(ii) A full application of this principle may lead to a rate of dividend which fluctuated widely. We have already implied that this would be undesirable. The dividend would obviously vary both with the profit and with the investment opportunities which were currently available.

(iii) With a business which was expanding rapidly because there were abundant attractive investment opportunities open to it these may absorb the whole of the profit and still require further equity finance, i.e. in effect a negative rate of dividend. In real life it is most unlikely that a company could continuously raise new capital if it never paid a dividend.

(iv) The capital budgeting decision may indicate that a dividend in excess of profit should be paid (by distributing also the proceeds of asset realisations). This would not be allowed by law. The privilege of limited liability may sometimes, therefore, be gained at the cost of investing to yield a return at below the cost of capital.

16.6.2 It should be pointed out that the approaches to dividend payment discussed here are not necessarily incompatible if we take the long view. Certainly a precise year by year application of the analysis just described would probably not lead to stable dividends. Taking a longer, say five or ten year, planning horizon, however, may well make a reconciliation possible.

Summary

(i) The payment of a dividend is an important decision of financial management and there are a number of constraints affecting it. These may be categorised as legal, conventional, liquidity and financial constraints.

(ii) **Legal.** Company law allows the payment of a dividend only out of profits calculated on conventional accounting principles. A dividend may exceed current profits where there are accumulated revenue reserves earned in the past but not otherwise.

(iii) **Conventional.** It has become part of the lore of the stock market that a company is favoured by investors if its dividends are basically stable over time. A gentle upward movement is to be desired but violent fluctuations in either direction are not. This coupled with the legal factors often leads to a very cautious dividend policy.

(iv) **Liquidity.** Regardless of other considerations a company will be unable to pay a dividend if cash is not available to do so. It may, however, sometimes borrow, e.g. by bank overdraft, for this purpose.

(v) **Financial.** Financial analysis suggests that profits should be retained when they can profitably be invested within the business but not otherwise. Dividends are then the residue, i.e. the profit for which there is no profitable use. The analysis is quite straightforward – retained earnings becoming a component of the cost of capital.

Review questions

(i) What are the legal constraints on distribution policy?

(ii) *Paradox, plc has paid a dividend to its shareholders and is at the same time making a rights offer of new shares. Comment on this.*

(iii) *Could either the borrowing of money or the liquidation of investment projects to provide cash for the payment of a dividend ever be justified?*

(iv) *'Retained earnings are no different from any other source of equity capital.' 'The retention of earnings is the best way to finance expansion.' Comment on these two statements by directors of different companies.*

(v) *Describe the conventions which surround the distribution decision. What might be the consequences of (a) passing a dividend (i.e. not paying one) or (b) paying a dividend at double the rate of the previous year.*

(vi) *'But for the requirements of company law a rational management would wish to vary the capital of the company downwards as well as upwards as a regular review of circumstances might dictate.' Explain.*

(vii) *'The dividend decision is not affected by the level of profits.' Discuss.*

(viii) *How important are considerations of liquidity to the distribution decision?*

Exercises

1. *At the Annual General Meeting of Bright, plc a shareholder says, 'Our chairman has just told us that we have made a record profit in the past year and that many highly profitable projects have been commenced so that we have a bright future. How, then, can he tell us that the company cannot afford to increase the dividend and so enable us to benefit from this?' How might this be answered?*

2. *Hope, plc has made a profit over the past year of £120,000. Its gearing ratio is .4 and its costs of capital are:*

Equity	22% per annum
Retained earnings	20% per annum
Debt	10% per annum

   Four projects are under consideration and particulars are as follows:

Project	Investment required	Internal rate of return
	£	
A	60,000	19%
B	50,000	18%
C	80,000	17%
D	20,000	16%

What dividend should be paid?

3. *The directors of Hindsight, plc always pay a dividend equal to one-tenth of the profits of the previous five years. What may justify this policy and what are its consequences?*

4. *'The legal imposition of constraints on dividends will encourage badly needed investment in British industry.'*

    'An effective capital market requires that companies are free to distribute whatever proportion of their profits they choose.' Comment on these opposing points of view.

5. *Consider the following extreme circumstances and comment on the likely consequences:*

    (i)   *A pays no dividend but invests all retained funds in projects yielding more than its cost of capital.*

    (ii) *B pays no dividend but has no profitable use for the funds retained.*

    (iii) *C pays out all its profits as dividend forgoing investment opportunities in order to do so.*

    (iv) *D pays out all its profits as dividend having no profitable investment opportunities to lead it to do otherwise.*

6. *Beautiful, plc has its dividend covered twice by earnings according to its most recent accounts. It has pursued, over the years, a conservative distribution policy and that degree of cover has come to be regarded as normal for the company.*

    In the current year a profit has been made of £530,000, after tax, and the Board of Directors has to take a decision as to what dividend to recommend. At the same meeting it is considering several well-suported investment projects, brief particulars of which are given below.

Project	Investment required	Internal rate of return
	£	% per annum
W	150,000	20
X	250,000	19
Y	100,000	18
Z	90,000	$17\frac{1}{2}$

Beautiful's cost of equity capital is 19% per annum and of retained earnings 18% per annum. The weighted average cost of capital is 16% per annum.

What relevant points might you expect to be made at the meeting of the Board and what might their ultimate decision sensibly be?

17: Financial Ratios

17.1 The Importance of Ratios

17.1.1 The figures appearing in a set of accounts convey a considerable amount of information in terms of their absolute amounts. We can, for example, learn how much profit a business has made or what value of resources it has tied up in fixed assets. Such information may be very useful. Very often, however, the relationship between one figure and another can be a great deal more useful. The computation of financial ratios is a development from this principle.

17.1.2 One good case for the calculation of ratios is illustrated by a consideration of a figure for profit. A certain business has made a profit in the year just ended of £100,000 and we wish to comment on how satisfactory a performance this is. Clearly in order to do this we must relate the profit to some measure of the effort expended in earning it or of the resources committed to this end. If the profit arises from a turnover of £500,000 and an invested capital of £750,000 it may seem to represent a good level of performance. If turnover is £2,000,000 and invested capital £5,000,000 it will seem much less satisfactory.

17.1.3 Valuable though ratios are, a warning must be given against too glib an interpretation of them. No given value can automatically be regarded as 'good' or as 'bad'. It must be related to the type of business which is being carried on and to the accounting processes which have produced the figures on which it is based. There is potentially a large number of ratios which might be calculated. Some of the more useful and important ones are illustrated and discussed below.

17.2 Measures of Effectiveness

17.2.1 A fundamental measure of commercial effectiveness is the gross profit rate. This is calculated as the percentage rate which gross profit bears to sales turnover. So:

$$\text{Gross profit rate} = \frac{\text{Gross profit}}{\text{Sales}} \times 100\%$$

Other things being equal the higher the gross profit rate the more effective the basic profit earning activity of the business. No general view can, however, be taken on an appropriate target value. Typical rates of gross profit vary considerably between one type of business activity and another. Thus one might expect a retailer to make a gross profit on sales of 30% or more, whilst a supplier of heavy machinery might make 15%. This reflects the much greater effort which needs to be made, per £1 of sales, in the former case.

17.2.2 It should be noted that a business can, within limits, select its own gross profit rate through its pricing policy. If it is a profit maximiser this freedom will be constrained by the market situation. If prices are increased in order to improve the gross profit rate there will, at some point, be such a fall off in turnover that the absolute level of gross profit is reduced.

17.2.3 An unexpected reduction in the gross profit rate should be taken seriously. It may be sign of any or all of the following situations on which action is required:

(a) Careless stock control leading to losses and pilferage of stock.

(b) Defalcations of cash received from sales.

(c) Rising costs which have not been passed on to customers in higher prices.

(d) A change in the sales mix caused by changing conditions of demand.

(e) An error in the stock taking records.

17.2.4 Example. The following information is taken from the trading account of Duck, plc. Calculate the gross profit rate for each of these two years and comment.

	Year ended	
	31st March 19-1	**31st March 19-2**
Sales	£1,000,000	£1,500,000
Cost of sales	750,000	1,200,000
Gross profit	£250,000	£300,000

17.2.5 The gross profit rate for the first year is

$$\frac{£250,000}{£1,000,000} \times 100 = 25\%$$

and for the second year

$$\frac{£300,000}{£1,500,000} \times 100 = 20\%$$

The business has apparently suffered a fairly sharp decline in its basic profitability. Turnover has, however, improved by a substantial amount and this has lead to an improvement in the absolute level of gross profit. Subject to any consequent changes in the level of administrative costs or of capital employed this would appear to be an improved situation. It may have come about (a) by a reduction of selling prices which has attracted extra customers or (b) by an absorption of increased costs again, perhaps, favourably received by the market as competitors have passed on such extra cost.

17.2.6 The effectiveness of a business's administrative function, as opposed to its business activity, can be tested by calculating a percentage of administrative costs to sales. We will call this the administrative percentage and it is calculated as:

$$\text{Administrative percentage} = \frac{\text{Administrative costs}}{\text{Sales}} \times 100\%$$

The supposition underlying the calculation of this figure is that, given a particular level of sales, the administrative costs of servicing it should be kept as low as possible. It should be noted, however, that the cost of the administrative process cannot be separated from its quality. A low administrative cost achieved by inadequate staffing or poor facilities is a false economy and may be very expensive in terms of lost business, high bad debts or customers' complaints.

17.2.7 It will be characteristic of many administrative costs (e.g. office staff salaries, rent, rates and insurance) that they will be fixed, or only semi-variable, relative to sales. Where this is the case the percentage will depend in part on the level of sales. If sales increase while, because of the fixed components, administrative costs remain constant or increase less than proportionately, the administrative cost percentage will fall. This does not necessarily carry any implication of improved efficiency.

17.2.8 It is important to remember that the overall total of administrative costs will contain a large number of components varying considerably in nature. It may be useful to analyse these components in order to consider them separately. Thus it might be seen that, say, rising telephone costs are obscured by, say, savings on staff or that an overall poor percentage is caused by one or two identifiable items on which action can be taken once they have been isolated.

17.2.9 Example. The following figures are summarised from Duck's profit and loss accounts.

	Year ended	
	31st March 19-1	**31st March 19-2**
Gross profit	£250,000	£300,000
Less Administrative costs	100,000	120,000
	£150,000	£180,000

17.2.10 Using the sales figures given in the previous example we can see that administrative costs, although rising in absolute terms, have declined as a percentage of sales. This percentage in the first year is 10% and in the second 8%. Duck is getting more out of its administrative system than before which in consequence is represented as being more efficient. Final judgment should be reserved until some check has been made on quality to ensure that the administration is not under pressure sufficient to impair its effectiveness.

17.3 Measures of Short Term Solvency

17.3.1 However profitable a business might be in the long run, its survival depends, amongst other things, on its immediate ability to pay its bills as and when they fall due. If its funds are overinvested in fixed assets (i.e. it is underfinanced relative to its scale of operations) this may not be possible. Creditors may thus be given the power to foreclose. The current ratio and the liquidity ratio are two important measures of short term solvency.

17.3.2 The current ratio is the relationship between the current assets and current liabilities. It is an important part of the structure of a balance sheet. It is calculated as:

$$\text{Current ratio} = \frac{\text{Current assets}}{\text{Current liabilities}}$$

and is quoted as a single figure (not a percentage). Although no hard and fast rule can be laid down, as different types of business operate under different conditions, a current ratio of around 2 is generally considered to be about right. This means that short term obligations can be met approximately twice over by existing short term sources of funds. This allows for the fact that, although all current liabilities will have to be settled in cash, not all current assets can be converted into cash immediately. Such things as stock, for example, will be a permanent component of current assets.

17.3.3 A more stringent test of short run solvency which is sometimes used is the liquidity ratio. This is given by:

$$\text{Liquidity ratio} = \frac{\text{Liquid assets (i.e. debtors, bank and cash)}}{\text{Current liabilities}}$$

This ratio is generally regarded as satisfactory if it is equal approximately to 1 or is just above that figure.

17.3.4 It is very important that current and liquidity ratios are kept to an appropriate level, given the nature of the business's activities and its financial situation. A retail business, where debtors are few and turnover rapid, would be safer on a lower current ratio than would a business whose customers take long periods of credit and where there is a lengthy manufacturing process. If a business had substantial easily realisable investments in securities or access to large overdraft facilities it could, again, afford to operate on a tighter liquidity position than otherwise. A large well known company may, by its reputation and market power, be able to secure favourable terms of credit which reduce its need for immediate liquidity.

17.3.5 The following might be the consequences of too low current and liquidity ratios:

(a) payment of creditors is delayed (and discounts, perhaps, lost);

(b) there is a constant problem of how to find enough cash to pay weekly wages;

(c) creditors withhold supplies because of late payment;

(d) essential maintenance and replacement of fixed assets is frequently postponed;

(e) investment plans are delayed or shelved.

17.3.6 If the current and liquidity ratios are too high all anxiety over cash flow will be removed but equally undesirable consequences may follow. Examples are:

(a) capital will be tied up unproductively so that the overall rate of return is reduced;

(b) unnecessarily large stocks will be maintained so that storage costs and stock losses of various kinds are higher than they need be;

(c) a valuable discipline on the credit control section will be lost so that an unwise amount or length of credit may be advanced to customers.

17.3.7 Example. Included in the balance sheet of Duck, plc at 31st March is the following section:

	31st March 19-1	31st March 19-2
Current assets		
Stock	£82,000	£79,000
Debtors	44,000	45,000
Cash	10,000	8,000
	136,000	132,000
Less **Current liabilities:**		
Creditors	62,000	55,000
Net current assets	£74,000	£77,000

Calculate suitable ratios giving a measure of short term solvency and comment.

17.3.8   The ratios are:

	Current	Liquidity
31st March 19-1	2.19	.87
31st March 19-2	2.40	.96

The ratios appear to be fairly healthy and have improved from the first year to the second.

17.4 Measures of Performance of Working Capital Management

17.4.1   Where management operates a policy of managing the credit which it grants to customers the average collection period for debts will be a useful test of the effectiveness of implementation. In all cases it casts useful illumination on what is often a key factor in working capital. If the value of debtors is calculated as a proportion of sales and then this fraction is applied to the length of time occupied by the accounting period, this will give us the average length of time which customers are taking to pay. If we take it that there are 365 days in the year.

$$\text{Average collection period for debts} = \frac{\text{Debtors}}{\text{Sales}} \times 365$$

Putting in the relevant figures for Duck, plc, taken from the examples above we get for the first year

$$\text{Collection period} = \frac{£44,000}{£1,000,000} \times 365$$

$$= 16.06 \text{ days}$$

and for the second year

$$\text{Collection period} = \frac{£45,000}{£1,500,000} \times 365$$
$$= 10.95 \text{ days}$$

17.4.2 It should be noted that we have assumed that all sales are on credit. If this is not the case cash sales must be excluded from the bottom line of the fraction. We should also note that for a seasonal business the figure given above may be misleading. At the busy part of the year debtors will bear a higher proportion to annual sales than at the slack period even if the true average collection period remains unaltered. The value of calculating the collection period is that it can be compared with the 'official' period of credit offered. This is a good test of the effectiveness of credit control. The effects of policy changes, e.g. offering cash discount for prompt payment or increasing sales by taking on slightly less credit-worthy customers can be assessed.

17.4.3 Example. Assume that in the year ended 31st March 19-1 50% of Duck plc's sales were on credit terms but that in the year ended 31st March 19-2 this proportion had dropped to 40%. Determine the average period for the collection of debts on each of the two years and comment.

17.4.4 For the year ended 31st March 19-1

$$\text{Collection period} = \frac{£44,000}{£500,000} \times 365$$
$$= 32.12 \text{ days}$$

For the year ended 31 st March 19-2

$$\text{Collection period} = \frac{£45,000}{£600,000} \times 365$$
$$= 27.38 \text{ days}$$

It can be seen that the average collection period has declined, pointing to a (slight) increase in the efficiency of collection.

17.4.5 Stock turnover is another important ratio having relevance to the management of working capital. It measures the rate at which stock moves through the business and is thus the inverse of the length of time that stores remain on hand. It is calculated as follows:

$$\text{Stock turnover} = \frac{\text{Cost of sales (materials component)}}{\text{Average stock}}$$

A very high stock turnover indicates a relatively low level of stocks and conversely slow moving stocks signify that they are high relative to usage.

17.4.6 Example. Determine the stock turnover for Duck, plc for the year ended 31st March 19-2 and comment.

17.4.7 We will take it that the average stock for the year is the average of its opening and closing values. This is:

$$\frac{£82,000 + £79,000}{2} = £80,500$$

Stock turnover is

$$\frac{£1,200,000}{£80,500} = 14.9 \text{ times per annum}$$

The validity of this calculation depends on the assumption that cost of sales is wholly the cost of materials drawn from stock. If it includes any amount for labour this would have to be excluded before the calculation was done. As with other ratios it is important to note that stock turnover is an average figure and may conceal important differences between one type of stock and another. It may, therefore, sometimes be useful to do separate calculations for stock turnover for different types of material.

17.5 Rate of Return on Capital

17.5.1 The rate of return on capital is sometimes regarded as the ultimate test of business success. It is calculated as follows:

$$\text{Rate of return} = \frac{\text{Net profit}}{\text{Average capital employed}} \times 100\%$$

Accounting technicalities make this a notoriously unreliable figure. Where the accounting statements are prepared on a consistent basis trends in the rate of return may be of some significance but, even then, its absolute level must be interpreted with extreme care. A greatly simplified example will indicate some of the pitfalls.

17.5.2 Example. Eggs, plc and Bacon, plc, each commenced in business on 1st January with identical physical resources identically financed. The balance sheet shown below thus applies equally to either of them:

Balance sheet at 1st January

Share capital	£100,000	Fixed assets		£80,000
Current liabilities	40,000	Stock		40,000
		Cash		20,000
	£140,000			£140,000

During the ensuing year each company experienced precisely the same trading conditions and entered into identical transactions. The accounting policies underlying the statements of their results were, however, different. Eggs charged its goods issued on a first in first out basis while Bacon used last in first out. Eggs depreciated its fixed assets on a straight line basis over four years while Bacon used the reducing balance method and a depreciation rate of 30%. Neither company paid a dividend during the year. Determine the indicated rate of return on capital in each case.

17.5.3 Summarised profit and loss accounts appear below:

Profit and loss accounts for the year ended 31st December

		Eggs		Bacon	
Sales			£120,000		£120,000
Less Cost of sales	£40,000			£43,000	
Other costs	32,000			32,000	
Depreciation	20,000		92,000	24,000	99,000
Net profit			£28,000		£21,000

The summarised balance sheets (in vertical form) are:

		Eggs		Bacon	
Fixed assets			£60,000		£56,000
Net current assets:					
Stock	£48,000			£45,000	
Cash	62,000			62,000	
	110,000			107,000	
Less Current liabilities	42,000		68,000	42,000	65,000
			£128,000		£121,000

Financed by:

	Eggs	Bacon
Share capital	£100,000	£100,000
Revenue reserve	28,000	21,000
	£128,000	£121,000

The rate of return can then be calculated:

	Eggs	Bacon
Average capital invested	£114,000	£110,500
Profit	£28,000	£21 000
Indicated rate of return	24.6%	19.0%

Thus, although identical to Bacon, Eggs is reported to be earning a higher rate of return on its capital.

Summary

(i) The relationship between figures is often of more significance than the absolute values of those figures. Many financial calculations, e.g. those relating to financial structure and to profitability, are based on this idea. Ratios computed from the financial accounts are just one more application of this principle.

(ii) Ratios must not be used blindly as they can mislead if too simply interpreted. In particular overall average ratios may conceal important detail and ratios based on conventional accounting valuations may be inappropriate where decisions involve entering the market have to be taken.

(iii) Some important ratios are:

(a) Gross profit rate. This is a measure of the effectiveness of the basic profit earning activity of the business.

(b) Ratio of administrative costs to sales. This is a measure of the efficiency of the business's administration.

(c) Current and liquidity ratios. These are tests of the short term solvency of the business.

(d) Collection period for debtors. This is a test of the efficiency of the credit control system.

(e) Stock turnover. This is a test of the efficiency of the stock control system.

(f) Rate of return on capital. This is often seen as the ultimate measure of business success as it purports to show the return which is being earned on the funds employed by the business. It has, however, perhaps a greater capacity to mislead than any other ratio.

Review questions

(i) *Your company has experienced a sharp fall in its rate of gross profit in the current year as compared with the previous one.*

List some of the possible causes of this and suggest appropriate action.

(ii) 'Administrative costs represent an unproductive burden on a business. They should be ruthlessly pruned and kept at a minimum possible level.' To what extent do you agree?

(iii) 'Return on capital employed is the ultimate test of business success.' What reservations would you have in supporting this view?

(iv) Your company has too low a current ratio. How would you expect this to make itself felt?

(v) Explain the calculation and the significance of the collection period for debtors.

(vi) Why are accounting ratios important to the financial manager?

(vii) A very high stock turnover leads to a minimum investment of funds in financing stock and a minimum cost in terms of storage charges. In what circumstances, therefore, could high stock turnover be a cause of anxiety?

(viii) A ratio sometimes calculated is the rate of turnover of fixed assets. It is the relationship between sales and the value of fixed assets. Of what significance would such a ratio be?

Exercises

1. Mr. Swann owns a small shop and it has been suggested to him that the time has come for him to retire. He could sell the shop and invest the proceeds in securities which it is expected would yield him 12% per annum. He points out that the latest annual accounts for the business reveal an invested capital of £100,000 and a profit for the year of £20,000. Thus it would appear that his investment in the shop is earning 20% per annum and ought not, therefore, to be disturbed. Can you throw more light on the situation. Use illustrative figures where these are helpful.

2. In what circumstances might management plan for a reduced gross profit rate? What factors could lead to an unplanned reduction?

3. To what extent is it true to say that a financial manager should keep an especially close watch on the current and liquidity ratios?

4. Your managing director, seeking economies which will improve the profitability of the business, has suggested that administrative costs should be brought down from their present level of

15% of sales to a figure of about half of this. Comment on the suggestion.

5.   The following figures and ratios are extracted from recent accounts of Moorhen, plc.

Sales for the year	£1,000,000
Gross profit rate	30%
Stock turnover	5
Collection period for debts	30 days

It is proposed to enter an entirely new market with a product which has not been handled by Moorhen before. This will lead to additional annual sales of £200,000 having a gross profit rate of 20%. Customers will expect 60 days credit and additional stocks of raw materials equal to three months' usage will be needed. Raw material costs, on existing products as with the new product account for 75% of all cost of sales. If the proposal is implemented how will it affect Moorhen's key ratios?

6.   The Chairman of Gander, plc announces the following at a meeting of the Board of Directors:

'*Our latest results look good and I am particularly pleased with the following improvements in key ratios*

(a)   *gross profit rate is up from 20% to 25%*

(b)   *collection period for debtors is down from 38 days to 29 days*

(c)   *administrative costs to sales is down from 10% to 7%*

(d)   *the rate of return on capital is up from 8% to 9%* '

What reservations would you have about judging these figures as favourable signs and what other information would you seek before doing so?

18: Stock Market Investment

18.1 Investment in Securities

18.1.1 So far we have been looking at things from the point of view of the financial manager within a productive business who has to make decisions about where to raise finance and how to deploy it. In this chapter we are going to look at things, as it were, from the other side of the window in order to see how a provider of finance, and in particular an equity investor, is led to his decision as to where he will place his funds.

18.1.2 The importance of doing so is two-fold. First of all it will clearly be helpful to a financial manager if he knows something of the impulses which govern the providers of his funds. This will enable him, when he wishes to attract finance, to strike a fair balance between making unattractive and therefore unsuccessful offers and making ones which are attractive but unnecessarily expensive. Secondly, in certain kinds of commercial activity the financial manager will himself be investing in securities rather than in directly productive assets and he will need to know how to evaluate the opportunities which are available to him. Examples of this kind of business are given by life assurance companies, investment trusts and unit trusts.

18.1.3 Before embarking on our analysis we must state a warning. The stock market performs a serious and vital function in the finance of the nation's economic machine. Nevertheless it has gathered about itself an aura of mystery and excitement which draws something from the casino, the racetrack and Aladdin's cave. This makes it a highly emotional place and investors' emotions, not always rational, can have a substantial impact on what occurs there, especially in the short term. Post-holiday depression can lop as much off prices as can the resignation of a cabinet minister. Bad news can sometimes perversely boost prices as an expression of relief that it is no worse. This means that the whole market is permeated with rumour, with theory and with tribal ritual in praise of the gods. Every theory about the future course of stock market prices can be proved right and every theory can be proved wrong. Our warning, therefore, is that however apparently scientific our analysis might be, it will never guarantee success in the investment process and, indeed, more cynical observers would believe with some justification that it will do no more than give us the confidence to make our mistakes the more boldly.

18.2 Fundamental Analysis

18.2.1 One very important school of thought on the investment appraisal scene is that of fundamental analysis. The essence of this idea is that every business has an intrinsic long term worth quite apart from any transitory value that is placed on it currently by the market. This worth is as much an inherent part of the company as is a person's intelligence or an engine's horse-power. It is further believed that this intrinsic value can be discovered by an assembly and analysis of financial information about that specific company derived from its annual accounts. Where the intrinsic value of the business appears to be above the current market value of the shares, this is to be taken to be a signal to buy the shares and, where it is below, a signal either not to buy or, if already held, to sell.

18.2.2 For fundamental analysis to work successfully requires the truth of a number of assumptions. These are:

(a) That a business has an intrinsic value;

(b) that this can be determined by analysis of company generated data;

(c) that this value may go unrecognised by the market in the short term;

(d) that it will eventually be recognised by the market in the long term.

18.2.3 Let us now look at some of the ratios which a fundamental analyst might calculate and the interpretation which we could expect him to place upon them.

Earnings per share. This is a somewhat special ratio in that it has been given 'official' recognition in an Accounting Standard, SSAP 3, as amended by FRS 3. This means that it has to be calculated on a consistent basis by the company itself and quoted in its annual report. The definition of EPS given in that standard is: 'The profit in pence attributable to each equity share, based on the profit of the period after tax, minority interest and extraordinary items and after deducting preference dividends and other appropriations in respect of preference shares, divided by the number of equity shares in issue and ranking for dividend in respect of the period.'

18.2.4 Example. X, plc has equity share capital ranking for dividend consisting of 250,000 ordinary shares of £1 each. Its after-tax profits available to equity holders total £125,000. What is the figure for earnings per share?

$$\text{EPS} = \frac{\text{Net earnings}}{\text{No. of ordinary shares ranking for dividend}}$$

$$= \frac{£125,000}{250,000}$$

$$= \underline{\underline{50p}}$$

Note that the amount of the dividend, i.e. that part of earnings which happens to be distributed, is irrelevant in calculating earnings per share.

18.2.5 SSAP 3 also introduces the important concept of 'fully diluted earnings per share'. Current holders of shares ranking for dividend are the only ones entitled to a share in the current profit. There may, however, exist other people who will or may come to share in profits in the future. These are:

(a) holders of shares (perhaps newly issued) not ranking for dividend currently but to do so in the future,

(b) holders of convertible debentures which may become shares if the option to convert is exercised,

(c) holders of warrants or options giving the right to acquire shares.

Where any of these exist the value of EPS calculated on the existing capital may be misleading. In these circumstances the Standard requires that both EPS and fully diluted EPS (i.e. taking into account both actual and potential share capital) are stated.

18.2.6 Example. X, plc of our previous example had made a rights issue on a one for ten basis immediately before its year end. These shares did not rank for dividend until the following year. Determine the fully diluted EPS.

18.2.7 Fully diluted EPS is determined as follows:

$$\text{fd EPS} = \frac{\text{Net earnings}}{\text{Total number of shares}}$$

$$= \frac{£125,000}{250,000 + 25,000}$$

$$= \underline{\underline{45.45p}}$$

18.2.8 Price earnings ratio. Obviously as to whether a particular absolute level of earnings is attractive or not depends on how much has to be invested in order to obtain it. The price earnings ratio merely demonstrates this relationship. It has to be calculated by the analyst himself as the company will not publish it. Indeed it is rare anywhere in its annual report for a company to make any explicit reference to the market price of its shares. The ratio is merely the market price of a share divided by the earnings attributable to it.

18.2.9 Example. X's shares stand at £4.50 each in the market. What is the price earnings ratio?

$$P/E = \frac{\text{Market price of one ordinary share}}{\text{EPS}}$$

$$= \frac{£4.50}{50p}$$

$$= \underline{\underline{9}}$$

A high earnings ratio indicates prima facie an expensive share but may, of course, be an expression of market confidence in the company's expansion potential or of its susceptibility to an attractive take over offer. It need by no means necessarily imply that it would be a bad buy. P/E ratios of 20 or 30 are not uncommon even though this implies a very low rate of immediate return on the investment.

18.2.10 Earnings yield. This is merely the inverse of the price earnings ratio. It is, however, sometimes calculated by the analyst as it gives rise to a figure which is more in line with what is normally understood as a rate of return on an investment.

18.2.11 Example. What is the earnings yield of X, plc?

$$\text{Earnings yield} = \frac{\text{Dividend}}{\text{Share price}} \times 100$$

$$= \frac{50p}{£4.50} \times 100$$

$$= \underline{\underline{11.1\%}}$$

18.2.12 Dividend yield. The ratios we have referred to so far all relate to the amount which a company *earns* for its equity holders during a year. They say nothing about the amount which he actually *receives*. This is, effectively, at the discretion of the directors and will range between zero and the full amount of the earnings. The dividend yield, then, gives the actual cash received by the investor as a rate of return on his investment.

18.2.13 Example. X, plc pays a dividend totalling 25p per £1 share. What is the dividend yield?

$$\text{Dividend yield} = \frac{\text{Dividend}}{\text{Share price}} \times 100$$

$$= \frac{50p}{£4.50} \times 100$$

$$= \underline{\underline{5.6\%}}$$

Note that the dividend yield is not the same as the rate of dividend declared by the company. X, plc would state that it was paying a dividend of 25%, i.e. relating the payment to the nominal value of the shares. Dividend yield relates it to the market value.

18.2.14 Dividend cover. This is a measure derived from others we have calculated. It states how many times over the actual dividend could have been paid from the available profits and it is regarded as a measure of how secure a dividend is, i.e. how likely it is to be maintainable in the future.

18.2.15 Example. What is the dividend cover for X, plc?

$$\text{Dividend cover} = \frac{\text{EPS}}{\text{Dividend per share}}$$

$$= \frac{50p}{25p}$$

$$= \underline{\underline{2}}$$

Obviously a dividend twice covered is relatively safe. Profits would have to fall by one half in future years before they failed to cover the present rate of dividend and, moreover, the company is currently putting to reserve enough to pay the dividend for one further year even in the complete absence of profits. Dividend cover and interest cover are sometimes also calculated for preference shares and debentures respectively. They are inevitably much higher than for equity, perhaps even 25-50 times covered, reflecting the very considerable security of income given by these investments. Equity dividend cover may sometimes be fractional (i.e. less than one). This implies that current earnings fall short of dividends and are being supplemented from accumulated reserves. This situation cannot persist indefinitely.

18.2.16 Gearing. We have discussed elsewhere the financial risk which may be caused by gearing (the partial use of debt for financing) and that a measure of gearing can easily be calculated. It is a ratio which the fundamental analyst may wish to compute from a company's balance sheet. In investment analysis, however, it is normally done in terms of nominal value where, in our discussion on the cost of capital, we have used market value.

18.2.17 Example. X plc, in addition to its ordinary shares referred to above, has in issue 100,000 preference shares of 50p each and debentures to a nominal value of £75,000. It also has reserves totalling £50,000. What is its gearing?

$$\text{Gearing} = \frac{\text{Nominal value of loan capital}[1]}{\text{Nominal value of loan capital} + \text{Nominal value of equity}[2]}$$

$$= \frac{£125}{£425,000}$$

$$= \underline{\underline{5.6\%}}$$

[1]including preference capital

[2]including reserves

18.2.18 Asset cover. This quantity is often calculated by the fundamental analyst in an attempt to find the intrinsic worth of the business. It appears to be based on the view that value depends on what is there – the potential tied up in assets – as much as on the actual results of its current use which income derived measures highlight. It is determined quite simply by dividing net assets (i.e. equity capital plus reserves) by the number of equity shares in issue.

18.2.19 Example. Y, plc has an issued ordinary share capital of 500,000 shares of £1 each. It also has revenue reserves totalling £300,000 and a capital reserve of £80,000. What is its asset cover?

$$\text{Asset cover} = \frac{\text{Net assets*}}{\text{Number of ordinary shares}}$$

$$= \frac{£880,000}{500,000}$$

$$= \underline{\underline{£1.76 \text{ per share}}}$$

*£500,000 + £300,000 + £80,000

If the market price of the shares is below £1.76 each the inference is that the investor is buying the underlying assets at a bargain price. The logical weakness of this is that the valuation derives from the balance sheet values of the assets. These are usually cost based and need bear no relationship to the current realizable value. In any case a minority shareholder has no means of realising the value. It is locked in and can manifest itself only through whatever it is capable of earning. There are, however, some who would argue that if the value exists it must eventually be recognised by one means or another in the stock market price.

Living proof of the fallacy of this is given by investment trusts (see 4.9) which, historically, have permanently maintained a share price below the value of their net assets. This is despite the fact that those assets consist largely of quoted securities and are thus highly realisable and readily valued.

18.3 The Valuation of Business and of Securities

18.3.1 The ratios discussed in the previous section may be seen as a useful framework within which published accounting information may be considered. They do not, however, lead directly to computations of value which the theory underlying fundamental analysis requires. The valuation of a business or of a marketable security follows the same general principle as the valuation of an individual asset. The present value, that is to say, is the discounted value of the expected future returns.

18.3.2 There are special difficulties involved in the valuation of a business by someone who is outside it and who has no control over it. Some of these are:

(a) it is difficult to estimate future returns because of limited access to information and because this depends on managerial activity over which he has no control;

(b) the life of the business is, normally, indefinite whereas the life of an individual productive asset is relatively short;

(c) the appropriate discount rate, which must allow for risk, is not easy to determine.

18.3.3 The problems are overcome by making general assumptions, based on observations of past trends and existing conditions, and by placing some reasonable time horizon on predictions. The valuation of a business determined in this way will normally exceed the apparent value of the assets as shown by the balance sheet. The difference between the two is often described as 'goodwill' which may be a valuable measure of the business's success as a going concern. It should be treated with some reservation, however, unless there is confidence in the balance sheet valuations of tangible assets.

18.3.4 Example. Fortune, plc, a business manufacturing board games, has the balance sheet which is summarised below:

Fortune, plc

Summarised balance sheet at 31st December 19xx

	£000's		£000's
Share capital	1,000	Fixed assets	1,320
Reserves	520	Current assets	490
Current liabilities	290		
	1,810		1,810

Predicted profits for the years following the balance sheet date are also available:

Years	1	2	3	4	5	6 and onwards*
Profit (£000's)	186	192	205	220	240	250

*Beyond five years no progression or fluctuations in profit can be forecast. A steady annual profit of £250,000 is the best estimate which can be given.

An appropriate rate of return on investment in a business of the type conducted by Fortune is 12% per annum. Determine the value of the business and hence of its goodwill. Ignore taxation.

18.3.5 It should be noted that in this example a time horizon has been placed on predictions at five years in the sense that no attempt at accurate prediction is made thereafter. The time horizon is, however, infinite in the sense that the business is regarded as having an indefinite life. This can be dealt with analytically by placing a value on the business in this steady state at year 5 and then discounting that, along with the cash returns, at the appropriate rate.

Thus value at year 5 is $£250,000 \times \dfrac{100}{12} = £2,083,333$

Discounting all returns gives a valuation as follows:

Year £000's	Profit 12%	Discount factor £000's	Present value £000's
1	186	.893	166
2	192	.797	153
3	205	.712	146
4	220	.636	140
5	240+2,083	.567	1,317
			1,922

Thus the business is valued at	£1,922,000
The balance sheet value of net assets is	1,520,000
The value ascribed to goodwill is, therefore	£402,000

18.3.6   Valuation of shares. The valuation of shares in a company is based on the same principles as the valuation of the business itself, i.e. of discounting future returns. It might be thought, therefore, that having valued the business the value of the shares is a pro rata part of that figure. This is not necessarily the case, however, for a package of shares not large enough to confer control. This is because neither dividend policy nor the employment of retained earnings can be determined by the shareholder. Another factor is that an investor in shares is not the purchaser of a business and does not necessarily, therefore, have the same required rate of return.

18.3.7   Example. Fortune's shares currently stand in the market at £1.20 each. The most recent dividend paid by the company was 10p per share (again ignore taxation). Predicted dividends for the next five years are:

Year	1	2	3	4	5
Dividend per share	10p	11p	11p	12p	12p

At the end of year 5 the share is expected to have a market value 15% above its present level. An investor has a required rate of return of 10% per annum and wishes to determine the value of the share to him.

18.3.8 Future cash flows, including the terminal value of the share are discounted as shown below:

Year	Cash now	Discount factor(10%)	Present value
1	10p	.909	9.09p
2	11p	.826	9.09p
3	11p	.751	8.26p
4	12p	.683	8.20p
5	12p+ £1.38	.621	93.15p
			127.79p

The value of the share is thus £1.28 (rounded) and a purchase at the present price of £1.20 would appear to be indicated.

18.3.9   Dividend valuation model. An investor in shares may be as interested in the prospect of capital gains as in dividend income. There is a model for evaluating shares based on predictions of both dividends and growth in capital value. The formula is:

$$V = \frac{D\,(1+g)}{r-g}$$

where   V = value of share

D = current dividend

g = growth

r = cost of capital

18.3.10 Example. The shares of Y, plc currently stand at £1.20 each. The latest dividends totalled 2.5p per share for the full year and the company is expected to grow at the rate of 10% per annum for the foreseeable future. Determine whether an investor having a cost of capital of 12% per annum should buy the shares.

18.3.11
$$V = \frac{D(1+g)}{r-g}$$

$$= \frac{2.5p\,(1+.10)}{.12-.10}$$

$$= \frac{2.75p}{.02}$$

$$= £1.375$$

At £1.20 the shares would appear to be a buy.

18.3.12 Valuation of debentures. The valuation of debentures is a quite different process from the valuation of shares. Debentures are, to all intents and purposes, risk free investments and their value is therefore largely determined by prevailing rates of interest. A calculated value, such as shown below, is likely to be very close to the market value and is rarely of any particular help in a buy-or-sell decision.

18.3.13 Example. Alert, plc has in issue two debentures. It is a strong company with a good profit record. The debentures are:

(i) $5\frac{1}{2}\%$ irredeemable debentures

(ii) 7% debentures redeemable in four years' time at par.

The current market rate of interest on investments of this kind is 9% per annum. What are the values of the two debentures?

18.3.14 Debentures are quoted at a value per £100 nominal stock. Hence the value of the $5\frac{1}{2}\%$ irredeemable debenture is

$$\frac{5\frac{1}{2}}{9} \times 100 = £61.11$$

The value of the 7% debenture must be determined by discounting because of the cash repayment after four years. Thus:

Year	Cash now	Discount factor	Present value
	£	9%	£
1	7	.917	6.42
2	7	.842	5.89
3	7	.772	5.40
4	107	.708	75.76
			93.47

The debenture is valued at £93.47

18.4 Market Analysis

18.4.1 We turn now to the other main idea underlying security investment appraisal. This is that taken by those we will term the market analysts. Their view is that whatever the accounts of a company reveal about the business, the value of its shares, in the case of a quoted company, depends on the interplay of market forces. If fundamental analysis seems to indicate that a share is worth, say, £1.50, this is of no significance at all, say the market analysts, if the market price is, say, £1.25. This would not, to them, imply that the shares were cheap and should be bought but rather that fundamental analysis was wrong and should be disregarded. The market price represents a consensus view. The information contained in a company's accounts will have contributed to the formation of this view but so will many other factors, including an assessment of the general economic situation.

18.4.2 How then do market analysts make their investment decisions? If market prices are always fair then there would appear to be no decision to make. Every investment is an equally good buy. The view is, however, that the market assessment is constantly changing and that there is a somewhat ponderous adjustment by the market to a new situation. Thus trends of price movements are constantly being established.

The investor should aim to buy his shares early in a rise and sell early in a fall.

18.4.3 A highly specialised form of market analysis is that practised by those known as chartists. Share price movements are carefully graphed and it is claimed that patterns can be discerned which give a pointer to emergent trends which can thus be predicted.

Some of these rely on the existence of so-called 'resistance levels'. These are the upper and lower bounds of the movements of a share price set by investors' present attitude to the shares. The breach of a resistance level indicates a change in that attitude and is, therefore, a predictor of a substantial movement of the share price either upwards or downwards depending on the direction of the breach. This is illustrated in figure 18.1 where a breach in the lower resistance level occurs at time A and a chartist would then predict a major downward re-evaluation of the share.

Other shapes are also looked for by chartists. Figure 18.2 shows a 'head and shoulders' formation which would be taken to indicate a reversal of a previously rising trend in the share price. Figure 18.3 illustrates a convergence of resistance levels. The share price must break out of this in one direction or another where the lines meet.

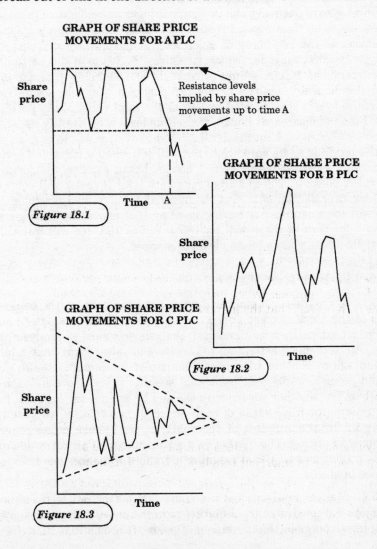

GRAPH OF SHARE PRICE MOVEMENTS FOR A PLC

Share price

Resistance levels implied by share price movements up to time A

Time   A

Figure 18.1

GRAPH OF SHARE PRICE MOVEMENTS FOR B PLC

Share price

Time

Figure 18.2

GRAPH OF SHARE PRICE MOVEMENTS FOR C PLC

Share price

Time

Figure 18.3

18.4.4 Mechanical trading systems have been devised which rely for their success on the idea that the market makes major movements in one direction or another with, superimposed on these, smaller movements which sometimes go against the major trend and sometimes reinforce it. The trick of successful investment is to buy a share (or portfolio of shares) before a major upward movement and to sell it before a major fall without being diverted from this either by selling on a minor retrenchment in a major upward movement or buying on a minor reversal of a long term downward movement.

A typical system might select a 'filter' of 10%. Price movements within 10% are deemed to be insignificant and movements of greater than this to be significant. Investment is made in a certain portfolio of shares at the beginning of a predicted major upward movement. Let us say that an index which measures the value of the portfolio then stands at 100. A selling price is set at 10% below this, i.e. 90 and should the index reach this the portfolio would be sold. The potential loss is thus limited to 10% of the total value of the portfolio. If the index rises, as hoped, the selling level is constantly revised to be 10% below each successive 'high'. The investor will thus remain in the portfolio as its value rises but will sell when a major fall (evidenced by a greater than 10% fall) occurs. Let us say that the portfolio index peaks at 200 and then falls back. Our investor will sell at 180 (an overall gain of 80% of the original value of his investment). He will then establish a buying level at 10% above the successive 'lows'. The first of these will be 180 + 10% = 198. He will buy the portfolio again when a buying level is reached.

18.5 The Efficient Market

18.5.1 A great deal of empirical work has been done on the behaviour of the stock market and much evidence has been amassed to suggest that neither fundamental analysis nor market analysis is likely to be of much assistance to investors in gaining any particular advantage over other investors. The use of fundamental analysis would seem to imply that individual security prices move independently of one another governed in the end by a tendency to revert to the unique intrinsic value of each share. It can readily be shown, however, by the simplest of observations, that share prices move strongly in unison. The market as a whole moves either up or down. It is on this basis only that meaningful indices of market movements can be produced.

18.5.2 Market analysis has not come any better out of research findings. Although a chart of market movements will appear to show long term trends in the movement of prices, it seems that these can be observed only with hindsight and that the establishment or continuance of a trend cannot be predicted. There is strong evidence for the so-called random walk theory of stock market movements. This states quite simply that movements are random and, therefore, unpredictable. In any historical random series coincidences can be discovered or patterns imputed after the event if one wishes to do so but that does not imply that these could have been forecast.

18.5.3 The implication of all of this is that the stock market is what is known as an 'efficient market'. This is a technical term and implies that the market assimilates and responds to new information so rapidly that there is no source of information which will enable an individual investor to gain a permanent advantage over his fellows.

18.5.4 There are three forms of the efficient market theory. These sometimes form the subject of examination questions and should, therefore, be known. They are:

(a) The 'weak' form. This states that all the information conveyed by past movements of the market has been incorporated into the current market price. No other information has been taken into account. Under this form of the theory a chartist cannot predict the future course of a share's price but a fundamental analyst might be able to do so.

(b) The 'semi-strong' form. This states that the current market price for a security has been determined by a market which has assimilated all publicly available information. This will include information about the course of previous market movements but will also include company generated information such as that given in its annual accounts and information about the general state of the economy and other matters. If the market is semi-strong efficient neither a chartist nor a fundamental analyst can make more than normal profit from share dealing activities but an insider, having access to confidential information might do so.

(c) The 'strong' form. This states that all information, whether public or private, has been taken into account in determining market prices. This would imply that even insider dealing will be unable to achieve a more than normal reward.

18.5.5 It seems highly likely, though it is difficult fully to test, that, in fact, the market is semi-strong efficient. It is in this belief that insider trading has been made a criminal offence on the ground that this involves taking unfair advantage of privileged information. On the assumption that no insider dealing takes place no private information could come to the attention of the market and the semi-strong form of market efficiency would be reinforced.

Summary

(i) Stock market investment analysis is of interest to a financial manager:

    (a) because it gives an insight into the thinking of the providers of finance and;

    (b) because it may contribute to some investment decisions which he himself must make.

(ii) The stock market is not ruled by scientific laws but by the actions of human beings. These are capable of being motivated by emotion just as much as by a rational assessment of reality. No precise guides for action which will guarantee success can, therefore, be given.

(iii) One very important school of thought on investment appraisal is that of the fundamental analyst. He believes that every business has an intrinsic value which can be determined by an informed consideration of its accounts and of ratios derived from them. It is implicit in fundamental analysis that the market valuation of a security will sometimes stray from this intrinsic value but that over time it will tend to revert to it.

(iv) Important quantities calculated by the fundamental analysis are:

    (a) Earnings per share

    (b) Price earnings ratio

    (c) Earnings yield

    (d) Dividend yield

    (e) Dividend cover

    (f) Gearing

    (g) Asset cover

(v) The actual valuation of businesses and of securities is done by discounting expected future cash flows at an appropriate rate.

(vi) Another important school of thought is that of the market analyst. The underlying idea here is that the value of a security can be determined only by the market which, in consequence, is always 'right'. Because market adjustments take place over a considerable period of time the market analyst believes that long term trends develop and that these can be predicted.

(vii) Research suggests that the stock market is an efficient market. This means that it absorbs and responds to new information very rapidly. The implication of this is that neither fundamental analysis nor market analysis would give an investor any advantage over his contemporaries. Stock market movements follow a 'random walk' and cannot be predicted.

Review questions

(i) *'A careful study of accounts will enable the stock market investor to make profitable decisions.' To what extent is this true and what does it imply?*

(ii) *In what way is 'Earnings per Share' a more useful measure of the value of an investment in a company than 'Dividend Yield'?*

(iii) *Distinguish between 'fundamental analysis' and 'market analysis'.*

(iv) *The price earnings ratio for Company Y is double that for Company X. What might this imply?*

(v) *It is believed by some that asset cover is the ultimate test of the value of a share. Explain this view and present arguments to refute it.*

(vi) *Why is it impossible to predict the future movements of an efficient market?*

(vii) *'The random walk hypothesis implies that no investor can make long term capital gains.' Is this a fair statement?*

(viii) *'Share prices are based more on emotional reactions than they are on a hard-headed assessment of business prospects.' Discuss.*

Exercises

1. *The following information is taken from the accounts of Rainyday, for last year:*

Issued share capital

    1,000,000 ordinary shares of £1 each, fully paid

Issued loan capital

    £250,000 10% debentures

Reserves

Capital	£200,000
Revenue	£800,000

Profit and distribution

Profit for the year   £600,000 (after tax but before dividends
or interest)

Ordinary dividend   20%

*You are also told that the current market price of Rainyday's
ordinary shares is £3.20 each and of its debentures is £90 per
cent.*

*Calculate some ratios which are likely to be of interest to an
investor or potential investor in Rainyday. Comment on each.*

2. *A well-known automatic system for profiting from stock market
movements operates as follows. The value of an index of share
prices is plotted day by day until it rises to a value which is 10%
above a previously recorded record low. A portfolio of shares is
then purchased and held until the index falls 10% below its subsequent record high. The intention is that an investor will be 'in'
shares during a rising market and 'out' of shares during a
falling market.*

*In a certain year the share index fell to 228 and then subse-
quently rose to 389 before falling again to 250. How much would
an investor operating the system with a capital of £1,000 have
made? (Ignore dealing costs and taxation). On what theory of
investment is the system based? Would you expect it, in the long
run, to succeed?*

3. *How is it helpful to the financial manager with a manufacturing concern to understand how investors appraise securities?*

4. *'The £1 ordinary shares are a bargain at their current price of
90p. Asset cover is in excess of £2 per share.' (Comment in an
investment journal on a company in whose shares you are interested.) What is meant by 'asset cover'? Do you agree with the
interpretation?*

5. *The following figures have been extracted from the annual
accounts of Umbrella. Calculate some ratios likely to be of interest to a shareholder.*

Share capital	£5,000,000
Reserves	£1,200,000
Loan capital	£1,200,000
Profit after tax and loan interest	£550,000
Dividend	£300,000

The current market price of the shares is £1.50 each.

6. *Define briefly the following terms and indicate their value in fundamental analysis:*

(a) *Earnings per share*

(b) *Price earnings ratio*

(c) *Earnings yield*

(d) *Dividend yield*

(e) *Dividend cover*

(f) *Gearing*

19: Mergers and Take-Overs

19.1 The Process of Merger

19.1.1   A merger is the result of a process whereby two or more previously autonomous concerns come under common control. It is a regular feature of the world of corporate business operations. The process would normally be described as a takeover if the party initiating it were much larger or more powerful than the other party. Mergers have important implications in a number of subject areas, economics, law and financial accounting being the most obvious. Here we are going to consider purely the financial management implications. Thus it will not be our concern that mergers reduce competition and perhaps concentrate an undesirable degree of power. Nor shall we give any attention to the details of consolidated accounts. We shall be concerned with the financial decision making process which leads a company to decide on a merger, to determine the terms on which it should be carried through and to plan how it should be financed.

19.1.2   There are frequently commercial advantages in sheer size. Some of these are:

(a) **Economies of scale:** large scale production may lead to lower unit costs than small scale production.

(b) **Monopoly power:** large firms have a greater degree of market influence than small.

(c) **Risk reduction:** size gives the opportunity for rational diversification to reduce risk.

(d) **Lower cost of capital:** a big 'name', perceived by investors as financially well-based, may raise funds at lower cost than a lesser known concern.

19.1.3   Size can be achieved by a policy of growth from within and this may lead to all the advantages mentioned above. It is, however, quite commonly achieved by a process of merger. We might refer to this as 'external' growth in distinction to 'internal' growth. It will be helpful to list some of the reasons why it might be preferred.

(a) **Financing:** Growth requires financing, either from internally generated funds or from externally raised debt or equity. A merger can often be arranged whereby the existing finance of an acquired company is retained. Its shareholders become shareholders in the enlarged concern and its lenders continue their loan. This is a cheap and certain way of obtaining finance.

(b) **Speed:** Growth is obviously achieved much more rapidly by means of a merger than by any other means. The advantages of size can thus be gained more quickly.

(c) **Risk reduction:** The driving force behind growth is, as indicated above, very often a desire to reduce risk, e.g. by diversification. There are, however, considerable risks attached to the actual process of growth particularly if this requires expansion into areas in which management has no experience. Expansion by the acquisition of an established business with a proved record may be much less risky.

(d) **The existence of an exploitable situation:** The business to be taken over may have badly utilized assets, e.g. idle land ripe for development, patents for a good product badly marketed or idle cash reserves. The management of the merging concern may see opportunities which it can exploit and to which it could gain access in no other way.

(e) **Competitive considerations:** A company may wish to undertake a merger in order to prevent this from being done by a rival. Regardless of any other benefits which the merger might confer, it may be justifiable if it prevents a competitor from gaining a particularly dominant position.

19.1.4 There are technically several ways in which a merger can take place although they are not all equally well-used in practice. If A, plc has decided that its business can profitably be combined with that of B, plc, it can:

(a) buy the *assets* of B for cash. B would then be wound up and its shareholders would receive the proceeds.

(b) buy the *shares* of B for cash. This has much the same implications as (a) for the existing shareholders of B but B retains its legal identity which, if it has a well-known name, may be valuable.

(c) acquire the shares of B, by exchanging for them, on an agreed basis, new shares of its own. The previous shareholders of B then become shareholders in A.

(d) form a holding company, e.g. C, to issue its own shares in exchange for the shares of both A and B. All existing shareholders of both companies then become shareholders in C.

Some mixture of methods might be used, e.g. acquisition of shares partly on an exchange basis and partly for cash. Probably (c) is the commonest form of merger and it will be used to illustrate our examples.

19.2 Financial Basis for Mergers

19.2.1 A basic requirement for any transaction is that, to secure agreement, it must be, or seem to be, of advantage to both sides. Let us look at an example with that point in mind.

19.2.2 Example. A, plc and B, plc have balance sheets as set out below. A is proposing to take over B by means of an issue of its own shares in exchange for those of B and has to decide on the terms of its offer.

	A, plc £	B, plc £
Ordinary share capital (£1 shares)	1,000,000	500,000
Preference share capital	200,000	
Share premium account		20,000
Profit and loss account	380,000	40,000
10% Debentures	150,000	50,000
	£1,730,000	£610,000
Fixed assets	1,220,000	350,000
Net current assets	510,000	260,000
	£1,730,000	£610,000

Other information concerning the two companies is as follows:

	A, plc	B, plc
Maintainable annual profit after tax attributable to equity	£240,000	£150,000
Current market price of ordinary share	£2.40	£2.70
Current EPS	24p	30p
(Hence) P/E ratio	10	9
Current market price of debentures	£125%	£125%

What offer should the directors of A make to the shareholders of B?

19.2.3 We can see something of the complexity of the problem if we consider some of the bases on which A might determine its offer. We shall initially assume that the merger makes no difference to the position or prospects of either company. There is also a presumption that the shareholders of each company wish to be as well off after the merger as they were before.

19.2.4 (a) **Net asset value**

$$\text{Net asset value} = \frac{\text{Value attributable to equity}}{\text{Number of ordinary shares}}$$

$$\text{NAV for A} \quad = \quad \frac{£1,380,000}{1,000,000}$$

$$= £1.38$$

$$\text{NAV for B} \quad = \quad \frac{£1,380,000}{1,000,000}$$

$$= £1.12$$

For the net asset value to be preserved for all members of the enlarged A, whether currently they are shareholders in A or in B, requires A to issue 112 of its own shares in exchange for every 138 of those in B which it acquires. If it makes a more generous offer than this then its existing shareholders will see their net asset value decline and, if less generous, then this will occur for the existing shareholders in B.

To acquire the whole of the issued share capital of B, A should issue

$$\frac{500,000}{138} \times 112 = 405,797 \text{ new £1 shares.}$$

19.2.5 (b) Earnings per share

$$\text{Earnings per share} = \frac{\text{Total earnings attributable to equity}}{\text{Number of shares}}$$

$$\text{EPS for A} \quad = \quad \frac{£240,000}{1,000,000}$$

$$= 24p$$

$$\text{EPS for B} \quad = \quad \frac{£150,000}{500,000}$$

$$= 30p$$

The fair terms on this basis, i.e. those which preserve the EPS attributable to all parties, are 30 new shares in A for 24 existing shares in B. This leads to a total issue of:

$$\frac{500,000}{24} \times 30 = 625,000 \text{ new £1 shares.}$$

It will be noted that this basis is quite different from the one calculated in the previous paragraph. It is not, therefore (except in very unusual circumstances), possible to devise a basis for the share exchange which maintains the shareholders' existing entitlements in all its aspects.

19.2.6 (c) Market value

The current market price of A's shares is £2.40 and of B's shares is £2.70. To maintain the market value of any individual's holding (still assuming, of course, that the combined market value of the two companies is unaffected by the merger) A should issue 9 new shares for each 8 of B's shares (270 for 240 simplified). The total number to be issued is:

$$\frac{500,000 \times 9}{8} = 562,500 \text{ new £1 shares}$$

19.2.7 (d) Financial analysis

A's current cost of equity (assuming no expected growth) is:

$$\frac{\text{Maintainable annual profit}}{\text{Market value of equity}} = \frac{£240,000}{£2,400,000}$$

$$= 8\% \text{ per annum}$$

A's current cost of debt is

$$\text{Coupon rate} \times \frac{\text{Nominal value}}{\text{Market value}} = 10\% \times \frac{£150,000}{.0965}$$

$$= 8\% \text{ per annum}$$

The after tax cost of debt is therefore 5.2% per annum.

A's weighted average cost of capital is:

$$\frac{10 \times £2,400,000 + (5.2 \times £187,500)}{£2,587,000} = 9.65\% \text{ per annum}$$

The most that A would be prepared to pay for B for this to be an acceptable 'project' under conventional capital project appraisal methods would be:

$$\frac{\text{Earnings of B}}{\text{Cost of capital}} = \frac{£150,000}{.0965}$$

$$= £1,554,404$$

This implies issuing $\dfrac{£1,554,404}{£2.40}$ = 647,668 new shares in A for the

equity in B, i.e. an offer of about 130 new shares in A for 100 shares in B.

19.2.8 It would seem from all this that it is almost anybody's guess what the terms of a takeover offer will be and, again, almost anybody's guess as to whether an offer is fair. To some extent this is true but we have somewhat stronger guidelines in practice than might seem apparent at the moment.

19.3 Synergy

19.3.1 A very important point that we have so far disregarded is that of any advantages which will flow from the merger as such. We have made our calculations on the assumption that the financial parameters of the combine are merely the sums of those for A and B considered separately. If this were really true there would be no advantage in the merger and therefore no justification for it. It would not warrant the cost of arranging it. In a real life situation we would expect to find that the conglomerate formed by the merger was greater than the sum of its parts. This is a phenomenon known as synergy. The synergistic effect may be so considerable that there are obvious large benefits to be obtained by both parties to the merger and there is merely the question of how to apportion them. In the last resort this is a matter of bargaining rather than of the strict application of rules. In the real world this finds reflection in the not-uncommon rejection of an initial take-over bid followed by an improved offer from the prospective acquiring company. If a second buyer enters the market bidding may become brisk and even reckless. Nevertheless, insofar as the synergistic effects are recognised in the financial parameters, we can apply some logical analysis to the situation.

19.3.2 Example. The following expectations are held about the prospective combine to be formed when A takes over B:

Group earnings attributable to equity	£448,500 (i.e. about 15% higher to than merely A + B)
P/E ratio	12 (representing risk reduction and consequent adjustment to the cost of capital)

Hence the market value of A's shares after the merger is

$$12 \times £448,500 = £5,382,000$$

Which exceeds the current market value of A plus that of B by £1,632,000 (over 30% up). Obviously there is great scope here for an offer with advantage to both sides.

A might, for instance, offer 1 new share of its own for every existing share in B (a one-for-one offer). Its own members would then see the market value of their shares rise from a current £2.40 per share to

$$\frac{448,500 \times 12}{1,500,000} = £3.59 \text{ per share}$$

and current shareholders in B would be receiving, in effect, this price for shares having a current value of £1.70.

19.3.3 Examination questions on mergers are rarely susceptible to cut-and-dried solutions and this reflects, as we have tried to show, the real life situation. If a person were purchasing a house the price paid may be as much dependent on the persuasiveness of the estate agent or on how desperate to sell is the vendor as it is on an objective assessment of the characteristics of the property. Similarly takeover terms are, in the ultimate, determined by the bargaining power and the expectations of the parties to it. This is evidenced by the substantial improvement in the initial offer which is often made where a takeover bid is contested by others or opposed by the directors of the company for which the offer is made. Accounting information may help us to analyse the situation more fully but will usually, in the end, provide merely a range within which bargaining will take place. One must be prepared, therefore, to put forward proposals and to support them with arguments reasonably supported (but not necessarily confirmed by) the available data.

Summary

(i)   A merger is said to occur when two or more formerly independent concerns come under common control. It is a regular feature of the business world.

(ii) The explanation for the occurrence of mergers is twofold. There are frequently commercial advantages in sheer size so that businesses are encouraged to grow. Some of the more important advantages are:

(a) Economies of scale.

(b) Monopoly power.

(c) Risk reduction.

(d) Reduction in cost of capital.

(iii) Merger represents one method of growth with the advantages that:

(a) It is readily financed by absorbing existing sources.

(b) It is rapid.

(c) It is relatively free of risk.

(d) It may provide access to investment opportunities not otherwise available.

(e) It may frustrate the acquisition of market power by a competitor.

(iv) Merger may be achieved by:

(a) A purchase of the assets of another business for cash.

(b) A purchase of the shares of another business for cash.

(c) An acquisition of the shares of another business by an exchange issue of shares in the acquiring company.

(d) The formation of a holding company to hold the shares of both parties to the merger.

(v) Agreement to the terms of a merger usually requires that both sides see benefits in it. The phenomenon of synergy, i.e. that the combined organisation will give a better performance than that achieved as a mere sum of its parts, provides the benefit. Bargaining will determine how it is to be shared and it is not, therefore, possible to calculate the 'right' terms for a merger. Calculation can, however, establish a range within which bargaining is likely to take place.

Review questions

(i) Define the term merger.

(ii) In what ways could a merger, once decided upon, be achieved?

(iii) What are the commercial advantages of size? Are there any disadvantages?

(iv) Why is growth by merger often preferred to growth by expansion?

(v) What may be the disadvantages of a merger?

(vi) How can it be argued, as it often is, that both parties to a merger can benefit from it?

(vii) *Why should the government sometimes outlaw particular proposed mergers?*

(viii) *The holder of 100 shares in X, plc receives the offer of either £2.50 in cash for each share or 3 shares in Y, plc for each share. What factors should the holder take into account in deciding whether to accept either offer and as to which one is preferred?*

Exercises

1. *As part of a policy of diversification, Solo, plc wishes to expand into a field of activity new to it. Two alternatives seem to be available. One is to acquire the existing business of Tandem, plc a well established concern in the new field. The other is to invest in manufacturing capacity of its own financing it by funds raised on the market. Discuss the factors which will influence a decision.*

2. *Dum, plc is proposing to take over Dee, plc by means of an issue of its own shares in exchange for those of Dee. Relevant information is as follows:*

	Dum	**Dee**
Ordinary share capital, £1 shares fully paid	£2,000,000	£1,500,000
Reserves	520,000	140,000
Loan capital	500,000	100,000
	£3,020,000	£1,740,000
Fixed assets	£1,810,000	£1,230,000
Net current assets	1,210,000	510,000
	£3,020,000	£1,740,000

Other information:

Maintainable annual profit attributable to equity	£500,000	£200,000
Current market price of ordinary shares	£3.00	£1.20

It is expected that the combination, if it takes place, will earn profits of about 10% higher than the present combined profits of Dum and Dee and that the market will value the shares on the basis of a price earnings ratio of 15.

Discuss the factors which might be taken into account during negotiations and suggest fair terms for the offer.

3. *'Synergy is the necessary mainspring of a successful merger.' What is synergy? Explain the statement.*

4. The Boards of Directors of Black, plc and White, plc have concluded discussions which lead them to believe that a merger of the two businesses, which are in many respects complementary in their activities, will be desirable. The favoured plan is to create a new holding company, Grey, plc which will issue its ordinary shares to the existing ordinary shareholders of Black and White on a basis to be agreed.

Summaries of the balance sheets of the existing companies appear below:

	Black £	White £
Fixed assets	2,140,000	925,000
Net current assets	930,000	595,000
	3,070,000	1,520,000

Financed by:

	Black	White
Ordinary share capital (£1 shares)	2,500,000	1,000,000
Share premium account	–	100,000
Revenue reserves	570,000	420,000
	3,070,000	1,520,000

Other information:

	Black	White
Maintainable annual profit	£420,000	£244,000
Current dividend rate	10%	12%
Price earnings ratio	8	10

Valuations of the goodwill of each business have been made and agreed at £500,000 for Black and £300,000 for White. Economies of scale and competitive advantages are expected to give the group profits 15% higher than the combined profits of the constituent companies and the market is expected to value the shares in the new holding company on the basis of a price/earnings ratio of 9.

Decide on fair terms for the issue of Grey's shares in exchange for those of Black and White and show how you come to your decision.

5. There appears to be a long term trend towards industrial concentration, achieved largely by merger. Discuss the advantages and disadvantages to an individual company seeking to pursue a policy of growth by merger.

6. Square, plc and Triangle, plc have mutually agreed to a merger but still have to agree on how this should be achieved. Three possibilities have emerged. These are:

(a) Square should purchase all the shares in Triangle for cash at a fair price.

(b) Square should issue new shares in exchange for the shares in Triangle.

(c) A new company should be formed to acquire all the shares of both Square and Triangle, issuing its own shares in exchange.

Discuss, in general terms, any advantages and disadvantages you see in each of these possibilities.

20: Management of Working Capital: Stock

20.1 Investment in Working Capital

20.1.1 We have given a great deal of attention to the economical deployment of capital funds by a financial manager. We have looked at some of the important techniques available to him in deciding whether or not to invest in a particular capital project. It is now time to turn our attention to the equally important matter of investment in working capital and its control.

20.1.2 Working capital supports and is necessitated by the operations of the fixed assets. Whenever a project involving investment in fixed assets is evaluated, therefore, an inclusion should be made for the additional investment in working capital which is required. Only in this way can it be ensured that working capital earns an appropriate rate of return on the investment in it as do other assets. This idea was explained and exemplified in 9.10.

Once a project is proceeding its working capital merges with that of all other activities and separate monitoring becomes impossible. It is, therefore, necessary for the financial manager to exercise control over working capital as a whole and this is the subject of our consideration now.

20.1.3 The diagram on the following page (Figure 20.1) illustrates what is known as the working capital cycle and shows the interrelationship between one component and another. Its relationship with the source and application of funds statement developed in chapter 2 will be obvious.

20.2 Stock

20.2.1 In this chapter we shall look at the problems of working capital management as related to stock. In subsequent chapters we will look at debtors and cash. Stock may be of raw materials, of finished goods which have emerged from a manufacturing process or of items for resale in the case of a retail or wholesale business. In all three cases the principles are broadly the same but our examples will draw on the case of raw materials to be used in a manufacturing process. This will most conveniently illustrate all the points which need to be made.

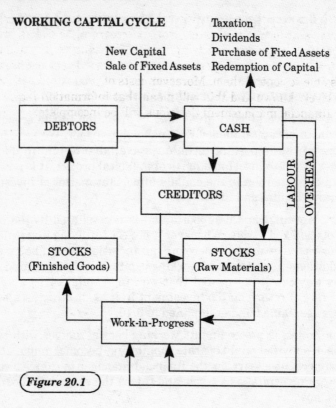

WORKING CAPITAL CYCLE

Taxation
Dividends
New Capital — Purchase of Fixed Assets
Sale of Fixed Assets — Redemption of Capital

Figure 20.1

20.2.2 The primary requirement is that stock levels should be optimal, i.e. neither too large nor too small. We should be aware in general terms of the penalties for a business lying in divergence from the optimum.

(a) If stocks are too high:

  (i) excess capital is tied up unproductively;

  (ii) costs of storage, e.g. warehousing and insurance, have to be met;

  (iii) there is a risk of deterioration due to the length of time in storage;

  (iv) there is a risk that changes in demand or technology will leave surplus stock unusable.

(b) If stocks are too low:

  (i) there is a risk of interruption to production due to shortage;

  (ii) frequent ordering, with associated costs, will be necessary;

  (iii) any economies resulting from bulk buying are lost.

20.2.3   Before any decision rules can be applied to the management of stocks a proper system of control and recording of stocks must be instituted. If stocks are left lying around in heaps for any one to use as required it will be impossible to know their level and therefore impossible to control them. Moreover costs of production will be very imprecisely known and this will mean that information required for other financial management decisions will be incomplete.

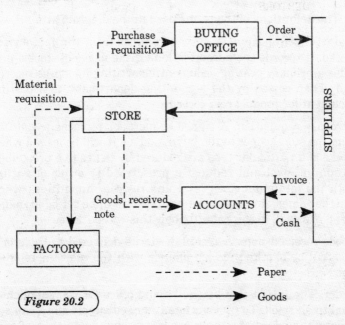

Figure 20.2

20.3 Stock Control

20.3.1   A proper system of stock control will have the following elements:

(i)   Physical security of the stocks. Stocks should be properly stored in a lockable section controlled by a responsible storekeeper. Security will include such things as dry storage for stocks vulnerable to damage from damp and safe containment of poisonous or inflammable stocks as well as protection from theft.

(ii)   Diversified control of stock ordering and usage. Usage of stock should be authorised by works personnel, issue and receipt by stores personnel, buying by the buying office and payment by the accounting department. This built in check and double check will make error or fraud much less likely.

(iii) Careful documentation of all stock movements and of stock levels. Only in this way can proper information be obtained for stock control and other purposes.

20.3.2 A simple system of stock control which contains the elements identified above is shown diagrammatically above (Figure 20.2). Most stock control systems are elaborations of this basic model.

20.3.3 The definitions of the terms used in the diagram are:

1. Material requisition: A signed request from the factory for stocks. It records the authorisation for the usage of stocks, provides a primary posting document for writing up stores records and, when costed by the accounting department, is a posting document for product cost records.

2. Purchase requisition: A signed request for replacement stocks from the storekeeper to the buying office. It will be issued when stocks of a particular type are reduced by issues to a prescribed minimum level and request a prescribed re-order quantity. Both the minimum stock level and re-order quantities, which together determine average stock levels, will be set by management. We shall discuss shortly how this will be done.

3. Goods received note: A record of stocks delivered to the store, this will be checked for compliance with the relevant requisition.

4. Order: The instruction by the buying office for the supplier to send fresh stock. To prevent unauthorised supply suppliers are generally advised that only goods supplied against an official order will be paid for.

5. Invoice: This is the suppliers 'bill' for the goods. It will be paid when verified against the purchase order and the goods inwards note i.e. when it is confirmed that a valid order has been correctly fulfilled.

20.3.4 The store-keeper will keep a ledger (probably in card index form or in a computer) recording the quantity of stock received and issued and serving to prompt him when recording is necessary.

It may look as illustrated below:

Stock; ½ Inch steel rod   RE-ORDER LEVEL: 100m
RE-ORDER QUANTITY: 200 m
MAXIMUM STOCK: 250 m
MINIMUM STOCK: 25 m

Date	Received	Issued	Stock
1st January Stock brought forward			120
3rd January Mat. req. 5682		30	90
10th January Mat. req. 5926		25	65
19th January Mat. req. 6897		40	25
23rd January Goods received M987	200		225

This stock would have been re-ordered at 3rd January when the stock level first fell below the re-order level.

20.4 Re-Order Quantities

20.4.1 We now need to see how management will set the re-order quantity and the re-order level. The analysis will assume initially that all costs are known and that delivery times and consumption rates can be predicted with certainty. In practice some degree of approximation and estimation may have to take the place of precise knowledge.

20.4.2 Let Q equal the re-order quantity of a certain type of stock. Ideally, in order to minimise the unnecessary stock holding, the stock will just be exhausted when new deliveries arrive. Maximum stock will thus be Q and minimum zero. Average stock level, assuming even consumption, would be Q/2. There are costs associated with the holding of stocks. Let these equal C per unit per annum. Annual holding costs then total CQ/2. The more frequently re-ordering takes place the smaller is the average stock holding and therefore the smaller is the total holding cost.

20.4.3 There is another side to the picture. Let N be the number of units of stock used in a year. The number of orders placed must be N/Q. There is a cost associated with ordering and buying (i.e. clerical costs, transport, etc.) which will designate as B per order. Total ordering costs must therefore be BN/Q per annum. This will be the smaller the fewer is the number of orders.

20.4.4 Combining our two costs the total annual cost of stock holdings is (CQ/2) + (BN/Q). Since one component of this is falling as stocks rise and the other is rising we may expect the combination to have a minimum at a certain value of Q. This is that value of the order quantity known as the Economic Order Quantity or EOQ. It can be determined by calculation that

$$\text{EOQ} = \sqrt{\frac{2BN}{C}}$$

20.4.5 Example. Eeyorquant, plc uses red paint at the rate of 10,000 litres per annum. The holding cost of the paint is 20p per litre per annum and the buying cost is £50 per order. Determine the economic order quantity and verify by the calculation of order quantities on either side of it.

20.4.6 The economic order quantity is determined as follows:

$$EOQ = \sqrt{\frac{2BN}{C}}$$

$$= \sqrt{\frac{2 \times 20 \times 10,000}{.2}}$$

$$= \underline{\underline{2,236 \text{ litres}}}$$

The economic order quantity is thus 2,236 litres giving an average stock of red paint of 1,118 litres. We will now verify our calculation by determining total annual stock cost at three levels of order quantity, 2,000, 2,236 and 3,000 litres. This cost is given by (CQ/2) + (BN/Q).

At 2,000 litres:

$$\frac{CQ}{2} + \frac{BN}{Q} = \frac{.2 \times 2,000}{2} + \frac{50 \times 10,000}{2,00}$$

$$= £450 \text{ per annum}$$

At 2,236 litres:

$$= \frac{.2 \times 2,236}{2} + \frac{50 \times 10,000}{2,236}$$

$$= £447 \text{ per annum}$$

At 3,000 litres:

$$= \frac{.2 \times 3,000}{2} + \frac{50 \times 10,000}{3,000}$$

$$= £467 \text{ per annum}$$

20.4.7 Having seen how to determine the economic order quantity we need to consider how to decide the re-order level, the stock level at which the order should be initiated. Ideally this should be at the point where there remains just enough stock to cover the period of waiting for the order to be delivered. It thus depends on delivery times. If D is the delivery time in weeks the re-order stock level R is given by DN/W, where W is the number of working weeks in the year.

20.4.8 Example. Where Eeyorquant orders red paint, delivery usually follows in six weeks. The factory works for 44 weeks in a year. What is the re-order level for red paint?

20.4.9 The re-order level is determined as follows:

$$R = \frac{DN}{W}$$

$$= \frac{6 \times 10,000}{44}$$

$$= 1,364 \text{ litres}$$

The picture is now complete. The storekeeper should be told to re-order 2,236 litres of paint whenever the stock held falls to 1,364 litres. Average stock will turn out to be 1,118 litres.

20.4.10 In practice our figures might not work out quite so well as they do in our examples. If the red paint is supplied in 1,000 litre batches, for instance, an order of 2,236 litres will not be acceptable. In that case we must choose a 2,000 litre order as being the nearest possible to our theoretical optimum. We may find that consumption fluctuates a little. In that case there will be a risk of shortage if we delay reordering until the level indicated by our calculation. We could then order at a level of, say, 1,500 litres rather than 1,364 in order to be on the safe side.

20.4.11 It should be noted that these matters are not the only ones which impart a lack of precision to the figures used in practice. Holding costs and buying costs are very difficult to ascertain and may indeed, not be fully attributable to specific lines of stock. In such cases estimates will have to be used.

20.5 Stocks of Finished Goods and Work in Progress

20.5.1 So far we have referred only to stocks of raw materials. A considerable amount of finance may, however, be tied up at the other end of the production chain (finished goods) and during production (work in progress).

20.5.2 Finished goods levels can be determined in precisely the same way as can stocks of raw materials. The issues from this stock are governed by the level of sales and the inputs to it by the level of activity in the factory.

20.5.3 The amount of work in progress is governed by the length of the production cycle which is largely a technical matter. The only control which can be exercised by the management of the business is to ensure that the cycle is not unnecessarily prolonged by slackness or by holdups arising from disputes or from stock shortages.

Summary

(i) Investment in working capital, of which stock is a large component, can be very sizeable and ought to receive the same careful consideration as investment in fixed assets.

(ii) The first essential in doing this is that stock be systematically controlled. This implies a proper authorisation and documentation of the purchase, use and movement of all stock.

(iii) A consideration of the costs of, on the one hand, carrying stocks and, on the other hand, ordering fresh supplies will lead to a determination of an economic order quantity. This is the order quantity which minimises the overall cost of stock management.

(iv) Associated with the economic order quantity will be a re-order level, i.e. that minimum level of stock at which a new order will be initiated. It is derived from the rate of usage of the material and the delivery delay.

(v) Stocks of finished good and work in progress tie up large amounts of capital and should also be carefully monitored.

Review questions

(i) What is meant by stock control?

(ii) Distinguish between a re-order quantity and re-order level.

(iii) Distinguish between a material requisition and a purchase requisition.

(iv) 'Frequent small orders are costly to process and should therefore be avoided.' Discuss.

(v) Define the term economic order quantity and show how it is calculated.

(vi) What are the undesirable consequences of too high a level of stock?

(vii) What are the undesirable consequences of too low a level of stock?

(viii) Itemise the most important components of the costs of (a) holding stock and (b) ordering stock.

Exercises

1. Sugar and Spice are retail grocers. One of their best selling lines is a particular brand of soap. It can be bought wholesale in boxes of 1,000 tablets and buying costs amount to £5 per order regardless of its size. An order is delivered eight weeks after it is placed. Retail sales average 200,000 tablets per 48 week year and holding costs are 50p per annum per 1,000 bars. Calculate the economic order quantity, re-order stock level and average stock level for this soap.

2. Careless, plc manufactures a range of products from a variety of raw materials. These are stored wherever space is available in the factory and operatives help themselves to what they require. Set out the undesirable consequences which you would expect to follow from this policy.

3. Papyrus, plc uses a large quantity of salt in a manufacturing process. The annual consumption is 60,000 tons over a 50 week working year. It costs £100 to initiate and process an order and delivery follows an average of two weeks later. The storage costs for the salt amount to 10p per ton per annum. The current practice is to order twice a year when the stock falls to 10,000 tons. Recommend an appropriate ordering policy and determine the cost of the current policy. What would be your recommendation if told that delivery had occasionally followed the order by as late as four weeks and that to run out of this material was very costly in terms of production holdups?

4. Cardinal, plc uses two important materials in its productive process. A shortage of either of these will cause very costly delays in production. The materials are, however, corrosive and therefore difficult to store as well as being expensive to handle.

   Relevant information is:

	Material X	**Material Y**
Annual usage	24,000 litres	15,000 kgs.
Holding costs	5p per litre per annum	10p per kg. per annum
Buying costs	£100 per order	£80 per order
Delivery time	5 weeks	10 weeks

   Determine the economic order quantity and the re-order level for each material. Assume a fifty week working year.

5. 'Cash invested in working capital is idle, earning no return as does cash invested in fixed assets. It should therefore be regarded as a necessary evil but kept to an absolute minimum.' Discuss.

6. *Turf and Toil are landscape gardeners. They use large quantities of concrete slabs and have a regular monthly delivery of 5,000 slabs which approximates to their average usage. The cost of processing an order is £100 regardless of its size. It costs £2 per slab per annum to store the slabs. Slabs have to be ordered two weeks (i.e. half a month) before they are delivered. Could a better ordering procedure be devised and would any savings be worthwhile?*

21: Management of Working Capital: Debtors

21.1 Credit Policy

21.1.1 In this chapter we shall look at the problems concerned with the management of trade debtors, another important component of working capital. For two reasons it is less easy to treat this in an analytical way than was the case with stocks. The first is that the constraints, because they are not physical, are very much less clear cut and the other is that writers in the area have generally not given so much attention to this topic and so fewer concepts have become developed.

21.1.2 In principle every business wants to be paid for the goods or services it supplies as soon as possible. Once a sale has been made the profit making cycle is completed but the resources employed in the process cannot be set working on another cycle until they are released by payment. The convention of the trade is a very powerful factor in determining how long it takes for a customer to pay. In the retail trade, for example, a very high proportion of all business is done on a cash basis. Where one business sells to another, however, the giving of some credit is almost universal.

21.1.3 Most people would expect to pay cash if buying, for example, a cauliflower. They would expect up to three months' credit for telephone calls on a private line. They would take up to three years to pay for a car. It should be noted that the amount of credit given by a firm may not be what it seems. Although British Telecom has large debtors for unbilled telephone calls most car dealers trade effectively on a cash basis because the credit is supplied by a specialist finance firm. Its business is to lend money, on which interest is charged, so for it debtors is very much a productive asset.

21.1.4 It will be clear from the above that in many cases a trader will be virtually tied to particular terms of credit because they are conventionally offered by his competitors. There is no point in demanding cash with order if one's competitors give one month's credit. Only a very pronounced price or quality advantage would enable one to retain custom in these circumstances. On the other hand there is usually little point in offering more credit than competitors. This would tie up a great deal of extra working capital and, although it might attract a little more custom, there is a risk that this will be less credit worthy leading to higher bad debts.

21.1.5 Management needs to establish a policy on its trade debtors and there are several factors to be considered. These are:

(a) Cash discount to be offered for prompt or early payment.

(b) Official period of normal credit offered.

(c) Assessing credit worthiness of customers.

(d) Action to be taken regarding late payments.

These factors will be discussed separately but it should be noted that each will have an effect both on the general level of investment in debtors and on the firm's competitive position. A balance between the two will have to be achieved.

21.1.6 Some firms offer a cash discount for the prompt settlement of accounts. Typically an invoice might state 'Terms: $2\frac{1}{2}\%$ cash discount within 7 days, otherwise 30 days net'. This means that the debtor is allowed up to 30 days to pay his bill at the stated amount. If it is paid within the first 7 days of this period he may deduct $2\frac{1}{2}\%$ from the total. Since the effect, where the debtor takes up the offer of a discount, is to reduce the average level of trade debtors, one would expect that the amount of the cash discount would be related to the firm's cost of capital. In fact it is usually on a more generous scale than this (in the above example $2\frac{1}{2}\%$ for three weeks represents over 40% per annum!) This is because early payment not only reduces capital requirements but also saves administrative costs in pursuing outstanding debtors and may reduce the overall risk of bad debts as well. Cash discounts are a relatively expensive way of improving the inflow of cash and most companies would prefer to avoid them by raising extra working capital at a more advantageous market rate. There may, however, sometimes be an element of price reduction in the cash discount. It is a concealed way of offering lower prices to a sector of the market which might otherwise go to competitors.

21.1.7 The period of credit in most cases is set by the convention of the trade and very little flexibility is afforded to the individual business. It is usual to offer variously credit terms of 30 days, 60 days or 90 days, i.e. payment is to be made within that interval following the date of the invoice. Where he has a choice in the credit terms which he may offer, the manager should bear in mind that a longer period of credit is not only expensive in terms of tied up capital but that it may increase the risk of bad debts. This does not arise so much because an individual debtor becomes more likely to default after a lapse of time. It comes from the fact that firms in financial difficulties are likely to be attracted to suppliers offering the longest credit. Thus to offer these terms will certainly draw customers away from competitors but this customer group is likely to have an above average risk of default.

21.1.8 Before allowing any customer credit the good debt manager should assess his credit worthiness. This may be done directly by an examination of his accounts (which, if the customer is a limited company, are publicly available) or indirectly through trade sources or by means of a bankers' reference. Credit worthiness is rarely assessable in terms of absolutes and it will be a matter of judging the risk in each case and categorising the customer accordingly. Some risk is inevitable where business is done on credit. Although some potential customers in a very high risk category may not be acceptable at all, others, where the risk exists but is not so great may be offered credit restricted to an overall maximum. This keeps the debt within the debtor's adjudged capacity to pay and also, should the worst happen, limits the maximum loss which can occur. It should be borne in mind that, although a great deal of business can be gained by offering credit to those with whom others will not trade, the costs of legal action in pursuit of debts can be very high and the cost of bad debts can be devastating. One large bad debt will wipe out the profit earned on a very large volume of sales.

21.1.9 The final point to be considered in the management of trade debtors is the follow-up action to be taken regarding late payments. Obviously a system must be maintained which signals outstanding debts which go past their due date of payment. Some discretion is then possible, however, over the amount of pressure which is then applied. There are many sanctions ranging from polite reminders, through solicitors' letters and the withholding of supplies to action through a Court and the speed with which this process is followed needs careful judgment.

21.1.10 A service sometimes used by a business to reduce its investment in debts without restricting the amount of credit offered to customers is that of debt factoring. This involves 'selling' book debts to an organisation set up for the purpose of acquiring them. Since this organisation earns its income by acquiring the debts at less than their face value this amounts to the same thing as the giving of a cash discount.

21.1.11 A practice which has grown up relatively recently is for a business to sell goods on a contract which includes a clause reserving title in the goods until payment has been made. This is a device to minimise the risk of bad debts. Under a normal contract of sale title to the goods passes to the buyer when he obtains possession. From that point on the seller may sue for payment but not for the return of the goods. In the event of the buyers' bankruptcy or liquidation the seller then ranks equally with other creditors and might not be paid in full. If, however, he has reserved title to the goods he may retrieve them in so far as they remain in the buyer's stocks and can be identified. In this way he may recover in full.

21.2 Principles for Guidance

21.2.1 Within the broad ground rules discussed above the formulation of a sound credit control policy will be achieved by a combination of appraisal, experience and instinct. In these circumstances it is very difficult to lay down any firm principles for guidance. Some attempt at analysis can be made, however, although it should be realised that it rests on estimates which may prove to be very unreliable. The analysis depends on judging the effect which defined courses of action will have and can usually be made only in terms of subjective probabilities.

21.2.2 Example. Sellers, plc makes all its sales on credit. Its terms are $2^{1}/_{2}$% cash discount within seven days, otherwise net within thirty days. The value of its annual sales is £500,000. The gross margin on sales is 30% and Sellers cost of capital is 15% per annum. Customers can be divided into three categories as shown in the following table.

Category	Annual sales	Average period of credit taken	Proportion of bad debts
A	£50,000	7	Nil
B	250,000	30	Nil
C	200,000	75	2%

In an effort to reduce the level of trade debtors and the losses due to bad debts the following policies are proposed. All references to sales value are in annual terms.

(i) To offer 3% cash discount for payment in 7 days. This would induce customers for £50,000 to move from category B to category A and customers worth £20,000 to move from category C to category A.

(ii) To offer 5% cash discount for payment in 7 days. This would increase to £100,000 the value of customers moving from category B to category A and to £50,000 the value moving from category C to category A.

(iii) To withdraw credit terms from category C customers altogether. This would result in a loss of business worth £20,000.

(iv) To tighten up the procedure on late payment. This would reduce the period of credit taken by category C customers to 50 days on average and would improve the proportion of bad debts to $1\frac{3}{4}\%$. It would result in a loss of business worth £15,000.

21.2.3 We can assess each of these terms of costs and benefits.

(i) Average debtors now is:

Category A	$\dfrac{7}{365} \times$ £50,000 =	£959
Category B	$\dfrac{30}{365} \times$ £250,000 =	20,548
Category C	$\dfrac{75}{365} \times$ £200,000 =	41,096
		£62,603

if we increase cash discount to 3% average debtors will become

Category A	$\dfrac{7}{365} \times$ £120,000 =	£2,301
Category B	$\dfrac{30}{365} \times$ £200,000 =	16,438
Category C	$\dfrac{75}{365} \times$ £180,000 =	36,986
		£55,725

There is a reduction in debtors of £6,878 which (at 15% p.a.) gives a saving in financing cost of £1,032 per annum. Added to this there is a saving in bad debts from those who move from category C to category A of 2% × £20,000 = £400. The total benefit is £1,432 per annum.

The cost is the increase in discount:

Currently this is $2\frac{1}{2}\% \times$ £50,000	=	£1,250
Under this proposal it will increase to 3% × £120,000	=	3,600
The total increase in cost is		£2,350

This action would result in a net loss of £918 per annum and is thus not worthwhile.

(ii) If the cash discount is raised to 5% average debtors will become:

$$\text{Category A} \quad \frac{7}{365} \times £200,000 = \qquad £3,836$$

$$\text{Category B} \quad \frac{30}{365} \times £150,000 = \qquad 12,329$$

$$\text{Category C} \quad \frac{75}{365} \times £150,000 = \qquad 30,822$$

$$\overline{\underline{£46,987}}$$

The reduction in debtors is £15,616 and in financing costs £2,342. Bad debts saving is £1,000 and thus total saving is £3,342 per annum.

The increase in discount can be determined. It will become:

5% × £200,000	= £10,000
From its present level	1,250
	£8,750

This is even less worthwhile than the first proposal losing £5,408 p.a.

(iii) To withdraw credit facilities from category C will save financing costs of

$$15\% \times £200,000 \times \frac{75}{365} = £6,164 \text{ p.a.}$$

There will also be a saving in bad debts of

$$2\% \times £200,000 = £4,000.$$

Total saving is £10,164. The cost will be the loss of gross margin:

$$£20,000 \times 30\% = £6,000$$

This proposal is worth implementing as it improves the situation by £4,164 per annum.

(iv) If we tighten up the procedure operated against late payers there will be a financing cost saving:

$15\% \times \dfrac{75}{365} \times £200,000$	= £2,055
Bad debt saving is G % of £200,000	= 500
Total gain	£2,555

The cost is 30% margin on £15,000 = £4,500. This proposal, then, would lead to a net loss of £1,945 per annum and is not worthwhile. Clearly the best thing to do is to withdraw credit facilities from the slow players. This would not be a general conclusion, of course, and depends entirely on the estimates and assumptions which Sellers has made.

Summary

(i) It is important that a policy should be established over trade debts. This will cover such matters as:

    (a) Cash discount to be offered for prompt or early payment;

    (b) Official period of normal credit offered;

    (c) Assessing credit worthiness of customers;

    (d) Action to be taken regarding late payments.

(ii) The costs associated with debtors are:

    (a) The cost of the capital tied up in them and

    (b) The cost of bad debts.

(iii) Factoring is a device sometimes used to reduce the investment in debtors. Debtors are 'sold' to the factor at a discount for cash.

Review questions

(i) *Why does management sometimes have very little flexibility in the terms of credit which it may offer?*

(ii) *What are the costs of an unwisely liberal credit policy?*

(iii) *Is it worth offering discounts to debtors to encourage prompt payment?*

(iv) *What is debt factoring?*

(v) *'A bad debt of £100 costs us only £70 because we make 30% profit on sales. We can therefore afford a proportion of bad debts.' Do you agree?*

(vi) *A certain business never offers credit to its customers but insists on cash with order. What are the advantages of such a policy? Are there any disadvantages?*

(vii) *Why should offering an extended period of credit encourage defaulters?*

Exercises

1. *What would you expect to be the elements of an efficient credit control policy? Indicate the likely consequences of a policy which is (i) too tight, (ii) not tight enough.*

2. *I.O.U., plc categorises prospective credit customers according to a credit rating based on a number of criteria. The categories and the expected experience of them are listed below:*

Category	Average collection period	Proportion of bad debts
A	20 days	$\frac{1}{2}$%
B	30 days	2%
C	40 days	5%
D	50 days	10%

   The company's cost of capital is 20% per annum. Currently only customers in categories A to C are granted credit facilities. Comment on the consequences of extending credit facilities to category D.

3. *Quickstep, plc sells a product which yields a marginal contribution of 20% of sales (i.e. £1 of additional sales increases net profit by 20p). Its debtors at the last year end stood at £350,000. The average collection period is 25 days and bad debts are of negligible amount. The company recently introduced a $2\frac{1}{2}$% cash discount offered to all customers for payment within seven days. This has had the effect of reducing the collection period only slightly, to 24 days, as only half of all customers take it up. It has, however, attracted new business which has had the effect of increasing total debtors to £400,000. Should the cash discount offer be continued? Quickstep has a cost of capital of 15% per annum.*

4. *Gloomy, plc has an annual average sales turnover of £2 million. It has grown over the years and its management policies have not kept pace with expansion. In particular credit control is very slack and amounts to little more than accurate record keeping. The bad debts record has deteriorated and the average collection period has lengthened. Bad debts now amount to 10% of all sales and the average debtor takes 60 days to pay. A consultant, called in to examine the problem, has made the following recommendations:*

   (i) Establish a proper credit control department. This will require a permanent investment of £100,000 for equipment

and office space and there will be annual operating costs of £30,000 for wages, etc.

(ii) Withdraw credit facilities from that category of customer who is least credit worthy. This will result in a loss of business estimated at £200,000 per annum but the average bad debt record should improve to 5% of all sales. The marginal contribution of sales is 15%.

(iii) Insist on payment within 30 days and ruthlessly follow up late payers. This is expected to bring the average period of collection down to 30 days.

Determine the net benefit to Gloomy of adopting the recommendations. Its cost of capital is 18% per annum.

5. Cloudy and Co. operates in the retail trade selling on a cash only basis and earning an average gross profit of $33\frac{1}{3}\%$ on sales. The manager wishes to start offering monthly credit terms in an effort to increase sales and he estimates that turnover would increase by £50,000 per annum if this were done. All the new sales would be on credit and a further £50,000 of existing cash customers would probably take advantage of the credit facility. The manager is quite realistic about the risks involved in advancing credit in this trade and expects a bad debt rate of about 15% but still feels that the policy is worthwhile. He produces the figures given below:

Extra sales generated by new policy	£50,000
Less Expected bad debts 15% × £100,000	15,000
Net extra sales	35,000
Less Cost of extra sales O × £50,000	33,333
Net gain from policy	£1,667

Criticise and correct these figures assuming any other quantities required.

6. Earlybird, plc has annual sales of £1,000,000, about one quarter of which are on credit with an average collection period of 40 days. Bad debts average only 1% of all credit sales. A recent review of credit control procedures has suggested that sales on credit should be encouraged in an effort to win more trade. It is believed that this would increase sales by 30% and that, of this enlarged volume, 40% would be on credit. The average collection period could be reduced to 35 days but bad debts would increase to $1\frac{1}{2}\%$ of all credit sales. The company's cost of capital is 14% per annum and the marginal contribution of sales is 15p in the

£. The annual cost of the clerical labour involved in the change would be £10,000.

Evaluate the proposal.

22: Management of Working Capital: Cash Budgets

22.1 The Cash Budget

22.1.1 In the first chapter we referred to the importance not only of selecting profitable projects and providing finance for them at minimum costs but also of providing finance at the right time. Where major projects are concerned this is relatively straightforward and is largely a matter of making appropriate arrangements. A fresh issue of capital, for example, may be timed to coincide with the payment for a new factory or with the repayment of a debenture. Timing is, however, more difficult and more attention needs to be given to it in the case of the finance of working capital. A highly profitable manufacturing and sales plan can be seriously impeded if cash is not available at the right time to pay for necessary supplies. Conversely there will be less than optimum use of resources if the business carries large cash balances at a time when it is borrowing money expensively from elsewhere.

22.1.2 In this chapter we shall be looking at the preparation of cash budgets which are an essential tool of the financial manager in providing the proper finance of working capital. The ideas underlying them are very simple although, in a real life situation, the arithmetic may sometimes become quite involved. The cash budget is derived from a consideration of (a) the master budget and (b) the structural factors which govern the timing of the cash flows. An example should make this clear.

22.1.3 **Example.** Foresight, plc has produced a plan for its activities for a forthcoming financial period of six months. This can be summarised in the form of a budgeted profit and loss account for the period.

Foresight, plc – Budgeted profit and loss account for the forthcoming six months

	£	£
Sales (50,000 units @ £10 each)		500,000
Less Cost of sales:		
Material	100,000	
Labour	75,000	
Variable overhead	100,000	275,000
Operating profit		225,000

Less Fixed overhead	125,000	
Depreciation	20,000	145,000
Net profit for the six months		80,000

Foresight's (summarised) balance sheet immediately prior to the commencement of the six months was as follows:

	£	£
Fixed assets		99,000
Current assets:		
Stocks of raw material	20,000	
Stocks of finished goods	44,000	
Debtors (80% previous month's sales)	32,000	
Cash	50,000	146,000
		£245,000

Represented by:

	£	£
Share capital and reserves		200,000
Creditors (previous month's supplies)	20,000	
(supplies of month before that)	25,000	45,000
		£245,000

Foresight's trade is seasonal and its forecast sales for the next full year (of which the current budget is months 1-6) are:

Month	Sales	Month	Sales
1	40,000	7	140,000
2	40,000	8	80,000
3	60,000	9	60,000
4	80,000	10	60,000
5	120,000	11	50,000
6	160,000	12	40,000

It is Foresight's policy to hold stocks of finished goods equal to the requirements of the next two months' sales and stocks of raw materials equal to the next one and a half months' production requirements. It pays its creditors for supplies, on average, two months after the goods are delivered but labour and variable overheads are paid for in the month in which they are incurred.

Fixed overheads are paid quarterly in advance. Eighty per cent of the company's sales are to credit customers (the rest being for cash) and debtors are allowed one month's credit. Depreciation is a composite figure made up of the appropriate amounts for each of the fixed assets in use. No cash receipts or payments are expected during the six months of the budget period except those referred to above.

22.1.4 Obviously it would be much too naive an approach for us merely to argue that, since there is a planned profit, cash receipts must exceed cash payments and that therefore no cash shortage can arise. A lot depends on the timings and synchronisations of those receipts and payments. We must now look at the situation in detail.

22.1.5 We will look first at the cash inflow. Schedule I below shows how this may be determined.

Schedule 1

Month	1	2	3	4	5	6
	£	£	£	£	£	£
Cash sales (1)	8,000	8,000	12,000	16,000	24,000	32,000
Cash from credit customers (2)	32,000 (3)	32,000	32,000	48,000	64,000	96,000
	42,000	40,000	44,000	64,000	88,000	128,000

(1)   at 20% of current month's sales
(2)   at 80% of previous month's sales
(3)   debtors as shown on opening balance sheet.

22.1.6 We now turn to the cash outgoings. Since it is the company's policy to hold stocks of finished goods enough for the forthcoming two months' sales, production must always be two months in advance of sales. Schedule 2 shows this and hence determines the level of production and expenditure accrued month by month.

Schedule 2

Month of production	1	2	3	4	5	6
Month of sales	3	4	5	6	7	8
Hence number of units produced	6,000	8,000	12,000	16,000	14,000	8,000
Costs incurred:	£	£	£	£	£	£
Material	12,000	16,000	24,000	32,000	28,000	16,000
Labour	9,000	12,000	18,000	24,000	21,000	12,000
Variable overhead	12,000	16,000	24,000	32,000	28,000	16,000

We shall also need the information that production in month 7 and month 8 are each to be 6,000 units and that, therefore, the material requirement for each of these months will have a cost of £12,000.

22.1.7 In the case of materials we must now look further at the relationship between the incurring of the cost and the payment. Since at any time we must hold stocks sufficient for the next one and a half month's usage, we must buy in a month sufficient for the second half of the *next* month and for the first half of the month after that.

For example, given the stockholding policy stated, Foresight will enter month 1 of this budget period with sufficient raw material to fill the manufacturing requirements of month 1 and the first half of month 2. An examination of the opening balance sheet and of Schedule 2 will confirm that this is the case. In order to maintain this stock the company must buy during month 1 enough for the remainder of month 2 and for the first half of month 3. Having consumed in month 1 (obviously) the manufacturing requirement of that month, the company will enter month 2 with the manufacturing requirement of that month and of half of month 3. Schedule 3 shows the material purchases of the company.

Schedule 3

Month	1	2	3	4	5	6
Purchase half of next month's requirement	8,000	12,000	16,000	14,000	8,000	6,000
Next month's but one requirement (1)	12,000	16,000	14,000	8,000	6,000	6,000
Total purchases	£20,000	£28,000	£30,000	£22,000	£14,000	£12,000

(1) Figures computed from Schedule 2 and accompanying note.

22.1.8 The actual cash outflow relating to material purchases will, because of the period of credit obtained, be delayed by two months from the purchases. Schedule 4 shows this.

Schedule 4

Month	1	2	3	4	5	6
Month purchased	-2	-1	1	2	3	4
Cash paid	£25,000*	£20,000*	£20,000	£28,000	£30,000	£22,000

*Taken from the opening balance sheet.

22.1.9 Labour and variable overhead are paid for in the months in which they are incurred. The cash payments will therefore tally in amount and timing with the figures given for those items in Schedule 2. Fixed overhead totals £125,000 and is paid quarterly in advance. This means that two payments each of £62,500 will be made, one in month 1 and one in month 3. There will be no cash outflow associated with depreciation which requires simply a book entry.

22.1.10 We can now put together all these pieces of information and determine our month by month cash position.

Foresight, plc – Cash budget for the forthcoming six months

Month	1	2	3	4	5	6
£	£	£	£	£	£	£
Cash inflow (1)	40,000	40,000	44,000	64,000	88,000	128,000
Cash outflows:						
Creditors for						
materials (2)	25,000	20,000	20,000	28,000	30,000	22,000
Labour(3)	9,000	12,000	18,000	24,000	21,000	12,000
Variable overhead (3)	12,000	16,000	24,000	32,000	28,000	16,000
Fixed overhead	62,500			62,500		
	£108.500	£48,000	£62,000	£146,500	£79,000	£50,000
Change on month	-£68,500	-£8,000	-£18,000	-£82,500	+£9,000	+£78,000
Cash balance (4)	-£18,500	-£26,500	-£44,500	-£127,000	-£118,000	-£40,000

(1) From schedule 1
(2) From schedule 4
(3) From schedule 2
(4) Takes account of opening balance of £50,000.

22.1.11 It can be seen from this that, despite profitable working, there is a progressive increased requirement for cash building up to a peak of £127,000 in month 4 before it begins to decline again. It would have been a gross mistake for us to have assumed that our opening cash balance of £50,000 would have adequately financed our working capital.

22.2 Budgeted Balance Sheet

22.2.1 The budgeted balance sheet of Foresight, plc as it should appear at the end of the six months can readily be constructed from figures already calculated. It is given below but the reader is left to determine the sources of its figures for himself.

Foresight, plc – Budgeted balance sheet at the end of the forthcoming six months

	£	£
Fixed assets		79,000
Current assets:		
Stocks of raw material	18,000	
Stocks of finished goods	121,000	
Debtors	128,000	267,000
		£346,000

Represented by:

Share capital and reserves	280,000
Creditors	26,000
Bank overdraft	40,000
	£346,000

22.2.2 Our example has shown very clearly the value of a cash budget in giving advance warning of a squeeze on cash resources. If this had not been anticipated it could have caused great difficulty. The budget does not, however, show how to deal with the matter and this is a responsibility of the financial manager. In the balance sheet in 22.2.1 we have incorporated the assumption that the shortfall was to be met by means of a bank overdraft and, for most cases of a temporary cash shortage, this will be entirely appropriate. It should not be overlooked, however, that action is needed to arrange this with the bank. The bank may require evidence of the time scale over which repayment will be made and the cash budget could have another use for this purpose.

22.3 Basic Working Capital Requirement

22.3.1 The special feature of the case of Foresight was that, because of the seasonal nature of its trade, there was an ebb and flow in its working capital financing requirement. A comparable position might arise where a company needed a heavy commitment of funds to a new project in order to set it up (and this will include working capital, our present concern) but that thereafter its own cash generation quickly released some of this initial outlay. In either case, underlying the temporary cash requirement there is a permanent, 'steady state', requirement which it would not be appropriate to provide from short term sources.

22.3.2 Let us illustrate this point with some assumed figures for Foresight, plc. These are not calculated directly from the figures previously given.

	£
Average level of current assets	
Stocks of raw materials	24,375
Stocks of finished goods	89,375
Debtors	65,000
Fixed overheads paid in advance	15,625
	194,375
Average level of current liabilities	
Creditors	32,500
Average long term level of working capital	£161,875

This basic level of working capital must be seen as a permanent investment in the business which should be financed on a permanent basis, i.e. by share capital, by long term loans or, eventually, by retained earnings. These sources of finance were more fully discussed in chapter 3.

22.3.3 It should not be assumed that the financial manager should accept without question the working capital requirement indicated to him by a first draft of the cash budget. In 22.1.3 we referred to the structural factors which underlie the budget. These need not necessarily be seen as rigid and adjustment to them may be both possible and profitable.

22.3.4 Any of the following courses of action would have the effect of reducing the basic working capital requirement although all have negative aspects which must not be overlooked .

(a) Reduction of debtors.

This can be achieved by:

(i) Reducing the period of credit offered to customers.

(ii) Enforcing more stringently the allowed period by tight credit control (chasing late-payers, more care in assessing credit worthiness, etc.)

(iii) Offering cash discounts for early payment.

(iv) Debt factoring.

Care must be taken that too inflexible an attitude to credit does not lose the company customer goodwill. The giving of discounts and debt factoring may prove to be unwarrantably expensive.

(b) Reduction of stocks.

Many businesses keep stocks of both raw materials and finished goods at an unnecessarily high level. This increases the risk of deterioration and puts up storage charges as well as tying up extra working capital. Inadequate stocks will lead to delays in production and in supply to customers but careful stock control including an efficient re-ordering system may make it possible to work on a narrower stock margin.

(c) Increase in creditors.

If a company is a large purchaser of materials and is therefore a valued customer to its suppliers it may be able to negotiate longer terms of credit, e.g. three months to pay instead of two. No financial manager should condone, however, the deliberate late payment of creditors as a device for conserving working capital. Apart from the doubtful honesty of this practice, it may lead the supplier to retaliate by restricting supplies or withdrawing credit facilities altogether. It will certainly, in the long run, impair the company's overall credit rating.

22.4 Cash Surpluses

22.4.1 So far we have discussed the management of working capital in terms of coping with a shortage. It is obvious, however, that the converse may occur. With a seasonal business, like that of Foresight, plc in our example, if the working capital is supported by permanent finance based on the average requirement, the shortages of one part of the year will be counterbalanced by surpluses at another. The active and effective financial manager will ensure that such surpluses do not merely lie idle. Neither, however, should they be regarded as available for investment in any long term project.

22.4.2 Useful homes for short term cash surpluses include the following:

(a) Early payment of creditors in order to claim cash discount;

(b) A bank deposit account where interest would be earned but the cash remains easily accessible;

(c) Loans to associated companies (in the case of a group) where one company's period of greatest surplus may coincide with another company's period of greatest shortage;

(d) Forward buying of raw material where price rises are foreseen and where the materials can be stored without risk;

(e) Purchase of readily marketable securities, e.g. government stocks or shares in other companies. This method is to be used with great caution owing to the risk of loss due to market fluctuations. The rate of return may, however, be better than for other short term investments. It should not be overlooked that market dealing costs are fairly high and that this use of funds will usually be profitable only where the surplus persists for some time.

Summary

(i) Planning in advance for cash requirements is always important for the financial manager. The financing of working capital, however, frequently causes more problems than those associated with fixed capital.

(ii) A cash budget is a useful device to draw attention to future requirements so as to enable proper preparations to be made. It is derived by reference to:

   (a) the master budget and,

   (b) the structural factors which govern the timings of cash flows.

(iii) Timing of cash inflows is related to the level of sales and the period of credit given to customers. The timing of cash outflows is related to the level of production, the period of credit given by suppliers and the level of stocks carried.

(iv) The cash budget is effectively a forecast summary of the cash account and when complete should integrate with the budgeted profit and loss account and balance sheet.

Review questions

(i)   *What are the likely consequences of a failure to budget for cash requirements?*

(ii) *What might cause a business to alternate between situations of cash surplus and cash shortage?*

(iii) *'We expect to make a good profit so cash flow should be no problem.' Why is this too simple a view?*

(iv) *What is the significance of a budgeted balance sheet in the context of a cash budget?*

(v) *A cash budget normally shows a steadily improving cash situation over the life of any capital project. Why would you expect this to be the case?*

(vi) *How can temporary cash surpluses be profitably employed?*

(vii) *From what sources should a temporary cash shortage be met?*

(viii)*What factors would be included in a calculation of the basic long term working capital requirement of a business?*

Exercises

1.   *Mendip proposes to set up a small manufacturing business as from 1st July Year 1. His bank has agreed to grant him overdraft facilities of up to £20,000 and he has £50,000 capital of his own. His friend Cotswold has agreed to give him a loan of £25,000 at a rate of interest of 18% per annum paid six monthly in arrear.*

For the first month Mendip will manufacture for stock only and will also, in that time, build up his raw material stock. He considers that it will be necessary to carry finished stocks equal to one months's future sales and raw material stocks equal to $1\frac{1}{2}$ months' future manufacturing requirements.

He has made the following forecasts of sales and costs. Sales (units): August 10,000; September 12,000; October 15,000; thereafter 18,000 per month. The product will sell at £1 per unit. Material costs will be 15p per unit and labour and variable overhead will each be 20p per unit. Fixed overhead will be £40,000 per annum, including the rent of the premises. Machinery and equipment having an expected life of ten years will have to be bought in July and will cost £60,000 payable immediately.

Creditors for materials and variable overheads will allow one month's credit. Wages will be paid one week in hand (i.e. always one-quarter month owing). Debtors will take $1\frac{1}{2}$ months to pay and fixed overhead will be paid quarterly in advance.

Bank interest and taxation may be ignored. Mendip will make no drawings for the time being.

Prepare:

(a) Manufacturing and material buying schedules for the first six months of operations,

(b) A cashflow forecast up to 31st December Year 1,

(c) A budgeted profit and loss account for the six months ended 31st December Year 1 and a budgeted balance sheet as at that date.

2. Stargazer, plc plans to establish a subsidiary to manufacture and sell a new product. The following estimates of sales and production have been made for the first eight months of the life of the new company, this being regarded as the critical setting-up period.

Month	Sales (000's)	Production (000's)
1	Nil	15
2	Nil	20
3	10	20
4	20	20
5	30	20
6	30	25
7	25	25
8	20	25

After this time production will settle down to 30,000 units per month. Sales will be made at a price of £10 per unit and half of them will be for cash and the other half on one month's credit.

Variable costs of production are expected to be:

Material	£1 per unit
Labour	2
Overhead	3
	£6 per unit

All materials will be purchased on credit, one and a half months being taken for payment. Labour will be paid one week (one quarter month) in arrear and variable overhead will be paid one month after the expense is incurred. Fixed overhead will amount to £300,000 per annum and will be paid quarterly in advance. In the first month machinery costing £450,000 (payable immediately) will be bought and this is expected to last for five years. Stocks of raw material equal to three months' usage will also be bought at that time and this level of stocks will be maintained by purchases in subsequent months.

Stargazer is able to provide £500,000 of permanent finance to be subscribed for shares in the new subsidiary. It will also make an initial loan of a further £300,000 to be repaid in four equal instalments in months 5 to 8.

Prepare a cash budget for the subsidiary for the period for which data are given and forecast its balance sheet at the end of that period.

3. *Starship, plc is considering the investment of £50,000 in new manufacturing capacity and is concerned at the overall burden which this will place on its financial resources. From the following information you are required to prepare a cash budget for its first six months of operations.*

(i) *Schedule of production and sales*

Month	Sales (units)	Production (units)
1	–	2,000
2	–	3,000
3	1,000	4,000
4	2,000	5,000
5	4,000	5,000
6	5,000	5,000

Production and sales will both level out at 5,000 per month after month 6.

(ii)   *Unit contribution*

	£	£
Selling price		6.00
Less Variable cost:		
Material	2.00	
Labour	1.00	
Overhead	1.50	4.50
		1.50

(iii) There will also be avoidable (i.e. direct) fixed cost of £2,000 per month.

(iv) An initial stock of materials will be purchased in month 1 equal to the first three months' usage. Future purchases will be calculated to maintain stock at that period of usage. Suppliers of raw materials give one and a half months' credit. Labour is paid half a month in arrear and variable overhead is paid in the month following that in which it is incurred. Fixed overhead is paid quarterly in advance. Sales will be 50% for cash and 50% on two months' credit.

23: The International Dimension

23.1 International operations

23.1.1 It is often said that the world is steadily becoming a smaller place. What is meant by this is that improved communications make it easier to contact people in other countries by means of telephone or fax and that physical travel to those countries is facilitated by a network of fast and efficient transport services, especially air transport.

23.1.2 To us all, therefore, other countries are becoming less foreign in the sense that they are more familiar. Travel to distant countries is accessible to all and the idea of selling one's product to a customer living in Singapore is no more strange than the idea of selling it to a customer in Sheffield.

23.1.3 The significance of this to financial management is that companies can now regard themselves as operating in markets much larger than that provided by their home nation. This is obviously the case for markets for their ultimate products. Less obviously there are also markets in financial resources. A company may be owned in England, have productive factories in France, sell its goods in America, raise equity finance in Germany and borrow short term funds from Sweden.

23.1.4 All of this increases the complexity of the financial management process but does not change its essential nature. It will still be concerned with making the optimum use of resources to achieve a desired goal but a wider range of resources will be available and new risks will emerge. The dimensions of the decision making process will thus be enlarged.

23.1.5 Foreign trade is by no means a new phenomenon. Britain has always been a trading nation and our ships have carried goods to and from distant parts of the globe since the middle ages and before. In earlier times, however, we traded our manufactured goods for raw materials obtained from abroad. Foreign trade is now multidirectional. It presents not only the opportunities of greater profit from exploiting overseas markets but also contains the threat of competition in the home market from imported goods.

23.2 Opportunities

23.2.1 There are many opportunities offered to a business enterprise by overseas trade and investment and some of the more important of these are set out overleaf:

a) The world market is much larger than the home market so there is an opportunity for greatly increased sales;

b) The cost of capital varies from one country to another so that there may be better investment opportunities in other countries;

c) the cost of labour and other factors of production varies so it may be possible to undertake production more cheaply in another country than one's own;

d) tariff barriers set up by other countries may be overcome by creating production facilities within them and selling goods which do not then have to be imported into the host country;

e) Some countries have a more favourable tax environment than others.

23.2.2 There are also special risks attached to overseas trade and investment which need to be taken into account. Some of these are:

a) The political risk that property may be expropriated by a hostile regime or that the transfer of funds may be restricted or prevented;

b) The risk of currency exchange rate fluctuation which make transactions less profitable than planned;

c) The risk that cultural differences will make it difficult for the company to be accepted into the country concerned, e.g. a prejudice against foreign goods.

23.3 Foreign trade and comparative advantage

23.3.1 The traditional explanation of the economist for foreign trade is that of comparative advantage. It does not require a country to be better at producing a certain product than another for trade to be beneficial to both. It requires only that it be relatively better.

23.3.2 **Example.** The Republic of Cleverland can use a certain unit of resource (i.e. a combination of land, labour and capital) to produce either 20 units of product A or 10 units of product B or any intermediate pro rata combination of these products (e.g. 10 units of product A plus 5 units of product B). In Cleverland, therefore, product B costs twice as much as product A. The Kingdom of Dulland can use the same unit of resource as is used in Cleverland but can produce only 15 units of product A or 5 units of product B. In every way, therefore, production in Dulland is less efficient than it is in Cleverland and the people of that kingdom will enjoy a lower standard of living than the people of Cleverland.

23.3.3 At first sight it might seem that there could be no advantage in trade between the two countries. This is not, however, the case. In Dulland product B costs three times as much as product A. Although product A is more expensive to produce in Dulland than it is in Cleverland in absolute terms is relatively cheaper to produce in terms of the amount of product B which has to be forgone. If trade between the countries exists each country can specialise in what it makes best and exchange this for the product which the other country makes best.

23.3.4 Cleverland should devote its resources to the production of B and will make 10 units. Dulland should devote its resources to the production of A and will make 15 units. Cleverland may now obtain the supplies of B which it requires by trade with Dulland. It will be content if it is able to do so on terms better than 2 units of A for 1 unit of B (because this is what could be achieved internally). Similarly Dulland can obtain the supplies of B which it requires by trading with Cleverland and will be happy to do so on terms better than 1 unit of B for 3 units of A. An actual rate of trade can be established between these limits will give advantage to both countries. For example a rate of exchange of 5 units of A for 2 units of B will enable both countries to benefit. Cleverland's potential ranges between 25 units of A and 10 units of B. Dulland's potential ranges between 15 units of A and 6 units of B. At all points where trade occurs (i.e. where a mixture of products is consumed) both countries are better off. The precise terms of trade will depend on the relative bargaining strengths and skills of the countries.

23.4 Foreign investment

23.4.1 In addition to trade in the sense that goods are sold or purchased abroad there is also the possibility of making investments overseas or of making use of foreign capital.

23.4.2 A company in the UK may invest in an overseas country in one of several ways:

a) It may take a stake as a shareholder in an enterprise which is already established overseas.

b) It may set up an overseas subsidiary using capital raised in the country in which the subsidiary is situated.

c) It may set up an overseas subsidiary using capital raised in the UK.

d) It may set up a branch overseas financing it from internal sources.

23.4.3 Capital budgeting. The capital budgeting process for overseas investment is essentially the same as that for investment at home. There are two important dimensions which, however, may cause special problems. Firstly they may be a much higher degree of uncertainty about the size and duration of future cash flows. Secondly the cash flows to the project may differ from the cash flows to the investing company.

23.4.4 The uncertainties about future cash flows derive from the distance between the investing company and its investment both physically and culturally. When investing in the UK a company will be thoroughly familiar with the environment in which it operates. It will have the benefit of a government operating within constitutional parameters which are clearly understood. It will be in a position to influence events either economically or politically. Investment overseas, however, may be subject to risk from economic uncertainties on which poorer data had been available and to political risks from the unstable regimes which have power in some parts of the world.

23.4.5 In same cases cash flows reaching the investing parent may be the same as total cash flows for the project, subject only to exchange rate fluctuations, about which more is said later. This will be the case when all proceeds are remitted home. Sometimes, however, there may be restriction on the flow of funds so that a portion of the amounts available must be reinvested in the overseas country. Where this occurs it may be wiser to base the evaluation of the investment project on the cash flows which may actually be remitted. This again may have tax implications in the home country.

23.4.6 Sources of finance. Both loan and equity capital may now be raised in world markets thus making it possible to seek the least cost package of finance. Again uncertainties may arise from the possibility of exchange rate and interest rate fluctuations which makes the evaluation of the cost of capital rather more difficult.

23.5 Exchange rate exposure

23.5.1 One of the risks specially associated with overseas operations is that there will be a change in the rate of exchange between the domestic currency and the overseas one. Exposure to this risk has three dimensions which may be categorised under three headings. These are transactions exposure, operating exposure and translation exposure. All of these may lead to unforeseen losses or, of course, unforeseen profits.

23.5.2 The risk from transactions exposure relates to the possibility that the rate of exchange will change after a contract has been entered into but before settlement has been completed.

23.5.3 Example. Worldwide plc agrees to buy 10,000 control valves for 2FF each from France at a time when 9.5FF is equal to £1. It takes one month's credit. When payment falls due the rate of exchange is 8.7FF to £1. Transactions exposure has thus resulted in a loss of £193.59 as calculated below.

Cost as calculated when goods are accepted

$$\frac{10,000 \times 2}{9.5} = £2,105.26$$

Cost when goods are paid for

$$\frac{10,000 \times 2}{8.7} = £2,298.85$$

There is, therefore an unexpected loss of

$$£2,298.85 - £2,105.26 = £193.59$$

23.5.4 The risk from operating exposure relates to the fact that uncertainty about future rates of exchange compounds the normal commercial uncertainty about the amount payable for supplies (if these are obtained from abroad) or the amount receivable from customers (if they are resident abroad). There is not usually any action which can be taken to eliminate this source of risk but it should be taken into account as an extra dimension of overseas operations.

23.5.5 Translation exposure relates to the changes in valuations of assets or in profit which may occur when accounting statements made up in a foreign currency are translated into the domestic currency for the purposes of consolidation. Although they may make a difference to the perception of results they differ from the other exposure risks in that they do not result in any variations in actual real cash flows.

23.6 Foreign exchange market

23.6.1 One of the most pressing needs of trade and investment between countries is a method whereby the currency of one country can be exchanged into the currency of another. If a company in England sells to a customer in Germany, either the English company will have to exchange the marks received for pounds or else the German customer will have to buy pounds for marks and then remit these to the English company for settlement to be achieved.

23.6.2 Not surprisingly there has arisen a world wide market in foreign exchange in which dealers provide this service at, of course, a price which provides an income for themselves. The market is not only world wide but also operational twenty four hours a day. This is because there are financial centres distributed over the globe in such a way that there is always one or more operational.

23.6.3 The foreign exchange markets offer three facilities. These are spot exchanges, forward exchanges and swap contracts. Each of these is described below and we shall see their value in different situations.

23.6.4 Spot Exchanges. This term refers to an immediate purchase or sale of one currency in terms of another at a rate of exchange known as the spot rate. Because the market makers in foreign currency (like those in the Stock Market) have to make an income a given client will pay more for buying a foreign currency than would be received on selling it. The quotation of spot rates will reflect this.

Example. The spot rate for German marks against sterling is 2.30 – 2.35 DM to £1. A UK company wishing to purchase 100,000 marks to pay for purchases in Germany or to make an investment there would have to pay

$$\frac{100,000}{2.30} = £43,478.26$$

If the company had received the 100,000 marks from a German customer it would receive for them

$$\frac{100,000}{2.35} = £42,553.19$$

23.6.5 Forward exchange. This is an agreement to buy or sell now, for immediate settlement, foreign exchange for delivery at a specified time in the future (say three months hence). Rates will be quoted which reflect the expected rate of exchange at that future time, the degree of certainty with which that expectation is held and the time value of money. If, for a given pair of currencies, exchange rates were very stable then the forward rate would differ from the spot rate by an amount which allowed for little more than interest on the money. If the relationship is more volatile the two rates may differ considerably. Forward rates are related to spot rates by being quoted as a difference. This is a premium if the currency is expected to strengthen and discount if it is expected to weaken.

23.6.6 Example. Let us suppose that our UK company has made purchases in Germany for 100,000 marks but is allowed credit so that this is payable in three months time. The mark is expected to weaken in terms of the pound so that, whereas the spot rate is 2.30 – 2.35, the three months forward rate is 0.05 – 0.03 discount. Marks can be deposited in Germany at a rate of interest of 12% per annum. The company has three alternatives. These are:

a) Wait for three months and then buy the required German currency in the market at the then spot rate;

b) Buy the marks now in the spot market and deposit them in Germany at interest until required;

c) Buy the marks now in the forward market for delivery in three months.

The cost of alternative (a) cannot currently be determined as it depends on the rate of exchange in three months' time. This can be predicted but not known. If our company adopts this alternative it exposes itself to the full risk of exchange rate movements which may lead to unanticipated loss or profit. Although some companies may be willing to take this risk, most would see it as a speculation and not within their preferred range of activities as traders.

The cost of alternative (b) can be calculated with more certainty. In order to have available 100,000 marks in three months time our company will have to deposit in Germany at 12% per annum interest (i.e. 3% for the three months) the amount of

$$\frac{100,000 \times 100}{103} = 97,087.38 \text{ marks}$$

In order to purchase this currency in the spot market it would have to pay:

$$\frac{97,087.38}{2.35} = £41,313.78$$

The cost of alternative (c) can also be calculated. The currency is purchased forward at the current forward rate:

$$\frac{100,000}{2.35 - 0.03} = £43,103.45$$

Clearly the better alternative is (c). The advantage of both of these alternatives is that the outcome is certain. The company has been able to avoid any exchange rate fluctuation risk by a process which is termed hedging.

Let us now suppose that it had chosen to accept the risk of a change in the rates of exchange and that, in fact, the spot rate for marks against the £ after the three months had proved to be 2.17 – 2.22. Settlement of the debt would then cost:

$$\frac{100,000}{2.17} = £46,082.95$$

Meanwhile the company would also have had the use of the funds for three months and could have earned interest on them. If the rate of interest had been the same in the UK as in Germany (12% per annum) the net cost in brought down to:

$$\frac{£46,082.95 \times 100}{103} = £44,740.72$$

Although this lies between the two other alternatives it must be stressed that this could not have been predicted in advance. It might as easily have been inferior to both of them or better than both of them.

23.6.7 Swaps. A swap is a single transaction made up of a matched pair consisting of a forward contract for the sale of an amount of foreign currency and a forward contract for the purchase of a foreign currency but with different dates. It is a method whereby a company may finance a trading transaction by, in effect, borrowing foreign currency whilst depositing its own currency as a security for that loan.

23.7 Futures and options markets

23.7.1 In addition to the direct market for foreign exchange described in the previous paragraph there also exists an indirect market in the form of futures and options.

23.7.2 A future is an enforceable agreement to deliver a specified amount of foreign currency at a specified price on a specified future date. It is for a convenient round amount. There might, therefore, exist a future requiring the delivery of 125,000 German marks in three months time at a cost of £50,000. This agreement is traded in a market during its lifetime. The holder may at any time sell the agreement thus parting with both the right and the obligation which it contains. The price at which the sale takes place is determined by supply and demand in the market and will be influenced by the changing rates of exchange between the pound and the mark.

23.7.3 An option is the right to buy (a call option) or sell (a put option) a specified amount of foreign currency at a specified price on a specified future date. If at the specified date rates of exchange have moved so that it is not worth exercising the option it will be allowed to lapse. Otherwise it will be enforced. The price of an option will be much lower than the price of a future and the markets in options will be influenced again by the changing rates of exchange between the two currencies. Unlike a future an option may become completely worthless.

23.8 Commercial documents

23.8.1 A number of commercial documents have become of particular importance in facilitating foreign trade and a number of these are defined below.

23.8.2 **Bill of exchange.** The bill of exchange is a document which allows a trader who gives credit nevertheless to receive immediate cash in respect of the transaction. It operates very like the cheque which actually developed out of the bill of exchange.

Example. Armadillo sells goods having a value of £10,000 to a foreign customer, Bear, on the terms that they will be paid for in three months time. Armadillo draws a bill of exchange for this amount on Bear who signifies (by writing on its face) that it is accepted. The bill of exchange is merely a document which requires Bear to pay the agreed sum to Armadillo or to some other person on Armadillo's order the £10,000 at the agreed date. Armadillo may then sell this bill to others, a banker or another trader, or use it in settlement of a debt at a discount which depends on the time to maturity and the financial status of the drawer and the acceptor. The bill may pass freely from one person to another by endorsement. At the end of the three months it will be presented by its current holder to Bear for payment. Should Bear default, Armadillo and all subsequent endorsers may be pursued for payment.

23.8.3 **Letter of credit.** A letter of credit is issued by a bank and enables a trader to give credit to an overseas customer not well known to him with confidence that the debt will be settled.

Example. Cat, an overseas customer, wishes to buy goods from Dog in the UK for £20,000 with payment due on delivery. Cat is unknown to Dog who does not have the information necessary to make a proper credit rating. Cat is, however, financially reliable and this is known by the Elephant Bank, a bank which operates in Cat's country but which is internationally respected. Elephant, therefore, issues a letter of credit to Dog on behalf of Cat. The effect of the letter is that Elephant guarantees payment of the debt to Dog when Cat receives the goods. It will then be the responsibility of Elephant to recover the money from Cat. Dog is thus relieved of the risk of the transaction.

23.8.4 Bill of lading. A bill of lading is, in effect a receipt from the carrier for the goods which are to be delivered to an overseas customer. Since it is proof of despatch it may be used to claim payment under a letter of credit.

23.9 Translation of foreign currency

23.9.1 Where a business operates through a subsidiary located in a foreign country it will face the problem of the translation of accounting information from that subsidiary stated in a foreign currency into the home currency so the information can be consolidated into its own group accounts. If the rate of exchange fluctuates this will have the effect of creating the potential for distortion in that process.

23.9.2 One way of undertaking a translation is to convert all values at the rate of exchange prevailing at the date of the statement. This is known as the closing rate method. It has the merit of giving an apparently up-to- date picture and of being simple to calculate since the translated amounts will remain in balance. It can, however, lead to apparent fluctuations in the values of fixed assets which are meaningless in terms of real events.

23.9.3 Example. Temperate plc has a wholly owned subsidiary company, known as Hot plc, operating in the Republic of Tropicania where the unit of currency is the teak. The rate of exchange between the teak and the pound sterling fluctuates considerably but at 31 December 19x5, Temperate's year end it stood at 50 teaks = £1. This represented a considerable net change since 1 January 19x5 when it had stood at 30 teaks = £1. At 31 December 19x5 Hot produced a summarised balance sheet as follows:

	Teaks millions
Fixed assets at 1 January 19x1	240	
Less depreciation	40	
		200
Net current assets		150
		350
		250
Share capital		
Revenue reserve at 1 January 19x5	120	
Add profit for year	80	
	200	
Less Dividends paid to Temperate	100	
		100
		350

23.9.4 In order to translate this balance sheet at the closing rate we merely divide each amount by 50. This gives the balance sheet shown below which can easily be consolidated with Temperate's own.

	£000s
Fixed assets at 1 January 19x1	4,800	
Less depreciation	800	
		4,000
Net current assets		3,000
		7,000
		5,000
Share capital		
Revenue reserve at 1 January 19x5	2,400	
Add profit for year	1,600	
	4,000	
Less Dividends paid to Temperate	2,000	
		2,000
		7,000

23.9.5 Although simple in a technical sense this has had strange consequences. The value of fixed assets on 1 January 19x5 is shown in this balance sheet as £4.8 million would have appeared in the previous year's balance sheet (as the closing figure) as £8 million (240,000/30). What the figures are telling us is that there has been a very large loss in the value of fixed assets between the two dates. Unless there has been some change in the productive potential or in their realisable value in Tropicania this does not reflect any actual economically significant change.

23.9.6 There is an alternative method of foreign currency translation which is known as the temporal method. Under this method all physical assets, i.e. fixed assets and stocks, are translated at the exchange rate existing when they were acquired. This puts them on the same basis of valuation as home acquired assets, i.e. cost to the group in the group's home currency.

23.9.7 Liquid assets present a different case and one which can best be exemplified by looking at cash. If Hot holds a cash balance of, say, 500,000 teaks then this is the amount which might be remitted home and, if it were, it would be converted at the current exchange rate. Logic thus suggests that cash and similar liquid assets, e.g. debtors, should be converted at the current rate of exchange.

23.9.8 A precisely similar line of argument can be applied to liabilities as to assets. Thus we would argue that long term liabilities such as the share capital should be valued at the exchange rate prevailing when they were set up, i.e. the actual sterling value of the funds remitted as the original investment. Current liabilities should be valued at the current exchange rate as they will have shortly to be settled out of liquid assets which have been valued on this basis.

23.9.9 This leaves us with the problem of dealing with those amounts representing a flow of items over the period. This includes most profit and loss account items and cash remitted home. The general principle here is that these should be converted at the rate existing at the date on which the transaction occurred. Thus cash remitted home will be translated into the sterling amounts actually received. In the case of the profit and loss account, profits and losses on exchange which impinge on the liquid assets representing profits after they are earned, are separated from profits earned on trading which emerge before these occur. In practice, because of the difficulty of converting every small transaction at its current rate of exchange, an average rate for the whole period is often applied to the total amount concerned.

23.9.10 Example. Hot's balance sheet is as given before in 23.9.3. Conversion is now to be made on the temporal basis. At the time the original capital was subscribed and the fixed assets purchased the rate of exchange was 25 teaks = £1 and the average rate for the year ended 31 December 19x5 was 40 teaks = £1. The amounts remitted in the year realised £2,630,000. The depreciation charged in the profit and loss account was 10 million teaks and the figure for retained profits in the previous balance sheet had been £3,750,000.

23.9.11 Converting on this basis we get:

		£000s
Fixed assets at 1 January 19x1	9,600	
Less depreciation	1,600	
		8,000
Net current assets (3)		3,000
		11,000
Share capital		10,000
Revenue reserve at 1 January 19x5	3,750	
Add profit for year (1)	1,850	
	5,600	
Less Dividends paid to Temperate	2,630	
	2,970	
Add loss on exchange (2)	1,970	
		1,000
		11,000

1)	Teaks million	£000s	
Profit for year	80		
Add back depreciation	10		
	90	2,250	Average
Less depreciation	10	400	Rate when assets acquired
	80	1,850	

2) The "difference" on the balance sheet due to conversion.

3) Assumed, in the absence of other indication to be all liquid.

23.9.12 It is suggested that, since foreign investment is not generally undertaken primarily in order to speculate in exchange variations, differences on exchange should be separately shown and not be "lost" in the main profit and loss account. It is further suggested that the normal accounting convention of conservatism indicates that we should write off against profits any exchange *losses* but that exchange *profits* should be held in reserve to provide for future possible losses.

23.10 Accounting standard

23.10.1 SSAP 20, which was issued in May 1983, deals with foreign currency translation in published accounts. The standard draws a distinction between the situations of individual UK based companies undertaking some transactions denominated in a foreign currency and companies having overseas subsidiaries wishing to translate their accounts for the purposes of consolidation.

23.10.2 Individual companies are required by the standard to translate their foreign currency transactions on the temporal basis and this will also apply to companies operating overseas branches which have no autonomy and are merely a medium through which frequent overseas transactions take place. They will translate each transaction at the rate prevailing at the date of occurrence of the transaction except that for monetary assets and liabilities conversion will be at the rate prevailing at the balance sheet date. Exchange gains and losses may occur and will be included in overall profit or loss.

23.10.3 Example. At the beginning of a financial year Here, plc bought a warehouse in There, an independent republic where the unit of currency is the droll. The warehouse cost 1 million drolls at a time when 10 drolls = £1. Stock was bought at a cost of 500,000 drolls and £49,500 was remitted to pay for this. Stock which had cost 400,000 drolls was sold for 600,000 drolls when the rate of exchange was 10.5 drolls = £1. Cash was received of 500,000 drolls and remitted to the UK where it realised £47,500 after expenses. The rest of the sales remained as debtors at the end of the financial year when the rate of exchange was 11 drolls = £1. The warehouse is to be depreciated over 10 years. Show the accounts of the foreign warehouse in drolls and in £.

23.10.4 HERE PLC
Foreign Warehouse
Profit and loss account

	drolls	Rate of exchange	£
Sales	600,000	10.5	57,143
Cost of sales	400,000	actual	39,600
Depreciation	100,000	10.0	10,000
	500,000		49,600
Profit	100,000		7,543
Balance Sheet			
Fixed asset			
Warehouse	900,000	10.0	90,000

Current assets			
Stock	100,000	actual	9,900
Debtors	100,000	11.0	9,091
Cash	500,000	actual	47,500
	1,600,000		156,491
Investment	1,500,000	actual	149,500
Profit on trading	100,000		7,543
Loss on exchange			(552)
	1,600,000		156,491

23.10.5 In consolidated financial statements, where the subsidiary company operates autonomously within a foreign country, all amounts in the subsidiary's accounts are to be translated at the rate current at the date of the holding company's balance sheet. The only exchange difference which may then arise is a discrepancy between a figure brought forward on reserves translated at the previous year's current rate and that same figure re-translated at the current year's rate. Any such difference should be shown separately as a movement on reserves.

Summary

i) The main components of international operations are:

    a) trade with overseas customers and suppliers;

    b) investment in productive resources in foreign countries;

    c) use of foreign sources of finance.

ii) All of these areas both widen opportunities and increase risk. The operation of comparative advantage provides the incentive for foreign trade.

iii) One special risk of overseas operations is that of variation in the rate of exchange between sterling and foreign currencies. This has ramifications which affect cash flows from foreign investment, amounts received from customers or paid to suppliers and the presentation and interpretation of accounting results. A company can, at a cost, protect itself from this risk by hedging. This is done by appropriate use of foreign exchange markets.

iv) Foreign exchange markets offer a variety of transactions. Some are:

    a) Exchange of currencies at spot rates;

    b) Exchange of currencies for future delivery at forward rates;

c) Swaps;

d) Futures and options.

v) A variety of commercial documents are used to facilitate foreign trading transactions. Those most likely to be encountered are:

a) bills of exchange;

b) letters of credit;

c) bills of lading.

vi) The translation of accounts prepared in terms of a foreign currency may be done by either the closing rate method or the temporal method. SSAP 20, which currently governs translation for reporting entities in the UK, requires the use of the temporal method.

Review questions

i) *Overseas operations are likely to carry greater risk than those at home. Why, then, should companies wish to extend their activities overseas?*

ii) *Discuss the problems involved in the translation of information given originally in terms of foreign currency into sterling.*

iii) *What is meant by hedging? What is its purpose and what are the mechanisms by which it can be undertaken?*

iv) *What is the difference between the forward market and the futures market?*

v) *"New investment has the same implications and should be evaluated in the same way whether it be at home or overseas." Do you agree?*

vi) *"All companies should develop their export business" (Government spokesman). Is this sound advice?*

Exercises

1. *Smith has sold goods in Spain to Escamillo. The total invoiced price of the goods is 2m pesetas payable in three months' time. In order to hedge against exchange rate fluctuations Smith may either:*

   a) *Borrow such sum in Spain as will with interest at the current Spanish rate of 12% per annum be settled exactly when Escamillo pays his account and sell this at the current spot rate of 169 – 172 pesetas = £1 or;*

b)   Sell 2m pesetas at the forward rate of 3 – 4 premium.

Which alternative would you recommend?

2.   Jones has purchased supplies from Luigi in Italy to an invoiced
value of 5m lire payable in three months' time. His is considering:

a)   Buying sufficient lire at the current spot rate of 2249 - 2282
lire = £1 so that invested at the current Italian interest rate
of 8% per annum it will yield the required 5m lire in three
months.

b)   Buying the 5m lire at the three months' forward rate of 8 -
10 discount.

Advise Jones.

3.   On 1 January Manchester plc remitted £500,000 to the island
republic of Tonica, which was to set up a subsidiary with a capital of 1,000,0000 gins (the local unit of currency). In the first
year of operation fixed assets were acquired for 800,000 gins at
a time when the rate of exchange was 2.4 gins = £1. The average
rate for the year was 2.1 gins = £1 and the average rate for the
last three months of the year, over which period the stock were
acquired, was 2.2 gins = £1. The rate of exchange at 31 December was 2.3 gins = £1. The subsidiary's balance sheet at that
date, in local currency units was:

	gins 000s	gins 000s
Fixed assets		
Cost	800	
Less depreciation	100	
	——	
		700
Current assets		
Stock	330	
Debtors	140	
Cash	150	
	——	
	620	
Current liabilities		
Creditors	120	
	——	
		500
		——
		1,200
		====

Share capital		1,000
Profit for year	520	
Less dividends remitted	320	
	——	
		200
		——
		1,200
		══

The amounts remitted during the year realised £152,000. Translate this balance sheet into sterling using the temporal method.

Appendix 1: Answers to exercises

Chapter 1

Exercise 1.1

(i) We must answer this from our knowledge of Financial Accounting but within the context of Financial Management as outlined in the chapter. A balance sheet shows a present position and this will have been arrived at following a series of decisions and of events in the past. Some of these will have left no mark on the balance sheet. Where investments have been made in projects which are now completed and the profits earned and distributed, then there will be nothing to show on the face of the current balance sheet. What is now there is the unfinished business - the ongoing investment activities.

(ii) We can see that there is a total of £144,780 invested in fixed productive assets and that this has required the support of £39,800 of current assets. It is useful to regard the current assets as being financed in part by the current liabilities describing the surplus (i.e. current assets − current liabilities) as working capital. Thus we would regard the creditors as financing the stocks which they supplied and the bank overdraft as financing debtors (the credit we allow to our customers). This balance sheet layout facilitates this approach and shows the working capital at £18,700. This has to be financed out of permanent sources.

(iii) Long term finance is provided from three sources. These are:
  (a) Shareholders (equity finance) £100,000;
  (b) Amounts retained (or saved) from earnings, £33,480 (both General Reserve and Profit and Loss Account fall into this category);
  (c) Amounts borrowed at a fixed rate of interest (debt finance) £30,000.

(iv) We might note that the current liquidity situation appears to be adequate, the current ratio being

$$\frac{£39,800}{£21,100} = 1.89$$

and the liquidity ratio being

$$\frac{£22,800}{£21,100} = 1.08$$

293

but that if the business wishes to expand by investment in further fixed assets, it will require to raise extra long term funds as there appears to be no surplus.

Note our financial manager's concern with the sources of finance, the uses of which that finance is put and the opportunities for future development.

Exercise 1.2

(i) We should first of all see that the fact that available projects are less profitable than existing ones may be disappointing but should not affect any decision we make. The issue is whether the available projects are profitable enough to warrant the raising of the finance for them.

(ii) Since finance costs the company 15% per annum any project yielding more than this will be profitable. Projects A and B are clearly in this category and should be undertaken. Project C is what we would call 'marginal' i.e. we are indifferent as to whether to invest in it or not. Project D is not worth while as it will yield less than we must pay for its finance.

(iii) In real life the following complications may occur:

   (a) Finance is unlikely to be available in unlimited amounts at a given rate.

   (b) There may be a multiplicity of market rates for finance and it may be difficult to decide on the one which is appropriate.

   (c) The returns stated for projects must (since they are future enterprises) be forecasts. In the event these may turn out to be incorrect.

   (d) Projects A to D are the ones which have been located and evaluated by Dodo. There may exist other possibilities of which it is unaware.

Some of these difficulties will be discussed further in later chapters.

Exercise 1.3

(i) **Bad timing for capital raising**. If finance is raised too early it will lie idle pending use and thus earn nothing although it is being paid for. If it is raised too late this may hold up the start of a profitable project and may also lead to disruptions elsewhere in the business. Such a holdup may have to be overcome by the raising of expensive short term finance which would not otherwise have been required.

(ii) **Inefficient capital raising**. If the cheapest available forms of finance are overlooked and more expensive ones used this will have a considerable effect on which projects can be undertaken and on the overall profitability of the business. Another aspect of efficiency in capital raising is that a failure to foresee the long term needs for finance may lead to a series of small capital raising operations each with its own associated costs. A single large funding would generally be more efficient.

(iii) **Inefficient use of funds**. If att2ention is not given to locating the best available projects and evaluating them properly, profits will be much lower than potentially they might be. Actual losses may be incurred.

Exercise 1.4

(i) There is a conflict here between long and short term objectives and between profitability and risk. If the research programme is undertaken the immediate effect on the profit will be at best neutral and at worst quite adverse (depending on how the research expenditure is accounted for). Only in the very long term will there be any pay off in terms of profit.

(ii) The conflict here is to balance the cost of the strike against the cost of the high wages. It is complex in that the increased wages will be for the indefinite future whereas the impact of the strike will be immediate and very substantial. Management will also need to judge whether to give way now and thus save the cost of the strike might make labour more inclined to use the strike threat in future negotiations.

(iii) There is a timing conflict here. Management will frequently find that it will be advantageous to raise funds at one point in time but advantageous to invest them at another. Careful cash budgeting can be of value here and will sometimes allow funds to be raised in advance of requirements in order to take advantage of low interest rates. Another possibility is to finance long term projects on a temporary basis pending a negotiation of better terms in the future.

(iv) There is a conflict here between what a company may see as its moral responsibility to inform its customers of the flaw and its short term interest in disposing of stocks at the best possible price. If the failure (e.g of a motor vehicle component) will put life at risk the company must clearly draw attention to it. If it will merely cause inconvenience (e.g. part of a washing machine) a way round the problem might be to offer repairs and modifications to those customers whose machines do fail.

Exercise 1.5

The managing director's argument is not convincing. A pound tied up in current assets is just as costly to the company as a pound tied up in fixed assets and ought to be considered as carefully. Although individual current assets may be of short term duration the general item current assets occupies a permanent place on the balance sheet and represents a significant permanent employment of funds. The evaluation of benefits may be difficult but it is also frequently difficult in the case of fixed assets. Criteria can be established for an appropriate level for current assets, e.g. the minimum level consistent with a smooth flow of business activities. Frequently particular investments in fixed assets imply associated investment in current assets. For example a new machine may require the creation of a stock of raw materials for its use and may generate debtors in respect of the product which it makes. This should be taken into account in evaluating the project.

Exercise 1.6

Taxation

All business profits are subject to a heavy burden of taxation and any effort directed towards the reduction of this burden will be worthwhile. Thus a financial manager should be aware of any tax concessions which are available to him, e.g. when investing in a development area, and make full use of them.

In addition to reducing the cash flows deriving from any investment, the rules for calculating tax will alter the pattern of cash flows. Taxation will also have a differential effect on the cost of capital from various sources. These factors may profoundly effect the outcome of an investment decision.

Overseas operations lead into another field where a knowledge of taxation both in the overseas country and in the U.K. will be valuable. Double taxation may, for example arise and there may be tax considerations involved in deciding what proportion of profits should be remitted to the home country.

Law

The law is inextricably woven into every aspect of life and particularly business life. An important area of law of concern to the financial manager is the law of contract. This will govern all activities involving parties outside his own company. These include customers and suppliers, employees and the providers of capital. The company will be bound in civil law to observe the terms of its contracts and company law will also constrain the freedom of its activities. A company may not, for example, engage in any activity not permitted by the objects clause in its Memorandum of Association and it may not normally make any distribution to its shareholders until profits have been earned. The law relating to title in assets is fundamental in protecting the ownership of the assets required to operate the business.

Economics

A financial manager is part of a team which is operating an economic unit. This will thus be a part of the greater economic process of applying scarce resources to desirable ends. A knowledge of the workings of this economic process should be helpful in the quest for maximum profits derived from the supplying of a community need.

There are many occasions on which a knowledge of economics will be of direct relevance to financial management decisions. One example is that of the formulation of forecasts of cash flows in investment appraisal and another is in determining the appropriate cost of capital.

Quantitative methods

The financial manager is seeking to quantify economic events and here the relevance of quantitative methods is obvious. Quantitative techniques of specific importance are time series analysis (for forecasting), correlation and regression (for analysing the behaviour of costs), index numbers (for calculations relating to inflation) and probability (for the assessment of risk).

Chapter 2

Exercise 2.1

RED RUM PLC
Cash Flow Statement for the year ended 31 December 19x2

	£000s	£000s
Operating activities:		
Trading profit	3,681	
Amount written off goodwill	30	
Depreciation	690	
Increase in stock	(2,883)	
Increase in debtors	(12)	
Increase in creditors	741	
Net cash inflow from operating activities		2,247
Servicing of finance: Dividends paid		(975)
Taxation		(789)
Investing activities:		
Purchases of plant and machinery	(1,560)	
Sales of plant and machinery	630	
		(930)
		447

Notes on calculations

The net cash flow is:	£000s
Cash at 31 December 19x1	810
Cash at 31 December 19x2	363
	447
Dividends paid:	
Proposed dividend at 31 December 19x1	675
Dividend paid in year	300
	975
Sales of plant and machinery:	
Book value	210
Surplus on sale	420
	630

Exercise 2.2

WASP PLC
Cash Flow Statement for the year ended 31 December 19x4

	£000s	£000s
Operating activities:		
Trading profit	25,230	
Depreciation	3,423	
Increase in stock	(510)	
Increase in debtors	(1,706)	
Increase in creditors	2,420	
Net cash inflow from operating activities		28,857
Returns on investments and servicing of finance:		
Dividends from		
associated company	9	
Dividends paid	(4,800)	
		(4,791)
Taxation		(11,010)
Investing activities:		
Improvements to freehold		
land and buildings	(6,000)	
Disposals of freehold		
land and buildings	4,200	
Purchases of plant		
and machinery	(8,400)	
Sales of plant		
and machinery	1,740	
Purchases of motor vehicles	(795)	
Sales of motor vehicles	339	
		(8,916)
		(4,140)

Notes on calculations

	£000s
The net cash flow is:	
Cash at 31 December 19x3	8,580
Cash at 31 December 19x4	12,720
Net cash outflow	4,140
Dividends paid:	
Proposed dividend at 31 December 19x3	3,000
Dividend for year	5,400
	8,400
Proposed dividend at 31 December 19x4	3,600
	4,800
Depreciation:	
Plant and machinery	2,940
Motor vehicles	483
	3,423
Sales of plant and machinery:	
Book value	210
Surplus on sale	420
	630

Exercise 2.3

Just as a balance sheet summarises a business's position at the end of a financial period and a profit and loss account summarises the outcome of trading operations, so a cash flow statement summarises the major sources and dispositions of liquid resources. It may thus be regarded as a statement showing the effect of a financial manager's activities.

The statement is prepared from information already given in the final accounts in a different form with some further analysis or amplification. Its main categories of cash flow are:

> Operating activities
> Returns on investments and servicing of finance
> Taxation
> Investing activities
> Financing

Any business, however profitable, has to have proper regard to its cash flow. Investment opportunities cannot be taken if the funds for finance are unavailable. Existing operations cannot be properly maintained if suppliers and workers are not promptly paid and if adequate stocks and customer credit are not available. The management of cash is thus as important an area of management as any other.

A cash flow statement enables a shareholder to judge the extent to which proper attention is being paid to the business's liquidity position. It can be verified that there is a correct balance between the absorption of funds by development and maintenance and their supply. Liquidity shortages and surpluses can be analysed and explained. A distinction can be made between short and long term finance and a judgment made on the appropriateness of the balance.

Exercise 2.4

Claverton Plc
Cash Flow Statement for the year ended 31 December 19x7

Operating activities	£000s	£000s
Trading profit	1,063	
Loss on revaluation and disposal of investments	(93)	
Depreciation	540	
Increase in stock	(300)	
Reduction in debtors	50	
Increase in creditors	120	
		1,380
Servicing of finance		
Dividends paid		(600)
Taxation		(950)
Investing activities		
Improvements to buildings	(400)	
Purchases of plant and machinery	(1,090)	
Sales of plant and machinery	350	
		(1,140)
Financing		
Issue of ordinary shares		1,100
		(210)

Notes on calculations:

	£000s	£000s
Net cash flow		
Cash at 31 December 19x6	200	
Investments at 31 December 19x6	540	
		740
Cash at 31 December 19x7	40	
Investments at 31 December 19x7	490	530
		(210)
Sales of plant and machinery		
Net book value	290	
Profit	60	
	350	

Chapter 3

Exercise 3.1

Table showing how the profits of Rex, plc were distributed over the five year period.

Year	1	2	3	4	5
	£	£	£	£	£
Profit	80,000	40,000	20,000	50,000	25,000
Debenture interest (1)	6,000	6,000	6,000	6,000	6,000
	74,000	34,000	14,000	44,000	19,000
Preference dividend (2)	18,000	18,000	14,000 (3)	22,000 (4)	18,000
	56,000	16,000	nil	22,000	1,000
Ordinary dividend (5)	28,000	8,000	nil	11,000	500
Retained profit	28,000	8,000	nil	11,000	500
Rate of ordinary dividend (6)	5.6%	1.6%	nil	2.2%	0.1%

Notes

(1) 6% of £100,000. Payable regardless of profits (or losses).
(2) 9% of £200,000. Maximum, depends on the availability of profits.
(3) Dividend curtailed because there is insufficient profit.
(4) Includes arrears from previous year. They are 'cumulative' shares.
(5) 50% of the amount available.
(6) Calculated as a percentage of nominal value.

The income of the debenture holders is very secure. Even in the worst year there were profits of over three times the amount required to meet the interest. If there were a loss this interest would still be paid thus increasing the loss. In the last resort the debenture holders could force a winding up to obtain payment of their interest and repayment of their principal.

The advantages of the preferential rights can clearly be seen in the case of the preference dividends. Normally adequate profits are available to cover these. Where this was not so (in Year 3) most of the 9% maximum dividend was met and the shortfall was comfortably made up in the following year. We should, however, note that, unlike debenture holders, preference shareholders have no ultimate protection against loss.

The profits of the company fluctuate widely and these fluctuations are communicated in magnified form to the ordinary dividends. Note that where profits fall by one half, as they do between Year 1 and Year 2 and again between Year 4 and Year 5, the ordinary dividend falls by much more than this proportion. This is because of the fixed entitlements of other investors and it will be discussed further later.

Retained profit is obviously an erratic and unreliable source of new investment funds. There is no guarantee that its availability will coincide with the availability of good investment projects.

Exercise 3.2

For a short term shortage of funds it will be quite inappropriate to consider the issue of shares or debentures. There are considerable costs associated with these operations which are disproportionately high when the amounts are relatively small and, once the short term problem is over, there will be the problem of how profitably to use the funds thereafter.

As it is expected that the proposed expansion will shortly be self-financing, we can infer that the difficulty is caused by the necessity to build up stocks of raw material in advance of production and of finished goods in advance of a sales drive together with an expansion of the total amount of credit given to customers. We might, perhaps, comment that we should first of all minimise the extent of our problem by ensuring that debts are collected promptly and that stocks are kept moving as quickly as possible.

The sources of finance we should explore are:

(i) **Creditors**. We may be able to negotiate longer terms of credit if we are now becoming better customers to our suppliers by buying more. This form of finance has the advantages that it is interest free and that its amount rises and falls automatically with an important component of the amount required.

(ii) **Bank overdraft**. Our bank will almost certainly be prepared to allow us an overdraft for a few months at normal rates of interest. We must calculate carefully how much we are likely to need as the bank will give us an overdraft limit and this must not be exceeded once agreed. The bank may also require detailed projections of cash flows showing how we intend to repay the loan within the stipulated time.

(iii) **Debt factoring**. If factors are to be a substantial cause of the requirement for finance, we might consider using the services of a debt factor who will advance immediately cash up to an agreed proportion of all sales. A disadvantage of this method is that it may be inconvenient to enter into an agreement of this kind on a very short term basis.

Exercise 3.3

So-called 'off balance sheet' financing is that form of financing for specific assets which does not give rise to a freestanding liability appearing in the balance sheet. It can best be described by contrasting it with conventional financing in an example.

Hatter is proposing to acquire a new piece of plant which will cost £100,000 and which will last for three years. Two forms of financing are under consideration:

(i) Raising a bank loan to be paid off over the life of the plant. This we might term conventional financing. The plant will appear with other fixed assets on the balance sheet and the bank loan will appear amongst liabilities. Except that the acquisition of the plant provided the reason for seeking the loan, there is no connection between the two transactions. The bank is lending money. Hatter, is buying the plant. The bank acquires no ownership interest in the plant.

(ii) Leasing. Under this method a leasing company will buy the machine on behalf of Hatter, and will then rent it to that company for the whole of its life on agreed terms. There is no liability to the leasing company provided that instalments are met as they fall due* nor is the plant owned by Hatter. The transaction does not, therefore, appear in Hatter's balance sheet at all.

The advantage of off balance sheet financing is that it does not 'use up' conventional financing. There will be a limit to what a bank will lend to any one business. If Hatter uses a leasing agreement in con-

---

* There may be a contingent liability in the event of breach of the contract.

nection with this purchase, the bank loan will still be available for another where, perhaps, leasing could not be arranged.

A domestic example will clarify this. Mr Happy has £5,000 and wishes to do two things. These are (a) to buy a £5,000 car and (b) to gamble £5,000 in Monte Carlo in the hope of winning a fortune with it. If he buys the car for cash he will probably find it extremely difficult to borrow another £5,000 for playing the tables. On the other hand it will be relatively easy to buy the car on hire purchase (off balance sheet) and use the cash for gaming.

Exercise 3.4

No one type of investment can be described as better than another in all circumstances. It is necessary to assess the characteristics of each investment and judge the extent to which they match up with the requirements of the investor. An elderly person with no other source of income than from his investments will be looking for a safe return. A young person with spare funds to invest and personal commitments easily met by the salary from a safe job may be willing to take a risk for the prospect of a higher return.

Preference shares have the following advantages:

(i) The income from them is relatively secure and has a low probability of failure.

(ii) In the event of a winding up there is a high probability that the invested capital will be recovered in full.

They have the disadvantages that:

(i) The income is not protected from inflation and is therefore likely to decline in real terms.

(ii) Recovery of capital, except in a winding up, relies on the price of the share in the stock market.

(iii) The holders of preference shares have no say in the running of the company as they have no vote at meetings.

(iv) When the company does exceptionally well the benefit is denied to preference share holders except to the extent of a minimal improvement in their safety. There is no prospect of an improved income and little prospect of any capital gain.

Ordinary shares have the following advantages:

(i) When the company does well dividends improve, possibly dramatically.

(ii) Dividends and the market value of the shares tend, normally, to rise in line with inflation.

(iii) The holders have, through their vote, a say in the management of the company.

(iv) There is a prospect of large capital gains, e.g. if a takeover bid is made.

They have the disadvantage that

(i) When a company runs into difficulty income and capital value may be reduced substantially or even be totally eliminated.

The friend should be advised that preference and ordinary shares are different investments and their characteristics should be matched against his personal situation and requirements in making his choice.

Exercise 3.5

The advantages of convertible debentures to the company are:

(i) They may be easier to sell because of this added attraction.

(ii) As they are converted the company is relieved of the burden of interest.

(iii) As the terms of conversion need only to be pitched at a level which may be favourable in the future it may be an inexpensive way of redeeming debt.

The advantages for the investor are:

(i) He has the present security of a fixed interest investment but with the option to get into the equity when some of the risks of doing so are over.

(ii) His investment is likely to be more marketable than a pure debenture.

(iii) While conversion is a possibility the market price of the debenture is likely to rise if the price of the equity rises. The fixed interest entitlement, however, will limit the extent of any fall.

It should be noted that the terms of conversion give a right which is restricted as to time and which becomes progressively less favourable. It is obviously administratively convenient to specify a limited number of occasions for conversion. The declining value of the option reflects the uncertainty which makes assessment of the equity value more difficult in the long run.

Exercise 3.6

Equity capital

All businesses must be financed to a substantial extent by equity capital as this bears the risk inevitably associated with enterprise. An equity investor in a company thus acquires a right to a share in the outcomes of its activities and this right cannot be expressed in terms of a measurable financial commitment .

A company has a legal obligation to call meetings of its members at which they are entitled to vote on resolutions and it must accept the result of those votes. It also has an obligation to keep members informed through the medium of regular accounting reports of prescribed minimum content.

There are some less positive constraints imposed on a company by its shareholders. Although it is not obliged to pay them a dividend even where profits allow there will be pressure on it to give its members a reasonable cash return on their investment. Whatever a company does is always liable to challenge by any shareholder who will have considerable power if his holding is large or if he is able to gain the support of others. This ultimate sanction imposes a general constraint on the activities of the company which will need to be seen as being broadly in the interests of the shareholders.

Secured debentures

When a company borrows money by means of an issue of debentures it enters into a binding contract to pay an agreed rate of interest at agreed intervals of time (usually six monthly). In the case of redeemable debentures it also agrees to repay the principal at some time in the future.

Like shareholders, debenture holders have the right to receive annual accounts but they do not have the right to attend and vote at meetings of shareholders. Provided that the terms of the deed establishing the debentures are meticulously observed the debenture holders will have no power to interfere or comment on the management of the company. Where debentures are, as here, secured on specific assets such as a building this fact will restrict the company's right to deal with the asset. In particular it will be impossible to sell or to pledge the asset without the permission of the debenture holders. This is not likely to be given unless some other adequate security for their interests can be offered.

Should the company get into difficulties so that the debenture holders' security of either capital or income becomes in jeopardy they will acquire considerable powers to intervene in the company's operations. This power will be directed towards safeguarding their own position and will not necessarily be exercised in a way which will be of benefit to the company or to its shareholders.

Bank overdraft

A bank overdraft is normally used by a company requiring short term finance through a period of liquidity shortage. It is an arrangement negotiated with the bank as an individual lender and will be on such terms as arise from that negotiation. The terms will include the rate of interest to be charged (which will be variable and related to the bank's base rate) and the amount of the overdraft and length of time for which it will be available.

The essence of a bank overdraft is that it enables a company to draw cheques against its current account in excess of the funds deposited therein. A limit will be set and the level of the overdraft is likely to fluctuate within that limit. Before agreeing to provide overdraft facilities a bank may require that some readily realisable asset (e.g. investments) is offered as security.

It will usually also require accounts of the business so that it can judge its capacity to meet the interest and principal repayments on the overdraft. An overdraft facility may usually be terminated at short notice and this is clearly a constraint on a company which seeks to use an overdraft to finance any long term project.

Chapter 4

Exercise 4.1

It cannot be denied that the Stock Exchange shares some of the characteristics of a gambling casino. There are undoubtedly speculators who buy shares and other securities with the intention of making short term gains for themselves and who are not motivated by any intention to make a long term investment in industrial enterprise. A gambling casino however, has the sole function of redistributing money on a basis determined by chance whilst the main function of the Stock Exchange is to provide a free and efficient market in securities. The stock market speculator can actually be said to contribute to the smooth running of the market as, by and large, he will be prepared to buy shares when others wish to sell them (and they are relatively cheap) and sell them when others wish to buy (and they are relatively expensive).

The Stock Exchange's part in the process of channelling new finance to industry is an indirect one. When one person buys shares in a company through the Stock Exchange he is not making any direct investment in industry but is acquiring rights in an investment already made some time ago. The company itself does not obtain any extra funds from this process. The existence of the Stock Exchange is, however, critical to the process of raising new funds as, if it did not exist, it would be much more difficult to find investors willing to venture their funds. This is because the investment would be virtually irrevocable with no opportunity for the continual reappraisal which the existence of the Stock Exchange allows.

Where a company does make a new offer of shares to raise extra money, the success of this issue may depend in large part on the activities of 'stags'. These are speculators who will subscribe for the shares believing that they can resell them at a profit as soon as dealings commence. It is of no significance to the company that it obtains its funds from this group as they will stand the risk of being unable to sell their shares while the company has obtained the finance which it needs.

Exercise 4.2

The volume of transactions taking place through the medium of hard cash (currency notes and coin), though substantial in absolute amount, is a relatively small part of the total volume of all transactions. Far more transactions are paid for by cheque and other forms of bank transfer (e.g. direct debits and standing orders). If a bank were to act as a mere storekeeper for money then cheque payments would need to be backed by currency stored in the bank's vaults. A bank, however, operates in a quite different manner from this and this enables it to create more money than is deposited with it.

People and firms who use a bank account do so, amongst other reasons, in order to avoid holding large amounts of cash. This is both inconvenient to them and carries a high risk of loss. This same reason will mean that a bank will never be asked to repay in cash all the funds deposited with it. Any profit seeking bank will use this as an opportunity to lend these deposited funds to others and to charge from them a rate of interest.

Let us suppose that customers deposit in Bank X £1,000. Experience shows the bank that only, say, 10% of this is likely to be demanded as a cash repayment whilst the rest will lie idly in its vaults. It may, therefore, safely lend £900 to other customers who will spend the amounts of their loans. If the whole of the banking system behaves in this way it is possible for transactions worth £10 to be financed by cash stored in the banks' vaults of only £1. This is the way in which the commercial banks can be said to create money and its value far exceeds that made in physical form by the Royal Mint.

Exercise 4.3

Direct investment

Any member of the public may invest directly in industrial shares. Opportunities to acquire new shares arise from time to time when companies raise finance by means of a public offer of shares. These can be bought by sending off an application form accompanied by the appropriate amount of money. Application forms are often printed in the daily press and the minimum application accepted is usually quite small bringing it well within the reach of the small saver. It should be noted, however, that small holdings are often uneconomic for brokers to handle. A subsequent sale of the shares may, therefore, be disproportionately expensive. Dividends are paid net of tax and non-tax payers are put to the trouble of reclaiming the tax. This may be a very small amount in respect of each holding and not always worth the trouble.

Unit trusts

A unit trust provides a useful medium whereby a small investor can acquire a stake in a wide spread of industrial shares. Most trusts will purchase existing shares from their previous owners but some investment in new issues may take place. A unit trust makes its units permanently available at a price reflecting the underlying stock market value of the fund and undertakes similarly to redeem them. The small difference between the bid and offer prices provide a 'turn' out of which expenses will be met and profits provided to the management company. A net cash inflow will be invested in newly purchased securities and a net cash outflow will be met by the realisation of securities.

Pension funds

Many people are investors in industrial securities without even knowing it through the medium of their pension schemes. The trustees of a pension fund will have the responsibility of managing the fund created out of the pension contributions of the members so that its value is maximised against the day when it will be required to support the actual payment of pensions.

Endowment life assurance

An endowment policy of life assurance gives to the beneficiaries an agreed sum, often with the addition of bonuses, in the event of death or on survival to an agreed date. Such a policy is therefore, for the policyholder, primarily a form of long term saving. The annual premiums have to be invested by the life assurance company in investments which will maintain or, if possible, improve in value over the years. Part of this money will find its way, through the medium of shares in industrial companies, into industrial investment.

Exercise 4.4

(i) As a consequence of the initial subscription for units £1,000,000 was received.

(ii) This amount was invested in a portfolio of shares conforming to the stated aims of the Crazy Unit Trust.

(iii) The value of the fund was £1,200,000. The offer price was thus:

$$£1.20 + 2\tfrac{1}{2}\% = £1.23 \text{ and the bid price:}$$

$$£1.20 - 2\tfrac{1}{2}\% = £1.17$$

(iv) and (v) An account of these events is:

Cash received for 500,000 units sold (£1.23 each)	£615,000
In respect of 350,000 existing units to be re-issued	430,500
Hence in respect of 150,000 new units	£184,500
Proceeds of resale of existing units (see above)	£430,500
Amount paid on repurchase by managers (£1.17 each)	409,500
Managers' 'turn' on re-issued units	£21,000
Proceeds of sale of new units (as above)	£184,500
Amount for investment in market (£1.20 each)	180,000
Managers' 'turn' on new units	£4,500

(vi) The value of the fund was £900,000. The offer price was thus:

$$90p + 2\tfrac{1}{2}\% = 92.25p$$

and the bid price:

$$90p - 2\tfrac{1}{2}\% = 87.75p$$

(vii) Value of investments realised in respect of net 500,000 units

repurchased from public	£450,000
Cash paid in respect of repurchases	438,750
Managers' 'turn' on units repurchased	£11,250

The management's income is derived partly from an accumulation of the 'turns' on dealing in units as illustrated above. It will also make an annual management charge to be set off against the income received from the investments before this is distributed to the unitholders.

Exercise 4.5

A public issue of shares

A public issue of shares is made where a company makes an offer of shares which can be applied for by the public at large. It is done by public advertisement and the making available of application forms by printing them in newspapers or by issuing them to banks (for issue to their customers). Certain legal formalities have to be complied with, chief amongst these being the issue of a prospectus giving prescribed information.

A public issue has the advantage of casting the net for funds as widely as possible and it may be the only suitable method where large amounts of capital are needed. It is, however, relatively expensive in terms of the incidental costs of the issue.

A rights issue of shares

A rights issue of shares is an issue on a pro rata basis to existing shareholders. It is made where the amount of additional capital required is small relative to the amount already in issue. A shareholder in a company making a rights issue of shares will receive a provisional allotment letter advising him of the number of shares allotted and the price which he must pay in order to take them up. If he does not wish to do this he may sell the rights through the market to some other person.

The advantage to the company of a rights issue is that it has lower incidental costs and it is directed towards people already known to be interested in the company. It also preserves, more or less, the existing pattern of control.

A placing

A placing is the issue of shares to one, or a small number of, substantial investor(s) introduced directly to the company, often by a merchant bank. They may be private individuals but more commonly are institutions, e.g. insurance companies or pension funds.

The method has the advantage of low cost but the disadvantage that it might concentrate a great deal of shareholder power in a small number of hands. This might limit the freedom of the directors in exercising their own judgment.

Exercise 4.6

No person who is not a member of the Stock Exchange may enter the trading floor. This means that the market in securities is not directly available to persons wishing to buy or sell securities as would be, for example, a retail market to the buyer of food. All business has to be conducted through members of the Stock Exchange who have gained their membership after being able to demonstrate professional competence and good character.

Stock brokers and market makers are both members of the Stock Exchange but they have rather different functions. The market maker will man one of the 'stalls' within the market offering to deal in securities which fall within a particular area of activity. All market makers specialise and there will be no point in seeking to deal in, say, government stocks by going to a market maker handling, say, shares in the oil industry. A market maker basically holds himself out as being willing to buy any securities which may be offered to him at his stated buying price and to sell any which may be required at his stated selling price. The difference between these two prices is known as the market maker's 'turn' and will be kept quite small by competition between one market maker and another. It is the market maker's role to set prices so that the number of shares offered to him is exactly the same as the number which he is required to supply.

Thus frequent upward and downward revisions are bound to occur in response to fluctuations in supply and demand. Sometimes a market maker will use his professional expertise to gauge in advance these fluctuations when they result from an announcement of important information. Thus a report on the day in the stock market might say that 'Market makers marked up prices at the outset on the news that Big company, plc had announced record profits. Demand, however, failed to materialise and prices fell back later.'

A broker is the Stock Exchange member who acts as intermediary between the public and the market maker. Thus all market makers' customers are brokers whilst brokers' clients are investors. A broker accepts from a client an instruction to buy or sell certain securities. Sometimes this may be conditional on market prices. Thus an instruction to 'sell my shares at £2.20 or better' means that the broker will sell them if he can obtain at least that price but not otherwise. The broker is responsible for completing all formalities relating to the purchase or sale of shares, i.e. preparing transfer deeds, obtaining signatures, stamping and registration with the company. For his services he will charge a commission based on the total value of the transaction.

Here is an example of the working of the Stock Exchange. A wishes to sell 100 shares in X, plc at the best price obtainable. He gives his instructions to B, his broker. B enters the market and asks J, the market maker, for a quotation for 100 shares but without indicating whether he is a buyer or a seller. J says, '£3.60, £3.80'. B says, 'I sell you 100 shares at £3.60'. Meanwhile W wishes to buy 100 shares in X, plc. He instructs his broker, K, to deal for him. K also approaches J and (if it is at the same time) receives the same quotation as did B.

He says 'I buy 100 shares at £3.80 '. A receives £360 less broker's commission. W pays £3.80 plus broker's commission. Thus the transfer is achieved and brokers and market makers are remunerated for their services.

Since the time of 'Big Bang' on 27th October 1987 most of the transactions described above have been done through computer links and trading by a physical meeting on the floor of the Stock Exchange has largely disappeared.

Chapter 5

Exercise 5.1

The cost of equity capital is equivalent to the yield received by an equity holder with an investment at the present market price. Although, no doubt, the presence of reserves is a factor contributing to the level of this, the actual figures for share premium and profit and loss accounts are irrelevant to our calculations. Hence:

$$E = \frac{d}{m} \times 100$$

$$E = \frac{20p}{£1.30} \times 100$$

$$= 15.38\%$$

Similarly cost of preference capital is given by:

$$p = \frac{d}{m} \times 100$$

$$E = \frac{3p^*}{40p} \times 100$$

$$= 7.5\%$$

*not 6p. They are 50p shares.

Cost of debt is given by:

$$p = \frac{i}{m} \times 100 \, m$$

$$E = \frac{£10}{£167} \times 100$$

$$= 6\%$$

To determine an average cost of capital we must now average these values using the market value of the securities as weights.

Security	Market value		Cost %	Mkt. Value × Cost
	£			£
Ordinary shares	650,000	(1)	15.38	9,997,000
Preference shares	60,000	(2)	7.5	450,000
Debt	208,750	(3)	6.0	1,252,500
	918,750			11,699,500

(1) $500,000 \times £1.30$

(2) $150,000 \times 40p$

(3) $125,000 \times \dfrac{167}{100}$

$$\text{Cost of capital} = \frac{\text{Market value} \times \text{cost}}{\text{Total market value}}$$

$$= \frac{11,699,500}{918,750}$$

$$= 12.73\%$$

Exercise 5.2

We assume that the existing capital structure is to be maintained and that therefore fresh issues are to be made in the same ratio of market values as at present exist. The respective costs of new capital are:

Equity

$$E = \frac{d}{m-c} \times 100$$

$$E = \frac{20p}{£1.20 - 2p} \times 100$$

$$= 16.95\%$$

Preference capital

$$P = \frac{d}{m-c} \times 100$$

$$= \frac{3p}{35p - 1\frac{1}{2}p} \times 100$$

$$= 8.96\%$$

Debt

$$D = \frac{i}{m-c} \times 100$$

$$= \frac{£10}{£167 - £1} \times 100$$

$$= 6.02\%$$

Weighting this as before we get:

Security	Market value		Cost %	Mkt. Value × Cost
	£			£
Ordinary shares	650,000	(1)	16.95	11,017,500
Preference shares	60,000	(2)	8.96	537,600
Debt	208,750	(3)	6.02	1,256,675
	918,750			12,811,775

$$\text{Marginal Cost of capital} = \frac{12,811,775}{918,750}$$

$$= 13.94\%$$

Exercise 5.3

On the assumption that Watson has attained a preferred capital structure, it is incorrect to think of a project as being financed by any specific source of funds such as either preference capital or debt. It should be thought of as being financed out of funds raised *pro rata* from all currently used sources. This is the case even if, for convenience, only one source is actually to be used. The assumption is that if debt is used on this occasion then that will oblige management to use equity on a future occasion to restore the capital structure. Thus the figure to use as the cost of capital in evaluating the project is the marginal weighted average cost of capital of 18%. On this basis the project is not, in fact, an acceptable one.

Exercise 5.4

The critical points will occur whenever there is a change in the marginal cost of capital. We must interleave the critical points for debt with those with equity. The presumed mix of equity and debt, however, is to be the 75:25 observed at present.

75% equity	25% debt	marginal cost	average cost
£250,000 (20%)	£83,333 (16%)	19% p.a.	16% p.a.
300,000 (20%)	100,000 (16%)	22.75% p.a.	16.32% p.a.
500,000 (25%)	166,667 (18%)	23.35% p.a.	17.43% p.a.
600,000 (30%)	200,000 (18%)	27% p.a.	18.13% p.a.

Exercise 5.5

Using the formula for cost of equity

$$E = \frac{d}{m-c} \times 100 + g$$

We get

$$18 = \frac{1200}{m - 2} + 10$$

$$8 = \frac{1200}{m - 2}$$

Thus: $m = 152$

It is suggested that the company offer 666,667 shares at a price of £1.50 each.

If the price is put higher than the calculated figure the issue might be expected to fail because not all the shares offered will be taken up. if the price is lower there will be an oversubscription. All the shares will then be sold but some of the benefit of the premium will go to the successful applicants, who will make an immediate profit, and not to the company. In practice Moriarty would be advised to pitch the offer price a little below £1.50 to guarantee the success of the issue and to allow for market fluctuations which may occur between the date of fixing the offer price and the actual date of the issue.

Exercise 5.6

There are two fallacies in the Board's thinking. The first arises from the assumption that a new 8% debenture would cost only 8% per annum. This would be true only if the debenture could be issued at par. With the existing, higher coupon, issue currently standing in the market at a discount, this is plainly impossible. The likely issue price would be given by

$$100 \times \frac{5}{11}\% = 45.45\%$$

It should also be noted that, to a debenture holder, the ultimate success or otherwise of a project is of very little significance as his income and capital repayments are secured by contract. Any exceptional success of the project will result in extra profit for equity holders and not for debenture holders.

The second fallacy arises in supposing that the proposed debenture issue can be regarded as being a project specific source of finance. In the long run the preferred capital structure of the company must be maintained and, therefore, the overall cost of capital should be applied in all cases regardless of the actual source of funds currently being tapped.

The cost of capital may be determined as follows. The cost of equity is given by:

$$E = \frac{d}{m} \times 100\%$$

$$= \frac{15p}{180p} \times 100 + 5\%$$

$$= \underline{\underline{13.33\%}}$$

The cost of debt is given by:

$$D = \frac{i}{m} \times 100 + g$$

That is,

$$D = \frac{10}{90.91} \times 100\%$$

$$= \underline{\underline{11\%}}$$

The weighted average cost of capital emerges as follows:

	Market value £	Cost %
Equity	1,800,000	13.33
Debt	181,820	11
Weighted average	1,981,820	13.12

The weighted average cost of capital is above the internal rate of return on the proposed project which would not, therefore, be worthwhile. The inclusion of costs of issue in the calculation of the cost of capital, ignored here, would lead to an even more unfavourable comparison.

Chapter 6

Exercise 6.1

The traditional view is that the cost of capital can indeed be reduced by increasing the proportion of debt to equity but that there is a limit to this process. Eventually the increased financial risk will increase the cost of both equity and debt prohibitively. Thus, if we increase our gearing ratio to 1, i.e. equal parts of debt and equity, our cost of capital should fall as shown below:

	Market value	Cost
Equity	£10 million	18%
Debt	£10 million	10%
Weighted average 14%		

If, however, we increase gearing ratio to 5, massively loading the financing in favour of debt, the effect of financial risk is clearly seen

	Market value	Cost
Equity	£10 million	25%*
Debt	£50 million	20%*
Weighted average 20.83%		

* These figures are illustrative and were not taken from data given in the question .

The position is illustrated graphically on the following page.

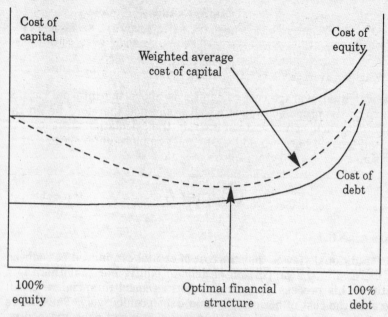

The view of the adherents to the Modigliani/Miller theory, however, is that the cost of capital is unaffected by the capital structure. As gearing increases the cost of equity increases such as precisely to off-set the reducing effect of the increased debt. Thus:

With gearing ratio of 1

	Market value	**Cost**
Equity	£10 million	24.54%*
Debt	£10 million	10%
	Weighted average 17.27%	

With gearing ratio of 5

	Market value	**Cost**
Equity	£10 million	53.62%*
Debt	£50 million	10%
	Weighted average unchanged at 17.27%	

* Adjusts itself through the mechanism of a fall in the share price caused by the market operation of arbitrage.

Again this is represented graphically on the following page.

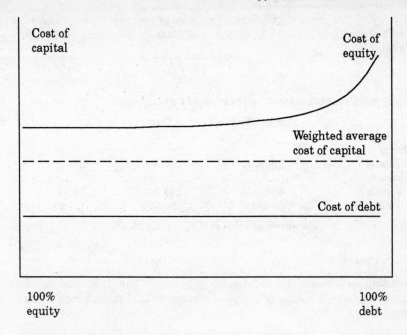

100%
equity

100%
debt

Exercise 6.2

On the Modigliani and Miller theory the total value of Order and Chaos must be equal as they are identical in every commercial sense. The position shown is one of disequilibrium as their market values appear to be unequal. Investors will sell shares in Order and buy shares in Chaos until the total value is equalised.

This can be demonstrated as being worthwhile to them as follows:

	Value	**Income**
Previous holding in Order (say)	£1,000	£250
Invest this sum in Chaos	£1,000	
Less sufficient reduction in borrowing (or actual lending at the market rate) to equate gearing to that of Order, i.e.		

$$\frac{300}{900} \times 1,000$$

	333	39.96
	667	237.50
Net income (higher than before)		£277.46

At equilibrium the valuation of the firms will be equal at, say, £950,000. Thus:

	Order	Chaos
Value of equity	950,000	650,000
Value of debt		300,000
	£950,000	£950,000

The cost of capital for each firm is then equal. Thus:

	Market Value £	Cost £	%
Order			
Equity	950,000	250,000	26.3
Chaos			
Equity	650,000	214,000	32.92
Debt	300,000	36,000	12.00

Weighted average cost of capital 26.3%

Exercise 6.3

Gearing expresses the relationship between the debt and equity components in a company's capital structure. It is determined by the formula:

$$G = \frac{D}{E}$$

where G = Gearing ratio

D = Market value of debt

E = Market value of equity

G may vary between 0 (all equity financed) and 1 (all debt financed). The higher the value of the gearing ratio the greater the proportion which the fixed interest is of the available profit and the more liable to fluctuation is the residue attributable to equity. A gearing ratio of .2, for example, implies that there is £1 of debt financing for every £4 of equity.

The theoretical justification for this level of gearing would rely on showing that it produced the minimum cost of capital. This would imply a rejection of the Modigliani/Miller theory and support for a traditional view. In practice it would be very difficult to obtain figures which would demonstrate that a minimum cost point had been reached. Alternatively empirical arguments could be mustered on the basis that the company had been well served in the past by this ratio and had found from experience that it gained the benefits of low cost debt financing without incurring the penalties of high financial risk.

Supporting arguments might be derived from a consideration of the corresponding ratios relating to other similar businesses.

Exercise 6.4

The cost of capital should be related to the long term gearing ratio, the current position being regarded as transitory. Thus the figure to be used for investment appraisal is:

	Weight	Cost
Equity	3	15% p.a.
Debt	1	10% p.a.

Average cost of capital is
13.75% per annum.

Future investment should be financed by debt, which is currently under-represented, until the gearing ratio is restored to .25. It is currently only .11.

Exercise 6.5

The risk free level of interest earned by debt is likely to be lower than the risky income received by equity. In the situation where a company is wholly equity financed a small increment in the amount of debt (from nil) does not markedly affect its risk. It is, therefore, almost certain to reduce the overall cost of capital. At the other end of the scale, where a company is almost wholly debt financed virtually all of the commercial risk falls on debt since there is no equity to provide a buffer. Its cost must, therefore, rise well above the risk free rate.

These suppositions do not necessarily imply a unique optimum gearing ratio. The curve may be very flat. MM would argue that it is a straight line with only its extremities diverging from this.

Exercise 6.6

If Polonius is wholly equity financed it means that all of its funds have been derived either from issues of ordinary shares or from the retention of profits otherwise available for the payment of dividends. Since its gearing is nil its equity holders are exposed directly to commercial risks and these are not magnified by the addition of financial risk. In the event of loss the shareholders are less vulnerable but in the event of high profits they cannot enjoy the magnification which gearing would give.

The effect on a company's cost of capital of its capital structure is a matter of crucial interest but no definitive theory has yet emerged to give positive guidance on this. Traditional theory would argue that debt is cheaper than equity because it is less risky to the investor (at low levels of gearing) and that therefore the ungeared company is missing the opportunity of 'diluting' its expensive equity.

Here is an example to illustrate this. We will suppose that Polonius's cost of capital (i.e. cost of equity) is 15% per annum. If debt were used to provide up to one tenth of the finance this would cost 10% per annum. By introducing gearing the overall cost of capital would be reduced to

$$(15 \times .9) + (10 \times .1) = \underline{\underline{14.5\%}}$$

The alternative theory of capital structure, attributed to Modigliani and Miller, states that the total value of a company is fixed regardless of its method of financing and that therefore gearing cannot affect this. Thus, extending our example and introducing more assumed information where necessary we obtain the following:

Absence of gearing	**Market value**	**Cost**
Equity	£1 million	15%
Gearing as before	**Market value**	**Cost**
Equity	£.9 million	15.56%*
Debt	£.1 million	10%
	Average cost of capital 15%	

* The theory indicates that in the event that debt were issued the cost of equity would rise so that there would be no overall change in the cost of capital. This could be interpreted as a rise in the cost of equity to compensate the holders for the increased risk which they now bear.

Thus it may be that Polonius's policy represents the loss of a valuable opportunity or it may be completely unimportant depending on which theory one supports. Most Boards of Directors seem to take the view that the existence of debt is a valuable part of capital structure. It would clearly have an advantage in another connection if any future contraction of the company were envisaged as generally it is easier to redeem debt than to redeem equity.

Chapter 7

Exercise 7.1

We must consider only relevant costs, i.e. those changed by the decision. This gives us the following statement leading to the contribution made by the branch:

Sales		£52,000
Cost of sales	£23,800	
Branch running costs	10,200	
Wages	12,500	
Manager's remuneration (1)	3,520	50,020
Contribution		£1,980

(1) This one may present some difficulty. Remember that this statement contains the costs avoided by the decision to close the branch. £1,000 of the manager's salary is not avoidable as he will continue to receive it as a 'premium' over and above the value of his new post.

Exercise 7.2

The fixed cost specific to the product is 75p × 4,000 = £3000

The unit contribution is £5 – £1 – £2 = £2

$$\text{The break even point is } \frac{\text{Fixed cost}}{\text{Unit contribution}} = \frac{£3,000}{£2}$$

$$= 1,500 \text{ units}$$

At the planned level of output there is a standard profit of 50p × 4,000, i.e. £2,000. The contribution will, however, be £2 × 4,000, i.e. £8,000. Of this, £3,000 will be absorbed by the fixed overheads specific to the project leaving £5,000 as a contribution to the overall position. Although £2,000 is given as the profit, therefore the profitability of the business overall will be improved by £5,000 if the product is made.

Exercise 7.3

Avoidable costs of producing the components are material, labour and variable overhead only. By definition fixed overhead will be unaffected by the decision to buy.

Costs are therefore:
Material	£2.80
Labour	3.20
Variable overhead	3.20
	£9.20

There is a net saving of 80p per 100 components in producing them and so prima facie it is better not to accept the works manager's recommendation to buy. The differential is fairly small, however, and the decision might go differently when other relevant factors are considered. Some of these are:

(i) Will buying rather than manufacturing release manufacturing capacity which can be profitably used elsewhere or profitably disposed of?

(ii) Can a better price be negotiated from the potential supplier if a long term contract is entered into?

(iii) Would outside supplies be more or less secure than those from Derwent's own factory?

(iv) Would it be possible to maintain lower stocks (or would these be higher) if we used outside suppliers?

(v) Is there any quality difference between own-made and bought out components?

(vi) Are there any market considerations? (E.g. being able to say that the product is of 100% British origin in advertising).

Exercise 7.4

The volume of production is the key factor in this decision. At low levels of production the manual process is better because of the low fixed component of its cost. As production levels rise and the fixed cost becomes a relatively small part of total cost then the lower variable cost of the machine process becomes more significant. The break even point between the two can easily be calculated.

Let x = the number of units processed at the break even point i.e. when the cost of either process is the same.

$$£x + £2,000 = £2x + £10,000$$
$$£8x = £8,000$$
$$x = 10,000 \text{ units}$$

If production is below 10,000 units the manual process will be cheaper. If above this level the machine process will cost less. It should be noted that changing between the two can probably be done only once i.e. having made the investment in the machine this could be realised only at great loss. The decision to mechanise, therefore, should be taken only if a *sustained* demand of over 10,000 units per annum is anticipated.

Exercise 7.5

The original cost of the raw material is irrelevant to the decision and should be left out of account. The consequence of adopting each suggestion should be assessed in terms of the net cash inflow or outflow which would result. These are:

(i) There will be a net inflow of £2,000

(ii) There will be a net inflow of:

Sales		£12,500
Less Additional material	£2,000	
Labour	4,000	6,000
		£6,500

(iii) There will be a net inflow of:

Saving	£6,000
Less Conversion cost	3,500
	£2,500

Proposal (ii) is clearly the one to choose.

Exercise 7.6

We should first set up a statement showing the results of the past year after taking into account only relevant costs. Thus:

	Total £	Knights £	Pawns £	Bishops £	Rooks £
Sales	188,000	73,000	62,000	39,000	14,000
Material	35,000	10,000	12,000	9,000	4,000
Labour	31,000	12,000	8,000	9,000	2,000
Variable overhead	41,000	15,000	10,000	12,000	4,000
Relevant cost	107,000	37,000	30,000	30,000	10,000
Contribution	81,000	36,000	32,000	9,000	4,000
Contribution per £ of labour		£3	£4	£1	£2

We have calculated contribution per £ of labour because labour is a limiting factor. It needs to be applied where it will be most beneficial. Pawns are thus best (i.e. most profitable) and we should use as much labour as possible on making them. Bishops are the least good product and we should minimise their production. The other two products can be ranked similarly.

The following calculation shows how labour will be allocated:

	Total £	Knights £	Pawns £	Bishops £	Rooks £
Minimum sales	150,000	58,400	49,600	31,200	11,200
(80% previous year)					
Labour used for this	24,800	9,600	6,400	7,200	1,600
Labour remaining	6,200	* 3,600	2,400	—	200
Total labour	31,000	13,200	8,800	7,200	1,800

* This is allocated in the following order of preference (based on contribution per £ of labour) Pawns, Knights, Rooks, Bishops. The maximum allocation is that which brings sales up to 110% of the previous year's level, i.e. a maximum of 3/8 of the labour already allocated.

The projected profit and loss account for the following year, with fixed overhead absorbed on the basis of sales as before, is:

	Total £	Knights £	Pawns £	Bishops £	Rooks £
Sales	192,300	80,300	68,200	31,200	12,600
Material	35,000	11,000	13,200	7,200	3,600
Labour	31,000	13,200	8,800	7,200	1,800
Variable overhead	40,700	16,500	11,000	9,600	3,600
Fixed overhead	46,500	19,417	16,492	7,544	3,047
Total cost	153,200	60,117	49,492	31,544	12,047
Profit/(Loss)	39,100	20,183	18,708	(344)	553

Chapter 8

Exercise 8.1

Calculate the trend by means of a moving average and determine the seasonal variations from this trend. This is done in the table below.

(Figures below are in £000's)

Year	Quarter	Sales	Sums of 4	Paired sums of 4	Moving average	Seasonal variations
19-4	1	53.1				
	2	49.2				
			209.6			
	3	52.4		418.4	52.30	+0.10
			208.8			
	4	54.9		416.7	52.09	+2.81
			207.9			
19-5	1	52.3		415.2	51.90	+0.40
			207.3			
	2	48.3		413.2	51.65	-3.35
			205.9			
	3	51.8		410.9	51.36	+0.44
			205.0			
	4	53.5		409.3	51.16	+2.34
			204.3			
19-6	1	51.4		407.0	50.88	+0.52
			202.7			
	2	47.6		404.7	50.59	-2.99
			202.0			
	3	50.2		403.5	50.44	-0 24
			201.5			
	4	52.8		401.5	50.19	+2.61
			200.0			
19-7	1	50.9		399.3	49.91	+0.99
			199.3			
	2	46.1		397.4	49.68	-3.58
			198.1			
	3	49.5		394.5	49.31	+0.19
			196.4			
	4	51.6		392 0	49.00	+2.60
			195.6			
19-8	1	49.2		390.4	48.80	+0.40
			194.8			
	2	45.3		388.3	48.54	-3.24
			193.5			
	3	48.7				
	4	50.3				

Summary and average of variations

Year	First quarter	Second quarter	Third quarter	Fourth quarter
19-4	+0.10	+2.81		
19-5	+0.40	-3.35	+0.44	+2.34
19-6	+0.52	-2.99	- 0.24	+2.61
19-7	+0.99	-3.58	+0.19	+2.60
19-8	+0.40	-3.24		
Totals	+2.31	-13.16	+0.49	+10.36
Means	+0.58	-3.29	+0.12	+2.59

The average decrease in trend is:

$$\frac{52.30 - 48.54}{15} = .251$$

Forecast 19-9

Quarter	Trend	Seasonal variation	Expected improvement	Price increase	Forecast
1	47.79	+0.58		+5%	50.79
2	47.54	- 3.29		+5%	46.46
3	47 29	+0.12	+2%	+5%	50.78
4	47 04	+2.59	+4%	+5%	54.20
					202.23

It should be noted when working with declining trends that (unlike rising trends) they must at some stage flatten out (unless the business is to end up with negative sales!)

Exercise 8.2

Rifleshoot, plc

	Sales volume relative to last year at 1% increased prices		
	90%	**100%**	**110%**
	£	£	£
Sales	1,105,231	1,228,035	1,350,838
Material	216,141	240,157	264,173
Labour	116,459	129,399	142,338
Variable overhead	115,903	128,781	141,659
Total variable cost	448,503	498,337	548,170
Contribution	656,728	729,698	802,668

	90% £	100% £	110% £
Fixed overheads	198,156	198,156	198,156
Depreciation	350,000	350,000	350,000
Loan interest	90,000	100,000	150,000
Total fixed cost	638,156	648,156	698,156
Net profit	18,572	81,542	104,512

It is interesting to note the very considerable effect which relatively small variations in sales are expected to have on profit.

Exercise 8.3

We might note first of all that what is proposed is an extension and formalisation of what is currently done rather than a completely new departure. The Board would have proper plans with which to compare actual results rather than having to apply a subjective judgment of what is satisfactory as they do now.

The preparation of detailed budgets would require:

(i) a forecast of future conditions and an analysis of their effect on the level of sales, costs and working efficiency;

(ii) a detailed analysis of current operations in terms of cost structures and of areas of control and responsibility;

(iii) the formulation of a plan based on the foregoing in which every aspect of business expense and revenue are included;

(iv) the construction of cash flow and capital expenditure plans which are required by the profit plan.

There are several advantages which might be expected to follow from the introduction of budgetary control. The more important are:

(i) the necessary review of current working is likely to draw attention to potential areas for improvement;

(ii) the whole of the management team and not merely the Board of Directors can become active in the formulation and achievement of plans;

(iii) the Board will be given consistent criteria for judging results and will more clearly see what action is required and in what area it is necessary;

(iv) it will be possible to attach firm responsibility for action to appropriate members of the management team;

(v) the effects of any divergences from plan can easily be quantified in terms of profit lost so that the important can be distinguished from the unimportant.

One objection which is likely to be raised to the introduction of budgetary control is the administrative and clerical cost involved. It can be pointed out that much of the detailed framework is already there as monthly accounts are already prepared and that the additional costs should be easily outweighed by the benefits.

Exercise 8.4

Actual profit has fallen short of planned profit by £43,043 and this shortfall should be analysed and, so far as possible, explained.

Sales	£
Planned sales were	1,489,487
The strike reduced this by $\frac{1}{12}$	124,124
To	1,365,363
Higher selling prices increased this by 2%	27,307
	1,392,670
The remainder was sales in excess of budget during the unaffected months	39,528
	1,432,198*

* At budget prices (for volume comparisons)

$$£1,432,198 \times \frac{100}{102} = £1,404,116$$

Materials

Budgeted material at actual level of sales

$$£536,214 \times \frac{1,404,116}{1,489,487}$$

	505,480
Second half of this increased by 5% price rise	12,637
	518,117
Increase usage over planned quantity	13,329
	531,446

Labour £
Budgeted labour at actual level of sales

$$£327,687 \times \frac{1,404,116}{1,489,487}$$

308,905

Increase due to unexpected part of wage rise

$$£308,905 \times \frac{2.5}{105}$$

7,354

316,259
Savings by improved efficiency 2,072

314,187

Factory overheads
Fixed portion 50% of £283,030 141,515
Variable portion budgeted at actual level of sales

$$£141,515 \times \frac{1,404,116}{1,489,487}$$

133,404

274,919
Extra due to reduced efficiency and/or price rises 743

275,662

Selling costs
Fixed portion 70% of £59,860 41,902
Variable portion budgeted at actual level of sales

$$30\% \text{ of } £59,860 \times \frac{1,404,116}{1,489,487}$$

16,929

58,831
Increased transport costs following strike 8,200

67,031
Extra due to reduced efficiency and/or price rises 1,917

68,948

Administrative costs
Fixed portion 80% of £86,290 69,032
Variable portion budgeted at actual level of sales

$$20\% \text{ of } £86,290 \times \frac{1,404,116}{1,489,487}$$

16,269

85,301

	£
Wage award £86,290 × .6 × $\dfrac{2.5}{105}$	1,233
	86,534
Saving due to increased efficiency and/or price falls	234
	86,300

Loan interest
As interest rates have been as expected, this amount must
be due to increased borrowing

	£
	2,180

Depreciation
This is very close to the budgeted amount. The small difference may be
accounted for by sales or purchases of fixed assets.

In order to avoid detailed examination of areas which do not warrant such attention, it is quite usual to set some arbitrary level
below which variances will be disregarded. We will set this at 1% of
budgeted profit, i.e. £1,142.

The following observations on variances in excess of this figure may
be made:

(i)   The transport strike was a matter beyond management control
but was by far the most important event of the year from the
point of view of its impact on planned profit. About 30% of the
lost volume was made up in other months and the price increase
helped to keep revenue losses to reasonable proportions.

(ii) The material price increase was not under management control.
The increased usage is serious and should be carefully investigated. It accounted for over 30% of the reduction in profit.

(iii) Again the wage increase is outside the control of this company.
It is, however, encouraging to see that nearly half of its cost was
recouped by improved efficiency.

(iv) The reduced efficiency of the selling costs is cause for concern
and should be carefully investigated.

(v)   A tight rein must be kept on borrowing which substantially
exceeded the plan. Areas to examine would be stockholdings,
debtors and cash holdings.

Chapter 9

Exercise 9.1

The amount to be invested in the project is not given directly in the question. It must, however, be the total amount shown in the accounts as depreciation, i.e. £6,000 × 5 = £30,000.

The returns given by the project for D.C.F. purposes are the sales less the direct costs. Depreciation has no part in the calculation. We must, therefore, recalculate the figures given.

	Year 1	Year 2	Year 3	Year 4	Year 5
Sales	£20,000	£22,000	£23,000	£16,000	£12,000
Direct costs	10,000	12,000	13,000	10,000	10,000
Returns	£10,000	£10,000	£10,000	£6,000	£2,000

We now calculate the net present value of the project in the ordinary way using the discount factors appropriate to a cost of capital of 12% per annum.

Year	Returns	Discount factor	Present value
	£		£
1	10,000	.893	8,930
2	10,000	.797	7,970
3	10,000	.712	7,120
4	6,000	.636	3,816
5	4,000	.567	2,268
			£30,104
Initial investment			30,000
Net present value			+£104

There is a positive net present value so the investment is (just) worthwhile.

Exercise 9.2

The methods discussed in the text are:

(a) Pay back method (section 9.3)

(b) Average rate of return (section 9.4)

(c) Discounted cash flow methods:
   (i) Net present value (section 9.6)
   (ii) Internal rate of return (section 9.7)

Although D.C.F. methods are conceptually superior to the others, the indications given may not be so very different. A crude method may be justified if, in practice, it gives acceptable results particularly where it enables relatively unimportant decisions to be taken rapidly at a low level of management. There are costs attached to the decision making process which, like any other costs, need to be justified by what benefits they bring.

Exercise 9.3

The internal rate of return is that rate which, if applied in a D.C.F. calculation, would lead to a net present value for the project of nil.

As a first approximation, in this case, calculate the average rate of return.

	£
Total returns	20,000
Less Initial investment	13,500
	£6,500

This is equivalent to $\dfrac{£6,500}{5}$ = £1,300 per annum

Average rate of return is $\dfrac{£1,300}{£6,750}$ = £19.26%

Since this method does not take into account the time value of money it will overstate the internal rate of return.

Let us, therefore, try 16% per annum.

Year	Returns	Discount factor	Present value
	£	(16%)	£
1	2,000	.862	1,724
2	4,000	.743	2,972
3	6,000	.641	3,846
4	5,000	.552	2,760
5	3,000	.476	1,428
			£12,730

Since this leads to a negative net present value we have selected too high a rate of discount.

Try 14% per annum.

Year	Returns	Discount factor	Present value
	£	(14%)	£
1	2,000	.877	1,754
2	4,000	.769	3,076
3	6,000	.675	4,050
4	5,000	.592	2,960
5	3,000	.519	1,557
			£13,397

About right. The actual rate is a little less than this, say 13.7% per annum.

Exercise 9.4

These are plainly mutually exclusive opportunities. They should therefore be ranked in terms of their net present values and the best one selected.

(i) The net present value here is simply £20,000.

(ii) The sum of the discount factors for 15% for five years is
.870+ .756 + .658 + .572 + .497 = 3.353

The present value of the rent is £5,000 × 3.353 = £16,765

(iii)

Year	Returns	Discount factor	Present value
	£		£
1	− £5,000	.870	−£4,350
2	15,000	.756	11,340
3	10,000	.658	6,580
4	8,000	.572	4,576
5	2,000	.497	994
			£19,140

It is therefore best to sell the land at once.

Exercise 9.5

We need to calculate the net present value of the project on the basis of the different retention periods possible. This is shown in a single table.

Year	Returns if kept	Abandonment value	Discount factors (18%)	PV of returns	PV of abandonment value	Cumulative
1	£4,000	£22,500	.847	£3,388	£19,058	£22,446
2	6,000	18,000	.718	4,308	12,924	20,620
3	10,000	16,000	.609	6,090	9,744	23,530
4	10,000	15,000	.516	5,160	7,740	26,686
5	10,000	12,500	.437	4,370	5,463	28,779
6	10,000	Nil	.370	3,700	Nil	27,016

Each figure in the final cumulative column is that line's present value of abandonment plus the present value of that line's and all previous lines' returns. It is clear from this that retention of the machine for less than four years leads to a negative net present value and is not to be recommended. Retention for five years is the best leading to a net present value of £3,779 (£28,779 − £25,000).

The company should be advised to invest in the project but to abandon it one year before the end of its economic life. Since all the figures on which this advice is based are predictions it will be wise to monitor the situation and amend them as more up-to-date information becomes available.

Exercise 9.6

The comparison of choices should be done on the basis of the net present value of each. These values are calculated below.

Choice A

$$\text{Net cash inflow} = \text{Value of product} - \text{running cost}$$
$$= £50,000 - £40,000 \text{ (two machines) p.a.}$$
$$= £10,000$$

15% discount factors summed for five years = 3.353 so present value of returns is £33,530. Net present value of Choice A is

$$£33,530 - £25,000 = £8,530$$

Choice B

$$\text{Net cash inflow} = £50,000 - £30,000$$
$$= £20,000 \text{ per annum}$$

15% discount factors summed for seven years = 4.161 so present value of returns is £83,220. Net present value of Choice B is

$$£83,220 - £75,000 = £8,220$$

Choice C

$$\text{Net cash inflow} = £50,000 - £37,500 \text{ (three machines)}$$
$$= £12,500 \text{ per annum}$$

15% discount factors summed for ten years = 5.019 so present value of returns is £62,738. Net present value of Choice C is

$$£62,738 - £52,500 = £10,238$$

The choice to be made is thus Choice C.

Other factors to be taken into account are:

(a) Will there be technological changes which will render the machines obsolete before the expected end of their economic life?

(b) To what extent might inflation and market changes invalidate the estimates on which the decision has been made?

Chapter 10

Exercise 10.1

Calculate 'expected' returns as the average of the possibilities
weighted according to probabilities. The results are recorded in the
'Expected Return' column of the table below:

Year	Expected return*	Discount factor	Present value
	£		£
1	2,900	.877	2,543
2	3,300	.769	2,538
3	3,500	.675	2,363
4	3,200	.592	1,894
5	1,300	.519	675
			10,013
Less initial investment required			10,000
Net present value			+£13

*Calculated for year 1, for example, as follows:

$$(£1,000 \times .2) + (£3,000 \times .5) + (£4,000 \times .3) = £2,900$$

This is just worthwhile at the stated cost of capital. Since we are
dealing with a situation where risk exists (and there is even a risk
that our assessment of risk is wrong) this margin is not very large.
The calculation also relies on the assumption that a large number of
projects subject to broadly similar risks are to be undertaken.

Exercise 10.2

The rational human being may be assumed to favour security and to
be averse to risk. The only way to avoid risk in the making of financial investments is to lend money to a substantial borrower on a contractual basis for the payment of interest and the repayment of principal. Such funds cannot then, however, be invested in risky projects
as this would threaten the ability to meet the terms of the contract.

The long term effective use of economic resources requires risk taking as this is the only way in which innovation can take place. All
entry into unexplored fields involves uncertainty about the outcome,
which is the essence of risk, and thus entrepreneurship requires the
taking of risks. Such activity must hold out the promise of rewards if
it is to be undertaken. Thus a person who would be willing to accept
a rate of return of (say) 10% per annum from a safe investment
might require a promised rate of (say) 15% per annum from a risky
project.

Since risk taking is seen to be an activity requiring the promise of reward if it is to be undertaken it is obvious that no business should be encouraged to take a 'leap in the dark'. This would imply that it should take risks for risk's sake. If it did so it would almost certainly not be profitable but would quickly come to the point of collapse. All risks must be carefully evaluated in relation to expected returns and taken only when the promise of profit seems to justify this. Thus whilst agreeing that risk taking is of the essence of entrepreneurship we do not agree with the conclusion that the entrepreneur should take reckless or uncalculated risks.

Exercise 10.3

A business is theoretically entitled to ignore risk where the pattern of actual returns from projects has a mean equal to the projected results and is distributed normally about that mean. For this to be given practical effect requires that individual investments are small relative to the total investment programme so that there is a large number of them.

What this implies is that for every project which falls short of expectations by, say, 2% per annum, there will be another which exceeds expectations by 2%. For every one 7% below there will be one 7% above. Risk can be ignored because the random variations cancel out. As a domestic example of this, if one were giving a party one might prepare two cheese rolls, amongst other things, for each guest. There is a risk that some guests will eat three or four of the rolls but this is offset by the 'risk' that some will eat none at all. So long as the average is vindicated the risk of variation can be ignored.

In practice it seems unlikely that actual returns will be distributed normally around anticipated returns. There is the psychological reason that those proposing investments will try to make the best case they can for a venture in which they believe. The projected returns are thus likely to overstate the actual results. There is the physical reason that most plans are based on the use of full or near-full capacity. It is thus possible to fall substantially below this utilisation but not to go far above it. Both these factors tend to make the distribution skewed (lop-sided).

Exercise 10.4

The use of a risk premium in discounting relies on the assumption that the general effect of risk is to reduce actual returns below what was expected, in other words that risk always has an adverse effect on returns. One might however envisage that risk would work in either direction, i.e. that things are just as likely to go better than expected as they are to be worse than expected. Where the operation of risk is neutral the use of a risk-loaded rate of discount will lead to the rejection of a proportion of projects which were in fact worthwhile and thus work against the maximisation of profit. It may indeed have the perverse effect of increasing risk by concentrating investment in the apparently more profitable (because more risky) projects.

In practice there are good reasons to think that risk is more likely to depress returns that it is to improve them. Most projects are evaluated on the basis that they will be worked at full or nearly full capacity. Returns greatly above those predicted are not then physically possible. The use of a risk premium will then reduce the probability of embarking on unprofitable projects but it may still, in the long run, lead to a less than maximum profit.

Exercise 10.5

Insurance is the classic case of the working of diversification. Although the individual contracts to which an insurance company is a party are risky the collection of all of its contracts is not. This can be explained in terms of portfolio theory and is exactly the same principle on which other business and individual investors seek to reduce risk by diversification.

The essence of successful diversification is that the individual component risks are uncorrelated so that they do not reinforce one another but rather cancel out or dilute one another. A careful insurer will pay very considerable attention to this. He will seek to avoid, for example, insuring against fire a large number of properties all in the same area. Six houses in the same street may all be destroyed together in the same fire (the risk is correlated). Six houses in different cities will not be subject to this common hazard. In marine insurance, where an individual vessel may be worth millions of pounds and it would not be possible for one insurer to cover enough ships to form a proper portfolio it is common practice for each insurer to cover a small fraction of each ship thus taking a share of a much more widely spread risk.

Exercise 10.6

Each of the proposed projects needs to be evaluated on a discounted cash flow basis, taking into account the risks involved.

Project X

	Cash flow	14% discount factors summed for 5 years	Probability	Expected present value
Most pessimistic	£13,500	3.432	.25	£11,583
Most likely	18,000	3.432	.50	30,888
Most optimistic	20,000	3.432	.25	17,160
				59,631
Initial investment				50,000
Expected net present value				+£9,631

The present value of the contingent liability for the penalty on patent infringement is:

$$£10,000 \times .675 \text{ (discount factor)} \times .1 \text{ (probability)} = £6,750$$

The project is thus worthwhile even taking into account the risk of patent infringement.

Project Y

The present value of the investment is

$$\frac{£50,000}{3} \times 2.321^* = £38,683$$

* 14% discount factors summed for three years.

The expected present value of the patent is

$$£200,000 \times .675 \times .5 = £67,500$$

This leads to an expected net present value of £28,817 so that the project is worthwhile.

Project Z

The present value of the firmly expected returns is

$$£8,000 \times 1.647 = £13,176$$

this leads to a negative net present value and the project should, therefore, be rejected. The uncertainty attaching to returns after the second year is so great that they must be taken as nil.

Chapter 11

Exercise 11.1

Alphabet, plc

Determine β for each project using the formula:

$$\beta = \text{Corr pi} \times \frac{s_i}{s_p}$$

For X
$$\beta = 0.58 \times \frac{1}{2.5}$$
$$= .232$$

For Y
$$\beta = 0.89 \times \frac{1.2}{2.5}$$
$$= .427$$

For Z
$$\beta = -.1 \times \frac{2.4}{2.5}$$
$$= -.096$$

Calculate risk premium on present portfolio:

$$
\begin{aligned}
\text{Rf} + \text{Rp} &= \ 15 \\
\text{Rp} &= \ 15 - 6 \\
&= \ 9\%
\end{aligned}
$$

For X $\quad \text{Rf} + \beta\,\text{Rp} = \ 6 + (.232 \times 9)$
$$= 8.09\%$$

For Y $\quad \text{Rf} + \beta\,\text{Rp} = \ 6 + (.427 \times 9)$
$$= 9.84\%$$

For Z $\quad \text{Rf} + \beta\,\text{Rp} = \ 6 + (-.096 \times 9)$
$$= 5.14\%$$

Finally we tabulate required and expected rates of return and indicate our decision:

Project	Required rate of return %	Expected rate of return %	Decision
X	8.09	10	Accept
Y	9.84	8	Reject
Z	5.14	6	Accept

Exercise 11.2

By risk aversion is meant the characteristic attributed to an investor that, for a given expected rate of return, he will prefer a less risky project to a more risky one. But for risk aversion no investor would wish to diversify as this is a policy for risk reduction rather than for increasing expected returns.

Sketches of the required indifference curves (not to scale) follow.

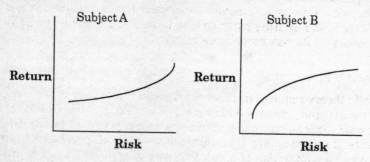

Subject A is risk averse but Subject B is risk seeking. We would therefore expect A to be a diversifier while B selected one risky investment and put all his resources into that.

Exercise 11.3

Calculate the variance of returns for the existing portfolio and the covariance of returns between the portfolio and the proposed new investment.

Probability	R_{pf}	R_i	$R_{pf} - \overline{R}_{pf}$ (a)	$R_i - \overline{R}_i$ (b)	$(a)^2 p$	(a)(b)p
.1	12	8	- 3.6	- 2.2	1.296	+.792
.2	14	10	- 1.6	- 0.2	.512	+.062
.2	15	12	- 0.6	+1.8	.072	-.216
.3	16	10	+0.4	- 0.2	.048	-.024
.1	18	14	+2.4	+3.8	.576	+.912
.1	20	6	+4.4	- 4.2	1.936	- 1.848
Averages	15.6	10.2		Totals	4.440	- .32

$$\beta = \frac{\text{Covar pi}}{\text{var p}}$$

$$= \frac{.32}{4.44}$$

$$= 0.72$$

Required rate of return is:
$$Rf + \beta\,Rp = 5 + (-.072 \times 10.6)$$
$$= \underline{4.24\%}$$

The expected rate of return is 10.2% and therefore the project should be accepted. Note that, although its expected rate of return is less than that of the existing portfolio, the project is a worthwhile addition because of its risk reducing property.

Exercise 11.4

Portfolio theory requires us to accept that the investor is risk averse. This means that, given a certain rate of return, he will require an additional inducement to invest in order to compensate him for risk. The rate of return on any investment or portfolio of investments can be seen as a summation of a risk free rate of return and a risk premium, the latter depending on the degree of risk.

Where an individual investment is to be evaluated the risk premium which it commands will be related to its riskiness when added to an existing portfolio rather than to its individual riskiness. Any investment having expected returns which vary inversely with the portfolio rate of return has the effect of reducing the variability of the portfolio rate of return. Logically the risk premium for such an investment will be negative. Of itself this merely means that the required rate of return on the investment will be less than the risk free rate of return. The investment is thus loss making in the relative rather than the absolute sense. In an exceptional case, however, the risk discount (or negative risk premium) would exceed the risk free rate of interest so that an investment would be accepted on its risk reducing properties even though it had a negative internal rate of return.

We must therefore support the financial manager in his statement that investment in loss making projects may sometimes be justified. We should however, point out that such cases are likely to be hard to find in the real world. This is because they require a very high degree of inverse correlation between portfolio rate of return and the returns on the proposed additional investment. Since most commercial projects are subject to broadly the same economic influences, doing well in a boom and suffering in a slump, such inverse correlation is like to be rare.

Exercise 11.5

In theory any investment project whether real, like the purchase of an industrial machine, or financial, like the purchase of shares in a company can form an element in a portfolio. A portfolio in this sense may be defined as a collection of ventures (usually of a similar type). Thus a pension fund might hold a portfolio of stock market securities, a property developer a portfolio of buildings and an insurance company a portfolio of policies. The essential commonality to which portfolio theory can be applied is that each component of a portfolio has its own individual risk/return profile and that, in a portfolio, it contributes to a total risk/return profile which may be quite different. Theory will give guidance as to how individual investments should be evaluated in terms of the contribution which they make to the overall portfolio.

The capital asset pricing model is portfolio theory applied to the world of investment in real projects. There are several important ways, however, in which this kind of investment differs from stock market investment. These are listed below and briefly discussed.

(i) Stock market securities can be bought in very small units whilst real investment may be available only in large indivisible amounts.

Suppose that a certain investment, X, is being evaluated. Pure portfolio theory might decree that, say, £10,000 should be invested in X as a component of the optimum portfolio. This is easily achieved where X is a marketable security. If X is, however, a real investment requiring the expenditure of, say, £25,000 to set it up then this ideal cannot be met. A decision has to be made either to invest the full amount or to invest nothing at all.

(ii) Disinvestment is easily possible from stock market securities but may be impossible with real capital projects. The central idea of portfolio theory is that there is an optimum portfolio containing a 'correct' mixture of securities drawn from the available choice. Adjustment to this optimum portfolio may as often require the disposal of investments as it does their acquisition. This is readily achieved for stock market securities. Real investment can, however, often be realised only at a considerable loss. This makes such adjustments very difficult or impossible in their case.

(iii) It is probably easier in practice to assemble the necessary information about risks and returns for stock market securities than it is for real investments. This is because the stock market is very closely documented and information about past price movements and rates of returns is easily obtained. There is also a homogeneity about securities which makes it reasonable to suppose that what holds good for one will hold good for another of a similar type. Real investments, however, are very diverse in type and in the influences to which they are subject. Information about the past behaviour of investments of a similar kind may be completely unavailable.

Exercise 11.6

A unit trust constitutes a mechanism whereby the small savings of a large number of investors are pooled and thus gives each of them the benefit of a stake in a much wider based portfolio than he could assemble independently. Some of the advantages of this relate to economies of scale. Dealing costs will be lower per £ invested and it will be possible to obtain the services of professional investment managers very economically. The specific advantage referred to in the question, however, refers to that of diversification. Obviously a small saver investing, say, £100 could not spread this over 200 companies as can the unit trust. Greater diversification of investment thus certainly does become available.

Portfolio theory tells us that diversification as a strategy for reducing risk will succeed where the individual risks of the components are uncorrelated. There is then the expectation that ill fortune in one sector will be, by the operation of chance, offset by good fortune elsewhere. Where all components are subject to the same risk, however, i.e. if one fails they are all likely to fail from the same cause, then diversification will not succeed as a strategy to reduce risk.

It is a fact of observation that security prices tend to move together. Indeed the unit trust publicity refers to 'a general upward movement of market prices'. There could thus just as easily be a general downward movement. We must conclude that, while a unit trust will protect the investor from the specific risks attaching to an individual company, e.g. the risk of unpredicted failure, it will not protect him from what is probably the commoner risk, that of major adverse market movements.

Chapter 12

Exercise 12.1

It is a central assumption of orthodox theory that the goal of financial management is the maximisation of the value of a company's equity. This derives from the economist's assumption that an entrepreneur will seek to maximise his profit. It is demonstrably true that capital rationing will be a barrier to the attainment of this goal. If a project yielding an internal rate of return of, for example, 20% per annum is forgone although it could have been financed with capital costing, say, 15% per annum, then an opportunity has been lost to increase the net present value of the company. Whether this implies that capital rationing *should* not be imposed, however, requires a judgment based on an acceptance or otherwise of the basic premise of value maximisation.

It seems likely that in real life this will be only one of the goals which management will set itself. Other possibilities are:

(a) to retain personal control of the business even though this means restricting its growth;

(b) to retain the 'family' atmosphere of a small concern because this is a more pleasant working environment;

(c) to avoid risk by restricting investment to a few projects which can be closely supervised;

(d) to avoid recourse to the market from a distaste for the associated publicity and formalities.

The existence of capital rationing may well promote goals such as these and be justifiable on that ground.

Exercise 12.2

(i) Where there is no capital rationing all projects should be accepted which have a positive net present value. This will occur whenever the internal rate of return of a project exceeds the cost of capital. In this case projects A to E should be accepted. Project F is marginal and it does not matter whether it is accepted or not.

(ii) Where capital rationing exists we should determine for each project its net present value at the stated marginal cost of capital. This is done by discounting the annual cash flow by the factors appropriate to 14% per annum. This has been done and the results recorded in the table below:

Project	Investment required	Net present value (cost of capital 14% p.a.)
	£	£
A	600,000	+236,106 *
B	100,000	+19,867
C	20,000	+3,385
D	80,000	+6,662
E	300,000	+14,569
F	400,000	Nil
G	200,000	+9,541
H	100,000	+5,125

* Calculated as follows:

As the annual returns are equal, sum the 14% discount factors over the life of the project, i.e. eight years:

$$.877 + .769 + .675 + .592 + .519 + .456 + .400 + .351 = 4.639$$

Multiply by the annual return:

$$4.639 \times £180,234 = £836,106$$

Subtract initial investment required:

$$£836,106 - £600,000 = £236,106$$

The others are calculated in a similar manner.

Where capital is rationed to £400,000 the investment programme should comprise projects B and E giving a net present value of +£34,436. If C and D, both more profitable than E, are undertaken this precludes E and thus leaves £100,000 of finance 'wasted' (i.e. yielding exactly 14% per annum). Where capital is rationed to £500,000 the investment programme should comprise projects B, C, D and E giving a net present value of +£44,483. Where capital is rationed to £600,000 we should invest only in project A giving a net present value of +£236,106.

Exercise 12.3

Where capital rationing is for one period only, the problem of the financial manager is to maximise net present value within that constraint for that year only. Where the constraint is maintained over a number of years the problem is to maximise net present value over a much wider time horizon. Since it is of the essence of capital rationing that some profitable projects are wasted, we must ensure that it is the least profitable which are lost. Investment this year may preclude more profitable investment next year. Clearly the situation requires very complex information not only on projects which are currently available but also on those which are to become available in the future. If linear programming is applied to these data, a long term strategy may emerge.

The data of the previous question indicate that some projects have very short pay back periods compared with others. If projects of future years are expected to surpass those currently available it may be better to invest now in projects of rapid payback (or even to with-hold investment altogether) than to invest in the long term projects which may be indicated by a single-period analysis.

Exercise 12.4

The first step is to calculate the net present value for each project using Lion's true cost of capital. This is done in the following manner.

A: NPV × £9,945 + (.870 + .756 + .658) − £20,000 = £2,714
B: NPV × £6,702 × (.870 + .756) − £10,000 = £897
C: NPV × £6,014 × (.870 + .756 + .658 + .572) − £15,000 = £2,176
D: NPV × £16,567 × (.870 + .756) − £25,000 = £1,938
E: NPV × £19,646 × (.870 + .756) − £30,000 = £1,944
F: NPV × £7,582 × (.870 + .756 + .658 + .572) − £20,000 = £1,654
G: NPV × £3,198 × (.870 + .756 + .658 + .572 + .497) − £10,000 = £723
H: NPV × £7,148 × (.870 + .756 + .658 + .572) − £20,000=£415
I: NPV × £15,375 × (.870 + .756) − £25,000 = Nil
J: NPV × £3,858 × (.870 + .756 + .658 + .572 + .497) − £15,000 = £2,064

Unrestrained investment would lead Lion to undertake all projects having an internal rate of return of over 15% per annum, i.e. Projects A to H inclusive. The combined net present value of these projects is £12,461 .

Lion's present policy will lead it to restrict investment to £100,000 and to deploy this in projects A to E inclusive. The combined net present value of these projects is £9,669. The cost of adopting this policy in terms of lost profits is therefore:

$$£12,477 − £9,669 = £2,808$$

It should be noted that even accepting Lion's desire to ration capital the device which it is using (of a high discount rate) is not the best. It would be better off by giving up Project E and using that £30,000 to invest in both of projects F and G which have a higher combined net present value. If this were done the investment programme would have a total net present value of £10,102. Thus the current policy, even given capital rationing, is costing it £433 (£10,102 − £9,669) more than it need.

Exercise 12.5

Any resource is in a sense 'rationed' by its price. This merely means that we must ensure that we can make economic use of anything which we buy. This is as true of material and labour as it is of finance. It is better to refer to this as a case of the scarcity of resources. In the case of finance the relationship between the cost of capital and the rate of return offered by available investments determines the optimum amount of finance to employ.

In conventional financial management terminology the rationing of capital refers to the case where the use of capital is artificially restricted so that not all potentially profitable projects can be taken up. It follows that the high price of capital (which automatically *limits* the use of capital) is no reason for rationing it.

Exercise 12.6

Panther should first rank its investment projects according to their net present value. The calculations are done below:

Project	Annual cash flow £	Number of years	Sum of discount factors (18%)	Present value £
R	34,143	5	3.127	16,765
S	20,808	4	2.690	5,974
T	48,115	4	2.690	9,429
U	94,967	3	2.174	6,458
V	26,169	5	3.127	1,830
W	18,587	4	2.690	Nil

There is no point in evaluating projects X, Y and Z which have internal rates of return below Panther's cost of capital. Net present value must be negative and the projects would not therefore be acceptable even if funds were available.

Projects are ranked according to net present value:

R,T,U,S,V,W

The best investment of the available £250,000 is thus R and T (leaving £40,000 uninvested). Unconstrained investment would lead to a total expenditure of £540,000 on projects R to V inclusive. W is the marginal investment.

Chapter 13

Exercise 13.1

For historical cost and CPP we need to make an assumption about the order of usage. We will use the first in first out basis.

Historical cost (valued at amount paid on purchase)

Cost of sales	15,000 is	10,000 @ £1.00	£10,000	
		5,000 @ £1.10	5,500	£15,500
	20,000 is	15,000 @ £1.10	16,500	
		5,000 @ £1.20	6,000	22,500
	25,000 is	10,000 @ £1.20	12,000	
		15,000 @ £1.30	19,500	31,500

Cost of sales	69,500
Stock is 5,000 @ £1.30	6,500
Purchases	£76,000

CPP (valued at amount paid on purchase indexed to accounting date)

Cost of sales	15,000 is	$£10,000 \times \dfrac{115}{100}$	£11,500	
		$5,500 \times \dfrac{115}{105}$	6,024	£17,524
	20,000 is	$£16,500 \times \dfrac{115}{105}$	18,071	
		$£6,000 \times \dfrac{115}{110}$	6,273	24,344
	25,000 is	$£12,000 \times \dfrac{115}{110}$	12,545	
			19,500	32,045

	73,913
Stock is as before	6,500
	£80,413

CCA (valued at replacement cost at time of consumption)

Cost of sales	15,000 × £1.10	£16,500
	20,000 × £1.20	24,000
	25,000 × £1.30	32,500
		73,000
Stock	5,000 × £1.30	6,500
		£79,500

Cost of sales adjustment as per SSAP 16 is £73,000 – £69,500 = £3,500. It will be charged in the profit and loss account and credited to current cost revaluation reserve.

Exercise 13.2

We will use the straight line method of depreciation

$$\text{CPP is } £10,000 \times \frac{£50,000}{5} = £10,000$$

$$\text{Historical cost is } \frac{115}{110} = £11,500$$

$$\text{CCA is } \frac{£50,000 + £60,000}{2 \times 5} = £11,000$$

This last calculation assumes that depreciation has taken place evenly over the year and should therefore be calculated on the average replacement value of the machine.

Exercise 13.3

Pneumatic, plc
Profit and loss account for the year ended 31st December

Sales (1)	£136,400
Less Cost of sales (2)	64,530
Net profit	£71,870

Balance sheet at 31st December

Share capital (3)		£56,700	Stock (4)	£57,000
Profit and loss account	£71,870		Cash (5)	67,500
Less Loss on holding cash	4,070	67,800		
		£124,500		£124,500

(1)	$(20,000 \times £4) + 8\%$	£86,400
	$10,000 \times £5$	50,000
		£ 136,400

(2)	$(25,000 \times £1.80) + 5\% + 8\%$	£51,030
	$(5,000 \times £2.50) + 8\%$	13,500
		£64,530

| (3) | $£50,000 + 5\% + 8\%$ | £56,700 |

(4)	$(10,000 \times £2.50) + 8\%$	£27,000
	$10,000 \times £3$	30,000
		£57,000

(5)

Proceeds of share issue			£50,000
Sales revenue			
30th June		£80,000	
31st December		50,000	130,000
			180,000
Less Purchases			
1st January		£45,000	
30th June		37,500	
31st December		30,000	112,500
			£67,500

(6)

Cash generated 1st January £5,000 loses 13.4%* i.e .	£670
Cash generated 30th June £42,500 loses 8% i.e.	3,400
Cash generated 31st December £20,000 loses nothing	-
*5% and 8% compounded	£4,070

Exercise 13.4

Profit and loss account
for the year ended 31st December

Sales	£130,000
Less Cost of sales (1)	80,000
Net profit	£50,000

Balance sheet at 31st December

Share capital	£50,000	Cash	£67,500
Revaluation reserve (2)	27,500	Stock (3)	60,000
Profit and loss account	50,000		
	£127,500		£127,500

(1)	20,000 × £2.50	£50,000
	10,000 × £3	30,000
		£80,000

(2)	Cost of sales adjustment	£22,500
	Stock adjustment	5,000
		£27,500

| (3) | 20,000 × £3 | £60,000 |

Exercise 13.5

Hot Air, plc

Profit and loss account for the year ended 31st December

Historical cost profit (before interest)		£50,000
Less Current cost adjustments (1)		5,200
Current cost profit		44,800
Gearing adjustment (2)	(£781)	
Interest	2,500	1,719
Current cost profit attributable to shareholders		£43,081
Deduct Dividend paid (12.5%)		12,500
Retained profit		£30,581

Balance sheet at 31st December

Share capital	£100,000	Fixed assets		£84,000
Current cost revaluation		Current assets		
reserve (3)	20,919	Stocks	£52,500	
Retained profit	30,581	Debtors	30,000	
		Cash	30,000	112,500
	151,500			
Loan capital	25,000			
Current liabilities				
Creditors	20,000			
	£196,500			£196,500

(1)	Cost of sales $\frac{15\%}{3}$ (average) × £80,000	£4,000
	Depreciation 10% (average) × £10,000	1,000
	M.W.C.A. (debtors − creditors) × 2%	200
		£5,200

(2) Gearing adjustment $\dfrac{25,000}{25,000 + 141,500} \times £5,200$ £781

(3) Stock revaluation 5% × £50,000   £2,500
    Fixed assets revaluation   14,000
    Profit and loss adjustments   5,200

                                                                  21,700
    Less Gearing adjustment   781

                                                                £20,919

Exercise 13.6

Deadloss
Historical cost
Profit and loss account for year ended 31st December

Sales		£35,000
Less Cost of sales	£15,500	
Expenses	10,000	
Depreciation	1,500	27,000
Net profit		8,000
Less Drawings		5,000
Retained profit		£3,000

Balance sheet at 31st December

Capital	£10,000	Machine	£4,500
Retained profit	3,000	Stock	5,000
		Cash	3,500
	£13,000		£13,000

Current purchasing power
Profit and loss account for year ended 31st December

Sales		£36,500
Less Cost of sales	£16,825	
Expenses	10,500	
Depreciation	1,815	29,140
Net trading profit		7,360
Less Loss on holding cash		265
		7,095
Less Drawings		5,250
Retained profit		1,845

Balance sheet at 31st December

Capital	£12,100	Machine	£5,445
Retained profit	1,845	Stock	5,000
		Cash	3,500
	£13,945		£13,945

Current cost
Profit and loss account for year ended 31st December

Sales			£35,000
Less Cost of sales		£18,000	
Expenses		10,000	
Depreciation		1,812.5	29,812.5
Net profit			5,187.5
Less Drawings			5,000
Retained profit			£187.5

Balance sheet at 31st December

Capital	£10,000	Machine	£6,000
Revaluation reserve	4,312.5	Stock	5,000
Retained profit	187.5	Cash	3,500
	£14,500		£14,500

Chapter 14

Exercise 14.1

We will set up our calculations in the form of a table.

No inflation

Year	Sales value	Costs	Net cash inflow	Discount factor	Present value
		£	£	£	£
1	25,000	12,000	13,000	.833	10,829
2	25,000	12,000	13,000	.694	9,022
3	25,000	12,000	13,000	.579	7,527
4	25,000	12,000	13,000	.482	6,266
5	25,000	12,000	13,000	.402	5,226
					£38,870

Less Initial investment	35,000
Net present value	+£3,870

General inflation at 15% per annum with no differential effects

All costs and revenues rise in money terms by 15% each year. This has no effect on their real values and therefore the net present value is still +£3,870 in terms of present £'s.

Differential inflation

Year	Sales value £	Variable costs f	Fixed costs £	Net cash inflow £	Deflator	Discount factor	Present value £
1	25,000	10,000	2,000	13,000	1	.833	10,829
2	28,000	11,400	2,400	14,200	.870	.694	8,574
3	31,360	12,996	2,880	15,484	.756	.579	6,778
4	35,123	14,815	3,456	16,852	.658	.482	5,345
5	39,338	16,890	4,147	18,301	.572	.402	4,208

	35,734
Less initial investment	35,000
	+£734

In either case the project exhibits a positive net present value and is therefore acceptable. Note, however, that the effect of differential inflation has been to make it much less attractive.

Exercise 14.2

(i) To discover the amount of the annual repayment we need merely to determine the annual amounts which, when discounted by the factors appropriate to 12% per annum, sum to £10,000.

$$\text{Annual repayment} = \frac{£10,000}{\text{Sum of 5 years discount factors (12%)}}$$

$$= \frac{£10,000}{3.605}$$

$$= £2,744 \text{ to nearest } £$$

(ii) the real cost of the loan capital will be determined by first using a deflator to calculate the current value of the future payments and then discovering, by trial and error, a set of discount factors which equates this to £10,000.

Year	Actual payments (money) £	Deflator (18%)	Actual payments (real) £
1	2,774	1.000	2,774
2	2,774	.847	2,350
3	2,774	.718	1,992
4	2,774	.609	1,689
5	2,774	.516	1,431
			£10,236

Since the total real value of the repayments is only just over £10,000 the discount factor we are seeking is very small. We will try 1%.

Year	Actual payments (money) £	Deflator (1%)	Actual payments (real) £
1	2,774	.990	2,746
2	2,350	.980	2,303
3	1,992	.971	1,934
4	1,689	.961	1,623
5	1,431	.951	1,361
			£9,967

By interpolation the rate is about .9% per annum.

(iii) Net present value of the loan to the bank.

Year	Cash received £	Deflator	Real value received £	Discount factor (6%)	Real present value £
1	2,774	1.000	2,774	.943	2,616
2	2,774	.847	2,350	.890	2,091
3	2,774	.718	1,992	.840	1,673
4	2,774	.609	1,689	.792	1,338
5	2,774	.516	1,431	.747	1,069
					8,787

Less Initial loan   10,000

Net present value   -£1,213

Comment Although it might seem that banks are thus frequently making unprofitable investments, inflation has an effect on their cost of capital which has been disregarded here. This, too, may be a negative quantity.

Exercise 14.3

We should first note that the avoidable cost of production is £1.30 per unit i.e. all but the indirect costs. This means that the contribution per unit at the contract selling price is 25p.

Assume no inflation Present value of total contribution is:

$$£0.25 \times 100,000 \times (.909 + .826 + .751 + .683 + .621) = £94,750$$

$$\text{Net present value is } £94,750 - £30,000 = £64,750$$

The project would appear to be very advantageous.

Assume inflation at 5% per annum

Year	Gross revenue	Money costs	Net return	Discount factors	Present value
1	£155,000	£130,000	£25,000	.909	£22,725
2	155,000	136,500	18,500	.826	15,281
3	155,000	143,325	11,675	.751	8,768
4	155,000	150,491	4,509	.683	3,080
5	155,000	158,016	–3,016	.621	–1,873
					47,981
Less initial investment					30,000
Net present value					+£17,981

At this rate of inflation the project is still worthwhile.

Assume inflation at 10% per annum

Year	Gross revenue	Money costs	Net return	Discount factors	Present value
1	£155,000	£130,000	£25,000	.909	£22,725
2	155,000	143,000	12,000	.826	9,912
3	155,000	157,300	–2,300	.751	–1,727
4	155,000	173,030	–18,030	.683	–12,315
5	155,000	190,333	–35,333	.621	–21,942
					–3,347
Less initial investment					30,000
Net present value					–£33,347

The project is thus not worthwhile while if an average rate of inflation in excess of between 5 and 10 per cent per annum is anticipated.

Exercise 14.4

Building society accounts contain no adjustment for the changing value of money. When a borrower uses a building society's services to enable him to buy a house he pays back the principal sum pound for pound. This does not set building societies apart from other sources of finance. What is a distinctive feature, however, is that the loan is very long term – typically twenty-five years – and that over that period inflation can have a catastrophic effect on the value of money. At an annual inflation rate of 10% a pound retains a real value of only 9p after 25 years!

The effect which this has on the cost of borrowing can clearly be demonstrated by considering an example over one year. We will assume a loan of £20,000 at a rate of interest of 15% per annum with an annual rate of inflation of 20%.

	Amount of loan (money terms)	**Real terms** (end-of-year £)
Year beginning	£20,000	£24,000
Add interest	3,000	3,000
	23,000	27,000
Less repayments (say)	3,100	3,100
Year end	£19,900	£23,900

Real loss to building society is £23,900 – £19,900 = £4,000

The effects which one would expect to observe (and which are, in fact, observed) are:

(i) High demand for loans of this kind (mortgage queues)

(ii) High prices for the properties purchased (rising house prices)

(iii) A transfer of wealth from the lender to the borrower (someone who borrows 90% of the price of his property and thus has a 10% interest in it quickly finds that as its value rises his proportionate interest increases).

Exercise 14.5

First we must evaluate the project ignoring inflation.

The sum of 8 years' discount factors (15%) is 4.488

The present value of the annual cash flows is thus

$$£50,000 \times 4.488 = £224,000$$

Net present value is £224,000 – £200,000 = +£24,400

The project is therefore worthwhile.

In order to allow for inflation we must recalculate the annual cash flow and this is done on the next page.

Total present value is £330,569

Net present value is £330,569 – £200,000 = £l30,969

	1 £	2 £	3 £	4 £	5 £	6 £	7 £	8 £
Sales	162,000	174,960	188,957	204,073	220,399	238,031	257,074	277,640
Material	39,375	41,344	43,411	45,581	47,861	50,254	52,766	55,405
Labour	27,500	30,250	33,275	36,603	40,263	44,289	48,718	53,590
Overhead	38,250	39,015	39,795	40,591	41,403	42,231	43,076	43,937
Total	105,125	110,609	116,481	122,775	129,527	136,774	144,560	152,932
Contribution	56,875	64,351	72,476	81,298	90,872	101,257	112,514	124,708
Deflator	.952	.907	.864	.823	.784	.746	.711	.677
Real cash flow	54,145	58,366	62,619	66,908	71,244	75,538	79,997	84,427
Discount factors	.893	.797	.712	.636	.567	.507	.452	.404
Present value	48,351	46,518	44,585	42,554	40,395	38,298	36,159	34,109

Inflation has had the effect of making the project more worthwhile than it had first appeared. A combination of factors has led to this.

These are:

(a) Selling prices are rising more rapidly than costs;

(b) Contribution has risen more rapidly than general inflation;

(c) Inflation has a favourable effect on the cost of capital.

Exercise 14.6

There are several areas where inflation will have an impact on the decisions of the financial manager. The most important are:

(a) **Investment appraisal**. Since investment projects invariably extend over a lengthy period of time it is important to take into account any expected inflation over that time. Failure to do so may mean acceptance and rejection of the wrong projects. Inflation may also have an effect on the cost of capital. This, too, is significant.

(b) **Credit management**. Outstanding trade debtors are always expensive to a business in terms of the cost of capital tied up in them. Inflation adds a new dimension to this. Any credit extended to customers allows them to pay for goods supplied in a currency worth less than that in which the deal was struck. The loss on each transaction from this cause may be quite small but cumulatively it can become a very significant amount.

(c) **Use of credit**. Borrowed funds are very advantageous in times of inflation as the principal sum declines in real value during the period of the loan. In some circumstances the real gain may exceed the real rate of interest so that the borrowing is effectively at negative cost. The financial manager should ensure that optimum use is made of trade credit and bank overdrafts.

(d) **Financial requirements**. If annual accounts are drawn up on an historical cost basis and distributions of dividend are based on the profits thus determined it may be that insufficient resources are retained in the business to maintain levels of activity. This will particularly show itself when major replacements of fixed assets have to be made (at greatly higher prices than the original purchases) but it will also result in a squeeze on the amount available for stock purchases. Additional permanent finance may from time to time have to be raised merely in order to maintain existing operations.

Chapter 15

Exercise 15.1

The important effects are:

(a) Differential effects on the cost of capital
   (discussed in section 15.3)

(b) Changes in pattern of returns
   (discussed in section 15.2)

Exercise 15.2

Calculation of net returns

Year	Gross returns £	Capital allowance £	Taxable return £	Tax due £	Tax paid £	Net return £
1	15,000	12,500	2,500	875	–	15,000
2	12,000	9,375	2,625	919	875	11,125
3	12,000	7,031	4,969	1,739	919	11,081
4	10,000	5,273	4,727	1,654	1,739	8,261
5	8,000	3,955	4,045	1,416	1,654	6,346
6	8,000	2,966	5,034	1,762	1,416	6,584
7					1,762	(1,762)

The residual value of the investment is £8,899.

Calculation of net present value

Year	Net return £	Discount factor (8%)	Present value £
1	15,000	.926	13,890
2	11,125	.857	9,534
3	11,081	.794	8,798
4	8,261	.735	6,072
5	6,346	.681	4,322
6	6,584	.630	4,148
7	(1,762)	.583	(1,027)
Present value of residual capital allowances			1,376

	£47,113
Initial investment required	50,000
Net present value	−£2,887

Thus the project is not worthwhile.

Exercise 15.3

(i) The Chancellor could favour the distribution of profits as dividend by dropping the requirement to pay advance corporation tax. Insofar as this led to increased distribution and hence reduced retentions, industrial investment would be reduced.

(ii) A more important influence could be achieved by an adjustment of capital allowances. He could reduce the rate of writing down allowance. This would not alter the total cash flow but would postpone part of it making the internal rate of return of any project lower. This would make some previously worthwhile projects not worthwhile and would thus reduce the level of investment.

(iii) He could increase the basic tax rate making all investment less profitable.

Exercise 15.4

Emu should evaluate all projects on an after tax basis. Thus a projected cash flow should be discounted using the after tax cost of capital. This is calculated below:

	Weighting	Net cost
Ordinary shares	£2m	14%
Preference shares	£.8m	12.6%
Debt	£.5m	7.8%

The weighted net cost of capital is 12.72% per annum.

Exercise 15.5

Original calculation

Year	Return	Discount factor (12%)	Present value
	£		£
1	15,000	.926	13,890
1	£10,000	.893	£8,930
2	8,000	.797	6,376
3	6,000	.712	4,272
4	6,000	.636	3,816
5	5,000	.567	2,835
			26,229
Less Initial investment			25,000
Net present value			+£1,229

Calculation including tax

Year	Gross returns £	Capital allowance £	Taxable return £	Tax due £	Tax paid £	Net return £
1	10,000	6,250	3,750	1,313	–	10,000
2	8,000	4,688	3,312	1,159	1,313	6,687
3	6,000	3,156	2,844	995	1,159	4,841
4	6,000	2,637	3,363	1,177	995	5,005
5	5,000	1,978	2,022	708	1,177	3,823
6					708	(708)

The residual value of the investment is £5,933.

Calculation of net present value

Year	Net return £	Discount factor (8%)	Present value £
1	10,000	.926	9,260
2	6,687	.857	5,731
3	4,841	.794	3,844
4	5,005	.735	3,679
5	3,823	.681	2,603
6	(708)	.630	(446)

Present value of residual capital allowances   991

	£25,662
Initial investment required	25,000
Net present value	+£662

The project is thus still acceptable after taking taxation into account.

Exercise 15.6

As Downunder has other profitable activities we can envisage negative as well as positive taxation (i.e. there may be a reduction of the tax liability arising from other sources).

The net cash flows are computed in the table below (negatives in brackets).

Year	Gross cash flow £	Tax £	Net return £	Discount factor	Present value £
1	(25,000)		(25,000)	.909	(22,725)
2	(25,000)	(12,500)	(12,500)	.826	(10,325)
3	(25,000)	(12,500)	(12,500)	.751	(9,388)
4	10,000	(12,500)	22,500	.683	15,368
5	30,000	5,000	25,000	.621	15,525
6	40,000	15,000	25,000	.564	14,100
7	50,000	20,000	30,000	.513	15,390
8	60,000	25,000	35,000	.467	16,345
9		30,000	(30,000)	.424	(12,720)

Net present value   +21,570

This is, therefore, a worthwhile investment.

Chapter 16

Exercise 16.1

Although the company is doing well and this is represented by an increase in its total value this value is not held in the form of cash but in the form of productive assets. These cannot be distributed as a dividend. The directors of the company have taken the view that they should invest in any project which yields more than the cost of capital. These have been forthcoming in large numbers and that explains how the profit has been absorbed as it has been earned. The implication of this is that the company is taking advantage, on behalf of its shareholders, of opportunities which are not available to them as individuals. They are therefore better off than they would have been had the profit been distributed. Given a responsive stock market this should be reflected in the market value of the shares. Any shareholder wishing, therefore, to realise all or part of this benefit in the form of cash could do so by selling part of his holding.

Exercise 16.2

First calculate the marginal cost of capital. This is:

Retained earnings	20% × 1=	20%
Debt	10% × .4 =	4%
		24%

$$\frac{24\%}{1.4} = 17.14\%$$

This rate applies until the earnings are exhausted, i.e. up to a total amount of

$$£120,000 + \text{related debt} = £120,000 + (.4 \times £120,000)$$
$$= £168,000$$

Thereafter the marginal cost of capital is

New equity	$22\% \times 1 =$	22%
Debt	$10\% \times .4 =$	4%
		26%

$$\frac{26\%}{1.4} = 18.57\%$$

Looking at the available projects we shall invest in A and B because these yield more than the marginal cost of capital. This will absorb £60,000 + £50,000 = £110,000 of finance. Of this

$$\frac{1}{1.4} \times £110,000 = £78,571$$

will come from retaining earnings leaving

$$£120,000 - £78,571 = \qquad £41,429$$

to be paid as dividend.

Exercise 16.3

This dividend policy will have the effect of stabilising dividends as only a prolonged increase or decrease in profits will affect the average sufficiently to have any appreciable effect on the size of the distribution. Since it is a conservative dividend policy – in the long run only one half of all profits will be distributed – there will be a substantial build up of retained earnings. This will certainly reinforce still further the consistency of dividends, which could for a while be maintained even in the face of actual losses. It may also relieve the company of having recourse to external sources of finance.

Since the retention, under this policy, bears no relationship to the availability of profitable investment opportunities, there is a risk that projects yielding less than the true cost of capital will be undertaken in order to absorb funds which would otherwise lie idle.

Exercise 16.4

From time to time Government has sought to encourage investment by constraints on distribution. These constraints may be either rigid, such that a fixed ceiling is placed on distributions, or flexible, whereby encouragement is given to profit retention by differential tax treatment. Although it is a fairly simple matter to cause profit retention to increase this is very far removed from the generation of profitable opportunities for the use of these funds. The pursuance of conventional management objectives should ensure that profits are retained when the opportunities for investment exist and are distributed when they do not. An effective capital market should then ensure that those distributions are invested by their recipients elsewhere.

Exercise 16.5

(i) In spite of the absence of dividend one would expect the value of the shares to rise reflecting the growing asset base of the company. Individual shareholders could obtain an income by selling part of their holding without reducing the value of the fund invested. In the long run, however, pressure would probably be exerted on the directors to make dividend payments.

(ii) B's return on capital would decline (by dilution) and hence the value of its shares would fall relative to the capital invested. This, together with the accumulation of cash or near-cash resources would make the company very vulnerable to a takeover bid.

(iii) C is adopting a policy of capital rationing. It is therefore not optimising its position. It may be possible for this situation to persist for a long time but a potential bidder might become interested.

(iv) D's policy is quite sound. If it cannot profitably invest its funds it should distribute them and allow its shareholders to make their own separate investment decisions.

In any case where a company pursues a misconceived distribution policy the extent to which this will persist depends on a number of factors. One of these is the tolerance of the shareholders, another is the determination of the directors, a third is the extent to which the deficiency becomes sufficiently apparent for a third party to become interested in the opportunities forgone.

Exercise 16.6

The relevant cost of capital for Beautiful to use in evaluating investment projects is the weighted average cost, i.e. here 16% per annum. On this criterion all four of the available projects are acceptable and should be accepted. The total investment required is a little more than the available profit and this might seem to indicate that no dividend should be paid and that the small additional sum required should be raised by means of a loan (e.g. a bank overdraft). This is, however, not necessarily a sensible conclusion.

The distribution policy of Beautiful is one of the factors which determines its share price and hence its cost of capital. If a dividend is not paid this is likely, as a sudden departure from previous practice, to be interpreted unfavourably by the market. The share price will drop and hence the cost of capital will rise. Some projects which were previously seen as acceptable will now become unacceptable. A strict application of distribution theory is therefore likely to be unhelpful here.

It is suggested that the Board should recommend a dividend in line with its previous policy, i.e. a twice covered dividend one half of the available profit. It should then give the shareholders the opportunity to reinvest this amount by making a rights issue of the financial requirement outstanding.

Thus:

Available profit	£530,000
Less Dividend	265,000
Retained profit	£265,000
Total of acceptable investments	£590,000
Less Retained earnings	265,000
Required to be raised by rights	£325,000

Chapter 17

Exercise 17.1

It should first be pointed out to Mr. Swann that the figure of £100,000 shown in his balance sheet is an accounting residue and does not necessarily represent the sum that would be made available should he decide to sell. This may be greater or smaller than £100,000 but for a number of reasons it is likely to be greater. The most important are listed as follows.

(i) Valuable goodwill is likely to have been built up over the years but this will not be valued in the balance sheet,

(ii) Conventionally conservative accounting methods (e.g. in respect of depreciation and stock valuation) are likely to have valued major assets at less than their market value.

Next we should note that the figure which appears as profit on the profit and loss account cannot be regarded as a pure return on capital. Part of it represents remuneration for the work and skill put into the management of the business by the proprietor. Again conventional accounting methodology will tend also, if anything, to understate the profits (Note the rule 'Anticipate no profit: allow for any foreseeable loss').

Some imaginary figures will show Mr. Swann how his perception of the situation might easily be incorrect:

Profit as shown in accounts	£20,000
Less Value of Mr. Swann's personal contribution	5,000
Pure return on capital	£15,000

Capital realised on sale of business £150,000

On this basis capital would appear to be earning only 10% currently and this yield would be beaten easily by the investment in securities.

Exercise 17.2

The situation in which one might expect management to plan for a reduced gross profit rate is where selling prices are cut in order to improve the business's competitive position. It follows that this is most likely where competition is fairly keen. The test of the success of the policy is whether the absolute level of gross profit is greater than it would have been otherwise. This can be illustrated by imaginary figures:

Estimated sales if a target gross profit rate of 25% is adopted £500,000.

Estimated sales if a target gross profit rate of 20% is adopted £700,000.

The lower gross profit rate actually leads to a higher gross profit i.e. £140,000 instead of £125,000 and, therefore, other things being equal, is the better one to aim for.

If the gross profit is unexpectedly reduced there are several factors which might be at work, the most important are:

(i) Costs have risen but prices have been raised insufficiently to recoup the increases:

(ii) Sales mix has changed so that a relatively higher proportion has been taken by production with a relatively lower gross profit rate;

(iii) Stock control is faulty so that there have been unnecessary stock losses through pilferage or deterioration;

(iv) There has been a misappropriation of cash;

(v) There have been delays or errors in the recording processes (e.g. the omission of sales invoices close to the year end).

Exercise 17.3

The current and liquidity ratios are the tests of the business's ability to meet its obligations in the short term. This may be poor even where long term solvency is not in question. This can be shown by the simple observation that one would expect to pay creditors out of immediate cash resources or those provided by payments from debtors. It would have undesirable commercial consequences if creditors could only be paid by an enforced sale of productive plant and machinery or other fixed assets.

There is a disease which often afflicts the fastest growing and most lively businesses known as overtrading. This means quite simply that the level of business activity has outstripped the amount of capital provision. Financial pressure thus caused may halt the expansion and cause damage to the business. Deterioration of the current and liquidity ratios are an early sign of overtrading and observation of this will allow remedial measures to be taken (e.g. the raising of extra capital). The good financial manager will, of course, not only observe these ratios but will also predict them and plan for desired levels.

It should not be overlooked that it is also undesirable for current and liquidity ratios to grow too large. This is a symptom of surplus cash which, whilst not imposing any pressures, does imply that expensive resources are being kept idle.

Exercise 17.4

The ratio of administrative costs to sales may be regarded as a measure of the efficiency of the administrative process. As such it should arguably be made as low as possible. A consideration of the cost of administration cannot, however, be separated from a consideration of its quality. If administration is poor because expenditure on it is skimped this can have disastrous commercial consequences in terms of loss of customer goodwill, loss of sales opportunities and losses through fraud and bad debts.

It is therefore dangerous for the managing director to determine an arbitrary percentage which is to be attained and much better for him to undertake a careful review of all administrative activity with a view to seeking and eliminating waste and improving efficiency. For example, it will be well worthwhile if a streamlining of procedures makes it possible for more work to be handled without taking on extra staff. It will, however, be a mistake to cut promotion expenditure if this will lead to a considerable loss of sales. The relationship between the level of sales and apparent administrative efficiency should not be overlooked and opportunities to increase the level of business within the existing setup should also be sought.

Exercise 17.5

We can reconstruct, in summary form, Moorhen's figures and add on the amounts relevant to the new product.

	Current	Proposed addition	Projected
Sales	£1,000,000	£200,000	£1,200,000
Less cost of sales	700,000	160,000	860,000
Gross profit	£300,000	£40,000	£340,000
Gross profit rate	30%	20%	28.33%

The stock currently is $1/5 \times .75 \times £700,000$	£105,000
Proposed addition is $1/4 \times .75 \times £160,000$	30,000
Projected total stock	£135,000

Stock turnover would become $\dfrac{.75 \times £860,000}{£135,000} =$ 4.78

Debtors currently are $\dfrac{£1,000,000}{12} =$ £83,333

Proposed addition is $\dfrac{£200,000}{6} =$ £83,333

£116,667

(rounded)

Period of collection of debts is projected as

$$\frac{£116,667}{£1,200,000} \times 365 = \underline{35 \text{ days}}$$

Exercise 17.6

Financial ratios should always be interpreted carefully, within a context, and not superficially in isolation. The following comments could be made on the ratios which the Chairman has quoted:

(a) Gross Profit Rate. Insofar as this is regarded as a measure of the effectiveness of the basic profit earning process an increase is a good thing. It did appear, however, to start from rather a low base and this raises, first, the question of whether this is a genuine improvement or whether it represents a recovery from a setback. This could be determined by examining accounts over a series of years from the past.

The gross profit rate should also be considered in the context of the absolute value of gross profit. A gross profit rate could be considerably improved by increasing prices to the final consumer. If, in a competitive situation, however, this meant a more than proportionate decline in sales, total profitability might be reduced.

(b) Debtors are an expensive current asset in terms of tied up capital and poorly controlled debtors may also lead to a cost for bad debts. Other things being equal, therefore, the reduction in the collection period for debtors must be welcomed. Enquiry ought to be made, however, into the way in which this has been achieved. If it is through a severe tightening up of credit control procedures it may drive customers away. Examples of this kind of policy might be increasing the evidence of credit worthiness required before credit is given or pressing debtors for payment when they are only marginally overdue. It might also have been achieved by the granting of generous cash discounts for prompt payment. This could be expensive and it should be evaluated to determine whether the expense is worthwhile.

(c) Although the cost of the administrative process is important, so is its quality. It is important to know how this very substantial saving has been achieved. If it has been by cutting out sources of waste and inefficiency then this is to be approved but if it is by reducing essential quality then there may be an overall adverse effect on profit. It should be noted that, because administrative costs often contain a high fixed element the percentage may show a marked reduction following a rise on the level of turnover.

(d) Other things being equal the higher the level of stock turnover the better. This minimises the costs of storage, the risk of deterioration and the capital tied up in the value of stock.

A high turnover may, however, be bought at the cost of the risk of stock shortages causing holdups in production and customer letdowns. Information should be sought on the composition of stocks and the turnover of its various components together with information on any shortages which have occurred.

(e) The rate of return on capital is a notoriously misleading measure when based on accounting figures. Both profit and the capital to which it is related are calculated according to a series of conventions which do not guarantee comparability between one situation and another nor between one time and another. Enquiry should be made concerning the consistency of the basis of calculation. The rates of return mentioned look to be on the low side even after the increase.

Chapter 18

Exercise 18.1

The following ratios may be calculated for Rainyday, plc:

(i) Earnings per share:

$$EPS = \frac{\text{Net earnings}}{\text{Number of ordinary shares}}$$

$$= \frac{£600,000 - 25,000}{1,000,000}$$

$$= \underline{\underline{57.5p}}$$

This is a measure of what the company is actually earning on behalf of its shareholders regardless of what it chooses to distribute as dividend.

(ii) Price earnings ratio:

$$PE = \frac{\text{Market price of one ordinary share}}{\text{E.P.S.}}$$

$$= \frac{£3.20}{57.5p}$$

$$= \underline{\underline{5.56}}$$

This is a measure of how 'expensive' a share is. This share can be bought for only a little over five and a half times its annual earnings – a payback period for the investor of about $5\frac{1}{2}$ years. It should be compared with the equivalent ratios for other similar investments. It is considerably affected by the degree of risk associated with the investment.

(iii) Earnings yield:

$$\text{Earnings yield} = \frac{\text{E.P.S}}{\text{Share price}} \times 100$$

$$= \frac{57.5p}{£3.20} \times 100$$

$$= \underline{\underline{17.97\%}}$$

This is a measure of the underlying annual yield of the investment. It is, of course, the inverse of the P/E ratio.

(iv) Dividend yield:

$$\text{Dividend yield} = \frac{\text{Dividend per share} \times 100}{\text{Share price}}$$

$$= \frac{20\text{p}}{£3.20}$$

$$= \underline{\underline{6.25\%}}$$

This is a measure of the cash yield of the investment. It will be misleading if no attention is paid to the profits which are retained. A fast expanding company will commonly exhibit a low dividend yield.

(v) Dividend cover:

$$\text{Dividend cover} = \frac{\text{EPS}}{\text{Dividend per share}}$$

$$= \frac{57.5\text{p}}{20\text{p}}$$

$$= \underline{\underline{2.875\%}}$$

This is a measure of the security of the dividend. Clearly a dividend which is covered nearly three times by the current profit is relatively invulnerable to future setbacks.

(vi) Gearing:

The investment analyst would almost certainly calculate gearing from the *relative nominal* values of debt and equity, i.e. using the figures available in the balance sheet.

$$\text{Gearing} = \frac{\text{Nominal value of loan capital}}{\text{Nominal value of loan} + \text{equity (inc reserves)}}$$

$$= \frac{£250,000}{£2,250,000}$$

$$= \underline{\underline{.11}}$$

The financial analyst would base his calculations on *market values*.

$$\text{Gearing} = \frac{\text{Market value of debt}}{\text{Market value of debt} + \text{equity}}$$

$$= \frac{£250,000 \times .9}{(1,000,000 \times £3.20) + (£250,000 \times .9)}$$

$$= .065\%$$

The lower the gearing the less vulnerable is the business to financial risk. The example here is of low gearing.

(vii) Asset cover:

$$\text{Asset cover} = \frac{\text{Net assets}}{\text{Number of ordinary shares}}$$

$$= \frac{£2,000,000}{1,000,000}$$

$$= £2$$

This figure attempts to reveal the underlying value of the business assets employed. It may be criticised as being based on purely balance sheet values which are not necessarily related either to realisable value or to earning capacity. It may also be objected to on the ground that the shareholder, unless he holds a controlling interest, has no direct access to the value contained in these assets.

Exercise 18.2

Assuming that our investor is 'out' of shares, i.e. is a holder of cash, at the time that low point is reached, he will continue observing the movement of the index until it rises to 228 + 10%, that is, in round figures, 251. He will then invest his available cash in a representative portfolio which can be expected to move in value in line with the index.

Now 'in' shares, the investor will continue to plot the progress of the index. He will note successive highs each of which will be superseded by new ones until the index reaches 389. When it has declined again to 389 – 10%, that is, 350 (round figures) he will sell his whole portfolio. His profit on the operation will be:

$$£1,000 \times = \frac{350}{251} - £1,000 = £394$$

This system is based on the theory accepted by market analysts – that long term market trends exist and that they can be predicted. Here the prediction is done in a mechanical way. It is argued that all short-term random fluctuations will be contained within a 10% band and that movements outside this signify the emergence of a new substantial trend.

There is considerable evidence in support of the 'random walk' theory of stock market behaviour which denies the existence of predictable trends. On this theory one would not expect this investment system to succeed as profitable operations would be offset by loss making ones. In the example examined, when the portfolio has been purchased at 251, if the market peaks at any level below 279 (because 279 – 10% = 251) a loss will be made. In the long run the investor should break even although, in the real world, the existence of dealing costs will ensure that he makes a loss.

Exercise 18.3

When a financial manager wishes to raise funds he will need to do so on the right terms and this can more readily be judged if he understands how investors themselves will appraise any offer which he makes. This amounts to saying that this knowledge is crucial to an accurate determination of the company's cost of capital.

Let us suppose that it is desired to raise £100,000 of equity finance and that this is additional to the £900,000 nominal value already in issue. If the new shares are issued at par their holders will become entitled to:

$$\frac{100,000}{900,000 + 100,000} = .1$$

of the future profits and future growth. If, on the other hand, the shares are issued at a premium, say at a price of £2 per £1 nominal share, then they will become entitled to a much smaller proportion of the benefit.

$$\frac{50,000}{900,000 + 50,000} = .05$$

It is essential that the issue terms are pitched so that the offer is marginally attractive to investors. If it is very attractive it will be oversubscribed but the funds will prove dearer than they need have done. If it is unattractive, it will be undersubscribed and the funds will not be forthcoming in full.

Exercise 18.4

Asset cover is the amount obtained by dividing the balance sheet value of net assets by the number of shares in issue. Unless the assets consist of cash or quoted securities it is a very misleading figure as there is no way in which an individual shareholder can gain direct access to the assets which his shares represent. Some investment analysts believe that in the long run asset value must be represented by share value but this depends much more on how the assets are used than it does on what they originally cost – the normal basis of balance sheet valuation. In the particular case quoted the shares stand in the market at a discount from their par value. This is an unusual situation suggesting considerable doubts about the future. Prospective investors should proceed with great caution.

Exercise 18.5

The following useful ratios can be calculated.

(i) Earnings per share:

$$EPS = \frac{\text{Net earnings}}{\text{Number of ordinary shares}}$$

$$= \frac{£550,000}{5,000,000}$$

$$= \underline{\underline{11p}}$$

(ii) Price earnings ratio:

$$PE = \frac{\text{Market price of one ordinary share}}{\text{E.P.S.}}$$

$$= \frac{£1.50}{11p}$$

$$= \underline{\underline{13.6}}$$

(iii) Earnings yield:

$$\text{Earnings yield} = \frac{\text{E.P.S}}{\text{Share price}} \times 100$$

$$= \frac{11p}{£1.50} \times 100$$

$$= 7.33\%$$

(iv) Dividend yield:

$$\text{Dividend yield} = \frac{\text{Dividend per share} \times 100}{\text{Share price}}$$

$$= \frac{6p^*}{£1.50}$$

$$= 4\%$$

$$* \quad \frac{£300,000}{5,000,000}$$

(v) Dividend cover:

$$\text{Dividend cover} = \frac{\text{EPS}}{\text{Dividend per share}}$$

$$= \frac{11p}{6p}$$

$$= 1.83\%$$

(vi) Gearing:

$$\text{Gearing} = \frac{\text{Loan capital}}{\text{Equity} + \text{loan capital}}$$

$$= \frac{£1,200,000}{£7,400,000}$$

$$= .16$$

(vii) Asset cover:

$$\text{Asset cover} = \frac{\text{Net assets}}{\text{Number of ordinary shares}}$$

$$= \frac{£5,000,000 + £1,200,000}{5,000,000}$$

$$= \underline{\underline{£1.24}}$$

Exercise 18.6

(a) Earnings per share is defined as the profit after tax attributable to ordinary shareholders divided by the number of shares. It is a measure of the profitability of the business as it concerns its equity holders.

(b) The price earnings ratio is defined as the market price of a share divided by the earnings per share. It may thus be seen as the number of years' purchase of earnings required to acquire a share. To the fundamental analyst it is a measure of how expensive a share is. It must be seen against the background of the price earnings ratio usual for shares in the same risk class and with similar prospects.

(c) Earnings yield is earnings expressed as a return on the market value of the shares. It indicates the ultimate profitability of an investment at current market prices.

(d) Dividend yield is the actual cash yield given on an investment in the shares at the current market price. It indicates the cash return which an investor may expect to obtain.

(e) The dividend cover is a measure of how secure a dividend is. It states how many times over the current dividend could be paid out of the current profit.

(f) Gearing is a measure of the company's reliance on debt. In fundamental analysis it is often calculated on the accounting values of debt and equity (i.e. their nominal values) rather than their market values as would be done in a calculation of the cost of capital. Gearing has a bearing on the degree of risk to which an equity investor is exposed.

Chapter 19

Exercise 19.1

Either of the methods of expansion available to Solo may be capable of achieving the required result and there is no fundamental reason for favouring either one or the other. The two possibilities should be evaluated like any other investment propositions and a selection made of the one which seems the more favourable.

There are several factors which might make the merger more attractive than setting up new capacity. Not all of these can necessarily be fully evaluated in cash terms and the decision might, therefore, be partly determined by a subjective assessment of their weight. These factors are:

(i) Tandem's activities already have their own finance – the equity and debt which Tandem has issued. If Solo acquires Tandem's shares by issuing its own shares in exchange for them it may effectively raise finance for the operation on more favourable terms than by recourse to the market. For one thing dealing costs will be considerably reduced. For another it will not be necessary to offer the discount often required to interest investors in a totally new proposition.

(ii) To set up its own capacity will take Solo time. Apart from the delay in building and equipping a factory and assembling and perhaps training a work force, markets will need to be created by advertising and other forms of promotion. The low profits or actual losses incurred during the build up period may represent effectively a substantial extra initial investment.

(iii) Solo has to face the prospect that its new venture may fail. It is expanding into a field in which its management have no experience and mistakes may be made. If it takes over Tandem it is acquiring an established business where the risks of the setting up period have already been overcome.

(iv) As an existing business Tandem will have acquired the goodwill of an established market and may own patents or trademarks which will inhibit the activities of a competitor. These important benefits can be obtained only by acquiring Tandem .

(v) If Solo does not acquire Tandem some other concern may do so. Tandem, backed by the resources of another organisation, could seriously prejudice Solo's chance of success if it expands into the new activity with new capacity which may never acquire a large enough market share to succeed.

Exercise 19.2

The market valuation of the two companies currently is:

Number of shares in issue × Market price of share

> For Dum this is $2,000,000 \times £3 = £6,000,000$

> For Dee it is $1,500,000 \times £1.20 = £1,800,000$

> The combined value is $£6,000,000 + £1,800,000 = £7,800,000$

If the combination takes place the market value of the group will be:

> Earnings × P/E ratio = $((£500,000 + £200,000) + 10\%) \times 15$

> $= £11,550,000$

The difference of £3,750,000 is a measure of the synergy created by the situation and represents the benefit to be apportioned between the parties to the negotiation.

We will calculate certain important financial parameters in the existing situation on the assumption that the equity holders of neither company will wish to see these deteriorate.

(i) Net asset value.

The net asset values for the two companies are:

$$\text{Net asset value} = \frac{\text{Value attributable to equity}}{\text{Number of ordinary shares}}$$

$$\text{For Dum} = \frac{£2,520,000}{2,000,000}$$

$$= \underline{\underline{£1.26}}$$

$$\text{For Dee} = \frac{£1,640,000}{1,500,000}$$

$$= \underline{\underline{£1.09}}$$

To maintain the net asset value the present shareholders of Dee would need to be offered:

$$\frac{1,640,000}{2,520,000 + 1,640,000} = .39 \text{ of the enlarged equity}$$

This is achieved by giving .85 of a Dum share for each Dee share.

(ii) Earnings per share.

$$\text{Earnings per share} = \frac{\text{Total earnings attributable to equity}}{\text{Number of shares}}$$

$$\text{For Dum} = \frac{500,000}{2,000,000}$$

$$= \underline{\underline{25\text{p}}}$$

$$\text{For Dee} = \frac{£200,000}{1,500,000}$$

$$= \underline{\underline{13.33\text{p}}}$$

On merger there would be enlarged total earnings of £770,000 (as calculated above) and to maintain the same equivalent E.P.S. Dee would require at least 200,000/770,000 of the equity of the enlarged Dum, achieved by giving .47 of a Dum share for each Dee share.

(iii) Market value.

Current total value of Dum's shares is
2,000,000 × £3 = £6,000,000

Current total value of Dee's shares is
1,500,000 × £1.20 = £1,800,000

Since the market value of the merged concern is expected to be £11,550,000 Dum would require at least 1.8/11.55 of its equity, i.e. .25 Dum share for each Dee share.

(iv) Financial analysis. Dum's current cost of capital, assuming no expected growth, is:

$$\text{For equity} = \frac{\text{Maintainable annual profit}}{\text{Market value of equity}} = \frac{£500,000}{6,000,000}$$

We do not know the cost of Dum's loan capital so we will take this figure as the overall cost of capital. Thus the most Dum would pay for Dee for this to be an acceptable project would be:

$$\frac{\text{Earnings of Dee} + \text{'synergistic' earnings}}{\text{Cost of capital}} = \frac{£270,000}{8.33\%}$$

$$= \underline{\underline{£3,241,297}}$$

This would involve issuing 1,080,432 shares given their market price of £3 per share.

The terms envisaged in all of the above are to issue in exchange for 1 share in Dee the following number of shares in Dum:

(i)   At least .85

(ii) At least .47

(iii) At least .25

(iv) Not more than .72

Suggested terms are 1 share in Dum for every 2 in Dee. This would be favoured by both parties on every criterion except net asset value.

Exercise 19.3

Synergy is the gain from the merger over what existed before. When two companies are amalgamated their combined profits will normally be more than the sum of what they would have earned separately. Hence their combined market value is likely to be more than the sum of the separate market values. These effects are manifestations of synergy.

If it were not for synergy there would be no justification for a merger. The combined business would be a mere summation of its parts each neither better off nor worse off than before. Every merger proposition would be a marginal case; it would not matter whether it took place or not. We would expect that occasional mergers would still take place, almost by accident, but there would be no general impetus towards business concentration .

Exercise 19.4

A number of possible bases for the allotment of shares in Grey should be explored to see whether there is any measure of agreement. The calculations are set out below. It is assumed in each case that Grey shares are of £1 each and are valued at par.

(a) **Net asset value**

Black:	balance sheet	£3,070,000	
	goodwill	500,000	£3,570,000
White:	balance sheet	£1,520,000	
	goodwill	300,000	1,820,000
			£5,390,000

Thus Black shareholders should receive:

$$\frac{3,570,000}{2,500,000} = 1.428 \text{ Grey shares for each Black share}$$

White shareholders should receive:

$$\frac{1,820,000}{1,000,000} = 1.82 \text{ Grey shares for each White share}$$

(b) **Earnings per share**

Since the group profit is expected to be 15% up on the present level each shareholder in both companies could expect to receive an equal increase of that amount. The total capital of Grey should be allotted between Black and White in proportion to their individual earnings:

Total earnings of group:	Black	£420,000
	White	244,000
		664,000
	Add 15%	99,600
		£763,600

(c) **Market value**

The total market value of the group is £6,872,400.

Market value of Black	£420,000 × 8 =	£3,360,000
Market value of White	£244,000 × 10 =	2,440,000
		£5,800,000

Shares allotted to Black

$$\frac{3,360,000}{5,800,000} \times 6,872,400 = 3,981,252$$

Black shareholders should receive

$$\frac{3,981,252}{2,500,000} = 1.59 \text{ Grey shares for each Black share}$$

Shares allotted to White

$$\frac{2,440,000}{5,800,000} \times 6,872,400 = 2,891,147$$

White shareholders should receive

$$\frac{2,891,147}{1,000,000} = 2.89 \text{ Grey shares for each White share}$$

The financial analysis method is not appropriate in this case as Grey is a new company whose prospective earnings are entirely derived from the existing businesses of Black and White. If pursued the method would give exactly the same results as the earnings per share method.

It is suggested that a fair compromise would be an allotment of shares in Grey as follows:

Black shareholders: 1.6 shares in Grey for each 1 share in Black
(a total allotment of 4,000,000 shares)

White shareholders: 2.4 shares in Grey for each 1 share in White
(a total allotment of 2,400,000 shares)

Grey would be formed with an issued share capital of 6,400,000 shares

If the new company planned to pay a dividend of 7½% this would give all shareholders a slightly higher income than they receive at present and it would be approximately as well covered by earnings.

Exercise 19.5

We should first consider the advantages of growth. These are:

(a) There may be economies of scale such that lower unit costs and hence higher profits can be expected from a greater size of operations.

(b) There may be market power accruing to a large business. Because customers have fewer alternative sources of supply it has more control over the price of the final product. A monopolist's prices are invariably higher than those which would be charged under competition. Similarly a large business may be able to negotiate more favourable terms with its suppliers if to them it is a substantial and valuable customer.

(c) Growth gives opportunities for diversification which, properly used, may reduce risk.

(d) A large company or group may be able to raise finance on lower cost terms than a small one.

It should be pointed out that these are the potential advantages of growth. If, in a particular situation, they do not apply then growth may not, in fact, be desirable. There should be no universal supposition that expansion is always either desirable or profitable.

As a method of growth merger has both advantages and disadvantages and these are briefly considered below:

Advantages

(a) Since the merging companies come complete with their own finance already arranged, this removes one barrier to expansion into new fields. The existing finance is also likely to be lower in cost than would be new finance.

(b) Growth by merger can be achieved much more rapidly than can growth by internal expansion.

(c) There may be less risk involved in expansion by merger because the merger can be made with a company already having a record of success.

(d) Mergers can sometimes be made with poorly managed companies which are not exploiting their opportunities properly. This may mean that the merger can be achieved on terms far more favourable than would otherwise be the case.

(e) Merger may bring under common control those who were previously competitors and thus strengthen market power even more effectively than other forms of growth.

Disadvantages

(a) If the merger is by an exchange of shares, as is commonly the case, the pattern of shareholder control of the business will be altered. This may not be desired by present substantial shareholders.

(b) A merger is a very public method of expansion which may provoke counter bids or other forms of retaliation from competitors.

(c) A merger is a fairly big once and for all step. It is very difficult to reverse it if, in the event, it turns out to be unsuccessful.

Exercise 19.6

The possibilities will be referred to one at a time.

(a) **A cash purchase of the shares of Triangle**

   Advantages

   (i) All future benefits of the merger go to the existing shareholders of Square.

   (ii) The control of Square remains in the same hands as at present.

   Disadvantages

   (i) A large amount of cash has to be raised.

   (ii) If a bid is unsuccessful (e.g. beaten by a counter bidder or refused by shareholders of Triangle) Square may be left with a substantial unwanted stake in Triangle.

(b) **Issues of Square shares**

   Advantages

   (i) No cash has to be raised.

(ii) Because of the future participation of the existing shareholders of Triangle they may be willing to agree to a merger on more favourable terms than if they are to be bought out completely.

Disadvantages

(i) Some measure of control passes out of the hands of Square.

(ii) Shareholders in Triangle may not like a situation in which Square becomes the senior company.

(c) **Formation of a holding company**.

Advantages

(i) No cash has to be raised.

(ii) The device emphasises the equality of the partnership which may be of psychological importance in gaining the agreement of directors and shareholders of Triangle.

Disadvantages

(i) It may be less easy to determine the appropriate terms for the merger.

(ii) There may be no leader which is often needed to make a merger successful.

Chapter 20

Exercises 20.1

We shall work in units of 1,000 tablets of soap.

$$EOQ = \sqrt{\frac{2BN}{C}}$$

$$R = \sqrt{\frac{2 \times 5 \times 200}{.5}}$$

$$= 63$$

The re-order quantity is thus 63,000 tablets.

The re-order level is the usage for the eight weeks waiting for delivery

$$R = \frac{DN}{W}$$

$$= \frac{8 \times 200}{48}$$

$$= 33.3$$

Re-ordering should be put in hand when stocks decline to 33,333 tablets. The average stock is half of the re-order quantity, i.e. 31,500 tablets.

Exercise 20.2

Poor or non-existent stock control is likely to have the following consequences:

(i) There will be over extravagant use of stock in production thus putting up costs.

(ii) Bad storage will lead to physical deterioration of stock.

(iii) There will be a high risk of pilferage.

(iv) Stock may not be located where it can readily be found when required and time may be lost in looking for it.

(v) There may be special hazards from corrosive, toxic or inflammable stocks not carefully stored.

(vi) Production costs will not be fully recorded and therefore will be difficult to control.

Exercise 20.3

$$EOQ = \sqrt{\frac{2BN}{C}}$$

$$R = \sqrt{\frac{2 \times 100 \times 60,000}{.1}}$$

$$= \underline{\underline{10,954 \text{ tons}}}$$

It should be ordered (just over five times per annum) when stocks fall to:

$$Q = \frac{DN}{W}$$

$$= \frac{2 \times 60,000}{50}$$

$$= \underline{\underline{2,400 \text{ tons}}}$$

Cost of this recommended policy

$$\frac{CQ}{2} + \frac{BN}{Q} = \frac{.1 \times 10{,}950}{2} + \frac{100 \times 60{,}000}{10{,}950}$$

$$= £1{,}095 \text{ per annum}$$

Cost of current policy

Stock is re-ordered in quantities of 30,000 tons whenever stock falls to 10,000 tons. Stock level, on delivery after two weeks, must be

$$10{,}000 - \frac{2}{50} \times 60{,}000 = 7{,}600 \text{ tons}$$

Minimum stock is thus 7,600 tons and maximum stock 37,600 tons. Average stock is 22,600 tons and holding cost $22{,}600 \times .1 = £2{,}260$ per annum. Order cost is $2 \times £100 = £200$ per annum. Total cost is £2,460 per annum. This exceeds the cost of the recommended policy by £1,365 per annum.

If it is very important not to run out of stock this can only be achieved by setting a re-order level appropriate to the longest delivery time expected, say four weeks. This would mean reordering at a stock level of 4,800 tons. It would increase average stock by 2,400 tons and annual holding cost by $2{,}400 \times .1 = £240$ per annum.

Exercise 20.4

First we must calculate the economic order quantities and re-order levels.

For X $\quad EOQ_x = \sqrt{\dfrac{2BN}{C}}$

$$= \sqrt{\frac{2 \times £100 \times 24{,}000}{5p}}$$

$$= \underline{\underline{9{,}798 \text{ litres}}}$$

$$R = \frac{DN}{W}$$

$$= \frac{5 \times 24{,}000}{50}$$

$$= \underline{\underline{2{,}400 \text{ litres}}}$$

For Y
$$EOQ_y = \sqrt{\frac{2BN}{C}}$$

$$= \sqrt{\frac{2 \times £80 \times 15,000}{10p}}$$

$$= \underline{\underline{4,899 \text{ kgs}}}$$

$$R = \frac{DN}{W}$$

$$= \frac{10 \times 15,000}{50}$$

$$= \underline{\underline{3,000 \text{kgs}}}$$

Since it is obviously very important that the company never finds itself out of stock it might be advisable to increase these re-order levels by, say, 50%. Whether or not this should be done would depend on the probability that delivery times would be met.

Exercise 20.5

Almost any investment in a productive fixed asset will render necessary a consequential investment in working capital. If, for example, the fixed asset is a machine producing a saleable product, it will be necessary to acquire and maintain a stock of raw materials so that production may flow smoothly without interruption caused by waiting for supplies. It will also be necessary to finance an appropriate level of debtors to facilitate sales of the product.

Quite clearly, then, investment in working capital is not idle since, without it, the projects which it supports would come to a halt. What may be true, however, is that it may be very difficult to identify and evaluate a rate of return on the investment in working capital. This difference, however, is more apparent than real. Because an investment in a fixed asset requires a corresponding investment in working capital then conceptually the investment is, in fact, the whole sum required including the working capital. The return can then be regarded as the cash flow from the total investment which can be appraised accordingly.

In a business which is a going concern the components of working capital are not always identifiable with the fixed assets to which they relate. The financial manager's efforts must thus be directed at optimising the amount invested in working capital. Optimisation is different from minimisation. An optimisation policy seeks to strike a balance between the costs of investment in working capital and the costs of being without it. A holding of stock, for example, incurs the cost of the capital tied up in it and the costs of storing and controlling it. An absence of stock incurs the costs of holdups leading to idle equipment and customer disappointment.

Exercise 20.6

We must determine the economic order quantity using the usual formula:

$$EOQ = \sqrt{\frac{2BN}{C}}$$

$$R = \sqrt{\frac{2 \times 100 \times 60,000}{2}}$$

$$= \underline{\underline{2,499}}$$

The slabs should therefore be ordered more frequently than they are at present – in lots of (say) 2,500 about twice in every month. This should be done when stocks fall to half a month's usage, i.e. 2,500 slabs.

If this policy is adopted average stock is 1,250 assuming even usage.

Holding cost is	£2,500
Ordering cost is	2,400
	£4,900

The original policy gave an average stock of 2,500 slabs

Holding cost is	£5,000
Ordering cost is	1,200
	£6,200

Saving is	£1,300 per annum

Chapter 21

Exercise 21.1

The elements which any credit policy must seek to control are:

(i)   discount or other incentives to be offered for prompt or early payment;

(ii) the length of credit granted;

(iii) the credit worthiness of the customers;

(iv) action to be taken regarding late payers.

If the credit control policy is too tight there are likely to be the following consequences (favourable and adverse):

(i)   The cost of financing debtors and that of bad debts will be relatively low;

(ii) Customers will go elsewhere and business will be lost;

(iii) A disproportionate volume of resources will be put into the credit control process (e.g. by chasing up debtors who are only a day or two late or by the meticulous researching of credit worthiness for a debt of a few pounds).

If the policy is too slack there may be the following consequences:

(i)   Customers will readily be found and sales are likely to be high;

(ii) The cost of financing debtors will be high because long credit periods will cause them to be relatively high as a proportion of annual sales;

(iii) Bad debts will be high because of the less credit worthy customers accepted and because late payers will not be dealt with promptly.

Exercise 21.2

Since the categorisation is based on the expected behaviour of different groups of customers we must anticipate that the proposed relaxation of the credit policy will not affect existing debtors. New debtors in category D will appear and this will lead to an increase in sales. We determine the cost of giving credit per £1,000 sales per annum below:

$$\text{Increased level of debtors } £1,000 \times \frac{50}{365} = £137$$

Cost of financing this is £137 × 20%		£27
Cost of bad debts is 10% × £1,000		100
So total cost is		£127

The additional sales need to make a contribution, therefore, of about 13% before this change in policy becomes worthwhile.

Exercise 21.3

We should first calculate the extent of the increased business which has been generated.

Sales before discount introduced £350,000 × $\dfrac{365}{25}$ =	£5,110,000
Sales after discount introduced £400,000 × $\dfrac{365}{24}$	6,083,333
Increase in sales	973,333
Increase in profit 20%	£194,667
Increase in financing charges	
(£400,000 – £350,000) × 15%	£7,500
Cost of discount $\dfrac{1}{2}$ × £6,083,333 × $\dfrac{2.5}{100}$	76,042
	£83,542
Net gain	£111,125

Exercise 21.4

Additional cost		
Investment of £100,000 – financing at 18% p.a.		£18,000
Running cost		30,000
		48,000
Loss of business £200,000 × 15%		30,000
		£78,000
Benefits		
Reduction in bad debts	– currently 10% × £2m	£200,000
	– projected 5% × £1.8m	90,000
		£110,000
Financing of debtors*	– currently £328,767 × 15%	£49,315
	– projected £147,945 × 15%	22,192
		£27,123

$$*£2,000,000 \times \frac{60}{365} = £328,767$$

$$£1,800,000 \times \frac{30}{365} = £147,945$$

Total benefits	£137,123
Net benefit	£59,123

Exercise 21.5

Cloudy's manager has failed to take into account the cost of financing the debtors. Below is presented a calculation showing the correct evaluation of the proposal assuming for the purposes of illustration that 10% of the credit sales turnover will be outstanding as debtors at any one time (i.e. a 36.5 day average collection period) and that Cloudy's cost of capital is 20% per annum.

Extra sales generated by proposed policy		£50,000
Gross profit at 33⅓%		£16,667
Less Bad debts incurred 15% × £100,000	£15,000	
Cost of finance 20% × £10,000	2,000	17,000
Net cost of implementing plan		£333

Exercise 21.6

The benefit from the proposal will be the contribution on the increased sales:

Increase in sales is 30% × £1,000,000		£300,000
Contribution is 15% thereof		£45,000
From this must be deducted the increased costs:		
(i) Clerical labour		£10,000
(ii) Bad debts:		
now $1\% \times \frac{1}{4} \times £1,000,000$	£2,500	
new policy 1½% × 40% × £1,300,000	7,800	5,300
(iii) Cost of capital:		
now $\frac{40}{365} \times \frac{14}{100} \times £250,000$	£3,836	
new policy $\frac{35}{365} \times \frac{14}{100} \times £520,000$	6,981	3,145
		£18,445
The net benefit from the new policy is		£26,555 p.a.

Chapter 22

Exercise 22.1

Manufacturing schedule

	Jul	Aug	Sep	Oct	Nov	Dec
Units to be manufactured	10,000	12,000	15,000	18,000	18,000	18,000

One month in advance of sales.

Material purchase schedule

	Jul	Aug	Sep	Oct	Nov	Dec
Material for (units)	29,500[1]	16,500[2]	18,000	18,000	18,000	18,000
Value @ 15p per unit	£4,425	£2,475	£2,700	£2,700	£2,700	£2,700

[1] Material used in July 10,000 units + material requirement for August, 12,000 + half of material requirement for September, 7,500 units.

[2] Material for remaining half of September 7,500 units and half of October, 9,000 units.

Cash flow forecast

	Jul £	Aug £	Sep £	Oct £	Nov £	Dec £
Payments :						
Creditors (materials)[1]		4,425	2,475	2,700	£2,700	£2,700
Creditors (var overhead)[2]		2,000	2,400	3,000	3,600	3,600
Wages[3]	1,500	2,300	2,850	3,450	3,600	3,600
Fixed overhead	10,000			10,000		
Machinery purchase	60,000					
Loan interest						2,250
	£71,500	£8,725	£7,725	£19,150	£9,900	£12,150
Receipts:						
Debtors[4]			5,000	11,000	13,500	16,500
Capital	50,000					
Loan	25,000					
	£75,000	Nil	£5,000	£11,000	£13,500	£16,500
Net change	£3,500	(£8,725)	(£2,725)	(£8,150)	£3,600	£4,350
Overdraft required		(£5,225)	(£7,950)	(£16,100)	(£12,500)	(£8,150)

[1] One month in arrear of material purchases.
[2] Previous month's manufacture @ 20p per unit.
[3] Three-quarters of current month's manufacture plus one-quarter of

previous month @ 20 per unit.
4   Half of previous month's sales and half of month before that @ £1 per unit.

MENDIP
Budgeted profit and loss account for the six months

	£	£
Sales		73,000
Deduct		
Variable cost of sales (73,000 × 55p)	40,150	
Fixed cost (six months)	20,000	
Depreciation (six months)	3,000	
Interest on loan (six months)	2,250	65,400
		£7,600

Budgeted balance sheet as at 31st December

		£	£	£
Fixed assets				
Machinery and equipment				57,000
Current assets				
Stocks of raw materials			4,050	
Stocks of finished goods			9,900	
Debtors			27,000	
			40,950	
Less	Current liabilities			
	Bank overdraft	8,150		
	Creditors: Materials	2,700		
	Variable overhead	3,600		
	Labour	900	15,350	25,600
				£82,600

	£
Financed by:	
Capital (including undrawn profit for six months)	57,600
Loan	25,000
	£82,600

Exercise 22.2
Subsidiary – Cash budget for first eight months £000's

	1	2	3	4	5	6	7	8
Payments:								
Creditors (materials)	-	55	20	20	25	25	25	30
Creditors (variable overheads)	-	45	60	60	60	60	75	75
Wages	22.5	37.5	40	40	40	47.5	50	50
Fixed overhead	75			75			75	
Machinery	450							
Loan repayment				75	75	75	75	
	547.5	137.5	120	195	200	207.5	300	230
Receipts:								
Cash sales	-	-	50	100	150	150	125	100
Debtors	-	-	-	50	100	150	150	125
Share capital	500							
Loan	300							
	800	-	50	150	250	300	275	225
Net change	252.5	(137.5)	(70)	(45)	50	92.5	(25)	(5)
Balance	252.5	115	45	Nil	50	142.5	117.5	112.5

Forecast balance sheet at end of period £000's

Share capital	500	Fixed assets		
Profit and loss account	240	Machinery		350
Current Liabilities		Current assets		
Creditors	117.5[1]	Stock (R.M.)	60	
		Stock (F.G.)	210	
		Debtors	100	
		Paid in advance	25	
		Cash	112.5	507.5
	857.5			857.5

[1]Material	30
Labour	12.5
Overhead	75
	117.5

Exercise 22.3

Starship, plc

(a) Materials

	1 £	2 £	3 £	4 £	5 £	6 £
Consumption (units)	2,000	3,000	4,000	5,000	5,000	5,000
Consumption (value)	4,000	6,000	8,000	10,000	10,000	10,000
Purchases (value)	18,000	10,000	10,000	10,000	10,000	10,000
Cash paid	-	9,000	14,000	10,000	10,000	10,000

(b) Labour

Usage (units)	2,000	3,000	4,000	5,000	5,000	5,000
Usage (value)	2,000	3,000	4,000	5,000	5,000	5,000
Cash paid	1,000	2,500	3,500	4,500	5,000	5,000

(c) Variable overhead

Usage (units)	2,000	3,000	4,000	5,000	5,000	5,000
Usage (value)	3,000	4,500	6,000	7,500	7,500	7,500
Cash	-	3,000	4,500	6,000	7,500	7,500

(d) Sales

Sales (units)	-	-	1,000	2,000	4,000	5,000
Sales (value)	-	-	6,000	12,000	24,000	30,000
Cash from cash sales	-	-	3,000	6,000	12,000	15,000
Cash from credit sales	-	-	-	-	3,000	6,000
Total cash	-	-	3,000	6,000	15,000	21,000

Cash budget for six months

	1 £	2 £	3 £	4 £	5 £	6 £
Payments						
Materials	-	9,000	14,000	10,000	10,000	10,000
Labour	1,000	2,500	3,500	4,500	5,000	5,000
Variable overhead	-	3,000	4,500	6,000	7,500	7,500
Fixed overhead	6,000	-	-	6,000	-	-
Purchase of machine	50,000					
	57,000	14,500	22,000	26,500	22,500	22,500
Receipts	-	-	3,000	6,000	15,000	21,000
Cash outflow	57,000	14,500	19,000	20,500	7,500	1,500
Cumulative	57,000	71,500	90,500	111,000	118,500	120,000

Chapter 23

Exercise 23.1

(a) The rate of interest of 12% per annum is 4% for three months.

The sum which has to be borrowed is:

$$2,000,000 \times \frac{100}{104} = 1,923,077 \text{ pesetas}$$

If sold at the spot rate this will yield:

$$\frac{1,923,077}{172} = £11,181$$

(b) If sold at the current forward rate the 2m pesetas receivable in three months' time will yield:

$$\frac{2,000,000}{172+4} = £11,364$$

Alternative (b) is preferable.

Exercise 23.2

(a) The rate of interest of 8% per annum is 2% for three months.

The sum which has to be invested is:

$$5,000,000 \times \frac{100}{102} = 4,901,961$$

Bought at the spot rate this would cost:

$$\frac{4,901,961}{2,249} = £2,180$$

(b) Bought at the forward rate:

$$\frac{5,000,000}{2,249 - 8} = £2,231$$

Jones should be advised to select alternative (a).

Exercise 23.3

Fixed assets	£	£
	000s	000s
Cost	333	
Less depreciation	42	291
Current assets		
Stock	150	
Debtors	61	
Cash	61	
	272	
Current liabilities		
Creditors	52	220
		511
Share capital		500
Profit for year	248	
Less dividends remitted	(152)	
loss on exchange	(85)	11
		511

Appendix 2: Past Examination Questions

Question 1   CIMA

(a) (i) Assume that the opportunity rate of return on equity capital
of companies in a particular risk class is 12½% and that this
is also the rate at which surplus funds can be re-invested.

The equity of X p.l.c. is in this risk category and the company
has a policy of paying annual dividends at the rate of 5% on
the market value of shareholders' funds at the beginning of
each year.

You are required to calculate what annual rate of growth
in share price X p.l.c. should achieve.   (5 marks)

(ii) X p.l.c. has under consideration a project costing £20,000, of
similar risk to existing activities, to be financed by an issue
of ordinary shares at par, and generating return cash flows
of £10,500 at the end of year 1 and £13,500 at the end of year
2.

You are required to demonstrate that this project will satisfy all the criteria derived from (a)(i) above, by preparing a
calculation of the net terminal value of the project. Ignore
taxation.   (5 marks)

(b) **You are required** to discuss

(i) whether all capital expenditure projects undertaken by an
enterprise should be expected to yield the same rate of
return; and

(ii) whether the cost of equity used in appraising projects would
be affected by an increase in the rate of interest at which
surplus funds could be re-invested.   (10 marks)
                                              (Total 20 marks)

Question 2   ACCA

The managing director of Lavipilon plc wishes to provide an extra
return to the company's shareholders and has suggested making
either:

(i) A 2 for 5 bonus issue (capitalisation issue) in addition to the normal dividend.

(ii) A 1 for 5 scrip dividend instead of the normal cash dividend.

(iii)A 1 for 1 share (stock) split in addition to the normal dividend.

Summarised balance sheet Lavipilon plc (end of last year)

	£m
Fixed assets	65
Current assets	130
Less: Current liabilities	(55)
	140
Financed by	
Ordinary shares (50 pence par value)	25
Share premium account	50
Revenue reserves	40
Shareholders' funds	115
11% debenture	25
	140

The company's shares are trading at 300 pence cum div. and the company has £50 million of profit from this year's activities available to ordinary shareholders of which £30 million will be paid as a dividend if options (i) or (iii) are chosen. None of the £40 million reserves would be distributed. This year's financial accounts have not yet been finalised

Required:

(a) For each proposal show the likely effect on the company's balance sheet at the end of *this* year, and the likely effect on the company's share price (9 marks)

(b) Comment upon how well these suggestions fulfil the managing director's objective of providing an extra return to the company's shareholders (3 marks)

(c) Discuss reasons why a company might wish to undertake

(i) a scrip dividend,

(ii) a share (stock) split. (5 marks)

(d) The managing director has heard that it is possible for the company to purchase its own shares. Explain why the purchase of its own shares might be useful to a company. Assume that the shares do not need to be cancelled after purchase. (8 marks)

(Total 25 marks)

Question 3 CIMA

MC Ltd is a small company (currently 19 employees) set up in 1982, which provides its clients with a consultancy service on electronic communications systems and which procures and instals the selected equipment.

Extracts from the accounts of the company for the past three years are given below.

MC Ltd
Extracts from annual accounts

Year ended 31st December	1985 £000	1984 £000	1983 £000
Profit and loss account			
Sales	3,700	2,600	1,600
Operating profit/(loss)	493	(32)	65
Interest receivable	103	130	18

Note: No dividends have been declared. No liability to corporation tax on operating results has yet arisen.

Balance sheets – year end

		1985			1984			1983
Fixed assets:								
Land and buildings		558			283			–
Plant and machinery at cost	263			82			48	
Less depreciation	48	215		26	56		10	38
		773			339			38
Current assets:								
Work-in-progress, at direct cost	1,457			783			46	
Less receipts on account	976	481		–	783		–	46
Debtors:								
Advance payments to suppliers	274			331			–	
Other	99	373		65	396		1	1
Cash at bank and in hand		1,007			1,090			294
		1,861			2,269			341
Current liabilities:								
Advance collections from customers	705			1,500			–	
Other	776	1481		855	2,355		257	257
Net current assets		380			(86)			84

Total assets less current liabilities	1,153	253	122
Less liabilities falling due after more than one year	140	111	78
	1,013	142	44

Share capital and reserves:			
Called-up ordinary share capital	20	20	20
Revaluation reserve	275	–	–
Profit and loss account	718	122	24
	1,013	142	44

You are required to:

(a) comment on the way in which the business has been financed over that period; (14 marks)

(b) indicate what appears to be the main weakness in financial management and suggest what actions might be taken to deal with it. (6 marks)

(Total 20 marks)

Question 4 ACCA

C plc and D plc are two companies in the printing industry. The companies have the same business risk and are almost identical in all respects except for their capital structures and total market values. The companies' capital structures are summarised below.

C plc	£000
Ordinary shares (25 pence par value)	20,000
Share premium account	45,000
Profit and loss account	36,500
Shareholders' funds	101,500

C's ordinary shares are trading at 140 pence.

D plc	£000
Ordinary shares (£1 par value)	25,000
Share premium account	8,000
Profit and loss account	44,000
Shareholders' funds	77,000
12% debentures (newly issued)	25,000
	102,000

D's ordinary shares are trading at 400 pence, and debentures at £100. Annual earnings before interest and tax for both companies are £25 million. Corporate tax is at the rate of 35%

Required:

(a) If you owned 4% of the ordinary shares of company D, and you agreed with the arguments of Modigliani and Miller explain what action you would take to improve your financial position.

(4 marks)

(b) Estimate by how much your financial position is expected to improve. Personal taxes may be ignored and the assumptions made by Modigliani and Miller may be used. (7 marks)

(c) If company C was to borrow £20 million calculate what effect this would have on the company's cost of capital according to Modigliani and Miller. What implications would this suggest for the company's choice of capital structure? (6 marks)

(d) Modigliani and Miller's theory of capital structure is sometimes considered to be unrealistic. Discuss the problems with this theory that might concern a financial manager who wishes to ascertain the appropriate capital structure for his company. (8 marks)

(Total 25 marks)

Question 5 CIMA

W, plc is a listed company engaged in the fabrication and erection of modular steel structures.

The company's recent history of sales and profits is as follows:

Year ended 30th September	1982	1983	1984	1985
Turnover Home (£000)	4,771	3,221	4,077	3,707
Export (£000)	4,441	7,362	8,152	4,773
Profit before tax as percentage of sales	9.7%	9.7%	9.3%	4.4%
Earnings per share	18.4p	30.9p	30.0p	8.9p
Ordinary dividend per share	7.7p	8.1p	9.1p	9.1p

Following publication of the 1985 annual report, a worried shareholder has asked for your independent comments on the financial management of the business during 1985.

The information you consider most relevant is reproduced in the following Appendices to this question:

Appendix A   Your own version of the 1985 Source and Application of Funds Statement

Appendix B   Abbreviated balance sheets as at 30th September, 1984 and 1985

Appendix C   Miscellaneous extracts from the annual report

You are required to set out your preliminary views (subject to further enquiry) on the financial management of the company during the year 1984/85, using the information provided and making any calculations you consider relevant.   **(30 marks)**

Appendix A
W plc
Source and Application of Funds Statement
for year ended 30th September 1985

	£000	£000
Profit before interest and taxation		380
Add : Items not involving the movement of funds:		
depreciation	521	
other	4	525
		905
Reduction in working capital (stocks, debtors and creditors)		1,109
Operating cash flow		2,014
Fixed assets: purchases	(921)	
sales	25	(896)
Cash payment on acquisition of new subsidiary (see Note below)		(1,425)
		(307)
Tax paid		(143)
		(450)
Reduction in liquid assets		361
Entity cash flow (out)		(89)
Equity cash flow:		
Dividends paid	(283)	
Shares issued	43	(240)
Lender cash flow:		
Interest paid	(7)	
Bank overdraft obtained	336	329
		89

Note: On 27th September, 1985 the company diversified its activities by the acquisition of the whole share capital of S Ltd. The total acquisition price was £3,658,000, satisfied by:

	£000	
Cash	1,425	
New ordinary shares	67	*
Unsecured borrowing	2,166	*
	3,658	

The net assets acquired were:		
Tangible fixed assets		624
Stocks		556
Trade debtors		669
Cash at bank		679
		2,528
Trade creditors	379	
Other liabilities	279	658
		1,870
Goodwill		1,788
		3,658

* These items are not shown in the Source and Application of Funds Statement.

Goodwill has been written off against Reserves.

W, plc Profit and Loss Account for the year ended 30th September, 1985 does not include any figures relating to S Ltd.

Appendix B
W, plc
Consolidated Balance Sheet at 30th September, 1985

	1985 £000	1984 £000
Fixed assets:		
Tangible fixed assets	4,283	3,290
Investments	1,437	1,399
	5,720	4,689
Current assets:		
Stocks and work-in-progress	3,141	2,792
Trade debtors	2,289	2,654
Other debtors	280	396
Cash at bank and in hand	792	522
	6,502	6,364

	1985 £000	1984 £000
Creditors – amounts falling due within one year:		
Bank overdraft	336	-
Trade creditors	1,382	806
Other creditors	1,387	1,513
	3,105	2,319
Net current assets	3,379	4,045
Total assets less current liabilities	9,117	8,734
Creditors – amounts falling due after more than one year:		
Unsecured loan	(2,166)	-
Deferred taxation	(593)	(229)
Net assets	6,358	8,505
Capital and Reserves:		
Called-up share capital	3,287	3,177
Revaluation reserve	487	449
Profit and loss account	2,584	4,879
	6,358	8,505

Appendix C
W, plc
Miscellaneous extracts from the Annual Report
for the year ended 30th September, 1985

1. Tangible Fixed Assets	Land and Buildings £000	Plant and Machinery £000	Total £000
Cost			
At 30th September, 1984	2,212	2,400	4,612
Additions	285	635	920
Subsidiary acquired	555	109	664
Disposals	(34)	(160)	(194)
At 30th September, 1985	3,018	2,984	6,002
Depreciation provision			
At 30th September, 1984	284	1,038	1,322
Provisions for year	227	294	521
Subsidiary acquired	-	40	40
Disposals	(34)	(130)	(164)
At 30th September, 1985	477	1,242	1,719

	£000	£000	£000
Net book value			
At 30th September, 1984	1,928	1,362	3,290
At 30th September, 1985	2,541	1,742	4,283

2. Stocks and Work-in-progress

		1985		1984
		£000		£000
Raw materials		635		682
Finished goods		1,950		1,680
Contract work-in-progress	847		440	
Less : progress payments received	291	556	10	430
		3,141		2,729

3. Profit and Loss Account Balance

		£000	£000	£000
Balance at 30th September, 1984				4,879
Profit for year ended 30th September, 1985:				
Before interest and tax			380	
Less:	Interest	7		
	Tax	95		
	Extraordinary item - provision for deferred taxation	496		
	Dividends	289	887	(507)
				4,372
Goodwill written off — acquisition of subsidiary				1,788
Balance at 30th September, 1985				2,584

4. Employees

	1985	1984
Average weekly number of employees:		
Manufacture	244	248
Selling	49	46
Administration	127	131
	420	425
Average remuneration per employee	£7,525	£7,300

Question 6 CIMA

A company needs to hold a stock of item X for sale to customers.

Although the item is of relatively small value per unit, the customers' quality control requirements and the need to obtain competitive supply tenders at frequent intervals result in high procurement costs.

Basic data about item X are as follows:

Annual sales demand (d) over 52 weeks	= 4,095 units
Cost of placing and processing a purchase order (procurement costs – Cs)	= £48.46
Cost of holding one unit for one year (Ch)	= £4.00
Normal delay between placing purchase order and receiving goods	= 3 weeks

You are required to

(a) calculate

(i) the Economic Order Quantity for item X, using the formula:

$$EOQ = \frac{2Csd}{Ch}$$

(ii) the frequency at which purchase orders would be placed, using that formula

(iii) the total annual procurement costs and the total annual holding costs when the EOQ is used; (6 marks)

(b) explain why it might be unsatisfactory to procure a fixed quantity of item X at regular intervals if it were company policy to satisfy all sales demands from stock and if

(i) the rate of sales demand could vary between 250 and 350 units per four-week period or

(ii) the delivery delay on purchases might vary between 3 and 5 weeks suggesting in each case what corrective actions might be taken; (6 marks)

(c) describe in detail a fully-developed stock control system for item X (or other fast-moving items), designed to ensure that stock holdings at all times are adequate but not excessive. Illustrate your answer with a freehand graph, not to scale. (8 marks)

(Total: 20 marks)

Question 7   ACCA

Ceder Ltd has details of two machines which could fulfil the company's future production plans. Only one of these machines will be purchased.

The 'standard' model costs £50,000, and the 'de-luxe' £88,000, payable immediately. Both machines would require the input of £10,000 working capital throughout their working lives, and both machines have no expected scrap value at the end of their expected working lives of 4 years for the standard machine and 6 years for the de-luxe machine.

The forecast pre-tax operating net cash flows associated with the two machines are:

Years hence (£)

	1	2	3	4	5	6
Standard	20,500	22,860	24,210	23,410		
De-luxe	32,030	26,110	25,380	25,940	38,560	35,100

The de-luxe machine has only recently been introduced to the market and has not been fully tested in operating conditions. Because of the higher risk involved the appropriate discount rate for the de-luxe machine is believed to be 14% per year, 2% higher than the discount rate for the standard machine.

The company is proposing to finance the purchase of either machine with a term loan at a fixed interest rate of 11% per year.

Taxation at 35% is payable on operating cash flows one year in arrears, and capital allowances are available at 25% per year on a reducing balance basis.

Required:

(a) For both the standard and the de-luxe machine calculate:
   (i) Payback period.
   (ii) Net present value.
   Recommend with reasons which of the two machines Ceder should purchase. (Relevant calculations must be shown.)

   (13 marks)

(b) If Ceder Ltd was offered the opportunity to lease the standard model machine over a 4 year period at a rental of £15,000 per year, not including maintenance costs, evaluate whether the company should lease or purchase the machine.   (6 marks)

(c) Surveys have shown that the accounting rate of return and payback period are widely used by companies in the capital investment decision process. Suggest reasons for the wide-spread use of these investment appraisal techniques.   (6 marks)

   (Total 25 marks)

Question 8 CIMA

(a) Security 'A' has an expected rate of return of 12%, with a standard deviation of 32.65%.

The expected rate of return is derived from three equal possibilities:

(i) that the actual rate of return will be the same as the expected rate of return;

(ii)/(iii) that the actual rate of return will differ from the expected rate of return by x%, either higher or lower.

You are required to calculate the two probable actual rates of return under (ii)/(iii) above. (6 marks)

(b) You are required to explain: (i) what information is conveyed to a potential investor by the standard deviation statistic; (ii) what factors would be taken into account by an investor when deciding whether to add to his portfolio either security 'A' or another security having lower values for standard deviation and expected rate of return. (10 marks)

(c) Given that the correlation coefficient of the return on security 'A' with the return on the market portfolio is 25% and that the standard deviation for the market portfolio is 13.5%, you are required to calculate the Beta factor for security 'A' and to interpret the result you obtain. (5 marks)

(d) Given that the risk-free rate of return is 8%, and using any relevant information supplied in parts (a)-(c) above, you are required to calculate the expected rate of return on the market portfolio.

(4 marks)

(Total 25 marks)

Question 9 ACCA

Killisick plc wishes to acquire Holbeck plc. The directors of Killisick are trying to justify the acquisition to the shareholders of both companies on the grounds that it will increase the wealth of all shareholders.

The supporting financial evidence produced by Killisick's directors is summarised below:

	£000	£000
	Killisick	*Holbeck*
Operating profit	12,400	5,800
Interest payable	4,431	2,200
Profit before tax	7,969	3,600
Tax	2,789	1,260
Earnings available to ordinary shareholders	5,180	2,340

Earnings per share (pre-acquisition)	14.80 pence	29.25 pence
Market price per share (pre-acquisition)	222 pence	322 pence
Estimated market price (post-acquisition)	240 pence	
Estimated equivalent value of one old Holbeck share (post-acquisiton)		360 pence

Payment is to be made with Killisick ordinary shares, at an exchange ratio of 3 Killisick shares for every 2 Holbeck shares.

Required:

(a) Show how the directors of Killisick produced their estimates of post-acquisition value and, if you do not agree with these estimates, produce revised estimates of post-acquisition values. All calculations must be shown. State clearly any assumptions that you make. (10 marks)

(b) If the acquisition is contested by Holbeck plc, using Killisick's estimate of its post-acquisition market price calculate the maximum price that Killisick could offer without reducing the wealth of its shareholders. (3 marks)

(c) The boards of directors of Holbeck plc later informally indicate that they are prepared to recommend to their shareholders a 2 for 1 share offer.

Further information regarding the effect of the acquisition on Killisick is given below:

(i) The acquisition will result in an increase in the total pre-acquisition after tax operating cash flows of £2.75 million per year indefinitely.

(ii) Rationalisation will allow machinery with a realisable value of £7.2 million to be disposed of at the end of the next year.

(iii) Redundancy payments will total £3.5 million immediately and £8.4 million at the end of the next year.

(iv) Killisick's cost of capital is estimated to be 14% per year.

All values are after any appropriate taxation. Assume that the pre-acquisition market values of Killisick and Holbeck shares have not changed.

Required:

Recommend, using your own estimates of post-acquisition values, whether Killisick should be prepared to make a 2 for 1 offer for the shares of Holbeck. (6 marks)

(d) Disregarding the information in (c) above and assuming no increase in the total post-acquisition earnings, assess whether this acquisition is likely to have any effect on the value of debt of Killisick plc. (6 marks)

(Total 25 marks)

Question 10   CIMA

XYZ Manufacturing, plc is a United Kingdom company producing industrial paints which, since 1981, have been marketed mainly through independent regional distributors.

Your own company, which has substantial resources, is a major user of these products and you have recently been asked by the financial director of XYZ Manufacturing, plc whether your company would provide medium-term loan finance to assist XYZ in improving its production facilities.

You have been given access to the accounts of XYZ Manufacturing, plc's accounts for the past five years, extracts from which are given in Appendix A on the following two pages.

You are required to:

(a) analyse the figures provided and comment on:

  (i) the liquidity of the company;

  (ii) the effectiveness of its utilisation of assets;

  (iii)its sources and uses of funds over the period under review, and

  (iv) the extent to which you consider it could expect to raise further loan and/or equity capital.

In answering, you should have regard to the nature and size of the business and to the economic conditions prevailing during the period. Calculations that are not relevant to the purposes outlined above are *not* required.

(b) list the actions that might be taken to improve fund flows through more effective working capital control *generally* by a manufacturing company and *specifically* by XYZ Manufacturing, plc.

(c) summarise briefly the main points in your answer to XYZ's request for financial assistance from your company.

(Total 40 marks)

APPENDIX A

XYZ Manufacturing plc. Extracts from Published Accounts. Years ended 31st December

£ millions

Balance Sheet	1982		1981		1980		1979		1978	
Fixed Assets										
Land and Buildings										
At cost, plus revaluation £12m 1981	59		47		35		35		35	
Depreciation provision	2	57	1	46	--	35	--	35	--	35
Plant and Machinery										
At cost, plus revaluation £40m 1981	164		144		93		85		78	
Depreciation provision	86	78	75	69	68	25	61	24	55	23
		135		115		60		59		58
Current Assets										
Stocks and Work in Progress	82		55		50		43		40	
Trade Debtors	55		42		33		27		26	
Other Receivables	2		1		2		3		1	
Bank Balances and Cash	--	139	--	98	--	85	--	73	4	71
Current Liabilities										
Trade Creditors	36		25		22		19		18	
Dividends	2		--		5		1		3	
Taxation	5		3		4		2		5	
Bank Overdraft	47	(90)	17	(45)	4	(35)	4	(26)	--	(26)
Total Assets *less* Current Liabilities		184		168		110		106		103
Loans repayable beyond one year		35		24		37		38		41

417

Ordinary Shareholders Funds	1982	1981	1980	1979	1978
Ordinary Shares of £1 each	31	31	13	13	8
Retained profits	66	61	60	55	54
Revaluation Reserve	52	52	--	--	--
	149	144	73	68	62

XYZ Manufacturing plc. Extracts from Published Accounts. Years ended 31st December

£ millions

Profit and Loss Account	1982	1981	1980	1979	1978
Sales	200	176	175	144	143
Operating Costs					
Depreciation (1982 based on revalued amounts)	12	8	7	6	6
Lease of Plant and Machinery	8	1	--	--	--
Other	150	156	145	130	118
	170	165	152	136	124
Operating Profit	30	11	23	8	19
Interest Payable	12	7	5	4	4
Profit before Taxation	18	4	18	4	15
Taxation	10	3	8	2	5
Profit Attributable to Shareholder	8	1	10	2	10
Dividends	3	--	5	1	3
Retained Profit for Year	5	1	5	1	7

Notes

1. Since 1981, Sales have been made partly through distributors instead of direct to end-users. Distributors (included in Trade Debtors) pay by cheque within the second month after receipt of an invoice.

2. It may be assumed that the general index of prices increased by 12% per annum over the five years.

Question 11   ACCA

The demerger of a large loss making conglomerate company resulted in the creation of four smaller firms and in the liquidation of the original company. While two of these companies have not survived, one of the new companies – Wood – appears successful and trading in its shares will shortly commence on the Unlisted Securities Market. The second surviving company – Holt – is currently experiencing severe liquidity problems and its future is uncertain.

Details of the two surviving firms are:

Holt is unable to pay the interest due on its only debt finance, the £3.5 million 12% debenture and is in breach of its trust deed. Due to Holt's poor financial position it would not be worthwhile for the debenture holders to exercise their right to appoint a receiver in an attempt to obtain repayment of the debenture. Instead Holt has suggested that the existing debenture be surrendered in exchange for either (i) 8 million newly issued ordinary shares of Holt, or (ii) £3 million non interest bearing convertible debenture. This convertible would be repayable at par in 3 years or could be converted, at the holders' option, into 6 million ordinary shares of Holt at that time.

Holt currently has 12 million ordinary shares in issue and will undertake not to issue any additional shares, or to pay any dividends, during the next 3 years if the debenture holders agree to one of the alternatives specified above.

If the convertible is issued and the holders choose not to exercise their conversion rights then Holt will be forced into liquidation in 3 years in order to obtain the funds needed to repay the debt liability.

Estimates of Holt's net realisable asset values in year 3, before considering repayment of outstanding debt, are:

Probability	Net Realisable Asset Values in Year 3 £ millions
0.1	1
0.2	2
0.3	4
0.2	8
0.2	10

Should Holt not be liquidated then its value as a going concern will be 50% higher than the net realisable value of its assets. If Holt is not liquidated then its share price will reflect its going concern value.

Wood is expected to have considerable investment opportunities but will pursue a policy of internally generated funding for growth. Earnings for the next year are expected to be £600,000 and these will continue in perpetuity unless reinvestment takes place. Details of investment opportunities, which are expected to be available indefinitely, are shown in the following table.

The rate of return required by investors is expected to be 15% but this could rise to 16% or 17% if earnings are retained.

Proportion of earnings retained	Growth rate of earnings	Possible increase in investor required returns
%	%	%
0	0	0
25	7	1
50	10	2

Required:

(a) Determine the expected money value at year 3 of each of the two alternatives offered to Holt's existing debenture holders.

Clearly indicate for each of the five year 3 asset values given, whether, in the event of the convertible debenture being issued, the conversion rights should be exercised. (8 marks)

(b) Determine the optimum retention policy of Wood, and the associated total equity value, if the return required by investors

(i) remains at 15%

(ii) increases with retentions.

Briefly explain why the required rate of return may change with retention policy. (8 marks)

(c) Outline the financial benefits, and disadvantages, inherent in a demerger and indicate circumstances where it might be an appropriate course of action. (9 marks)

(Total 25 marks)

Question 12 ACCA

(a) Pavlon, plc has recently obtained a listing on the Stock Exchange. 90% of the company's shares were previously owned by members of one family but, since the listing, approximately 60% of the issued shares have been owned by other investors.

Pavlon's earnings and dividends for the five years prior to the listing are detailed below:

Years prior to listing	Profit after tax £	Dividend per share pence
5	1,800,000	3.6
4	2,400,000	4.8
3	3,850,000	6.16
2	4,100,000	6.56
1	4,450,000	7.12
Current Year	5,500,000 (estimate)	

The number of issued ordinary shares was increased by 25% three years prior to the listing and by 50% at the time of the listing.

The company's authorised capital is currently £25,000,000 in 25p ordinary shares, of which 40,000,000 shares have been issued. The market value of the company's equity is £78,000,000.

The board of directors is discussing future dividend policy. An interim dividend of 3.16 pence per share was paid immediately prior to the listing and the finance director has suggested a final dividend of 2.34 pence per share.

The company's declared objective is to maximise shareholder wealth.

Required:

(i) Comment upon the nature of the company's dividend policy prior to the listing and discuss if such a policy is likely to be suitable for a company listed on the Stock Exchange.

(6 marks)

(ii) Discuss whether the proposed final dividend of 2.34 pence is likely to be an appropriate dividend: (1) If the majority of shares are owned by wealthy private individuals; (2) If the majority of shares are owned by institutional investors.

(10 marks)

(b) The company's profit after tax is generally expected to increase by 15% per year for three years, and 8% per year after that. Pavlon's cost of equity capital is estimated to be 12% per year. Dividends may be assumed to grow at the same rate as profits.

Required:

(i) Using the dividend valuation model give calculations to indicate whether Pavlon's shares are currently undervalued or overvalued. (6 marks)

(ii) Briefly outline the weaknesses of the dividend valuation model. (3 marks)

(Total 25 marks)

421

Question 13 **CIMA**

It is commonly accepted that a crucial factor in the financial decisions of a company, including the evaluation of capital investment proposals, is the cost of capital.

You are required to:

(a) explain in simple terms what is meant by the 'cost of equity capital' for a particular company; (5 marks)

(b) calculate the cost of equity capital for X plc from the data given below, using two alternative methods, i.e.:

    (i) a dividend growth model

    (ii) the Capital Asset Pricing Model;

Data:

X plc:		
Current price per share on Stock Exchange	£1.20
Current annual gross dividend per share	£0.10
Expected average annual growth rate of dividends	7%
Beta coefficient for X plc shares	0.5
Expected rate of return on risk-free securities	8%
Expected return on the market portfolio	12%

(10 marks)

(c) state, for each model separately, the main simplifying assumptions made and express your opinion whether, in view of these assumptions, the models yield results that can be used safely in practice. (10 marks)

(Total: 25 marks)

Question 14 **CIMA**

G Ltd sells purchased electrical equipment to building contractors and retail traders within a limited geographical area.

Its terms of sale require payment within one month of invoicing, but because the majority of its customers are well known to the managing director, no attempt has been made to impose strict credit control.

The company is in competition with other suppliers, but has had no difficulty in maintaining its monthly sales at a constant value of about £150,000.

At present the average pattern of payment by customers is as follows:

In month	1	15%
	2	35%
	3	30%
	4	15%
	5	5%

The company relies heavily on bank finance at an existing interest rate of 2% per month. The managing director is anxious to reduce the cost of finance, and has suggested two possible schemes:

Scheme 1. To give cash discount of 2½% for payment within one month. It is believed that this will give a revised payment pattern as follows:

In month		
	1	40%
	2	30%
	3	10%
	4	15%
	5	5%

Scheme 2. To grant 2 months' credit, but to institute stricter credit control. The forecast payment pattern under this scheme is:

In month		
	1	–
	2	80%
	3	15%
	4	5%

The additional cost of implementing improved credit control procedures would be £500 per month.

You are required to:

(a) (i) calculate for – each scheme whether it would be financially advantageous;

   (ii) comment on your findings; (12 marks)

(b) give an illustrative calculation of the effect on Scheme 2 if it were to result in an increase in invoiced sales of £20,000 per month (the purchase cost to the company is 80% of sales value, and one month's credit is taken from suppliers); (5 marks)

(c) distinguish briefly the circumstances under which the granting of credit should be regarded as: (i) a lending decision; and (ii) an investment decision; and indicate how your approach to evaluating the decision might vary between these two conditions; (5 marks)

(d) state the circumstances under which a customer might decide to take advantage of cash discount terms. (3 marks)

(Total: 25 marks)

Note: Present value tables are provided. The factors for periods in years at annual rates are equally applicable to periods in months at monthly rates.

Question 15   CIMA

(a) The table following sets out the year-end levels of the price of ordinary shares in W p.l.c. and of a representative Stock Exchange index.

Year	W p.l.c.	Index
	£	£
1	2.40	1280
2	2.50	1350
3	2.30	1500
4	1.80	1480
5	2.55	1510

You are required to use this information to calculate the beta coefficient of W p.l.c. ordinary shares ignoring any dividend payments.

Work to four decimal places only at each stage of calculation.

(12 marks)

(b) Assume an approximate beta coefficient of 1.5, a risk-free rate of 5% per annum and an expected return from equities generally of 8% per annum.

You are required to calculate the expected rate of return of W p.l.c ordinary shares. (5 marks)

(c) W p.l.c. has just paid a dividend of £0.30 per share and the market expectation is that this dividend will grow at a constant rate of 5% per annum. The 'cost of capital' for W p.l.c. may be taken as 10%.

You are required to calculate a market value for W p.l.c. ordinary shares using a dividend valuation model and assuming a perfect market. (3 marks)

(d) **You are required to** discuss whether it would have been correct in part (c) to use as the 'cost of equity capital' the expected rate of return computed in part (b) (5 marks)

(Total: 25 marks)

Question 16   CIMA

The following are abstracts from a notice published in the financial press:

'Notice is hereby given that GS, plc, will redeem on 15th September, 1985 all of its outstanding 4¾% Convertible Debenture Stock 1988 at the redemption price of 100% of the principal amount plus accrued interest from 15th May to 15th September, 1985. The debentures will no longer be outstanding after the date fixed for redemption and all rights with respect thereto will cease on that date except the right to receive the redemption price as set out above.

As the alternative to redemption, the debenture holders have the right on or before the close of business on 15th September, 1985, to convert their debentures into ordinary shares of GS, plc at the conversion price of £18.33 ⅓ per share. Fractional certificates will not be issued, but in lieu thereof GS, plc will pay in cash an amount equal to the market value of fractional shares computed on the basis of the Stock Exchange closing price of GS, plc ordinary shares on the conversion date. Upon conversion of debentures no payment or adjustment will be made for interest accrued thereon.'

Over the past six months the market price of GS, plc shares has fluctuated between £46.50 and £65.00, the current price being close to the higher figure. Half-yearly dividends of £0.25 per share have been paid regularly in recent years.

You are required to:

(a) calculate the minimum market price per share at which debenture holders upon conversion would receive ordinary shares and cash having a higher market value than the cash they would receive on redemption (ignoring any taxation implications);

(3 marks)

(b) discuss *three* possible reasons why GS, plc might have elected to redeem the debentures now, rather than at a later date;

(7 marks)

(c) suggest what factors might be taken into account by individual debenture holders in deciding between redemption or conversion.
(10 marks)
(Total: 20 marks)

Question 17
ACCA

Bewcastle Ltd has received an order from a potential new customer in an overseas country for 5,000 staplers at a unit price of £1.75, payable in sterling. Bewcastle's terms of sale for export orders are a 10% initial deposit, payable with order, with the balance payable in 180 days. The 10% deposit has been received with the order.

Customers from the overseas country have in the past usually taken approximately one year's credit before making payment, and several have defaulted on payment. On the basis of past experience Bewcastle's management estimates that there is a 35% chance of the new customer defaulting on payment if the order is accepted, and only a 50% chance of payment within one year.

Incremental costs associated with the production and delivery of staplers would be £1.25 per unit and, in addition, there is an estimated cost of £500 for special attempts to collect an overdue debt, this cost being incurred one year after the sale is made. When this extra cost is incurred there is a 30% chance of obtaining quick payment of the debt. If, after this action, payment is not received the debt is written off.

Bewcastle currently has some surplus funds which could be used to finance the trade credit. Prices, costs and interest rates are not expected to change significantly in the foreseeable future. Bewcastle's stapler production facilities have a large amount of spare capacity.

The company considers the granting of export credit to be a form of investment decision, with 14% per year as the appropriate discount rate.

Required:

(a) Evaluate whether Bewcastle should accept the order from the new customer:

   (i) On the basis of the above information.

   (ii) If there is a 50% chance that the order will be repeated at the same time next year. Following payment for a first order the probability of default for repeat orders is 15%. No special attempts to collect an overdue debt would be made at the end of year 2.

   (iii)If the overseas company has stated that it will definitely repeat the order in the second year.

   State clearly any assumptions that you make.   (14 marks)

(b) What other factors might influence the decision of whether or not to grant credit to this potential customer?   (5 marks)

(c) Discuss briefly other methods which might be used to evaluate the credit-worthiness of this potential customer.   (6 marks)

                                 (Total 25 marks)

Question 18   ACCA

Ceely plc is evaluating a high risk project in a new industry. The company is temporarily short of accountants, and has asked an unqualified trainee to produce a draft financial evaluation of the project. This draft is shown on the following page.

£000

Year [1]	0	1	2	3	4	5	6
Cash outflows							
Long term capital:							
Land and buildings	500	600					
Plant and machinery	700	1,700					
Working capital (cumulative requirement)	230	570	680	700	720	740	740
Sales		2,950	3,830	5,200	5,400	5,600	5,800
Direct Costs:							
Materials		487	630	858	891	924	957
Labour		805	1,043	1,420	1,474	1,529	1,583
Selling and distribution		207	267	364	378	392	406
		1,499	1,940	2,642	2,743	2,845	2,946
Overheads		370	480	630	642	655	660
Interest		214	610	610	610	610	610
Depreciation		240	700	700	700	700	460
Total cost		2,323	3,730	4,582	4,695	4,810	4,676

£000

Year [1]	0	1	2	3	4	5	6
Net profit before tax		627	90	618	705	790	1,124
Taxation at 40%		251	36	247	282	316	450
Net profit after taxation		376	54	371	423	474	674
Net cash flows	(1,200)	(1,924)	54	371	423	474	674
Cash flows discounted at 30% p.a.	(1,200)	(1,480)	32	169	148	124	140

The net present value is – £2,067,000

Conclusion: The project is not financially viable and should not be undertaken.

Notes:

[1] Year 0 is the present time, year 1 is one year in the future etc.

Cash flows have been discounted at a high rate because of the high risk of the project.

Assume that you have been engaged as a financial consultant to Ceely plc. The following additional information is made available to you.

(i)   The company has a six year planning horizon for capital invest-
       ments. The value of the investment at the end of six years is

estimated to be five times the after tax operating cash flows of the sixth year.

(ii) The project would be financed by two 15% debentures, one issued almost immediately and one in a year's time. The debentures would both have a maturity of 10 years.

(iii) 50% of the overheads would be incurred as a direct result of undertaking this project.

(iv) Corporate taxation is at the rate of 40% payable one year in arrears.

(v) Tax allowable depreciation is on a straight-line basis at a rate of 20% per year on the full historic cost of depreciable fixed assets. Land and buildings are not depreciable fixed assets and their total value is expected to be £1.1 million at the end of year six.

(vi) The company is listed on the USM. Its current share price is 273 pence, and its equity beta coefficient value is 1.1.

(vii) The yield on Treasury Bills is 12% per year, and the average total yield from companies forming the Financial Times Actuaries All Share Index is 20% per year.

(viii) Interest rates are not expected to change significantly.

(ix) The equity beta value of a company whose major activity is the manufacture of a similar product to that proposed in Ceely's new project is 1.5. Both company's have gearing levels of 60% equity and 40% debt (by market values). Ceely's gearing includes the new debenture issues.

Required:

(a) Modify the draft financial evaluation of the project, where appropriate, to produce a revised estimate of the net present value of the project. Recommend whether the project should be accepted, and briefly discuss any reservations you have about the accuracy of your revised appraisal. State clearly any assumptions that you make. (20 marks)

(b) You are later told that the draft cash flow estimates did not include the effects of changing prices. Discuss whether, on the basis of this new information, any further amendments to your analysis might be necessary. (5 marks)

(25 marks)

Question 19   CIMA

A company which imports electronic equipment into the USA will have to pay 14,385 yen to a Japanese exporter in three months time.

A survey in the financial press states that the trading range of the Japanese yen against the dollar during the previous year was 159.45 to 134.20. Last month's average rate was 143.27.

To-day's quotations are:

Spot-closing rate	136.45	–	136.66
One month forward	0.35	–	0.32 yen premium
Three months forward	1.12	–	1.08 premium

You are required to advise on the following points.

(a) How reliable are forward rates as estimates of future spot rates?
(5 marks)

(b) If the importer were to arrange a 3 month forward exchange contract with his bank, what would be the cost to him (ignoring commission and expenses) of the required 14,385,579 yen?
(5 marks)

(c) Would such a contract be advantageous or not, if the spot rate after three months might be at either extreme of last year's range (Give calculations)
(5 marks)

(d) What alternative actions might be taken if, as a result of some change in the order specification, the goods had not been received by the end of the three months, and payment would therefore not be made until a later date?
(5 marks)

(e) What are the features which distinguish between

    (i) a forward exchange fixed contract, and

    (ii) a forward exchange option contract?
(5 marks)

(Total: 25 marks)

Question 20
                        ACCA

Craig, plc is considering the purchase of 100% of the share capital of the all equity financed Earl, plc. Earl operates in two divisions – Red and Blue – and a head office. The divisions operate independently of each other; the only joint costs of Earl, not attributable directly to either division are those of the head office. Earls management are currently committed to operating both divisions for 4 years and have estimated operating cash flows and the taxable operating profits of each division as:

	Operating Cash Flows			Taxable Operating Profits		
	Division		Div'l	Division		Div'l
	Red	Blue	Total	Red	Blue	Total
Year	£'000s	£'000s	£'000s	£'000s	£'000s	£'000s
1	600	600	1,200	400	600	1,000
2	600	400	1,000	600	400	1,000
3	800	400	1,200	800	400	1,200
4	1,000	200	1,200	1,200	200	1,400

The above figures exclude

(i) Head office costs of £200,000 per annum.

(ii) Planned capital expenditure by Red division in year 1 of £400,000 and its tax consequences. This capital expenditure is necessary for Red divisions continued operations and the above figures assume it will be undertaken.

(iii) The salvage values of Earl's assets. Salvage values will be received at year 4 and are estimated at

	£'000s
Red division	1,200
Blue division	600

Equipment used at head office is all rented on short term operating leases and therefore has no salvage value to Earl at any time.

(iv) Earl's current tax liability of £600,000 which is due for payment at year 1.

The above details are widely known and would continue to apply to Earl after any takeover except that

(i) some of Earl's administrative activities would be undertaken by Craig resulting in savings of head office costs of 50% in years 1 and 2 and 75% in years 3 and 4;

(ii) at year 4 Red division's assets would be used by Craig to substitute for capital expenditure of £1.4 million planned for year 4.

Craig's Corporate Planning manager has suggested that if the takeover is completed then various options are available to Craig. He has detailed the options but has made no attempt to appraise their financial desirability. The details are:

(i) Early termination of Blue division's operations. This would change the estimated salvage values which would be realised immediately on termination of the division's activities. Early termination would also enable operating cash flows, and taxable profits, to be increased by a constant amount for each year of the division's revised life, the level of the constant increase being dependent upon the date of termination. The revised figures are:

Operations terminated at end of year	Blue Division revised salvage value	Increase in annual cash flows for each year until termination
	£'000s	£'000s
2	1,000	200
3	800	150

(ii) Craig's own transport department could be used to carry out Red division's deliveries thereby saving the division £30,000 per annum in transport costs. However this policy would cause Craig's transport department to modify its planned replacement cycle and expenditure of £80,000, scheduled for both year 3 and year 5, would be increased to £100,000 and would occur earlier, in year 1 and year 4. Thereafter all planned replacements would be unchanged.

(iii) By incurring additional advertising of £180,000 in year 1, sales of Red division would increase producing additional profit, and cash flow, of £120,000 for each of years 3 and 4.

Craig's Financial Director believes that an appropriate after tax discount rate to be applied to all cash flows relating to the consequences of the proposed acquisition is 18%.

The tax rate is 50% and the tax delay is one year. All capital expenditure is eligible for 100% First Year Allowances and sales of assets would be subject to tax Assume all cash flows occur on the last day in each year.

Required:

Using 18% as the appropriate after tax discount rate:

(a) Determine the market value of Earl, plc in the absence of any takeover possibilities. (4 marks)

(b) Advise Craig on the maximum amount it should be prepared to pay for Earl if the Corporate Planning manager's suggestions are completely ignored. (4 marks)

(c) Determine which of the Corporate Planning manager's suggestions should be undertaken and specify the optimum life of Blue division. Advise Craig of the maximum amount it should now be prepared to pay for Earl. (12 marks)

(Total 20 marks)

Question 21 CIMA

Two companies, V, plc and G, plc are in different market sectors of the same industry.

V, plc has been expanding rapidly over the past three years and is anxious to gain a significant position in the market sector in which G, plc operates. It has already acquired 20% of the issued share capital of G. plc for £55 million by private negotiation in exchange for an issue of its own shares. It is now ready to make an offer for the remaining 80% of G, plc share capital.

Extracts from the accounts of V, plc are given below.

V plc
Extracts from accounts for last three years
(Year 3 being the most recent)

Year:	3 £m	2 £m	1 £m
Fixed assets (including investment in G, plc)	301.4	249.7	190.0
Current assets	132.5	90.2	72.0
	433.9	333.9	262.0
Current liabilities	99.6	68.4	50.0
	334.3	271.5	212.0
Long-term liabilities	74.75	79.7	48.0
Net assets	259.55	191.8	164.0
Issued share capital (ordinary shares of £1 each)	50.0	36.8	27.0
Share premium	42.0	6.2	–
Profit and loss account	167.55	148.8	137.0
	259.55	191.8	164.0
Sales	660.3	448.0	340.0
Earnings after tax	25.75	18.8	13.6
Dividend	7.00	7.0	6.0
Retained profits	18.75	11.8	7.6

All that you know about G, plc is that it has 57 million shares in issue; total share capital and reserves are £342 million; earnings after tax in the most recent year were £42.6 million on sales of £626 million, which were double those of the previous year, and that it has an investment valued at £40 million (book and market) in a type of enterprise which might not be of interest to V, plc.

The current stock market prices per share are: V, plc 300p; G, plc 341p.

You are required to answer the following questions.

(a) At the above market prices, how many shares of V, plc would have to be issued to buy the rest of G, plc on a share-for-share offer? (2 marks)

(b) With regard to earnings and also the book value of assets per share, how would the above share-for-share offer affect the position of:

(i) existing shareholders in V, plc;

(ii) the 80% shareholders in G, plc whose shares were to be acquired? (10 marks)

(c) Assuming that the 80% shareholders in G, plc were prepared to accept £40 million 10% Loan Stock as part of the consideration:

(i) what advantages might there be for V, plc in this arrangement?

(ii) what total price could V, plc afford to pay without diluting the earnings per share of its existing shareholders?

(10 marks)

(d) If the board of G, plc decided to advise its shareholders not to accept an offer from V, plc, what arguments might they use including any derived from the financial information available about V, plc? (13 marks)

(Total: 35 marks)

Question 22   CIMA

(a) X is a government-owned business engaged in the manufacture and distribution of chemical products for which there is an increasing demand. Heavy capital expenditure is necessary each year.

The financial year of the business runs to 31 March. In accordance with a statutory requirement, its accounts are prepared on a current cost basis, though historic cost figures are also reported.

At 31 March 1988, the net assets of the business (after deducting a very small amount of external loans) were represented entirely by reserves. On 1 April 1988 the business was reconstituted as a commercial company, X p.l.c., with an authorised capital of 400 million ordinary shares of 25p each plus one special rights redeemable preference share of £1.

The preference share and 4 million ordinary shares were issued for cash at par to the government.

It was decided that further ordinary shares (number not yet agreed) should be issued to the government, credited as fully paid by capitalisation of part of the reserves, on 1 December 1988, and that 95% of the total number of ordinary shares then in issue should be offered to the public at a price of £1.40 per share.

The prospectus being prepared in connection with this offer contains the following information about profit after taxation:

Actual – year to	Forecast – year to 31 March 1988 £m	31 March 1989 £m
On historic cost basis	52.508	42.087
On current cost basis	29.498	26.570

There is disagreement, however, about the amount of ordinary share dividend to be forecast for the year to 31 March 1989 and the number of ordinary shares to be issued.

The board of the company proposes a dividend of £19.32 million which it considers would make possible a public issue of 285 million ordinary shares. The advisers to the government, however, suggest that a dividend of £21.256 million be forecast, and claim that this would enable a proportionately larger number of shares to be issued.

You are required to explain significant aspects of **each** of these **two** proposals, to indicate what information would be needed by the prospective shareholders, and to summarise possible arguments for and against each proposal. All relevant calculations should be given, including those of proceeds from the issue, earnings per share, gross yield and P/E ratio. (20 marks)

(b) In addition to the capital structure outlined in part (a), the company issued to the government an unsecured debenture, repayable by instalments over five years, by way of capitalisation of part of the reserves.

You are required to discuss possible reasons for the overall capital structure adopted, having regard to any relevant aspects of the government's concern with the business and to the presumed objectives of privatisation. (10 marks)

(Total: 30 marks)

Question 23 ACCA

Brookday, plc is considering whether to establish a subsidiary in the USA. The subsidiary would cost a total of $20 million, including $4 million for working capital.

A suitable existing factory and machinery have been located and production could commence quickly. A payment of $19 million would be required immediately, with the remainder required at the end of year one.

Production and sales are forecast at 50,000 units in the first year and 100,000 units per year thereafter.

The unit price, unit variable cost and total fixed costs in year one are expected to be $100, $40 and $1 million respectively. After year one prices and costs are expected to rise at the same rate as the previous year's level of inflation in the USA: this is forecast to be 5% per year for the next 5 years. In addition a fixed royalty of £5 per unit will be payable to the parent company, payment to be made at the end of each year.

Brookday has a 4 year planning horizon and estimates that the realisable value of the fixed assets in 4 years time will be $20 million.

It is the company's policy to remit the maximum funds possible to the parent company at the end of each year. Assume that there are no legal complications to prevent this.

Brookday currently exports to the USA yielding an after tax net cash flow of £100,000. No production will be exported to the USA if the subsidiary is established. It is expected that new export markets of a similar worth in Southern Europe could replace exports to the USA. United Kingdom production is at full capacity and there are no plans for further expansion in capacity.

Tax on the company's profits is at a rate of 50% in both countries, payable one year in arrears. A double taxation treaty exists between the UK and the USA and no double taxation is expected to arise. No withholding tax is levied on royalties payable from the USA to the UK.

Tax allowable 'depreciation' is at a rate of 25% on a straight line basis on all fixed assets.

Brookday believes that the appropriate beta for this investment is 1.2. The after-tax market rate of return is 12%, and the risk free rate of interest 7% after tax.

The current spot exchange rate is US $1.300/£1, and the pound is expected to fall in value by approximately 5% per year relative to the US dollar.

Required:

(a) Evaluate the proposed investment from the viewpoint of Brookday. State clearly any assumptions that you make.   (18 marks)

(b) What further information and analysis might be useful in the evaluation of this project?   (7 marks)

(Total 25 marks)

Question 24   ACCA

The £25 million annual credit sales of Whichford, plc are spread evenly over each of the 50 weeks of the working year. Sales within each week are also equally spread over each of the 5 working days.

Although Whichford operates from nineteen separate locations, all invoicing of credit sales is carried out by the central head office.

Sales documentation is sent by post daily from each location to the head office and from these details invoices are prepared. Postal delays affecting the receipt of documentation by the head office, delays and bottlenecks in processing at head office, together with the intervention of the non-working weekend period all contribute to the considerable range of delays in despatching invoices. As a result of these delays only some of the sales made on Mondays and Tuesdays of each week are invoiced that same week, the remainder of sales made on Mondays and Tuesdays and all sales made between Wednesdays and Fridays are not invoiced until the following week.

An analysis of the delay in invoicing, measured by the delay between the day of sale and the date of despatch of the invoice, indicated the following typical pattern:

No. of Days Delay in Invoicing (Days)	% of Weeks Sales Subject to this Delay (%)
3	20
4	6
5	40
6	22
7	12

A further analysis indicated that debtors take, on average, 35 days credit before paying. This period is measured from the day of the despatch of the invoice rather than the date of sale.

It is proposed to hire a number of micro computers to undertake invoicing at each of the nineteen sales locations. The use of computers would ensure that all invoices were despatched either on the day of sale or on the next *working* day. The revised delay in invoicing would result in 50% of invoices being despatched with no delay, 40% subject to a delay of one day, and 10% subject to a delay of 3 days.

A computer package, currently in the final stages of development, would assist the follow-up of debtors and, if used, is likely to reduce the number of days credit taken by customers to 30 – again this is measured from the date of the invoice.

Use of the micro computers would save head office and postage costs of £48,000 per annum spread evenly over the year.

Whichford finances all working capital from a bank overdraft at an interest rate of 15% per annum applied on a simple daily basis.

Required:

(a) *Ignoring tax*, determine the maximum monthly rental that Whichford should consider paying for the hire of the computers if they can be used

(i) only to speed the invoicing function,

(ii) to speed invoicing and reduce the period of credit taken from 35 to 30 days following the despatch of an invoice. (12 marks)

(b) Describe the main characteristics and features of a factoring agreement.

Clearly distinguish between factoring and invoice discounting. Outline the main issues which should be given consideration before entering into a factoring agreement and illustrate the circumstances in which entering into a factoring agreement may be desirable. (13 marks)

(Total 25 marks)

Question 25 ACCA

(a) Discuss the factors that are likely to influence the desired level of cash balance of a company. (5 marks)

(b) Mollet Ltd prepares a weekly cash budget. Based upon the experience of previous cash inflows and outflows it has estimated cash flows for the next week some of which are considered to be definite, and some of which have been assigned probabilities of occurrence.

Expected Cash Outflows		£	*Probability*
Wages and salaries:	Basic	50,000	1
	Overtime $\Big\{$	0	.5
		10,000	.5
Materials		70,000	1
Overheads		10,000	1
Expected Cash Inflows			
Cash from debtors	$\Big\{$	100,000	.4
		120,000	.6

Any surplus cash is invested in six month deposits in the money market and shortfalls of cash are funded by withdrawing cash from these money market investments. Mollet currently has £100,000 invested in the money market.

Transactions costs are estimated to be a fixed cost of £10 for each money market deposit and £8 for each money market withdrawal, with a variable cost of 0.05% of the transaction value on both deposits and withdrawals. All money market transactions must be of at least £10,000 in size and in multiples of £10,000.

If withdrawals are made from the six month money market deposits prior to the maturity of the deposits, a penalty equivalent to one weeks interest on the amount withdrawn is payable. No deposits are due to mature during the next week.

The interest rate on six month money market deposits is currently 12% per year.

Mollet's directors have decided that the company must maintain a minimum cash balance of £20,000. The cash balance at the start of the next week is expected to be £40,000.

Required:

Determine the level of investment in money market deposits at the start of the next week that will maximise the expected net return from the money market for the week. (12 marks)

(c) Outline the advantages and disadvantages of using short term debt, as opposed to long term debt, in the financing of working capital. (8 marks)

(Total 25 marks)

Question 26 ACCA

Amble plc is evaluating the manufacture of a new consumer product. The product can be introduced quickly and has an expected life of four years before it is replaced by a more efficient model. Costs associated with the product are expected to be as follows.

Direct costs (per unit)
Labour:
3.5 skilled labour hours at £5 per hour
4 unskilled labour hours at £3 per hour
Materials:
6 kilos of material Z at £146 per kilo
Three units of component P at £4.80 per unit
One unit of component Q at £6.40
Other variable costs: £2.10 per unit

Indirect costs
Apportionment of management salaries £105,000 per year
Tax allowable depreciation of machinery £213,000 per year
Selling expenses (not including any salaries) £166,000 per year
Apportionment of head office costs £50,000 per year
Rental of buildings £100,000 per year
Interest charges £104,000 per year

Other overheads £70,000 per year (including apportionment of building rates £20,000 N.B. rates are a local tax on property).

If the new product is introduced it will be manufactured in an existing factory and will have no effect on rates payable. The factory could be rented for £120,000 per year (not including rates) to another company if the product is not introduced.

New machinery costing £864,000 will be required. The machinery is to be depreciated on a straight-line basis over four years and has an expected salvage value of £12,000 after four years. The machinery will be financed by a four year fixed rate bank loan at an interest rate of 12% per year. Additional working capital requirements may be ignored.

The product will require two additional managers to be recruited at an annual gross cost of £25,000 each and one manager currently costing £20,000 will be moved from another factory where he will be replaced by a deputy manager at a cost of £17,000 per year. 70,000 kilos of material Z are already in stock and are not required for other production. The realisable value of the material is £99,000.

The price per unit of the product in the first year will be £110 and demand is projected at 12,000 17,500 18,000 and 18,500 units in years 1 to 4 respectively. The inflation rate is expected to be approximately 5% per year, and prices will be increased in line with inflation. Wage and salary costs are expected to increase by 7% per year, and all other costs (including rent) by 5% per year. No price or cost increases are expected in the first year of production.

Corporate tax is at the rate of 35% payable in the year the profit occurs. Assume that all sales and costs are on a cash basis and occur at the end of the year, except for the initial purchase of machinery which would take place immediately. No stocks will be held at the end of any year.

Required:

(a) Calculate the expected internal rate of return (IRR) associated with the manufacture of the new product.   (15 marks)

(b) What is meant by an asset beta?

If you were told that the company's asset beta is 1.2, the market return is 15% and the risk free rate is 8% discuss whether you would recommend introducing the new product.   (5 marks)

(c) Amble is worried that the government might increase corporate tax rates.

Show by how much the tax rate would have to change before the project is not financially viable. A discount rate of 17% per year may be assumed for part (c).   (5 marks)
(Total 25 marks)

Question 27   ACCA

Hempel, plc is considering setting up a production facility overseas in order to supply a market which it could not otherwise supply. Sales and costs of the venture on an accounting basis, all expressed in £ Sterling are:

	Per Year – Years 1 to 4	
	(£'000s)	(£'000s)
Sales		500
Materials expense	100	
Labour	80	
Overheads	70	
Head office charge	30	
Interest on loan	60	
Depreciation	120	460
Annual Profit		40

All sales and purchases of materials are for cash. Initial stocks of materials, required at the start of the project, will be £40,000. End of year stock levels will be £60,000 for years 1, 2 and 3 but zero at year 4.

'Labour' and 'Overheads' are incremental cash costs paid in the years to which they relate. 'Head office charge' is an apportionment of UK head office costs which, in total, will not be changed by acceptance of this proposal. 'Interest' relates to the loan used to finance this project – all cash flows relating to the loan occur in the UK 'Head office charge' and 'Interest' are the only expenses of the project paid in the UK.

'Depreciation' is based on the straight line method. Initial cost of fixed assets is £600,000 and the year 4 salvage value is estimated to be £120,000.

If the project goes ahead then Hempel will suffer a small reduction in its UK manufactured exports to those areas which have objections to Hempel's economic involvement with the country chosen for the siting of the new manufacturing venture. This will result in Hempel losing sales of 1,000 units of its Basic Product in each of years 1 to 4. Financial details, per unit, of the Basic Product are:

	Basic Product – Per Unit	
	Years 1 & 2	Years 3 & 4
	£	£
Sales price	90	110
Variable costs	60	70
Apportioned fixed costs	20	30

Included in 'Variable costs' is £15 relating to material X; this is the cost which Hempel has contracted to pay for each unit of this material. However, until the end of year 3, material X will be in short supply and any available quantities could be used elsewhere in Hempel to earn a contribution of £10 per unit in excess of cost. From year 4 material X will not be in short supply.

Hempel is unsure whether its proposed overseas project will be the only project it undertakes in that country or the start of a massive, long term, investment there. While cash flows from the project can be used for further investment in that country without restriction, cash flows for remittance to the UK are currently subject to the following restrictions:

(i) no cash can be remitted until 2 years after commencement of the project;

(ii) from year 2 cash remittances are limited to a yearly maximum of 30% of the initial investment in fixed assets;

(iii) all cash which cannot be immediately remitted – and which is not to be used to finance investment in the country – must be deposited, at zero interest, until the 30% limit permits remittance to the UK;

(iv) the limit of 30% applies to *all* cash flows from the project to the UK and includes any reimbursement of valid expenses initially paid in the UK as well as remittances of final salvage value of equipment.

These rules, which can result in cash from a project being remitted to the UK for many years after a project has ceased operating, are thought likely to apply for at least 8 but no more than 12 years – thereafter cash can be freely remitted. The exchange rate has been and is expected to be stable against Sterling.

All cash flows occur at the end of the year to which they relate, with the exception of the cost of the fixed assets and the cost of the initial stocks of materials, both of which will occur at the start of the first year. The required rate of return for the project is 15%.

Required:

(a) *Ignoring taxation*, determine the net present value of Hempel's project in each of the following separate conditions:

(i) Hempel will be pursuing a policy of substantial investment in the overseas country for the next 15 years, all cash flows from the project will be utilised for reinvestment and will reduce cash required to be remitted from the UK to facilitate Hempel's investment plans.

(ii) Hempel will not be investing further in the overseas country and requires the project's cash flows to be remitted to the UK at the earliest opportunity. (13 marks)

(b) Describe, and indicate the importance of, the additional factors which should be considered when appraising an overseas, rather than a domestic, capital investment. (7 marks)

(Total 20 marks)

Question 28
ACCA

You are required to analyse the following information from the view-point of the implications it has for working capital policy.

	Position as of now	Budget position one year from now
Sales	£250,111	£288,000
Cost of goods sold	210,000	248,000
Purchases	140,000	170,000
Debtors	31,250	36,000
Creditors	21,000	30,000
Raw Material Stock	35,000	60,000
Work-in-Progress	17,500	30,000
Finished Goods Stock	40,000	43,000

N.B. Assume all sales and purchases are on credit terms.

(Total 20 marks)

Question 29
ACCA

Below you are given a certain amount of financial information concerning two manufacturing companies. Comus, Ltd is contemplating making an offer for the shares of Rex, Ltd. The Comus company is quoted on the stock market, but the Rex company is not. The Comus company is interested in determining a number of alternative offers that it might make, each based on a technical approach to the subject. Summarised balance sheets of the companies as at 31 December 1978 are given below:

	Comus, Ltd (£000's)	Rex, Ltd (£000's)
Shareholders Funds		
Ordinary Shares (£1 par value)	200	150
Revenue Reserves	100	50
Current Liabilities	50	100
	350	300
Land and Buildings	25	100
Plant and Equipment	200	75
Current Assets	125	125
	350	300

Other relevant data are:

Earnings per share	£0.20	£0.15
Dividend per share	£0.08	£0.10
Expected annual % growth in dividends	10%	8%
Share Price as at 1 January 1979	£4.00	

Required:

(a) Assuming that the price of a company's equity share equals either

  (i) the present value of the future dividend stream or

  (ii) that it is based on some other share price evaluation model of your own choosing, calculate a price for the shares of Rex that the shareholders would expect if their company were quoted on the stock market. (If a discount rate is to be used in the calculation, it is to be the one that the stock market has used to arrive at the price of shares in Comus, Ltd). On the basis of this expected price suggest the terms of share for share offer that Comus Ltd might make for the shares of Rex Ltd that is attractive to shareholders. State explicitly how you have arrived at the share price for Rex Ltd. (7 marks)

(b) With a share for share exchange, what is the highest offer that Comus could make to Rex shareholders, before the offer results in diluting the earnings per share of Comus? (7 marks)

(c) The merchant banker that Comus is using has pointed out that an unusually large proportion of the assets of Rex Ltd are in the form of land and buildings. These have different risk characteristics to productive assets and are located in a desirable commercial district of a town. It has suggested that Comus should take this into account when considering the terms of the offer. How could this affect the offer, and if it is considered important, suggest terms that would allow for the structure of the assets to be acquired. (7 marks)

(d) Rex has constructed the following estimates of its future cash flows which it has made available to shareholders.

Year	Capital expenditure (£000's)	Profit after tax (£000's)	Depreciation (£000's)
1	20	25	7
2	25	30	8
3	15	35	10
4	14	40	11
Each year beyond 4	14	45	12

The cost of capital to Rex Ltd is 8%. Using this information and any other in the question you believe appropriate, what is the minimum price that Rex shareholders are likely to accept in exchange for the assets and liabilities of the company? (7 marks)

(Total 28 marks)

Question 30 ACCA

MBX is a holding company with two subsidiaries. It is late June and the finance director of MBX is worried about the cash flow position for the next six months commencing July. The group uses a centralised cash management system.

Subsidiary 1 is a manufacturing subsidiary. Sales in June are 82,418 units at a price of £10-60 per unit Sales have recently been increasing at the rate of 1.5% per month and this trend is expected to continue. Two months' credit is given to all customers, and one month's credit is received on all purchases. Materials, with a unit variable cost of £3.71 are purchased in order to meet expected sales in two months' time. Direct labour costs £318 per unit and wages are payable one month in arrears. Production levels are based upon expected sales in one month's time. Overheads, payable one month in arrears, are expected to be £95,000 per month (invoice value) for the next three months, and £101,000 per month for the following six months. Sales price, material and labour costs are expected to rise by 5% in early September. No other changes in price or costs are expected. Other forecast cash flows are:

Purchase of fixed assets;

(a) September – Replace 15 salesmen's cars at a net cost of £90,000.

(b) November – Purchase new machinery for planned expansion at a cost of £310,000

November Disposal of a small plot of land for the sum of £130,000 (receivable immediately)

Subsidiary 2 acts as an investment company for the group, and has investments in shares and gilts.

Holdings	Number held	Market price	Dividend or Interest due	PE ratio	Expected annual payout ratio
Alpha plc	812,000	152p	October	8	40%
Beta plc	326,000	346p	September	12	50%
Gamma plc	568,000	104p	December	8	50%
2.5 % consols (£100nominal value)	14,300	£33	November	–	–
12%, Exchequer 1998 (£100 nominal value)	10,000	£104	November	–	–

Dividends and interest are payable twice a year in equal amounts. Assume that there are no tax adjustments on dividends and interest payments.

The subsidiary has a £400,000 loan over one year ending next March, with a nominal annual rate of interest of 12%, with repayment by equal monthly instalments which include both interest and principal.

Administrative and other costs of this subsidiary are estimated to be £40,000 per month payable one month in arrears.

The holding company has administrative and other costs of £60,000 per month also payable one month in arrears and expects to pay a dividend of £400,000 in December and taxation of £470,000 in November. There will be an opening cash balance of £80,000 at the beginning of July.

Required:

(a) Evaluate whether MBX is likely to experience any cash flow problems during the next six months. Cash flows may be rounded to the nearest £1,000.

Discuss how any possible cash flow problems might be overcome.

The chairman of the company does not wish to dispose of any of its investments except as a last resort, and a maximum of £400,000 overdraft facility is available. The company does not wish to raise any external finance other than possible use of the overdraft.

State clearly any assumptions that you make. (19 marks)

(b) Explain how computerised cash balance management services offered by major banks and other organisations might assist a financial manager. (6 marks)

(Total 25 marks)

Question 31 **CIMA**

(a) You are required to summarise the advantages to a company of issuing convertible loan stock rather than ordinary shares or debenture stock. (10 marks)

(b) The 12% convertible loan stock of A p.l.c. is quoted at £131 per £100 nominal immediately after payment of the annual interest. The earliest date for conversion is in six years time, at a rate of 40 ordinary shares per £100 nominal loan stock. The share price now is £2.50.

You are required to calculate

(i) the average annual rate of growth in the share price that would be necessary for loan stockholders to achieve an overall rate of return of 8% compound over the next six years, including the proceeds of conversion, and

(ii) the conversion premium implicit in the data given. (9 marks)

(c) The following two quotations relating to the use of convertible loan stock have been taken from the financial press:

1. 'Convertibles are a security for issue in 'bull' markets.'

2. 'Only if the option to convert tomorrow is somehow overvalued by the same capital market that is depressing the share price to-day, will the company's owners gain any economic advantage.'

You are required to clarify and compare these two statements.

(6 marks)

(Total: 25 marks)

Question 32   ACCA

Using the Discounted Cash Flow Yield (Internal Rate of Return) for evaluating investment opportunities has the basic weakness that it does not give attention to the amount of the capital investment, in that a return of 20% on an investment of £1,000 may be given a higher ranking than a return of 15% on an investment of £10,000.

Comment in general on the above quotation and refer in particular to the problem of giving priorities to (ranking) investment proposals

Your answers should make use of the following information.

		Project A Cash flow	Project B Cash flow
		£	£
Y0	(Capital investments)	1,000	10,000
1	Cashflows	240	2,300
2	" " "	288	2,640
3	" " "	346	3,040
4	" " "	414	3,500
5	" " "	498	4,020
Cost of capital		10%	10%

Note:

1.	10%	15%	20%
The present value of the £ due in			
1 year	0.909	0.870	0.833
2	0.826	0.756	0.694
3	0.751	0.658	0.579
4	0.683	0.572	0.482
5	0.621	0.497	0.402

2. Taxation can be ignored   **(Total 20 marks)**

Question 33 **ACCA**

(a) Briefly outline the major functions performed by the capital market and explain the importance of each function for corporate financial management. How does the existence of a well functioning capital market assist the financial management function? (8 marks)

(b) Describe the efficient market hypothesis and explain the differences between the three forms of the hypothesis which have been distinguished. (6 marks)

(c) Company A has 2 million shares in issue and company B, 6 million.

On day 1 the market value per share is £2 for A and £3 for B.

On day 2 the management of B decide, at a private meeting, to make a cash takeover bid for A at a price of £3.00 per share. The takeover will produce large operating savings with a present value of £3.2 millions.

On day 4 B publicly announces an unconditional offer to purchase all shares of A at a price of £3.00 per share with settlement on day 15. Details of the large savings are not announced and are not public knowledge.

On day 10 B announces details of the savings which will be derived from the takeover.

Required:

Ignoring tax and the time value of money between day 1 and 15, and assuming the details given are the only factors having an impact on the share price of A and B, determine the day 2, day 4 and day 10 share price of A and B if the market is

(1) semi-strong form efficient, and

(2) strong form efficient, in each of the following separate circumstances:

  (i) the purchase consideration is cash as specified above, and (6 marks)

  (ii) the purchase consideration, decided upon on day 2 and publicly announced on day 4, is one newly issued share of B for each share of A. (4 marks)

  (Total 24 marks)

Question 34 **ACCA**

Discuss the factors to be considered in the formulation of a policy for credit control management, and use the following information in your discussion.

A study of the debtors of the XYZ Co. Ltd has shown that it is possible to classify all debtors into certain classes with the following characteristics:

	Average collection period days	Bad debts %
A	15	0.5
B	20	2.5
C	30	5.0
D	40	9.5

The average standard profit/cost schedule for the company's range of products is as follows:

		£	£
Selling price			2.50
Less:	Material	1.00	
	Wages	0.95	
	Variable cost	0.30	
	Fixed cost	0.05	2.30
Profit			£0.20

The company has the opportunity of extending its sales by £1,000,000 split between categories C and D in the proportions 40:60. The company's short term borrowing rate is 11½%

(Total 15 marks)

Question 35   CIMA

Part 1

The capital structure of a group of manufacturing companies as at 30th June, 1979 is shown below. **You are asked** to calculate the weighted average cost of capital to the group for the purpose of subsequent use in capital investment appraisal. Where you consider that alternative bases might be used you are required to explain the reasons for the basis you select.

Extract from balance sheet as at 30th June, 1979

	£000's
Ordinary share capital issued and fully paid, 300,000 shares of £0.50 each	150
Share premium account	30
Reserves, retained profit	250
Preference shares – 80,000 7% (4.9% plus tax credit) cumulative preference shares of £1 each	80
5% Loan stock 1985-1995	150
6% Unsecured loans	70

Notes:

1. Stock market prices at 2nd September, 1979:

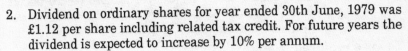

Ordinary shares	£0.66
Preference shares	£1.00
5% Loan stock	80

2. Dividend on ordinary shares for year ended 30th June, 1979 was £1.12 per share including related tax credit. For future years the dividend is expected to increase by 10% per annum.

3. Current liabilities at 30th June, 1979 were £140,000.

4. Profit before loan interest for the year ended 30th June, 1979 was £70,000.

5. The current rate of corporate tax may be taken as 50% and advance corporation tax as 30%.

Part 2

Outline the circumstances, if any, under which you would suggest that this group might use the marginal cost of capital in its investment appraisal, commenting at the same time on the group's financial ratios.

Part 3

The chief executive of the group now tells you that he personally has little confidence in calculations of the weighted average cost of capital.

His present policy is to use a rate of return of 25% after tax for the purpose of evaluating capital projects, plus or minus 10% dependent on whether a particular project appears to involve a high or low risk.

He points out that:

(i) a large number of alternative investment proposals are always available for review, and the group's only concern is to accept the most profitable;

(ii) the group is expanding rapidly, and a high target of return is necessary to compensate for the likely increase in central administration costs;

(iii) the group's cash position is not good enough for it to undertake low-yield proposals.

You are asked to give your own views on the strengths and weaknesses of this approach to investment evaluation.

(Total 35 marks)

Question 36   CIMA

A Limited (the lessee) enters into a leasing agreement with B Limited (the lessor), both United Kingdom companies, for an item of machinery costing £20,000 and eligible for 100% first year taxation allowance. The lease is for a five-year period, with annual rental of £4,800 payable in advance.

The effective rate of bank interest is 15% per annum before tax. It may be assumed that there is a delay of one year in the receipt of tax reliefs or liabilities; and that the rate of corporation tax is 50%

You are required to state:

(a) On the basis of the information given, whether the leasing agreement will be more or less profitable to A Limited than the outright purchase of the equipment taking into account the cost of finance at 15% per annum with tax relief thereon;

(b) the other facts that should be taken into account by A Limited in arriving at a final decision;

(c) whether the 15% borrowing rate is the most suitable for use by A Limited and B Limited respectively in evaluating the project, and the alternatives that might be available either generally or under conditions of inflation.

(Total 25 marks)

Question 37   CIMA

For the year ended 31st March 1979 the board of directors of A Limited proposes paying a final dividend of £0.05 per share on the ordinary share capital, making a total, the same as in the previous year, of £0.075 per share for the year, net of advance corporation tax at 30%

On 1st June 1979 it was announced that the board proposed to offer 20,000,000 new ordinary shares by way of rights at £0.90 per share, on the basis of one new ordinary share for every five shares currently held. The issue was forecast to yield £17,200,000, net of expenses. It was expected that the present rate of dividend per share would be maintained on the increased share capital. On the day following the announcement the market price of the existing ordinary shares fell from £1.20 to £1.05.

You have been asked by a shareholder in the company:

(a) to review the terms of the issue and to advise him whether, or not, to take up his rights;

(b) to suggest possible reasons why the company might choose to make an issue of this nature.

(Total 25 marks)

Question 38   **CIMA**

A manufacturing company, Y Limited, has just adopted a system of current cost accounting. For the purpose of its annual report to employees it has prepared an added value statement for the year ended 31st August 1979 and a balance sheet as at that date. Copies of these, with working notes, are given below and should be accepted as giving the message which the company wishes to convey.

You are required to prepare a simple statement of sources and application of funds linking the figure 'retained for expansion within the company' with the increase in cash and short-term investments.

Y Limited
Added Value Statement for year ended 31st August 1979

	£000's	£000's	£000's
Sales			393,786
Purchases of goods and services		328,289	
Depreciation of fixed assets		3,092	
Interest paid less interest received		396	
		331,777	
Current cost adjustments:			
Cost of sales	3,305		
Depreciation	1,264		
	4,569		
Gearing	701	3,868	335,645
			58,141
Share of losses of associated companies			538
Exceptional items including			
profit on sale of fixed assets			1,713
Added value available for disposal			55,890
Salaries, wages and other			
employee benefits			40,586
Taxation			8,190
Dividends to ordinary			
shareholders			1,892
Retained for expansion			
within company			5,222
			55,890

Y Limited
Balance Sheet as at 31st August, 1979

	31.8.78 £000's	*31.8.79* £000's	*Changes* £000's
Ordinary share capital	17,500	17,500	–
Retained profits	45,500	50,722	5,222
Loans	7,200	5,961	(1,239)
Capital maintenance reserve	–	5,172	5,172
	70,200	79,355	9,155
Current assets:			
Stock	30,000	33,622	3,622
Debtors	16,000	19,039	3,039
Cash and short-term investments	15,000	19,963	4,963
	61,000	72,624	11,624

	31.8.78 £000's	*31.8.79* £000's	*Changes* £000's
Current liabilities:			
Creditors	37,800	40,012	2,212
Taxation	6,000	10,883	4,883
Dividend	1,000	1,132	132
	44,800	52,027	7,227
Net current assets	16,200	20,597	4,397
Fixed assets	52,000	56,668	4,668
Associated companies	2,000	2,090	90
	70,200	79,355	9,155

Notes on accounts

1. **Fixed assets**

	£000's
At cost or valuation	
Balance at 31st August, 1978	80,000
Additions at cost	8,989
Less Sales at cost	(2,699)
Revaluation	1,984
	88,274
Depreciation provision	
At 31st August, 1978	28,000
Less Withdrawals (assets sold)	(750)
Depreciation for year on historical cost basis	3,092
Depreciation adjustment for year to CCA basis	1,264
	31,606

Net book value
At 31st August, 1978	52,000
At 31st August, 1979	56,668
Note: Proceeds of sales of fixed assets	2,321

2. **Stocks at 31st August, 1979**

At historic cost	33,038
Add Revaluation to current cost basis	584
	33,622

3. **Capital maintenance reserve**

Fixed assets	1,984
Stocks	584
Cost of sales adjustment	3,305
	5,873
Less Gearing adjustment	701
	5,172

(Total 25 marks)

Question 39   CIMA

The board of your group of companies wishes to declare a dividend for the year ended 31st August 1979 which will be 15% above that paid in the previous year, and to justify this on the grounds that the dividend cover would still be higher than that achieved over the past four years.

Given the following information you are asked whether this action would be justified.

	Year ended 31st August				
	1975	*1976*	*1977*	*1978*	*1979*
	£000s	£000s	£000s	£000s	£000s
Group trading profit	13,300	12,275	30,798	32,649	37,625
Add Share of profits of associated company	-	-	-	860	2,200
Total trading profit	13,300	12,275	30,798	33,509	39,825
Interest payable	800	900	1,000	950	750
Profit for the year before exceptional items	12,500	11,375	29,798	32,559	39,075
Taxation	6,500	6,264	14,900	14,879	18,766
Profit after taxation	6,000	5,111	14,898	17,680	20,309
Extraordinary items	-	-	(2,200)	(2,100)	291
Profit after extraordinary items	6,000	5,111	12,698	15,580	20,600 *Proposed*
Ordinary dividends	1,950	1,950	2,865	3,400	3,910
Profit retained	4,050	3,161	9,833	12,180	16,690
Dividend cover as calculated by board	3.25X	2.62X	4.43X	4.58X	5.27X

Notes:

1. Share of profits in associated company.

    The direct shareholdings by the parent company in this company are slightly less than 20%, but in view of the degree of influence which has always been exercised, it has been considered proper as from 1975 to treat it as an associated company. The profits for earlier years were: 1975-£200,000; 1976-£380,000; 1977-£400,000. The effective rate of taxation on the associated company profits may be taken as having been 50% throughout.

2. Research and development expenditure, amounting to £700,000 per annum, was carried forward as a deferred asset in the years 1975-77, but this was subsequently considered incorrect and the total amount was written off as an extraordinary item in 1978.

3. Deferred taxation, amounting to £500,000 in 1975, £455,000 in 1976 and £1,423,000 in 1977, was agreed to have been provided unnecessarily, and the total was credited in arriving at the taxation charge in 1978.

4. The extraordinary profit of £291,000 in 1979 arises from exchange rate adjustments relating to the current operations of an overseas subsidiary whose accounts are translated using the temporal method. A similar exchange gain of £2,718,000 in 1978 had been adjusted on reserves.

(Total 15 marks)

Question 40   CIMA

(a) For an investment portfolio consisting of a large number of securities, the important feature determining the riskiness of the portfolio is the way in which the returns on the individual securities vary together.

You are required to illustrate this statement by making calculations from the simplified data given in the table below in relation to a portfolio comprising 40% of Security A and 60% of Security B. You may ignore the possibility of nil correlation between the rates of return.

Probability	Predicted return Security A	Predicted return Security B
%	%	
0.2	12	15
0.6	15	20
0.2	18	25

(10 marks)

(b) In theory, an investor in risky securities is presumed to select an investment portfolio which is on the *efficient* frontier and touches one of his *indifference curves* at a tangent.

You are required to

(i) give a detailed explanation of the above statement, with particular attention to the expressions in italics;

(ii) illustrate your answer with a relevant freehand diagram.

(15 marks)
(Total 25 marks)

Question 41   ACCA

Holt, plc sells its products in two distinct and separate markets known within Holt as 'North' and 'South'.

Sales for the forthcoming year are expected to amount to £1.2 million, spread evenly throughout the year, and to be split 40% North and 60% South. All sales are on credit and the variable cost of Holt's products is 80% of sales price. It is expected that North's customers will take an average of 72 days credit whereas South's will take an average of 50 days; no bad debts are expected.

A change in the level of advertising would both increase total invoiced sales for the year by 20% and change the mix of sales to 60% North and 40% South. This increase in sales would be achieved without alteration to stock levels or creditors. However, such a change would increase the period of credit taken and cause bad debts to occur. Consideration is therefore being given to the introduction of a 3% cash discount for payment within 30 days with net terms for payment in 50 days. The expected pattern of receipts, both with and without the introduction of cash discounts, for the new level of sales is:

% of sales taking exact number of days credit

Exact Number of Days Credit Taken	No Cash Discounts		Cash Discounts	
	North	South	North	South
%	%	%	%	
30	10	8	60	30
60	20	10	-	8
90	68	80	39	60
Bad debts	2	2	1	2

However for both North and South only $\frac{2}{3}$ of those paying in 30 days will in fact take the cash discount.

Short term finance is readily available at a cost of 11% per annum.

Assume a 360 day year.

Required:

(a) *Ignoring the introduction of cash discounts*, determine

   (i) the effect of the introduction of the advertising campaign on Holt's debtors position net of bad debts;

   (ii) the maximum amount it would be worth paying, at the end of the year, for the advertising campaign.   **(10 marks)**

(b) *Assuming the advertising campaign is undertaken and the new sales levels will be achieved*, determine the annual benefit from the application of the cash discount terms to the sales of North and, separately, the sales of South. Is it worthwhile introducing the cash discount terms if they must apply to all Holt's sales without differentiating between markets?   **(8 marks)**

(c) Outline and explain the importance of the main factors to be considered in determining the method of financing the working capital requirements of a growing, but seasonal, firm.

Specify three potentially suitable types of short, or medium, term finance which may assist in the financing of working capital requirements and outline the merits, disadvantages and risks of each. (6 marks)

(Total 24 marks)

Question 42 ACCA

(a) A colleague has been taken ill. Your managing director has asked you to take over from the colleague and to provide urgently needed estimates of the discount rate to be used in appraising a large new capital investment. You have been given your colleague's working notes, which you believe to be numerically accurate.

Working notes
Estimates for the next 5 years (annual averages)

Stock market total return on equity	16%
Own company dividend yield	7%
Own company share price rise	14%
Standard deviation of total stock market return on equity	10%
Standard deviation of own company total return on equity	20%
Correlation coefficient between total own company return on equity and total stock market return on equity	0.7
Correlation coefficient between total return on the new capital investment and total market return on equity	0.5
Growth rate of own company earnings	12%
Growth rate of own company dividends	11%
Growth rate of own company sales	13%
Treasury bill yield	12%

The company's gearing level (by market values) is 1:2 debt to equity, and after tax earnings available to ordinary shareholders in the most recent year were £5,400,000 of which £2,140,000 was distributed as ordinary dividends. The company has 10 million issued ordinary shares which are currently trading on the Stock Exchange at 321 pence. Corporate debt may be assumed to be risk free. The company pays tax at 35% and personal taxation may be ignored.

Required:

Estimate the company's weighted average cost of capital using:

(i) The dividend valuation model.

(ii) The capital asset pricing model.

State clearly any assumptions that you make.

Under what circumstances would these models be expected to produce similar values for the weighted average cost of capital?

(10 marks)

(b) You are now informed that the proposed investment is a major diversification into a new industry, and are provided with the following information about the new industry.

Average industry gearing level (by market value)   1:3 debt to equity
Average payout ratio   55%
Average beta coefficient (β equity)   1.50

Required:

Using any relevant information from parts (a) and (b) prepare a brief report recommending which discount rate should be used for the investment. Any relevant calculations not included in your answer to part (a) should form part of your report.

(7 marks)

(c) Discuss the practical problems of using the capital asset pricing model in investment appraisal. (8 marks)

(Total 25 marks)

Question 43   CIMA

You are required to give brief answers to the following questions.

(a) What factors are said to affect security prices under the efficient market hypothesis in its semi-strong form? (4 marks)

(b) What formula should be used to express the ordinary shareholder's cost of capital on the assumption that the company's rate of dividend growth will be constant in perpetuity and given that 'D' is the dividend in Year 1? (4 marks)

(c) What is the meaning of 'systematic risk' in relation to the Capital Asset Pricing Model? (4 mark)s

(d) What is meant by the procedure of 'arbitrage' assumed by Modigliani and Miller in their 1958 paper on the capital structure of firms, and what factors might invalidate this procedure in practice? (4 marks)

(e) What is the nature of a Forward Option Contract in relation to foreign exchange transactions? (4 marks)

(Total: 20 marks)

Appendix 3: Model Solutions to Past Examination Questions

Note: The model solutions in this appendix have been composed by the author who accepts full responsibility for them. They do not, therefore, necessarily represent the views of the examiners on how the questions should be answered.

Question 1

Analysis

A reasonable knowledge of the concept of the cost of capital and its application to investment will see a candidate through the parts of this question. A total of 36 minutes is available for answering it.

Model solution

(a) (i) The equation giving the cost of equity capital is:

$$E = \frac{d}{m} \times 100 + g$$

where   E is the cost of equity
            d is the amount of the dividend
            m is the market value of the share
            g is the percentage growth

Substituting what is known in this equation we get:

$$12.5 = .05 \times 100 + g$$

Hence   G = 7.5%

The annual rate of growth which should be achieved in the share price for X plc is $7\frac{1}{2}\%$.

(ii) We should discount the expected cash flows at a rate of $12\frac{1}{2}\%$ per annum in the ordinary way:

Cash flow	Discount factor	Present value
10,500	.889	9,333
13,500	.790	10,666
		20,000

This gives a net present value of nil which was to be shown.

(b) (i) It cannot be expected that all capital projects undertaken by a business will yield the same rate of return. All that can be said is that they should all yield a return which is in excess of the company's cost of capital.

(ii) An increase in the rate of return on the investment of surplus funds will raise the company's cost of capital. Clearly it should not invest in any projects which yield less than this.

Question 2

Analysis

This is a fairly easy mark earner, requiring only a clear mind and a knowledge of how the value of a company might change. A quarter of the total time of the examination is available for it, i.e. 45 minutes.

Model solution

(a) The financing section of the company's balance sheet at the end of this year for each of the three alternatives is shown below:

	(i) £000's	(ii) £000's	(iii) £000's
Ordinary shares	35	30	25
Share premium account	40	50	40
Revenue reserves	60	85	60
Shareholders' funds	135	165	125
11% debenture	25	25	25
	160	190	150

(i) The dividend is equal to 60p per share. The first effect of the payment of the dividend is to make the ex div price of the share £2.40. The effect of the bonus issue is to give 7 shares the value previously attributable to 5 shares. The ultimate ex div price is, therefore:

$$£2.40 \times \frac{5}{7} = £1.71$$

(ii) Here the dividend is not paid so the basic ex div price is the same as the cum div price. After the issue of the new shares the price becomes:

$$£3.00 \times \frac{5}{6} = £2.50$$

(iii) The effect of paying the dividend is to reduce the price of the share to £2.40 as in (i). The effect of the stock split is then to halve this to £1.20.

(b) None of these actions should, in theory, affect the return to the shareholders in any way. It is possible that the attention drawn to the shares by the publicity surrounding the action may cause the share price to rise above its theoretical level at least temporarily.

(c) The purpose of a scrip dividend is to conserve within the company the funds which would otherwise have been used in paying the dividend. It is usual to give the shareholders the option of receiving the dividend in cash. The object of a stock split is to reduce the price of the shares and to increase their number so as to increase their marketability.

(d) The purchase of its own shares by a company might have the following objectives:

(i) To use surplus funds for which no attractive investment opportunity exists.

(ii) To buy out troublesome or dissenting shareholders.

(iii) To concentrate power in the hands of a particular group of shareholders.

(iv) To reduce the size of the business.

Question 3

Analysis

A 20 mark question for which, therefore, 36 minutes are available. It may present some candidates with difficulty as it is open ended. There is no clearly defined route to a solution. It does, however, allow scope for an imaginative interpretation of the figures and full advantage should be taken of this.

Model solution

Equity Financing

There has been no issue of shares during the period under review. There has, however, been a very large build up of retained profits which have thus formed an important component of financing. No dividends have been paid in any of the three years.

Although the value of the shares will, no doubt, have increased (as this is a private company there will be no stock market quotation), it is unusual not to provide shareholders with any income from their investment. It is, however, likely that the shareholders of this company are also directors so that they may receive adequate remuneration in the form of directors' emoluments.

Debt Financing

Debt finance has roughly doubled between 1983 and 1985. Because of the increase in equity the gearing ratio has actually declined over the period. Gearing was:

1983	64%
1984	44%
1985	12%

Liquidity

The company has built up very substantial cash balances. These are invested at interest so that interest receivable has provided a substantial part of total income. The current ratio has been:

1983	1.3
1984	.96
1985	1.25

These figures look to be low but are misleading. A high proportion of current liabilities are advance payments by customers which could legitimately be set off in part against work in progress. Part of work in progress is thus an investment of funds provided by customers rather than an investment of the company's own funds.

Source and Application of Funds

It may be useful to provide a statement of source and application of funds covering the whole period of the available information.

Source	£000's
Operating profit	461
Item not involving the movement of funds:	
depreciation	38
Funds generated by operations	499
Interest received	233
Additional long term funds	62
	794

Application	
Purchase of land and buildings	283
Purchases of plant and machinery	215
	498
Net application of funds	296

Question 4

Analysis

This is an interesting question on capital structure. It involves a knowledge of the theory of Modigliani and Miller and of the calculation of the weighted average cost of capital. The time allocation should be 45 minutes.

Model solution

(a) Modigliani and Miller would argue that the total value of the companies is independent of the capital structure except to the extent of the tax advantage enjoyed by debt. This is given by value of debt × tax rate. The values of the two companies are calculated below:

	£000's
Value of C	
80 million ordinary shares @ £1.40	112,000
Value of D	
25 million ordinary shares @ £4	100,000
£25 million debt	25,000
	125,000

Theoretically the value of D should exceed that of C by:

$$\text{value of debt} \times \text{tax rate} = £25 \text{ million} \times .35$$
$$= £8.75 \text{ million}$$

In fact the value of D exceeds that of C by £13 million. D is, therefore, overvalued relative to C. The investor in D can improve his financial position by arbitrage. This will be achieved by selling the holding in D, borrowing until personal gearing is the same as the gearing in the capital structure of D and then investing the proceeds in the shares of C.

(b) Income attributable to shareholders in the two companies is:

C	£000's
Gross earnings	25,000
Less tax at 35%	8,750
	16,250
D	
Gross earnings	25,000
Less Debenture interest	3,000
	22,000
Less tax at 35%	7,700
	14,300

The investor in D currently receives 4% of the income attributable to shareholders in D. This is:

$$.04 \times £14,300,000 = £572,000$$

He should sell shares in D realising

$$100,000,000 \times .04 = £4,000,000$$

He should borrow £1,000,000 to duplicate the gearing of D and then invest the combined total of £5,000,000 in the shares of C.

Income will become:

$$\frac{5}{112} \times £16,250,000 = \qquad £725,446$$

Less interest at 12% on borrowing	120,000
Income is	£605,446

which is £33,446 greater than before.

(c) If C borrows £20,000,000 Modigliani and Miller would indicate that its value will rise by:

$$\begin{aligned} \text{value of debt} \times \text{tax rate} &= £20,000,000 \times .35 \\ &= £7,000,000 \end{aligned}$$

Assuming that the debt replaces equity the value of C is £119 million of which the debt is £20 million. Equity is, therefore, £99 million. The earnings attributable to equity is calculated as:

	£000's
Gross earnings as before	25,000
Less interest on debt £20 million × .12	2,400
	22,600
Less taxation at 35%	7,910
	14,690

Cost of equity capital is

$$\frac{14,690}{99,000} \times 100 = 14.84$$

Weighted average cost of capital can now be calculated:

Debt 20 × (12 × .65)	156
Equity 99 × 14.84	1,469
	1,625

$$\frac{1,625}{119} = 13.66\%$$

(d) Some weaknesses of the Modigliani and Miller theory are:

(i) It assumes that arbitrage is a cost free process. In fact dealing costs may be quite high.

(ii) It assumes that personal taxation is irrelevant.

(iii) It assumes that personal gearing carries the same risks as corporate gearing.

(iv) It assumes that personal gearing has the same cost as corporate gearing.

Question 5

Analysis

We are given a great deal of information in this question. It is important to be selective and to highlight the key factors in the situation.

Model solution

Comments on the financial management of W, plc in 1984/85

Level of Activity

The company has suffered a very substantial drop in turnover in the year. Home turnover has declined by 9% and export turnover by 41%. Total turnover is down by 31%.

Profits and Dividends

Due to the drop in turnover profit has declined both absolutely and, because of the existence of fixed costs, as a proportion of turnover. Earnings per share is reduced by 70%. The dividend has been maintained at 9.1p and has therefore been paid at the expense of a depletion of reserves.

Source and Application of Funds

This document shows that cashflows were more or less in balance and the net reduction in liquid resources is only £89,000. There has, however, been a dramatic change in capital structure. A substantial net depletion of equity finance has been made up by an increase in borrowing. This borrowing has been in the form of a bank overdraft which cannot be regarded as a reliable long term source of finance. Consequent on the purchase of the new subsidiary there has also been a further substantial increase in borrowing making the company now very highly geared.

Consolidated Balance Sheet

Liquidity has deteriorated sharply but, for the moment, remains at a satisfactory level. The current ratio for 1984 was 2.7 and for 1985 2.09. The liquidity ratio for 1984 was 1.54 and for 1985 is 1.08. The company was probably overliquid prior to the acquisition of S, Ltd. Gearing has moved from nil to .25, i.e. the company is now about a quarter financed by debt.

Employment

In spite of the declining level of business the number of persons employed in all departments has remained about constant.

General

Clearly this has been a critical year for W. It is not yet in a position which should cause serious concern but a great deal depends on the contribution which the new subsidiary is going to make to group progress. Nearly half of the purchase price is accounted for by goodwill so that expectations would appear to be high.

Question 6

Analysis

This is a question on the control of stock. It is very easy if taken stage by stage. Candidates are not even expected to remember the formula for determining the economic order quantity which is, however, given incorrectly in the question! 36 minutes are available for answering it.

Model solution

(a) (i) The economic order quantity is given by:

$$\text{EOQ} = \sqrt{\frac{2C_s d}{C_h}}$$

$$\text{EOQ} = \sqrt{\frac{2 \times 48.46 \times 4,095}{4}}$$

$$= \underline{315}$$

(ii) The frequency with which the order would be placed is

$$\frac{4,095}{315} = 13 \text{ times per year}$$

(iii) The total annual procurement cost is

$$13 \times £48.46 = £630$$

The total holding cost is

$$\frac{315 \times 4}{2} = 13 \text{ times per year}$$

(b) It is suggested that the best way to deal with variable demand or variable delivery times is to re-order whenever the stock falls to a certain specified level. Since it is company policy to satisfy all orders from stock it must be accepted that average stock will be higher than if it was permissible for stock to be exhausted. This is the cost of satisfying the customer.

   (i) With a 350 unit consumption in four weeks and a three week delivery the minimum stock before re-order should be:

$$\frac{350}{4} \times 3 = 262 \text{ units}$$

   (ii) If delivery might sometimes take five weeks but usage is steady the re-order level should be:

$$\frac{4,095}{52} \times 5 = 394 \text{ units}$$

(c) The best way to handle a situation where stock usage is fast but irregular is to order regularly on an imprest system. At the beginning of each period the stock should stand at the maximum possible consumption during that period. Delivery should be arranged (giving as much notice as is required) so that this level is restored at the end of the period. This means that the size of the order will be equal to usage since the previous order. The following diagram shows how stock levels might move.

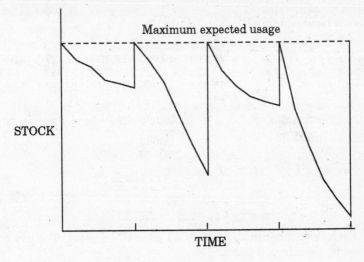

Question 7

Analysis

This is a type of question which is a favourite with the examiners. It involves a fairly straightforward application of DCF principles but is made complicated by the mass of information given and by the need to take into account taxation. It can be completed successfully only by clear thinking and by well laid out workings.

Model solution

(a) Standard Machine
Calculation of tax payments

Year	1	2	3	4	5
	£	£	£	£	£
Pretax cashflow	20,500	22,860	24,210	23,410	-
Capital allowances	12,500	9,375	7,031	5,273	15,820*
Taxable cashflow	8,000	13,485	17,179	18,137	
Tax @ 35%	2,800	4,720	6,013	6,348	

Net cashflow

Gross	20,500	22,860	24,210	23,410	
Tax payment	–	2,800	4,720	6,013	6,348
	20,500	20,060	19,490	17,397	(6,348)

Year	1	2	3	4	5
	£	£	£	£	£
Working capital released				10,000	
Value of residual capital allowances			3,730*		
Net cashflow	20,500	20,060	19,490	31,127	(6,348)
Discount factors 12%	.892	.797	.712	.636	.567
Present values	18,286	15,988	13,877	19,797	(3,599)

The total of present values is	£64,349
Initial investment is	60,000 (including working capital)
Net present value is	£4,349

*Value of residual capital allowances:
$$x_1 = £15,820 \times .25 \times .35 \times .892$$
$$x_2 = x_1 \times .75 \times .892$$
$$x_1 = x_2 + x_3 + \ldots\ldots = £3,730$$

Net cash flows total to about £60,000 after three years. The pay back period is, therefore, 3 years.

De-luxe Machine
Calculation of tax payments

Year	1	2	3	4	5	6	7
	£	£	£	£	£	£	£
Pretax cashflow	32,030	26,110	25,380	25,940	38,560	35,100	
Capital Allces.	22,000	16,500	12,375	9,281	6,961	5,220	15,662*
Taxable	10,030	9,610	13,005	16,659	31,599	29,880	
Tax @ 35%	3,511	2,403	4,552	5,830	11,060	10,458	

Net cashflow

	1	2	3	4	5	6	7
Gross	32,030	26,110	25,380	25,940	38,560	35,100	
Tax payment		3,511	2,403	4,552	5,830	11,060	10,458
	32,030	22,599	22,977	21,388	32,730	24,040	(10,458)
Working capital released						10,000	
Value of residual capital allowances						3,514*	
Net cashflow	32,030	22,599	22,977	21,388	32,730	37,554	(10,458)
Discount factors 14%	.877	.769	.675	.592	.519	.456	.400
Present values	28,090	17,379	15,509	12,662	16,987	17,125	(4,183)

The total of present values is	£103,569
Initial investment is	98,000
Net present value is	£ 5,569

*Value of residual capital allowances:
$$x_1 = £15,662 \times .25 \times .35 \times .877$$
$$x_2 = x_1 \times .75 \times .877$$
$$x_1 = x_2 + x_3 + \text{.......} = £3,514$$

Net cash flows total to about £98,000 after four years. The pay back period is, therefore, 4 years.

The de-luxe machine would appear to be the better one to buy as it has the higher net present value.

(b) Leasing of Standard Machine
Calculation of tax payments

Year	1	2	3	4	5
	£	£	£	£	£
Cashflow	20,500	22,860	24,210	23,410	
Lease payment	15,000	15,000	15,000	15,000	
Taxable cashflow	5,500	7,860	9,210	8,410	
Tax @ 35%	1,925	2,751	3,224	2,944	

Net cashflow

Gross	(15,000)*	5,500	7,860	9,210	23,410	
Tax payment			1,925	2,751	3,224	2,944
	(15,000)	5,500	5,935	6,459	20,186	(2,944)
Working capital released					10,000	
Net cashflow	(15,000)	5,500	5,935	6,459	30,186	(2,944)
Discount factors 11%	1.000	.901	.812	.731	.659	.593
Present values	(15,000)	4,955	4,819	4,722	19,893	(1,745)

*It is assumed that lease payments are made in advance, i.e. at the beginning of the year to which they relate.

Total present value is	£17,644
Initial working capital	10,000
Net present value	£7,644

It would be better to lease the standard machine.

(c) Some reasons why companies may use accounting rate of return and payback methods are:

(i) They are simple and easy to understand.

(ii) They are found to give acceptable results.

(iii) Ignorance or suspicion of more sophisticated methods.

Question 8

Analysis

An easy question for those who are happy with statistical calculations but tricky for those who are not. There is an implausibility in one of the figures given which seems likely to be a consequence of an error in the question.

Model solution

(a) The standard deviation is the root-mean-square of the deviations from the arithmetic mean. In this case there are three equally probable possibilities with deviations of -x, 0 and +x respectively. Therefore:

$$\sigma = \sqrt{\frac{2x^2}{3}}$$

$$\sqrt{\frac{2x^2}{3}} = 32.65$$

$$x = 40\%$$

This result seems implausible as it would lead to actual rates of

$$12 + 40 = \quad 52\%$$
$$\text{and } 12 - 40 = \quad -28\%$$

These are, however, correct on the figures given.

If the standard deviation had been given as 3.265% then

$$\sqrt{\frac{2x^2}{3}} = 32.65$$

$$x = 4\%$$

a more likely result and probably what was intended by the examiner. The two possible outcomes, other than 12%, would then be 16% and 8%.

(b) (i) The standard deviation is a measure of the variability of the predicted returns and hence of the degree of risk attached to the investment.

(ii) Factors to be considered by a potential investor are:

(1) The investor's attitude to risk. Does he require more safety even if this is associated with a lower prospective return?

(2) The investor's existing portfolio and the degree of correlation of A's returns with those of the portfolio. If A's returns are uncorrelated with those of the portfolio or are inversely correlated, the portfolio effect will reduce the investor's overall exposure to risk, without necessarily reducing overall return, if investment A is purchased.

(c) The formula for determining beta is:

$$\beta = \text{corr}_{pi} \times \frac{\sigma_i}{\sigma_p}$$

Where:
corr_{pi} is the coefficient of correlation between the portfolio and the investment

σ_i is the standard deviation of the returns of the investment

σ_p is the standard deviation of the portfolio returns.

$$\beta = .25 \times \frac{32.65}{13.5}$$

$$= .6$$

(d) $\quad R = R_f + \beta \, R_p$

where $\quad R$ is the return on investment A

R_f is the risk free rate of interest

R_p is the risk premium commanded by investment in the market.

471

$$12 = 8 + .6 R_p$$
$$R_p = 6.66$$

Therefore the market rate is risk free rate plus premium
$$8 + 6.66 = 14.66\%$$

Question 9

Analysis

This is the type of question, often favoured by examiners, which tests several pieces of knowledge within the context of a single case. No part is individually difficult but quite a large area of knowledge is tapped. The candidate may allow up to 45 minutes for answering it.

Model solution

The post acquisition values given by the directors of Killisick were calculated as follows.

Killisick
Total earnings   £5,180,000
Earnings per share   14.8p

Hence total number of shares is $\dfrac{£5,180,000}{£0.148} = 35,000,000$

Holbeck
Total earnings   £2,340,000
Earnings per share   29.25p

Hence total number of shares is $\dfrac{£2,340,000}{£0.2925} = 8,000,000$

Number of shares of Killisick after combination is:

$$35,000,000 + \frac{8,000,000 \times 3}{2} = 47,000,000$$

Total earnings is £5,180,000 + £2,340,000 = £7,520,000

Earnings per share is $\dfrac{£7,520,000}{47,000,000} = 16p$

Post-acquisition price of Killisick's shares is therefore:

$$£ 2.22 \times \frac{16.0}{14.8} = £2.40$$

Equivalent value of old Holbeck share is:

$$£\,2.40 \times \frac{3}{2} = £3.60$$

The fallacy has been to assume that the price earnings ratio for Killisick will be the same after the combination as it was before. There is also a presumption that there will be no synergistic effect in the combination so that there would seem to be very little justification for it.

Revised estimates
A more logical assumption is that the combined market value of the two companies will be the same after the combination as it was before.

The total current market capitalisation is:

Killisick	£2.22 × 35,000,000	£77,700,000
Holbeck	£3.22 × 8,000,000	25,760,000
Total		£103,460,000

Total number of shares is issue after the combination is 47,000,000 so that the market price of the shares should then be:

$$\frac{£103,460,000}{47,000,000} = £2.20$$

The post acquisition value of the equivalent of the old Holbeck share on this basis is

$$£2.20 \times \frac{3}{2} = £3.30$$

(b) Using Killisick's own valuation of its post-acquisition share price the market capitalisation would be:

£2.40 × 47,000,000 =	£112,800,000
Deduct pre-acquisition value	77,700,000
Maximum price payable is	£35,100,000

c) The effect of the further information is shown below:

Market capitalisation calculated above	£35,100,000
Value of increased cash flow £2,750,000 ÷ 14	19,642,857
Value of sale of machinery £7,200,000 × .877	6,315,789
Cost of redundancy payments :	
Immediate	(3,500,000)
In one year 8,400,000 × .877	(7,368,421)
Revised maximum value of bid	£50,190,225

If a 2 for 1 offer is made this is the equivalent of paying:

$$8{,}000{,}000 \times 2 \times \pounds2.22 = \pounds35{,}520{,}000$$

It is, therefore, worthwhile.

(d) It is clear from the large amount of interest shown in the profit and loss account that both companies have substantial amounts of debt. It is likely that the cost of debt is high. In so far as the combination is seen to reduce risk this may make debt more valuable by reducing its cost.

Question 10

Analysis

This is another 'big' question with a lot of information given. We have 72 minutes, a substantial allocation of time, to dig out the relevant ratios and draw some conclusions.

Model solution

(a) (i) Liquidity

Two ratios may be used to indicate the company's liquidity. These are:

$$\text{Current ratio} = \frac{\text{Current assets}}{\text{Current liabilities}}$$

$$\text{Liquidity ratio} = \frac{\text{Debtors} + \text{cash}}{\text{Current liabilities}}$$

A useful general guide is that the current ratio should stand at 2 or over and that the liquidity ratio, sometimes called the 'acid-test' ratio, should stand at around 1. The two ratios calculated for XYZ for the years for which we have information are given below:

Year	Current ratio	Liquidity ratio
1978	2.73	1.19
1979	2.80	1.15
1980	2.42	1.00
1981	2.17	.96
1982	1.54	.63

It can be seen from these ratios that the company now has serious liquidity problems and that these began to emerge in 1981. Prior to this the position appeared to be satisfactory.

(ii) Utilisation of assets

Asset turnover is a useful indicator of the utilisation of assets. It is calculated as follows:

$$\text{Asset turnover} = \frac{\text{Sales turnover}}{\text{net assets}}$$

The figures for the five years are shown below. In order that the revaluations which took place in 1981 do not obscure the figures an adjustment has been made to eliminate the effect of the revaluation.

Year	Asset turnover
1978	2.30
1979	2.12
1980	2.40
1981	1.91
1982	2.06

The utilisation of assets seems markedly worse in 1981 and 1982 than it had been previously.

(iii) Sources and uses of funds

This can best be displayed by preparing a statement of source and application of funds statement for the five year period. This appears below.

XYZ Manufacturing plc
Statement of source and application of funds
for the five years ended on 31st December 1982

£ millions

Source

Total trading profit for five years	44
Add Item not involving the movement of funds – depreciation	33
Total generated by operations	77
Proceeds of issues of shares	23
	100

Application

Purchases of land and buildings	12
Purchases of plant and machinery	46
Dividends paid	10
Taxation paid	23
Loan repayments	6
	97
Net generation of funds	3

It can be seen from this that a substantial part of the amount required to expand the business has been generated from operations. The net amount raised from shareholders (proceeds of issues less dividends) has been quite small.

(iv) Possibility of raising more capital

The company's difficulties seem to stem from the time when it began marketing through independent regional distributors and there is evidence in the figures that XYZ is, in effect, providing part of the finance of those distributors. The company would probably find it difficult to raise extra equity finance as it has had recourse to this source of funds twice in recent years. There may also be some difficulty in raising loan capital as, particularly taking into account the bank overdraft, the company has become quite highly geared. It is suggested that a thorough management review should be undertaken in order to stop the deterioration observed in the calculations made above. It may also be useful to make a bonus issue of shares and thus freeze part of the very substantial balance on the profit and loss account. This would make it easier to attract loan capital as it would increase the size of the equity buffer.

(b) The following actions might be taken to improve funds flow generally:

(i) Reduce the period of credit offered to customers.

(ii) Enforce the terms of credit more rigorously.

(iii) Offer cash discounts to encourage prompt payment of accounts.

(iv) Introduce rigorous stock control procedures so as to keep stocks at a minimum level.

(v) Seek to obtain longer terms of credit from suppliers. In XYZ's specific case we can observe two important elements of its problem. Its collection period for debtors in 1978 averaged 66 days and in 1982 100 days. Steps should immediately be taken to ensure that customers pay more promptly as it looks as though this has been allowed to slide. Stock turnover in 1978 was 3.6 and in 1982 2.4. Stock is therefore moving less rapidly than it did. This suggests that stock levels are being allowed to rise unnecessarily high and should be reduced.

(c) Before any loan was granted the following points would need to be answered:

(i) Has XYZ prepared detailed cash budgets which show that funds will become available to pay the interest and to repay the capital of the loan?

(ii) Is the company willing to introduce procedures to improve its credit and stock control?

(iii) Is the company willing to allow a charge on its land and buildings as security for the loan?

(iv) Is the company willing to make a bonus issue of shares so as to reduce the balance on the profit and loss account which is otherwise available for distribution?

(v) Is XYZ willing to allow representation of our company on its Board of Directors while the loan is outstanding?

Question 11

Analysis

This is an interesting question to which 45 minutes may be allocated. It is in three parts and each requires fairly simple calculations to demonstrate understanding of the principles involved.

Model solution

(a) Holt

Money value of shares is .4 (8 million out of 20 million) of total value of company.

Expected value of net realisable assets:

Probability	Value	Expected value
	£ million	*£ million*
.1	1	.1
.2	2	.4
.3	4	1.2
.2	8	1.6
.2	10	2.0
		5.3

Market value is £5.3 million × 1.5 = £7.95 million.

Market value of 8 million shares is

£7.95 million × .4 = £3.18 million.

Value of convertible is the best of (i) total net asset value up to a maximum of total par value and (ii) ⅓ of market value.

Probability	1/3 market value	Asset value	Par value	Probability x best of AV and MV	Conversion rights exercised?
	£m	£m	£m	£m	
.1	.5	1	3	.1	NO
.2	1.0	2	3	.4	NO
.3	2.0	4	3	.9	NO
.2	4.0	8	3	.8	YES
.2	5.0	10	3	1.0	YES
				3.2	

Value of convertible is £3.2 million and therefore this option appears to be slightly more favourable.

(b) Wood

If retention is nil then £600,000 is distributed to give 15% return on capital. Value of shares is:

$$£600,000 \times \frac{100}{15} = £4,000,000$$

If retention is 25% then £450,000 is distributed. If required return is still 15%, 7% is given by growth leaving dividend to yield 8%. Value of equity is:

$$£450,000 \times \frac{100}{8} = £5,625,000$$

If required return rises to 16% the dividend must yield 9% and value of equity is:

$$£450,000 \times \frac{100}{9} = £5,000,000$$

If retention is 50% then £300,000 is distributed. If required return is still 15%, 10% is given by growth leaving dividend to yield 5%. Value of equity is:

$$£300,000 \times \frac{100}{5} = £6,000,000$$

If required return rises to 17% the dividend must yield 7% and value of equity is:

$$£300,000 \times \frac{100}{7} = £4,285,714$$

(i) if the return required by investors remains constant at 15% the optimum distribution policy is to retain 50% of earnings which gives an equity value of £6,000,000.

(ii) if the return required by investors rises at higher levels of retention the optimum distribution policy is to retain 25% earnings when the equity value will be £5,000,000.

The required rate of return is likely to change with distribution policy to reflect the greater degree of risk associated with the retention of earnings for the purpose of investing in profitable but risky projects.

(c) The benefits and disadvantages inherent in a demerger are:

(i) Economies of scale might be lost.

(ii) Smaller units may be able to respond more flexibility to changing conditions.

(iii) Incompatible business segments can be separated from one another. Demerger would appear to be appropriate where a group had become unduly large and where some parts of its operations did not fit logically with its overall business profile.

Question 12

Analysis

This question tests a candidate's knowledge of how to evaluate Stock Market investment opportunities. Given the relevant knowledge it is not very difficult.

Model solution

(a) (i) Dividend policy

Year prior to listing	Dividend (p)	Dividend adjusted for changes ni capital (p)	Total dividend £	Cover
5	3.6	1.92^2	768,000	2.34^4
4	4.8	2.56^2	1,024,000	2.34
3	6.16	4.11^3	1,644,000	2.34
2	6.56	4.37^3	1,748,000	2.34
1	7.12	4.74^3	1,896,000	2.34
Current	5.5^1	-	2,200,000	2.50

(1) $5.5 = 3.16$ (paid) $+ 2.34$ (suggested).

(2) Dividend $\times \dfrac{100}{150}$

(3)   Dividend $\times \dfrac{100}{125}$

The company has clearly had a very conservative dividend policy. Cover of nearly two and a half times is high. The dividend has also been a very consistent proportion of profit which suggests that the size of the retention has been unaffected by the availability or otherwise of investment opportunities. A company listed on the Stock Exchange should be prepared to distribute a higher proportion of its profits, leaving its shareholders to decide how to reinvest this.

(ii) 1. The proposed final dividend may well be appropriate if the shares are owned by wealthy individuals. They will pay a high rate of income tax on distributions and may prefer the prospect of long term capital gains which are more lightly taxed.

   2. Institutional investors pay a flat rate of corporation tax and would usually prefer a higher distribution. This gives them the flexibility to reinvest the cash in other companies or to remain more liquid.

(b) (i) The dividend valuation model values shares on the basis of the discounted value of the flow of dividends which will emanate from them. The formula which incorporates the factor of growth is:

$$V = \frac{D(1 + g)}{r - g}$$

The operation of the formula requires g (growth) to be constant. To adapt this to the information given here, therefore, we evaluate cash flows for the next three years, during which growth is at 15%, and then add to this the projected value of the shares after three years. All values are appropriately discounted i.e. using the company's cost of capital.

Dividends for next three years
(growth 15% from base of 5.5p)

Year	Dividend (p)
1	6.325
2	7.274
3	8.365

Value of shares over three years

$$v = \frac{D(1 + g)}{r - g}$$

$$= \frac{8.365 \,(1 + .08)}{.12 - .08}$$

$$= 225.855$$

Total current value of shares

Year	Cash flow (p)	Discount factor	Present value (p)
1	6.325	.893	5.648
2	7.274	.797	5.797
3	234.220*	.712	166.765
			178.210

*225.855 + 8.365

Current share price is $\dfrac{\text{Market value}}{\text{No of shares}} = \dfrac{£78,000,000}{40,000,000} = £1.95$

Pavlon's shares would thus appear currently to be overvalued.

(ii) The weaknesses off the dividend valuation model are:

(a) It does not allow for risk.

(b) It does not allow for variable growth rates.

(c) It takes no account of market-wide factors.

Question 13

Analysis

This is a typical question testing the candidate's knowledge of the concepts underlying the cost of capital. It can be worked in less than the 45 minutes allowed given a rapid appreciation of what is required.

Model solution

(a) The cost of equity capital is the yield, taking account of both dividend income and the future growth in capital value, which a company needs to give in order to maintain its share price. This itself will have been determined by a combination of general factors affecting the whole market in equities and specific factors affecting investors' views about the particular company.

(b) Using the dividend growth model:

$$E = \frac{d}{m} \times 100 + g$$

$$= \frac{.10}{1.20} \times 100 + 7$$

$$= 15.33\%$$

Using the capital asset pricing model:

$$E = R_f + \beta R_p$$

Where R_f is the risk free rate of interest and R_p is the premium, i.e. excess returns, produced by a portfolio of risky investments.

$$= 8 + .5 \times 4$$

$$= 10\%$$

(c) The assumptions made are: For the dividend growth model:

(i) Growth will continue indefinitely at a steady rate.

(ii) Dividends will be maintained at the present rate.

(iii) The market price of the share will grow in proportion to the growth in earnings.

For the capital asset pricing model:

(i) There is a unique risk free rate of interest

(ii) Investors are risk averse.

(iii) The variation in returns of the company relative to variations in the market rate of return are constant i.e. is stable.

Question 14

Analysis

This question, for which 45 minutes may be taken, relates to credit control, an important component in working capital management It illustrates the interplay between credit control and competition in the market which is a feature of this activity.

Model solution

(a) (i) If all customers paid promptly the cash flow from sales would have a present value of the full amount of £150,000 in the month of the sales and the total flow (i.e. in perpetuity) would have a present value of:

$$\frac{£150,000}{.02} = £7,500,000$$

We can calculate these values for each of the payment patterns we are given.

Present pattern

	Cashflow	Discount factor	Present value
Immediate payment £150,000 × .15	22,500	1.000	22,500
After one month £150,000 × .35	52,500	.980	51,450
After two months £150,000 × .30	45,000	.961	43,245
After three months £150,000 × .15	22,500	.942	21,195
After four months £150,000 × .05	7,500	.924	6,930
Present value of sales in month of sales			145,320

$$\text{Value of flow in perpetuity} = \frac{£145,320}{.02} = 7,266,000$$

Scheme 1

	Cashflow	Discount factor	Present value
Immediate payment £150,000 × .975* × .4	58,500	1.000	58,500
After one month £150,000 × .30	45,000	.980	44,100
After two months £150,000 × .10	15,000	.961	14,415
After three months £150,000 × .15	22,500	.942	21,195
After four months £150,000 × .05	7,500	.924	6,930
Present value of sales in month of sales			145,140

$$\text{Value of flow in perpetuity} = \frac{£145,140}{.02} = £7,257,000$$

*To allow for cash discount

Scheme 2

	Cashflow	Discount factor	Present value
Immediate payment Nil			
After one month £150,000 × .80	120,000	.980	117,600
After two months £150,000 × .15	22,500	.961	21,623
After three months £150,000 × .05	7,500	.942	7,065
			146,288
Less monthly cost of credit control procedures			500
Present value of sales in month of sales			145,788

$$\text{Value of flow in perpetuity} = \frac{\pounds145{,}788}{.02} = \pounds7{,}289{,}400$$

(ii) Of the two schemes under consideration Scheme 1 is slightly less favourable than the present arrangement and should not be considered further. Scheme 2 is substantially better than either of the alternatives and should be adopted.

It should be noted that its success depends on the efficiency of the, as yet untried, credit control procedures.

(b) Effect on Scheme 2 if sales increase by £20,000 per month

Again we calculate the present value of one month's additional sales.

	Cash inflow £	Cash outflow £	Net cashflow £	Discount factor £	Present value
Immediate	Nil	Nil	Nil		
After one month £20,000 × .80	16,000	16,000*	Nil		
After two months £20,000 × .15	3,000		3,000	.961	2,883
After three months £20,000 × .05	1,000		1,000	.942	942
Present value of additional one month's sales					3,825

$$\text{Value of flow in perpetuity} = \frac{\pounds3{,}825}{.02} = \pounds191{,}250$$

*80% of sales proceeds deferred by one month.

It is assumed that the cost of the credit control procedures is unaffected by the higher level of turnover.

(c) The granting of credit may be regarded as a lending decision when:

(1) One customer is seeking extended credit terms substantially different from those offered to other customers.

(2) The amount involved is material having regard to the general level of debtors.

(3) The motive of the customer in seeking the terms is to avoid borrowing from other sources.

It should be regarded as an investment decision when:

(1) It involves the establishment of a general credit policy covering all customers.

(2) The motive for the granting of credit is to create goodwill and generate profitable business.

Where the granting of credit is seen as a lending decision regard should be had to the following:

(1) The credit worthiness of the customer concerned.

(2) The possibility of seeking security for the loan e.g. a charge on the goods supplied.

(3) The possibility of charging interest.

(4) The commercial benefit of making the loan e.g. to help a valued customer of long standing.

Where the granting of credit is seen as an investment in working capital regard should be had to:

(1) The amount of the investment and the expected return on it.

(2) General credit control procedures to monitor policy.

(3) The desirability of alternative policies.

(d) A customer might decide to take advantage of cash discount terms if:

(1) He has surplus cash otherwise lying idle.

(2) The discount is at a rate which makes early payment attractive even after taking into account the cost of interest on borrowed funds.

Question 15

Analysis

The first part of this question is quite difficult involving an involved calculation. Thereafter it is an easy mark earner. Time pressure is not too great as 45 minutes is allowed for the whole question.

Model solution

(a) Since we are to ignore dividends the returns from the investment in W plc and the market as a whole are represented by capital gains or losses. These can be determined for years 2 to 5 inclusive. We have calculated in the table below the quantities which we require to determine beta. W represents the return for W plc and I the returns on the market (index).

Returns W	Returns I	W − W̄	I − Ī	(W − W̄)(I − Ī)	(I − Ī)²
+4.1667	+5.4688	+.1434	+1.1504	+.1646	1.3233
−8.0000	+11.1111	−12.0236	+6.7927	−81.6726	46.1411
−21.7391	−1.3333	−25.7627	−5.6517	+145.6035	31.9420
+41.6667	+2.0270	+37.6431	−2.2914	−86.2553	5.2503
				−22.1598	84.6567

$$\beta = \frac{\text{Covar}_{wi}}{\text{var}_i}$$

$$= \frac{-22.1598}{84.6567}$$

$$= -0.2617$$

(b) Here the expected rate of return on shares in W is given by;

$$\text{Return} = R_f + (\beta \times R_p)$$
$$= 5 + (1.5 \times 3)$$
$$= 9.5\%$$

(c) The formula linking cost of capital, dividends, growth and the market price of the share is:

$$E = \frac{d}{m} \times 100 + g$$

$$10 = \frac{30p}{m} \times 100 + 5\%$$

$$M = \underline{£6.00}$$

(d) It would not have been correct in part (c) to use as the cost of equity capital the expected rate of return computed in (b). This is because that rate was based on the supposition that the invest-ment in W was going to be added to a portfolio. The rate of return required thus took into account the portfolio effect of the investment. This is the term used to describe the effect which the addition of an investment to an existing portfolio has on the overall risk of the portfolio.

Question 16

Analysis

A 36 minute question testing a knowledge of how investors in quoted securities might make their decisions.

Model solution

(a) The nominal amount of stock which is equivalent to one share is £18.33⅓.

The redemption value of this is the minimum share price which would make conversion just worthwhile. At any share price above this the value on conversion would be higher than the value on redemption. It is calculated as follows:

Principal sum	£18.33
Interest @ 4.75% for 4 months	.29
	£18.62

If the share price is £18.63 or over the value of conversion will be greater.

(b) The company may be redeeming the debentures now for the following reasons:

(i) Conversion now is on very favourable terms and it appears that they will become more favourable. It wishes, in effect, to force conversion at the existing share price on the holders of the stock.

(ii) Most holders of the stock may have already converted. It is administratively inconvenient to have a small amount of stock outstanding and the company wishes to resolve this.

(iii) The company happens currently to have surplus cash available which it wishes to use in this manner.

(iv) The company wishes to clear the way to issuing more loan capital, possibly on a non-convertible basis.

(c) In general terms the factors to be considered in deciding whether or not to convert the stock are:

(i) The future prospects of the company and whether its share price is likely to continue to rise in value.

(ii) The amount of income received from the investment. At the current level of dividend the shares yield a lower level of income than the equivalent amount of loan stock.

(iii) The capital value of the investment. In this case the value of the shares receivable on conversion is considerably higher than the redemption value of the stock.

(iv) The risk involved in investing in the shares of the company. At current price and dividend levels the investment is yielding only .38% per annum. This discounts prospective growth for many years into the future.

It should be noted in this case that the stock holders have no real choice but to convert. If they do not wish to hold the shares they may sell them and would, in this way, receive far more than they will on redemption.

Question 17

Analysis

Although the customer in this question is overseas the question does not relate to foreign currency. The candidate is required to calculate the expected value of each of the alternative courses of action in order to recommend the most favourable.

Model solution

(a) Assumptions made are:

  (i) Payment within one year is equivalent to payment after half year.

  (ii) Payment after one year is equivalent to payment at one year.

  (iii) If the customer does not default on the first order he will not default on the second.

Total value of order is $5,000 \times £1.75 = £8,750$

Immediate cash outlay if order is accepted is

$5,000 \times £1.25 =$	£6,250
Less Customers's deposit of	
$10\% \times £8,750 =$	875
	£5,375

The possibilities are:

Payment within one year £8,750 − £875 = £7,875 (probability .5)

Payment after one year £8,750 − £875 − £500* = £7,375 (probability . 15)

Complete default, payment nil (probability .35)

*cost of attempt to recover debt

Year	Discount factor 14%	Cashflow £	Present value (p) £
0	1.000	(5,375)	(5,375)
½	.938†	3,938	3,694
1	.877	1,106	970
Net present value			-711

† by interpolation

The negative net present value indicates that it is not worthwhile accepting this order.

Repeat order

Year	Discount factor 14%	Cashflow £	Present value (p) £
1	.877	(5,375)	(4,714)
1½	.823	3,938	3,240
2	.769	2,756	2,120
Net present value			646

If there is a 50% chance that a repeat order will occur the net present value of the present opportunity is

$$(£646 \times .5) - £711 = -£388$$

It is still not worthwhile accepting the order.

If the repeat order is certain the net present value now is:

$$£646 - £711 = -£65$$

The order, in these circumstances, is again not worth accepting.

(b) Factors which might influence the decision of whether or not to grant credit to this customer are:

(i) The possibility of other more valuable orders from the same customer in the future,

(ii) the benefits of breaking into a new overseas market,

(iii) the possibility of obtaining guarantees against the possibility of default by the customer,

(iv) the possibility of political risks to the contract in addition to the risk of default by the customer (e.g. he may be prevented by law from remitting funds).

(c) Methods which might be used to evaluate the credit worthiness of the potential customer are:

(i) Enquiries through credit agencies,

(ii) seeking a bankers' reference for the customer,

(iii) making enquiries from other suppliers to the same customer,

(iv) obtain and examine the financial reports of the customer.

Question 18

Analysis

This question requires a fair amount of knowledge and a lot of work for its 25 marks. It is very important to tackle it in a methodical manner if the large of amount of data is not to lead to hopeless complication. Although 45 minutes is allowed for this question a candidate will have to work hard in order to complete it in that time.

Model solution

(a) First we will calculate the trading cash flow and hence the amount of tax to be paid.

Year	1	2	3	4	5	6
	£000's	£000's	£000's	£000's	£000's	£000's
Sales	2,950	3,820	5,200	5,400	5,600	5,600
Materials	487	630	858	891	924	957
Labour	805	1,043	1,420	1,474	1,529	1,583
Selling and distribution	207	267	364	378	392	406
Overhead (i)	185	240	315	321	328	330
Direct costs	1,684	2,180	2,957	3,064	3,173	3,276
Trading cash flow	1,266	1,640	2,243	2,336	2,427	2,524
Depreciation (ii)	480	480	480	480	480	-
Taxable profit	786	1,160	1,763	1,856	1,947	2,524
Tax at 40%	314	464	705	742	779	1,009

(i) This is 50% of the total amount of overhead.

(ii) This is 20% straight line on the full amount of the depreciable capital expenditure.

We can now prepare a complete table of cash flows:

Year	0	1	2	3	4	5	6
	£000's	£000's	£000's	£000's	£000's	£000's	£000's
Land and buildings	(500)	(600)					1,100
Plant and machinery	(700)	(1,700)					
Working capital	(230)	(340)	(110)	(20)	(20)	(20)	
Trading cash flow		1,266	1,640	2,243	2,336	2,427	2,524
Tax (delayed one year)			(314)	(464)	(705)	(742)	(779)
Terminal value (iii)							7,575
Cash flow	(1,430)	(1,374)	1,216	1,759	1,611	1,655	10,420
Discount factors (iv)	1.000	0.847	0.718	0.609	0.516	0.437	0.370
Present value	(1,430)	(1,164)	873	1,071	831	1,082	3,855

The total net present value is **£5,118,000** and the project is, therefore, acceptable.

(iii) This is calculated as $(2,524 - 1,009) \times 5$

(iv) The discount factors are calculated on the basis of the company's cost of capital. This is:

cost of debt = 15% gross ($15\% \times .6 = 9\%$ net of tax).

$$\text{cost of equity} = R_f + \beta R_p$$
$$= 12 + (1.5 \times 8)$$
$$= 24\%$$

The weighted average cost of capital is then:

$$(9 \times .4) + (24 \times .6) = 18\%$$

Note that a beta value of 1.5 has been taken as being more likely to be applicable in the new situation that the existing level of beta.

The following reservations might be held about this appraisal:

(i) The estimate of the cost of capital is not very reliable.

(ii) The cost of capital may change over the period of the analysis.

(iii) The method of valuing the project at the end of six years seems to be very rough and ready.

(iv) The value of the land and buildings at the end of six years may be very difficult to estimate with accuracy.

(v) Over this period of time tax rates may change.

(b) If it is expected that there will be inflation this should be allowed for by adjusting the cash flows to what is anticipated. If

this is not done no allowance will be made for differential inflation and the combination of historical costs for depreciation and
current costs for other items will distort the figures.

Question 19

Analysis

This question tests various aspects of the candidates knowledge of
the problems connected with fluctuating exchange rates. No part is
individually difficult provided that the knowledge is there. 45 minutes is available to answer.

Model solution

(a) Forward rates are based on the market's estimates of how actual
exchange rates will move and might, therefore, be thought to be
the most reliable indication available of future spot rates. They
are not, however, particularly reliable. If rates could actually be
forecast in advance with any degree of accuracy the market in
futures would become unnecessary. The uncertainty is its ratio-
nale for existence.

(b) The cost of the yen on the proposed forward contract is:

$$\frac{14,385,579}{136.55 - 1.08} = £106,190$$

(c) If the spot rate at the end of the three months were at the one
extreme of last year's range the yen would have cost, at that
rate:

$$\frac{14,385,579}{£159.45} = £90,220$$

At that rate the forward contract is clearly not advantageous. At
the other extreme the cost would be:

$$\frac{14,385,579}{£134.20} = £107,195$$

This, by a small margin would not be advantageous.

(d) If the goods had not been received the alternative actions available to the company are:

(i) to resell the yen and arrange a new forward contract for the
revised date of the delivery;

(ii) to keep the yen and deposit them in an interest bearing
account until required.

(e) (i) A forward exchange fixed contract is one where there is an agreement that foreign currency shall be taken at an agreed rate of exchange at an agreed future time regardless of how actual rates of exchange have moved.

(ii) a forward exchange option contract is one where a sum is paid for the right to acquire currency at an agreed rate of exchange at an agreed date. The right need not necessarily be taken up and will not be taken up if the spot rate is more favourable.

Question 20

Analysis

This is a question on discounted cashflow. It involves evaluation of a number of alternatives and recommendations on the amount which should be invested. Tax provides a special complication.

Model solution

(a) Calculation of tax payments

Years	1 £000's	2 £000's	3 £000's	4 £000's	5 £000's
Taxable operating profit	1,000	1,000	1,200	1,400	
H.Q. costs	(200)	(200)	(200)	(200)	
Capital allowances	(400)				
Salvage values				1,800	
Taxable net profit	400	800	1,000	3,000	
Tax due	200	400	500	1,500	
Tax paid	600*	200	400	500	1,500

*already due

Current cashflows if no takeover

	£000's	£000's	£000's	£000's	£000's
Operating	1,200	1,000	1,200	1,200	
H.O. costs	(200)	(200)	(200)	(200)	
Capital	(400)			1,800	
Tax paid	(600)	(200)	(400)	(500)	(1,500)
Net cashflow	nil	600	600	2,300	(1,500)
Discount factors	.847	.718	.609	.516	.437
Present value	nil	430.8	365.4	1,186.8	(655.5)

Total present value is   £1,327,500

(b) If takeover occurs savings will take place.

Years	1	2	3	4	5
	£000's	£000's	£000's	£000's	£000's
H.O. costs	100	100	150	150	
Red's assets				200	
	100	100	150	350	
Tax		(50)	(50)	(75)	(175)
Net cashflow	100	50	100	275	(175)
Discount factors	.847	.718	.609	.516	.437
Present value	84.7	35.9	60.9	141.9	(76.5)

Total present value of change is   £246,900

The maximum amount which Craig should pay if the Corporate Planning manager's suggestions are ignored is

£1,327,500 + £246,900 = £1.574,400

(c) (i) Termination of Blue division

At year 2

Years	1	2	3	4	5
	£000's	£000's	£000's	£000's	£000's
Operating cashflow	200	200	(400)	(200)	
Salvage value		1,000		(600)	
	200	1,200	(400)	(800)	
Tax		(100)	(600)	200	400
Net cashflow	200	1,100	(1,000)	(600)	400
Discount factors	.847	.718	.609	.516	.437
Present value	169.4	789.8	(609.0)	(309.6)	174.8

Total present value is   £215,400

At year 3	£000's	£000's	£000's	£000's	£000's
Operating cashflow	150	150	150	(200)	
Salvage value			800	(600)	
	150	150	950	(800)	
Tax		(75)	(75)	(475)	400
Net cashflow	150	75	875	(1,275)	400
Discount factors	.847	.718	.609	.516	.437
Present value	127.1	52.8	532.9	(657.0)	174.8

Total present value is   £230,700

(ii) Use of Craig's own transport department for Red.

Years	1	2	3	4	5	6
	£000's	£000's	£000's	£000's	£000's	£000's
Operating cashflow	30	30	30	30		
Replacement	(100)		80	(100)	80	
	(70)	30	110	(70)	80	
Tax		35	(15)	(55)	35	(40)
Net cashflow	(70)	65	95	(125)	115	(40)
Discount factors	.847	.718	.609	.516	.437	.370
Present value	(59.3)	46.7	57.9	(64.5)	50.3	(14.8)

Total present value is £16,300

(iii) Additional advertising

Years	1	2	3	4	5
	£000's	£000's	£000's	£000's	£000's
Advertising	(180)				
Profit			120	120	
Tax		90	nil	(60)	(60)
Net cashflow	(180)	90	120	60	(60)
Discount factors	.847	.718	.609	.516	.437
Present value	(152.5)	64.6	73.1	31.0	(26.2)

Total present value is −£10,000

The optimum life for Blue is three years.

The best of the Corporate Planning manager's suggestions is that Blue should be operated for a further three years and then closed. It is also profitable for Craig's own transport to be used for Red division's deliveries. It is not profitable to undertake the additional advertising.

Question 21

Analysis

This is a fairly sizeable question (63 minutes may be allocated) on the valuation of shares. A number of different alternatives are given and need to be evaluated.

Model solution

(a) On the basis of market values G is worth

$$57m \times £3.41 = £194.37m$$

80% is being acquired and this will have a value of

$$£194.37m \times .8 = £155.496m$$

The number of shares to be issued is

$$\frac{£155.496m}{£3.00} = 51,832,000$$

(b) (i) Effect on existing shareholders in V:

Current earnings per share is $\dfrac{£25.75m}{50m}$ = 51.5p per share

Current earnings per share is \F(£25.75m,50m) = 51.5p per share

After the proposed share exchange total earnings will be

$$£25.75m + .8(£42.6m) = £59.83m$$

It is assumed that 20% of G's earnings is already included in V's accounts.

The number of shares becomes 50m + 51.832m = 101.832m

Earnings per share becomes

$$\frac{£59.83m}{101.832m} = 58.75p \text{ per share}$$

Current asset value is $\dfrac{£259.55m}{50m}$ = £5.19 per share

(Asset value attributable to V's own business is

£259.55m – £55m (the cost of g's shares) = £204.55m

Asset value of group is

$$£204.55m + £342m = £546.55m$$

Asset value per share is

$$\frac{£546.55m}{101.832m} = £5.37$$

(ii) Effect on existing 80% of shareholders in G

Current earnings per share is

$$\frac{£42.6m}{57m} = 74.7p \text{ per share}$$

After the share exchange it will become:

$$58.75p \times \frac{51.832}{57 \times .8} = 66.78p \text{ per share}$$

Current net asset value is

$$\frac{£342m}{57m} = £6 \text{ per share}$$

After the share exchange it will become

$$£5.37 \times \frac{51.832}{57 \times .8} = £6.10 \text{ per share}$$

(c) (i) The advantages to V in offering loan stock include:

1. The shareholders in G would be prevented from obtaining a majority of shares in the new group.

2. There would be a fixed rate of interest payable on the loan stock and this would be relievable against tax.

3. The effect of the gearing which would be introduced would probably be to increase the earnings per share available to the present holders of shares in V.

4. The part of G's business which is of no interest to V could be sold off to provide the cash to redeem the loan stock.

(ii) Determination of the price which could be paid for the 80% shares in G without diluting earnings per share.

If the loan stock is issued total earnings are

$$£59.83m - £2m = £57.83m$$

assuming the rate of corporation tax is 50% so that the net cost of the interest on the loan stock is £2m.

Solve for x in:

$$\frac{£57.83m}{50m + x} = .5875$$

where x is the number of shares which could be issued and .5875 represents the earnings per share available under the original scheme.

$$x = 48,434,043$$

The total price payable, allowing for the market value of the shares and for the value of the loan stock is:

$$(48,434,043 \times £3) + £40,000,000 = £185,302,129$$

Question 22

Analysis

An attempt has been made to make this a topical question by relating it to the government's privatisation policy. The main part of it, however, is concerned with the calculation of some conventional accounting ratios and their interpretation. It forms a major part of the whole examination and can be allocated 54 minutes of working time.

Model solution

(a) We look first at the original proposal to issue 285 million shares. The total proceeds would be 285m × £1.40 = £399m.
The total number of shares then in issue would be 95 = 300m
Earnings per share on historical cost earnings is:

This year: $\dfrac{£52.508m}{300m} = 17.5p$

Forecast: $\dfrac{42.087m}{300m} = 14.0p$

Earnings per share on current cost earnings is:

This year: $\dfrac{£29.498m}{300m} = 9.8p$

Forecast: $\dfrac{£26.570m}{300m} = 8.9p$

The gross yield is $\dfrac{\text{Total dividend grossed up}}{\text{Total market value of shares}} \times 100$

$= \dfrac{£19.32m \times 1.33}{300m \times £1.40} \times 100$

$= 6.12\%$

The price earnings ratio on historical cost earnings is:

This year: $\dfrac{£1.40}{17.5p} = 8$

Forecast: $\dfrac{£1.40}{14.0p} = 10$

The price earnings ratio on current cost earnings is:

This year: $\dfrac{£1.40}{9.8p} = 14.28$

Forecast:
$$\frac{£1.40}{8.9p} = 15.73$$

Dividend cover based on historical cost earnings is:

This year:
$$\frac{52.508}{19.32} = 2.72$$

Forecast:
$$\frac{42.087}{19.32} = 2.18$$

Dividend cover based on current cost earnings is:

This year:
$$\frac{29.498m}{19.32m} = 1.53$$

Forecast:
$$\frac{26.570m}{19.32m} = 1.38$$

Looking now at the alternative proposal to issue a larger number of shares. The number is to be in proportion to the dividend and so is:

$$285m \times \frac{21.256}{19.32} = 314m \text{ (about 10\% more)}$$

The total proceeds would be 314m × £1.40 = £439m

The total number of shares in issue would then be: $\frac{314}{.95} = 330m$

Earnings per share on historical cost earnings is:

This year:
$$\frac{£52.508m}{330m} = 15.9p$$

Forecast:
$$\frac{£42.087}{330m} = 12.8p$$

Earnings per share on current cost earnings is:

This year:
$$\frac{£29.498m}{330m} = 8.9p$$

Forecast:
$$\frac{£26.570m}{330m} = 8p$$

The gross yield is unaltered at 6.13%
The price earnings ratio on historical cost earnings is:

This year:
$$\frac{£1.40}{15.9p} = 8.8$$

Forecast:
$$\frac{£1.40}{12.8} = 10.9$$

The price earnings ratio on current cost earnings is:

This year:
$$\frac{£1.40}{8.9p} = 15.7$$

Forecast: $$\frac{£1.40}{8p} = 17.5$$

Dividend cover based on historical cost earnings is:

This year: $$\frac{52.508m}{21.256m} = 2.47$$

Forecast: $$\frac{42.087m}{21.256m} = 1.98$$

Dividend cover based on current cost earnings is:

This year: $$\frac{29.498m}{21.256m} = 1.39$$

Forecast: $$\frac{26.570m}{21.256m} = 1.25$$

The advantages of the larger issue are that it will raise more cash for the company and that it may make possible a somewhat wider ownership of the shares. Clearly the cash is needed as the company anticipates heavy capital expenditure in the future. The large discrepancy between the historical cost and current cost earning figures suggests that the company faces very rapidly rising prices which will make the impact of this capital expenditure even greater.

The disadvantages of the larger issue is that, although the dividend yield will be unchanged, all the financial ratios will deteriorate. Earnings per share, dividend cover and price earnings ratio all move against the shareholders.

Prospective shareholders will be concerned to know why the forecast earnings are so much lower than those experienced in the recent past. It would be helpful if the projection could be taken rather further into the future.

(b) The features of the capital structure which is being proposed are:

   (i) a large equity base;

   (ii) a special share reserved for the government;

   (iii) a debenture issue to the government repayable in the near future.

This has probably been selected firstly to give the possibility of as wide an ownership of the shares as possible. It has been part of the government's declared aim as part of its privatisation programme that wider share ownership should be encouraged. The function of the special preference share is to enable the government to retain certain special controls over the company. It is likely, for example, to enable the government to veto any proposed takeover of the company particularly if this would cause it to fall into foreign hands. The debenture issue, made from reserves, enables the government to draw past profits for its own benefit rather than leaving them in the hands of the company for the benefit of the new shareholders.

Question 23

Analysis

This is a lengthy question and the candidate will be pressed to finish it in the 45 minutes allocated to it. There are several elements to assemble to make up the total cash flow. Taxation may present some difficulty and there is also the necessity to make conversions from a foreign currency (American dollars).

Model solution
Brookday, plc

(a) Proposed USA subsidiary
Projected cashflow $000's

Year	0	1	2	3	4	5
Sales		5,000	10,500	11,025	11,576	
Purchase of subsidiary	19,000	1,000			(24,000)	
Variable cost		2,000	4,200	4,410	4,630	
Fixed cost		1,000	1,050	1,102	1,158	
Gross cash flow	(19,000)	1,000	5,250	5,513	29,788	
Tax [1]			(1,000)	625	756	10,894
Net cashflow	(19,000)	1,000	4,250	4,888	29,032	(10,894)
Exchange rate	1.300	1.235	1.173	1.115	1.059	1.006
£ value	(14,615)	810	3,623	4,383	27,414	(10,829)
Discount factors 13% [2]	1.000	.885	.783	.693	.613	.543
Present value	(14,615)	717	2,837	3,037	16,805	(5,880)

Total net present value is £2,901,000

(1) Tax

Gross cashflow	2,000	5,250	5,513	5,788	
Allowances	4,000	4,000	4,000	(16,000)	
Taxable amount	(2,000)	1,250	1,513	21,788	
Tax		(1,000)	625	756	10,894

*excluding capital transactions

(2) Determination of discount rate:

$$\text{Rate} = R_f + \beta R_p$$
$$= .07 + (1.2 \times .05)$$
$$= 13\%$$

Notes

(i) Royalties have been disregarded as they are merely transfer payments from one part of the business to another.

(ii) A balancing charge has been brought into account in respect of the value of the fixed assets at the end of the project's life.

On the analysis made above the project would appear to be worthwhile. It should be noted, however, that the positive net present value is quite small relative to the total sums involved.

(b) Other information and analysis which might be useful is:

(i) Whether any changes in the relative tax laws of the two countries are in prospect.

(ii) The degree of uncertainty attaching to the projected rate of inflation in USA.

(iii) The degree of uncertainty attaching to the projection of the future course of exchange rates between the pound and the dollar.

(iv) The extent to which the USA market can be further developed after the expiration of the present project.

(v) The opportunities which exist to terminate the project with minimum loss if it proves to be less successful than expected.

Question 24

Analysis

This is another question on a favourite topic, the control of debtors. More than one alternative has to be evaluated.

Model solution

(a)   Speeding invoicing saving:

(i) Daily amount outstanding is $\frac{£25,000,000}{50 \times 5}$ = £100,000

Average number of days delay:

$3 \times .2$	.60
$4 \times .06$	.24
$5 \times .4$	2.00
$6 \times .22$	1.32
$7 \times .12$	.84
	5.00

Interest is: £100,000 $\times \dfrac{15}{100} \times \dfrac{5}{250}$ = £300 per day

If computer is installed:

Average number of days delay:

$0 \times .5$	0
$1 \times .4$	.4
$3 \times .1$	.3
	.7

Interest is: $£100,000 \times \dfrac{15}{100} \times \dfrac{.7}{250} = £42$

Maximum rental payable is full amount of saving

$£300 - £42 = £258$

NB As a simplification it has been assumed that there are $250 \ (5 \times 50)$ working days (on which interest is charged) in a year.

(ii) Reduction in period of credit saves 5 days and the further saving is therefore:

$$\frac{5 \times £100,000}{250} \times \frac{15}{100} = £300$$

So the rental could now be as much as $£300 + £258 = £558$

(b) The main characteristics of a factoring agreement are:

(i) A factor purchases all rights in trade debts at a discount on their face value.

(ii) The cost of administering and waiting for collection is borne by the factor.

(iii) The risk of bad debts is assumed by the factor.

Invoice discounting also gives immediate (discounted) payment of trade debts but the cost of collection and the risk of bad debts remains with the trader.

The issues to be considered before entering into a factoring agreement are:

(i) The risk of bad debts and the amount that will be paid for freedom from this.

(ii) The cost of capital and thus the amount saved by immediate collection of trade debts.

(iii) The saving in administrative costs from using the factor.

(iv) Any restrictions placed on trading by the factor to protect his position.

(v) Any possible loss of customer goodwill caused by remoteness of communication with him after the goods have been supplied.

A factoring agreement may be desirable when a rapid expansion of business is likely to be held back by a shortage of liquid funds.

An alternative would be the raising of extra long term capital. Where the shortage of liquid funds is expected to be temporary, a bank overdraft may be preferable.

Question 25

Analysis

A slightly unusual question to which 45 minutes may be allocated. It can be tricky sorting out exactly what is required and there are several calculations to do.

Model solution

(a) The factors likely to influence the desired level of cash balances are:

(i) The predictability of future cash flows. If they are unpredictably higher, precautionary cash balances will have to be maintained.

(ii) The existence of readily realisable securities. If these are present smaller cash balances can be kept as they can readily be replenished when needed.

(iii) The availability of short term finance such as a bank overdraft.

(iv) The period of credit given by suppliers. If this is long then lower cash balances can be kept.

(b) Total cash outflows will be either £130,000 or £140,000, each with a probability of .5. Total cash inflows will be either £100,000 or £120,000 with probabilities of .4 and .6 respectively. Putting these together the following are the possible net cash outflows and their related probabilities:

Possible Outflow £	Probability
10,000	.3
20,000	.3
30,000	.2
40,000	.2

We can now calculate the net benefit of each of a number of levels for the opening money market balance.

	£
Money market investment of £120,000	
Cost of arriving at this (deposit £20,000)	−20
Interest earned in week £120,000 × .12 × 1/52	+276.9
Required withdrawal of £10,000 cost £36 probability .3	−10.8
Required withdrawal of £20,000 cost £64 probability .3	−19.2
Required withdrawal of £30,000 cost £92 probability .2	−18.4
Required withdrawal of £40,000 cost £120 probability .2	−24
	+184.5

	£
Money market investment of £110,000	
Cost of arriving at this (deposit £10,000)	−15
Interest earned in week £110,000 × .12 × 1/52	+253.8
Required withdrawal of £10,000 cost £36 probability .3	−10.8
Required withdrawal of £20,000 cost £64 probability .2	−12.8
Required withdrawal of £30,000 cost £92 probability .2	−18.4
	+196.8

	£
Money market investment of £100,000	
Cost of arriving at this (present balance)	Nil
Interest earned in week £100,000 × .12 × 1/52	+230.8
Required withdrawal of £10,000 cost £36 probability .2	−7.2
Required withdrawal of £20,000 cost £64 probability .2	−12.8
	+210.8

	£
Money market investment of £90,000	
Cost of arriving at this (withdraw £10,000)	−36
Interest earned in week £90,000 × .12 × 1/52	+207.7
Required withdrawal of £10,000 cost £36 probability .2	−7.2
	+164.5

	£
Money market investment of £80,000	
Cost of arriving at this (withdraw £20,000)	−64
Interest earned in week £80,000 × .12 × 1/52	+184.6
	+120.6

The level of investment in the money market at the beginning of the week which will maximise the expected net return is thus £100,000.

(c) The advantages and disadvantages of using short term debt in the financing of working capital are:

(i) Short term debt is likely to be more expensive than long term finance.

(ii) The level of finance is more readily varied with short term debt.

(iii) Short term finance may be unexpectedly withdrawn.

(iv) Short term debt requires constant renegotiation.

Question 26

Analysis

The main part of this question is a fairly standard discounted cash flow calculation. The usual problems of sorting out the relevant and nonrelevant costs occur. Although tax is an aspect of the question this is in a simplified form which should not present any problems. 45 minutes can be allocated.

Model solution

(a) Calculation of relevant costs

	Year 1 £000's	Year 2 £000's	Year 3 £000's	Year 4 £000's
Skilled labour (i)	210	328	361	397
Unskilled labour (ii)	144	225	247	272
Material Z (iii)	102	161	174	188
Component P (iv)	173	265	288	308
Component Q (v)	77	118	127	137
Other variable costs (vi)	25	39	42	45
Selling expenses (vii)	166	174	183	192
Other overheads	50	53	55	58
Rent (viii)	120	126	132	139
Managers (ix)	67	72	77	82
	1,134	1,561	1,686	1,818

Notes:

(i) £17.50 per unit escalating by 7% per annum.

(ii) £12 per unit escalating by 7% per annum.

(iii) First year: 6 × 12,000 kg required = 72,000. Of this 70,000 is for £99,000 and 2,000 £1.46 per kg totalling £101,920 (rounded to 102). Thereafter £8.76 per unit escalating by 5% per annum.

(iv) £14.40 per unit escalating by 5% per annum.

(v) £6.40 per unit escalating by 5% per annum.

(vi) £2.10 per unit escalating by 5% per annum.

(vii) £166,000 escalating by 5% per annum.

(viii) The opportunity rental of the buildings £120,000 should be used not the actual rental. Again escalating by 5% per annum.

(ix) Two managers at £25,000 plus one at £17,000. The total is £67,000 escalating at 7% per annum.

Calculation of net cash flows

	Year 1 £000's	Year 2 £000's	Year 3 £000's	Year 4 £000's
Sales	1,320	2,021	2,183	2,356
Less Cash outflows	1,134	1,561	1,686	1,818
Trading cash inflow	186	460	497	538
Less Tax payments*	(46)	50	63	77
After tax cash flow	232	410	434	461

* This is 35% of trading cash inflow-interest payments-tax allowable depreciation.

When the salvage value of the machinery is added to the year 4 cash flow this is increased from 461 to 473.

Use trial and error to determine the internal rate of return:
Try 20%

Year	Cash flow	Discount factor	Present value
1	232	.833	193
2	410	.694	285
3	434	.579	251
4	473	.482	228
			957
Less original investment			864
			93

The internal rate of return is higher than 20%
Try 25%

Year	Cash flow	Discount factor	Present value
1	232	.800	186
2	410	.640	262
3	434	.512	222
4	473	.410	194
			864
Less original investment			864
			Nil

So 25% per annum is the internal rate of return.

(b) An asset beta is a measure of the portfolio effect of that investment, i.e. the extent to which it increases or decreases overall
risk. The risk premium required from any given investment is:

$$R_f + R_p$$

where R_f is the risk free rate of return
R_p is the risk premium for the portfolio as a whole

In this case the required rate of return is:
$$8\% + (1.2 \times 7\%) = 16.4\%$$

This is comfortably exceeded by the internal rate of return indicating that the investment should be undertaken.

(c) Calculate the net present value at the present level of tax using a discount rate of 17%.

Year	Cash flow	Discount factor	Present value
1	232	.855	198
2	410	.731	300
3	434	.624	271
4	461	.534	246
	12	.534	6
			1,021
Less original investment			864
			197

A change in the tax rate will affect the first four figures of our table but not the residual value of the machinery. We calculate the proportion by which these elements would need to diminish to reduce the NPV to zero:

$$\frac{197}{1,015} = .194$$

The existing net cash flow is 65% of the gross amount. The tax rate would, therefore, need to increase by .194 ¥ 65% = 12.6% i.e. to 47.6%.

Question 27

Analysis

This is a fairly involved question on discounted cash flow. Although the proposed investment is overseas there is no translation of foreign currency as all figures are given in sterling. Exchange control regulations in the foreign country exist, however, and this will affect the outcome.

Model solution

(a) Cashflows overseas (all figures in £)

Years	0	1	2	3	4
Set up	(600,000)				120,000
Materials	(40,000)	(120,000)	(100,000)	(100,000)	(40,000)
Sales		500,000	500,000	500,000	500,000
Labour		(80,000)	(80,000)	(80,000)	(80,000)
Overheads		(70,000)	(70,000)	(70,000)	(70,000)
	(640,000)	230,000	250,000	250,000	430,000

Loss of contribution on Basic Product

	1	2	3	4
Sales	90,000	90,000	110,000	110,000
Variable cost	70,000	70,000	80,000	70,000
	20,000	20,000	30,000	40,000

(i) Net present value if cash used in overseas country

Year	Main cashflow £	Loan interest £	Loss of contribution £	Net cashflow £	Discount factor	Present value £
0	(40,000)*			(40,000)	1.000	(40,000)
1	230,000	(60,000)	(20,000)	150,000	.869	130,350
2	250,000	(60,000)	(20,000)	170,000	.756	128,520
3	250,000	(60,000)	(30,000)	160,000	.658	105,280
4	430,000	(660,000)+	(40,000)	(270,000)	.572	(154,440)
						169,710

*Net of loan   +Including repayment of loan

(ii) If the project's proceeds are to be remitted this will be limited to 30% of £600,000 i.e. £180,000 each year. The total proceeds are £1,160,000. This can be remitted at the rate of £180,000 per annum from year 2 to year 7 inclusive, leaving £80,000 to be remitted in year 8. The net present value of this situation is shown in the table below.

Year	Main cashflow £	Loan interest £	Loss of contribution £	Net cashflow £	Discount factor	Present value £
0	(40,000)*			(40,000)	1.000	(40,000)
1	Nil	(60,000)	(20,000)	(80,000)	.869	(69,520)
2	180,000	(60,000)	(20,000)	100,000	.756	75,600
3	180,000	(60,000)	(30,000)	90,000	.658	52,220
4	180,000	(660,000)	(40,000)	(520,000)	.572	(297,440)
5	180,000			180,000	.499	89,820
6	180,000			180,000	.432	77,760
7	180,000			180,000	.376	67,680
8	80,000			80,000	.327	26,160
						(17,720)

It appears from these figures that investment in the overseas project is worthwhile only if the net proceeds are reinvested overseas.

(b) The additional factors which should be considered when appraising an overseas capital investment are:

(i) The stability of the rate of exchange between the overseas currency and sterling. Exchange profits and losses are possible and if the exchange rate is unstable, the risks attaching to the project are increased.

(ii) The political stability of the overseas country. Conflict may lead to uninsurable loss of the investment. A change in political complexion may lead to the nationalisation, possibly without compensation, of the business assets.

(iii) The nature of the labour market overseas. It will be important to be able to staff the project with staff having the appropriate level of expertise.

(iv) The possibility of supplying the overseas market from home production. Export may turn out to be less risky and more profitable than setting up an overseas manufacturing facility.

Question 28

Analysis

A fairly straightforward question offering 20 marks to be earned in 36 minutes. It requires the calculation of a few key figures.

Model solution

Since we are given a budget position one year from now and not a forecast we must presume that these results are planned and our analysis is to be in terms of comment rather than recommendation. First we should determine the overall change in working capital:

Increases in current assets:	Debtors	£4,750
	Raw material stock	25,000
	Work-in-progress	12,500
	Finished goods stock	3,000
		45,250
Increase in current liabilities:	Creditors	9,000
		£36,250

There is thus a net increase in working capital of £36,250 which will involve a cost in terms of its finance. In spite of increased turnover there is no projected increase in gross profit and this is therefore a plan for a reduced absolute level of profit.

We should calculate the key ratios:

	Now	**In one year**
Debt collection period	$\dfrac{£31,250}{£250,000} \times 365 = 46$ days	$\dfrac{£36,000}{£288,000} \times 365 = 46$ days
Finished goods stock	$\dfrac{£40,000}{£210,000} \times 365 = 70$ days	$\dfrac{£43,000}{£248,000} \times 365 = 63$ days
Work in progress	$\dfrac{£17,500}{£210,000} \times 365 = 30$ days	$\dfrac{£30,000}{£248,000} \times 365 = 44$ days
Raw material stock	$\dfrac{£35,000}{£140,000} \times 365 = 91$ days	$\dfrac{£60,000}{£170,000} \times 365 = 129$ days
Creditors	$\dfrac{£21,000}{£140,000} \times 365 = 55$ days	$\dfrac{£30,000}{£170,000} \times 365 = 64$ days

It is interesting to note that it is planned to increase Raw Material Stock and Work in Progress relative to turnover quite substantially but to reduce (relatively) Finished Goods Stock. Perhaps there has been recent experience of production bottlenecks which have suggested this. Longer credit is to be taken from suppliers. It should be ensured that they will be willing to allow this and that there will be no consequent cost on the form of lost discounts.

Question 29

Analysis

50 minutes should be allowed for this question. It is made complex by the large number of different factors on which comment is required.

Model solution

(a) We cannot calculate a cost of capital for Rex since we have no market price for its shares. We can, however, calculate Comus's cost of capital and use this as a basis for our calculations. It is simple because the company is financed entirely by equity.

For Comus, cost of capital is given by:

$$E = \frac{d}{m} \times 100 + g$$

$$= \frac{8p}{£4} \times 100 + 10\%$$

$$= \underline{12\%}$$

For Rex (also wholly financed by equity) let m = market price of share

$$E = \frac{d}{m} \times 100 + 8\%$$

$$12\% = \frac{10p}{m} \times 100 + 8\%$$

$$m = \underline{£2.50}$$

A 'fair' share exchange would be 5 Comus for every 8 Rex. To make the offer attractive to Rex shareholders Comus might offer 2 for every 3.

(b) Current earnings

Comus .2 × £200,000 =	£40,000	
Rex .15 × £150,000 =	£22,500	
	£62,500	

In order to avoid dilution the maximum number of Comus shares in issue must be

$$\frac{£62,500}{.2} = 312,500$$

Allowing for the 200,000 already in issue this leaves 112,500 as the maximum that could be offered for Rex (i.e. 3 for 4).

(c) If it is argued that Rex is a less risky enterprise than Comus then it could be taken that its cost of capital is lower and thus its calculated share valuation higher. Comus would therefore need to make a higher offer in terms of its own shares. Alternatively it could 'pay' for the property element in Rex's structure with risk free debenture stock at a risk free rate of interest and pay only for the balance in its own equity.

(d) We should evaluate Rex's future cash flows, discounting at 8%.

Year	Net cash inflow[1] (£000's)	Discount factor	Present value (£000's)
1	12	.926	11.11
2	13	.857	11.14
3	30	.794	23.82
4	574.5[2]	.735	422.26
			468.33

[1] Profit after Tax + Depreciation − Capital Expenditure

[2] Value of perpetuity of 43. $\frac{43}{.08} = 537.5 + 37 = 574.5$

On this basis a single share in Rex is worth

$$\frac{468.33}{150} = £3.12$$

The minimum offer that Rex shareholders are likely to accept is

$$\frac{£3.12}{£4} = .78 \text{ of a Comus share per Rex share, i.e. about 7 for 9.}$$

Question 30

Analysis

This is a question on cash budgeting. The important requirement is to synchronise all cash flows correctly and in accordance with the information given. It is best to calculate all the elements separately before bringing them together in the full statement. The time allocation for this question is 45 minutes.

Model solution

(a) Cash inflow from Sales

These have a two months lag so will be the sales of May to October.

Sales month	Units	Price	Cash (rounded)
May (i)	81,200	£10.60	861
June	82,418	£10.60	874
July (ii)	83,654	£10.60	887
August	84,909	£10.60	900
September	86,183	£11.13	959
October	87,475	£11.13	974

(i) $82,418 \times \dfrac{100}{101.5}$

(ii) $82,418 \times \dfrac{101.5}{100}$ and so on for the other months.

Cash outflows for purchases

Purchases are two months in advance of production which is one month in advance of sales. They are paid for after one month's credit. The net effect of this is that cash flows are based on the sales of two months ahead i.e. September to February.

Sales month	Units	Price	Cash (rounded)
September	86,183	£3.71	320
October	87,475	£3.90	341
November	88,788	£3.90	345
December	90,119	£3.90	351
January	91,471	£3.90	356
February	92,843	£3.90	361

Cash outflows for wages

Labour is paid one month in arrear in respect of production one month is advance. It will , therefore, be paid concurrently with the related sales.

Sales month	Units	Price	Cash (rounded)
July	83,654	£3.18	266
August	84,909	£3.18	270
September	86,183	£3.18	274
October	87,475	£3.34	292
November	88,788	£3.34	297
December	90,119	£3.34	301

Cash inflows from investment income

Alpha $\dfrac{812,000 \times 1.52}{8} \times 40\% \times .5 = £30,856$ October

Beta $\dfrac{326,000 \times 3.46}{12} \times 50\% \times .5 = £23,500$ September

Gamma $\dfrac{568,000 \times 1.04}{8} \times 50\% \times .5 = £18,460$ December

$2^{1}/_{2}\%$ Consols $14,300 \times £100 \times .025 \times .5 = £17,875$ November

12% Exchequer 1998 $10,000 \times £100 \times .12 \times .5 = £60,000$ November

Putting this and other information together:

Cash budget for six months to December

	Jul	Aug	Sep	Oct	Nov	Dec
Opening balance	80	123	154	123	179	(325)
Sales receipts	861	874	887	900	959	974
Land sale					130	
Investments		–	24	31	78	18
	941	997	1,065	1,054	1,346	667
Creditors	320	341	345	351	356	361
Wages	266	270	274	292	297	301
Overheads	95	95	95	95	101	101
Purchases assets			90		310	
Repayments	37	37	38	37	37	38
Administration	100	100	100	100	100	100
Dividend						400
Taxation					470	
	818	843	942	875	1,671	1,301
Closing balance	123	154	123	179	(325)	(634)

Existing overdraft facilities will serve up until the beginning of December when, on present plans, they will start to become inadequate. The following are possible courses of action:

(i) Reduce the amount of the dividend. This is to be avoided if possible as it will not find favour with shareholders.

(ii) Postpone the purchase of the new machinery. A few months delay may not matter.

(iii) Acquire the machinery under a leasing arrangement.

(iv) Speed up the collection of debtors. Two months' credit seems a long time for them to be given.

(b) Computerised cash balance management can help a financial manager by relieving him with having to deal with cash shortages and surpluses on an ad hoc basis. All temporary surpluses of cash will be transferred to an interest bearing account and shortfalls will be covered by pre-arranged overdraft facilities. These will incur lower interest charges than unplanned overdrafts.

Question 31

Analysis

Although this is not explicitly mentioned this is a question which bears on the cost of capital. It should present few problems to the candidate who understands this and is able to perform discounting calculations. The available time of 45 minutes should be adequate.

Model solution

(a) There are the following advantages to a company in issuing convertible loan stock rather than ordinary shares or debenture stock.

(i) Because it provides the security of a debenture with the possibility of capital gains offered by ordinary shares the convertible may be more attractive to potential investors and therefore easier to sell.

(ii) Before conversion the interest payable on the debenture will be relievable against tax and this may reduce the net cost of the capital to the company during this period.

(iii) It may be possible to set the terms of the future conversion at such a level that the ordinary shares which are ultimately issued command a higher premium effectively than could have been achieved by a straight issue.

(iv) If the company wishes to do so it may repurchase its convertibles for cancellation before they have been converted. Unlike the purchase of its own shares this action will not deplete distributable reserves.

(v) As conversion takes place there will be a progressive reduction in the gearing of the company facilitating the issue of further debt.

(b) We must calculate the net present value of the debenture up to the date of conversion ignoring the value of the conversion. The sum of the discount factors for six years at a discount rate of 8% is 4.623. The discount factor for the sixth year is .630.

The total value of the interest payments on £100 nominal of stock for six years is:

$$12 \times 4.623 = £55.47$$

The cost of £100 nominal of stock now is £131 so the net present value is:

$$£131 - £55.47 = -£75.53$$

For conversion to yield the required 8% per annum the value of the shares acquired must be:

$$\frac{£75.53}{.630} = £119.89$$

Since this represents forty shares it implies a share price of almost exactly £3. For shares currently standing at £2.5 to be valued at £3 in six years' time requires an annual compound rate of growth of 3.1% per annum.

At the projected share price at conversion of £3, the total value of shares issued is £120 per £100 of stock. The conversion premium is, therefore, £20.

(c) (i) A 'bull' market is one where the prices of securities are rising and, by implication, are expected to continue to rise. It is in these circumstances that companies are able to offer convertibles on terms which imply the issue of equity in the future at a higher premium than is currently available. It is also in bull market that such securities are most attractive to investors as the potential gain on conversion will appear to be higher.

(ii) If the option to convert is overvalued relative to the current share price then this implies that the convertible issue will bring in more cash than will the issue of the equivalent amount of equity. The cost of capital is, thus, lower. It is in this way that the owners of the company will gain an economic advantage.

Question 32

Analysis

Worth 20 marks this question should be allocated 36 minutes. It is a very easy mark earner once the point has been spotted.

Model solution

The basic decision rule relating to investment opportunities is that an investment should be undertaken if it yields a return better than the firm's cost of capital. Ranking is therefore unimportant. All investments meeting the basic criterion will be undertaken and all which do not meet it will be rejected. There are, however, two situations where ranking becomes relevant. One of these is that of mutually exclusive projects and the other is that of capital rationing. In each of these cases ranking is important.

A method of ranking investments which allows not only for the rate of return but also for the amount of the investment is that of Net Present Value. All cash flows whether in or out are discounted by factors derived from the cost of capital. Projects are ranked according to their net present values. Normally all investments showing a positive net present value will be undertaken. For mutually exclusive projects or where there is capital rationing the total net present value of all projects taken together should be maximised subject to whatever constraints exist.

Trial and error will quickly establish that Project A has an internal rate of return of 20% per annum and B of 15% per annum. Thus, on this basis A would appear to be the better project. If we rank them on the basis of net present value, however, the position is different.

Project A	Year	Cash flow	10% discount factor	Present value
	1	£240	0.909	£218
	2	288	0.826	238
	3	346	0.751	260
	4	414	0.683	283
	5	498	0.621	309
				1,308
Less Initial investment				1,000
Net present value				+£308

Project A	Year	Cash flow	10% discount factor	Present value
	1	£2,300	0.909	£2,091
	2	2,640	0.826	2,181
	3	3,040	0.751	2,283
	4	3,500	0.683	2,391
	5	4,020	0.621	2,496
				11,442
Less Initial investment				10,000
Net present value				+£1,442

Where both projects can be undertaken they should be.

If A and B are mutually exclusive (i.e. undertaking one precludes undertaking the other) B should be ranked first.

Where capital is rationed A might be undertaken subject to consideration of how the remaining £9,000 would be invested. If it could be made to yield a net present value in excess of £1,442–£308 = £1, 134 A might be preferred to B

Question 33

Analysis

A straightforward question testing knowledge of the operations of the capital market. It should be allocated 43 minutes.

Model solution

(a) The capital market performs the following major functions:

(i) It enables new capital to be raised through the issue of securities. This provides the financial manager with funds as required.

(ii) It enables existing securities to be traded. This enables the financial manager continuously to monitor the cost of capital and to assess the terms on which he would be able to raise new capital. Because the market monitors the company's progress it also provides a discipline on the financial manager's activities. The existence of this secondary market makes the raising of finance in the first place very much easier than it would otherwise be.

(iii) It provides an outlet whereby surplus funds can be invested profitably in the short term or whereby long term strategic holdings in other companies can be built up.

(b) The efficient market hypothesis states that market prices are adjusted immediately in response to new information. The three forms of the hypothesis are:

(i) The weak form – the market responds only to information derived from its own past performance and trends. If this form of the hypothesis only prevails then fundamental analysts might make abnormal profits but market analysts will not.

(ii) The semi-strong form – the market responds to all publicly available information. If this form of the hypothesis holds then only persons with inside information can earn abnormal profits.

(iii) The strong form – the market responds to all information whether public or private. This form would make the earning of any abnormal profits impossible.

(c) (i) The cash offer

	Semi-strong		Strong	
	A	B	A	B
Day 2	£2.00	£3.00	£3.00	£3.20
Day 4	£3.00	£2.67	£3.00	£3.20
Day 10	£3.00	£3.20	£3.00	£3.20

(ii) The share offer

	Semi-strong		Strong	
	A	B	A	B
Day 2	£2.00	£3.00	£3.15	£3.15
Day 4	£2.75	£2.75	£3.15	£3.15
Day 10	£3.15	£3.15	£3.15	£3.15

Question 34

Analysis

27 minutes should be devoted to this question. It should offer no difficulty to a candidate who understands the basis on which working capital management operates.

Model solution

In formulating a policy for credit control management must be aware of the constraints under which it operates. Debtors tie up expensive capital and from this point of view should be minimised. Maximum sales, however, and therefore profit depend on offering credit on terms as favourable as those granted by competitors. Another important factor to be considered is the incidence of bad debts. These, as well as the investment in debtors, are likely to be higher if credit control is relaxed.

The particular matters on which management must take decisions are:

(a) the criteria to be used in assessing credit worthiness;

(b) the length of credit to be offered;

(c) the discount, if any, to be offered for prompt payment;

(d) the urgency with which later payers are to be pursued.

On the figures given in the question an estimate can be made of the profitability or otherwise of the proposed sales expansion. The contribution made per unit of sales is £0.25 (i.e. selling price less variable costs). Sales of £1,000,000 represents 400,000 units, a contribution of £100,000. Additional costs are:

Bad debts 5% × £400,000 =		£20,000
9.5% × £600,000 =		57,000
		£77,000
Financing 11 1/2% × 30/365 × £400,000		£3,781
11 1/2% x40/365 × £600,000		7,562
		£11,343
Total cost		£88,343
Net gain from expansion		£11,657

Although there is a small gain from the expansion and therefore acceptance seems to be indicated the amount is very small. Care should be taken that it will not be swallowed up e.g. by having to maintain larger stocks.

Question 35

Analysis

This is a major question and 63 minutes can be allowed for it. A candidate's success or failure in the exam. as a whole will turn on how well he or she tackles the question. Fortunately it is broken into three parts which are independent of one another and can therefore be treated separately.

Model solution

Part 1

First we must calculate the cost of the separate elements of capital. Since tax rates are given it is plainly the net of tax rate which is required.

Cost of equity

$$E = \frac{d}{m} \times 100 + g$$

$$= \frac{.084}{.66} \times 100 + 10$$

$$= 22.73\%$$

Cost of preference capital

$$P = \frac{d}{m} \times 100$$

$$= \frac{.049}{1} \times 100$$

$$= 4.9\%$$

Cost of loan stock

$$D1 = \frac{i}{m} \times 100$$

$$= \frac{.025^*}{.8} \times 100$$

$$= \underline{\underline{3.125\%}}$$

Cost of unsecured loan

$$D2 = \frac{i}{m} \times 100$$

$$= \frac{.03^*}{1} \times 100$$

$$= \underline{\underline{3\%}}$$

Since this is unquoted the nominal value is used as market value.

	Weighting (Market value) £000's	Cost %
Equity – 300,000 shares × £.66	198	22.73
Preference shares – 80,000 × £1	80	4.9
Loan stock-£150,000 × .80	120	3.125
Unsecured loan	70	3.0
	468	

Weighted average cost of capital is 11.70%

Part 2

The group should theoretically always use its marginal cost of capital in investment appraisal since investment absorbs new funds. In practical terms for relatively small increments of capital the average cost of capital is a good enough estimate of the marginal cost. Marginal cost is likely to diverge from average most where risk is seen to be growing with size and it is here that some of the financial ratios may be useful.

The gearing ratio is:

$$\frac{120 + 80 + 70}{198} = 1.36$$

This is a very high proportion of debt finance and this creates a considerable financial risk. Profit before loan interest is £70,000. After interest, tax and preference dividends it is £25,230. This only just covers the ordinary dividend of £25,200. Current liabilities seem very high at 16% of all liabilities.

Allows for corporation tax saving when loan interest is charged against profits.

Part 3

The following comments may be made on the chief executive's approach to investment evaluation:

(a) His method of allowing for risk is highly subjective and involves no proper evaluation of the risk involved.

(b) His required rate of return of 25% bears no relationship to our calculated cost of capital. He is likely to exclude a lot of worthwhile investments.

(c) His comment about accepting the most profitable of projects implies that he is applying capital rationing. If so a net present value calculation would be a sounder basis for ranking projects than the rate of return.

(d) Central administration costs should be allowed for explicitly in evaluating projects and not left to take care of themselves.

(e) The current cash position is irrelevant. Capital can be raised on the market and this should be done if it can be shown to be profitable. Again this idea implies capital rationing. The only strength of the method is that it is very simple and will probably give a reasonable, if not optimum, return.

Question 36

Analysis

45 minutes can be devoted to this question. It is fairly straightforward provided that DCF evaluation taking tax into account has been grasped.

Model solution

(a) We must calculate the present value of the cost of each alternative. The after tax of finance is $.5 \times 15\% = 7\frac{1}{2}\%$

Leasing

Year	Gross cash flow	Tax relief	Net cash flow	7.5% discount factor	Present value
0	−£4,800		−£4,800	1.000	−£4,800
1	−4,800	+£2,400	−2,400	.930	−2,232
2	−4,800	+2,400	−2,400	.865	−2,076
3	−4,800	+2,400	−2,400	.805	−1,932
4	−4,800	+2,400	−2,400	.749	−1,798
5	−4,800	+2,400	−2,400	.697	−1,673
6		+2,400	+2,400	.648	+1,555
					−£12,956

Buying

Year	Gross cash flow	Tax relief	Net cash flow	7.5% discount factor	Present value
0	–£20,000		–£20,000	1.000	–£20,000
1		+£10,000	+£10,000	.930	+9,300
					–£10,700

It is therefore cheaper to buy the machine.

(b) Other factors to be taken into account:

(i) Is the rate of interest charged by the bank an appropriate measure of the company's cost of capital?

(ii) A leasing commitment does not appear on the balance sheet. Should the use of external finance be 'saved' until it is the only way of financing a project?

(iii) On what terms, if any, can the lease be terminated before the five years is up?

(c) Both A and B should evaluate the project using their true net of tax cost of capital. Under conditions of inflation there is a transfer of wealth from a lender to a borrower. If this is taken into account it is likely that the real cost of capital is lower than the money cost. It may even be negative. This may, for A, reverse the decision as to whether to buy or lease. For B it may emerge that leasing is not profitable business.

Question 37

Analysis

There is nothing very complex about this question on which 45 minutes may be spent. It requires a few simple calculations.

Model solution

(a) Clearly the shareholder should take up his rights as he will be acquiring shares with a market value of £1.05 for only 90p. Whether he then retains them must depend on the rate of return as compared with the rates offered elsewhere in the market .

The rate of return currently offered is:

$$\frac{0.75}{1.20} \times 100 = 6.25\% \text{ per annum}$$

The rate on the new shares, valued at their cost is:

$$\frac{0.75}{9} \times 100 = 8.33\% \text{ per ann} \ldots \text{n}$$

The rate on the investment at prices established after the announcement is:

$$\frac{0.75}{1.05} \times 100 = 7.14\% \text{per annum}$$

The shareholders will thus gain an improved yield after the issue.

(b) A company makes a rights issue when it wishes to raise a relatively small amount of equity capital. Such an issue is less expensive and more certain than is a public issue. It also makes the fixing of the price of the issue less critical as any 'bonus' element does not benefit one group of shareholders at the expense of another.

The possible uses for the cash raised are:

(i) to finance a major expansion project, e.g. building and equipping a new factory;

(ii) to repay a bank overdraft thus replacing short term finance with long term funds;

(iii) to redeem a long term debt at its maturity date.

Question 38

Analysis

We have 45 minutes to answer this question. It is quite a tricky modification to the usual Source and Application of Funds Statement. Candidates must remember that CCA adjustments do not involve any movement of funds.

Model solution

We are required to link the amount 'retained for expansion within the company' with the increase in cash and short term investments. This will require an adaptation of the usual form of statement as per SSAP 10. First we will calculate historical cost profit which gives a figure to work to in the first part of the statement.

Sales			£393,786
Less	Purchases, goods and services	£328,289	
	Salaries, wages, etc.	40,586	
	Depreciation	3,092	
	Losses of associated company	538	
	Interest	396	
	Exceptional items	1,713	374,614
			19,172
Deduct Profit on sale of fixed assets (1)			372
Historical cost profit on trading			£18,800

Y, Limited – Statement of Sources and Application of Funds for the year ended 31st August, 1979

Sources

Retained for expansion within the company		£5,222
Appropriated for: Taxation		8,190
Dividends		1,892
CCA adjustments		3,868
	19,172	
Less Profit on sale of fixed assets		372
Historical cost profit		18,800
Adjustment for items not involving the movement of funds:		
Depreciation	£3,092	
Losses incurred by associated company	538	3,630
Funds generated by trading		22,430
Proceeds of the sale of fixed assets		2,321
		24,751

Applications

Repayment of loans	£1,239	
Purchase of fixed assets	8,989	
Tax payments	3,307	
Dividend payments	1,760	
Investment in associated company (2)	628	
Increase in net working capital (3)	3,865	19,788
Net increase in cash and short term investments		£4,963

1. Proceeds of sale of fixed assets		£2,321
Cost of sales	£2,699	
Less Depreciation	750	1,949
		£372

2. Balance at 31st August 1978	£2,000	
Less Share of losses written off	538	
	1,462	
Balance at 31st August, 1979	2,090	
Hence investment	£628	

3. Increase in debtors	£3,039	
Increase in stock	3,038	
	6,077	
Less Increase in creditors	2,212	
	£3,865	

Question 39

Analysis

Although there is a lot of information presented in this question the 27 minutes we can allocate to it make it clear that we shall not become involved in any very complex calculations. All that is required is a straightforward adjustment of accounts to put them on a comparable basis.

Model solution

On the figures for dividend cover calculated by the board their justification for the higher dividend is demonstrated. The notes show, however, that profits have been affected by extraordinary items and inconsistent treatment. We need, therefore, to calculate dividend cover after appropriate adjustments.

	Years ended 31st August				
	1975	**1976**	**1977**	**1978**	**1979**
	£000	**£000**	**£000**	**£000**	**£000**
Profit after taxation	6,000	5,111	14,898	17,680	20,309
Associated company (1)	100	190	200		
Research and development (2)	(700)	(700)	(700)	2,100	
Deferred taxation	500	455	1,423	(2,378)	
Exchange rate profit				2,718	291
Adjusted profit	5,900	5,056	15,821	20,120	20,600
Dividends	1,950	1,950	2,865	3,400	3,910
Cover	3.02×	2.59×	5.52×	5.92×	5.27×

The cover is thus lower in 1979 than in either 1977 or 1978. It is still, however, very high so the payment of the higher dividend can probably be justified on its own merits even though the claim made by the directors is not substantiated.

1. After tax at 50%. The adjustments for 1978 and 1979 had already been made.

2. Written back in 1978 and then left out of account.

Question 40

Analysis

Questions concerning the capital asset pricing model seem to be becoming increasingly popular with the examiners. If you know the terminology and the elements of the theory they are very simple. They may, otherwise, appear to be impossible – 45 minutes may be taken in working this question.

Model solution

(a) First assume that the returns from the two securities are perfectly positively correlated.

Predicted return Security A	Predicted return Security B	Weighted average return (W)	Probability (P)	W × P
12	15	13.8	0.2	2.76
15	20	18.0	0.6	10.80
18	25	22.2	0.2	4.44
				18.00

The average return is thus 18% but has a high degree of risk. It can vary between 13.8% and 22.2% .

Now assume that the returns from the two securities are perfectly inversely correlated.

Predicted return Security A	Predicted return Security B	Weighted average return (W)	Probability (P)	W × P
12	25	15.00	0.2	3.00
15	20	18.00	0.6	10.80
18	15	16.20	0.2	3.24
				17.04

The average return is 17.04% but the variability and hence the riskiness of the portfolio has been reduced. It can now vary between 15% and 18%.

This demonstrates that the risk of a portfolio depends on the degree of correlation between the elements rather than on their individual riskiness.

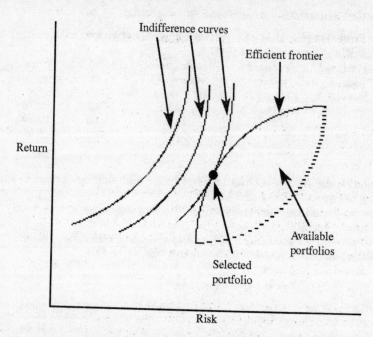

(b) (i) An investor will be faced by a collection of feasible portfolios. These are those which are offered by the market and are within his means to buy. The efficient frontier is the boundary of this collection which represents all the efficient portfolios. These are defined as those which, for a given degree of risk, maximise return or for a given return minimise risk.

The investor's indifference curves join points where he is indifferent as between one combination of risk and return and another. Each curve, however, represents a different level of satisfaction. Thus the investor will select the one of all the efficient portfolios available to him which enables him to reach the highest possible level of satisfaction.

(ii) See the diagram above.

Question 41

Analysis

This question requires the evaluation of the financial benefits of several courses of action so as to lead to a recommendation. It may be allocated 43 minutes.

Model solution

(a) (i) Current level of debtors.

North: Sales is £.48m outstanding on average 72 days.

North debtors is: $\dfrac{72}{360} \times .48m = £96,000$

South: Sales is £.72m outstanding on average 50 days.

South debtors is: $\dfrac{50}{360} \times .72m = £100,000$

Total debtors is therefore £196,000

Level of debtors after advertising

Total sales is £1.2m × 1.2 = £1.44m

North sales is £1.44m × .60 = £.864m

North debtors:

Days outstanding	*Amount*	Amount= $\dfrac{\text{Days outstanding} \times \text{amount}}{360}$
	£	£
30	86,400	7,200
60	172,800	28,800
90	587,520	146,880
	846,720	182,880

South debtors:

Days outstanding	*Amount*	Amount= $\dfrac{\text{Days outstanding} \times \text{amount}}{360}$
	£	£
30	46,080	3,840
60	57,600	9,600
90	460,800	115,200
	564,480	128,640

Total debtors is £182,880 + £128,640 = £311,520

(ii) Increase in debtors is £311,520 − £196,000 = £115,520
Additional finance charges are £115,520 × . 11 = £12,707

Increase in sales		£240,000
Increase in margin (20%)		£48,000
Less Additional interest	£12,707	
Bad debts	28,800	41,507
Maximum amount which should be paid		£6,493

(b) Debtors if discount given:

North:

Days outstanding	Amount £	Debtors £
30	518,400	43,200
60	–	–
90	336,960	84,240
	855,360	127,440

South:

Days outstanding	Amount £	Debtors £
30	172,800	14,400
60	46,080	7,680
90	345,600	86,400
	564,480	108,480

Total debtors		£235,920

	Total £	North £	South £
Saving in interest (11%)	8,316	6,098	2,218
Bad debts	8,640	8,640	–
	16,956	14,738	2,218
Cost of discount	13,824	10,368	3,456
Net benefit (cost)	3,132	4,370	(1,238)

The best policy will be to introduce the discount in respect of sales in the North only. If the discount terms must apply generally, however, it is still worthwhile to introduce them.

(c) The main factors to be considered are:

  (i) The basic amount of long term working capital which is required.

  (ii) The variation imposed on this by seasonal factors.

  (iii) The predictability of future cash requirements.

  (iv) The ease with which emergency funds could be obtained, e.g. through a bank overdraft, if required.

Three types of short or medium term finance which might be used are:

  (i) A bank overdraft. This has the advantage of being very flexible but it may not always be reliably available and it can be expensive if interest rates rise.

(ii) A term loan. This would be at a fixed rate of interest and would have to be repaid in full at the end of the term.

(iii) An extension of the terms given by creditors. If a better arrangement can be made with suppliers this is likely to be the cheapest form of finance for working capital available. It carries the risk that it may be withdrawn in more stringent times.

Question 42

Analysis

This question tests important knowledge about the different ways of determining the cost of capital. Candidates are likely to have the most difficulty in dealing with the capital asset pricing model. Working the question should take 45 minutes.

Model solution

(a) (i) The gross cost of debt is taken to be the same as the Treasury bill yield, i.e. 12%. The after tax cost is $12 \times .65 = 7.8\%$
The cost of equity is given by:

$$E = \frac{d}{m} \times 100 + g$$

$$= 7 + 11\%$$
$$= 18\%$$

The weighted average cost of capital is:

$$\frac{(7.8 \times 1) + (18 \times 2)}{3} = 14.6\%$$

(ii) The net cost of debt is as before. The cost of equity is given by:

$$E = R_f \times \beta R$$

To determine

$$\beta = \text{corr}_{pi} \times \frac{\sigma_i}{\sigma_p}$$

$$= .7 \times \frac{20}{10}$$

$$= 1.4$$

Thus

$$E = 12 + (1.4 \times 4)$$
$$= 17.6\%$$

531

Weighted average cost of capital is

$$\frac{(7.8 \times 1) + (17.6 \times 2)}{3} = 14.33\%$$

One would expect the two methods to give similar results if the company's returns are expected to be perfectly correlated with those of the market.

(b) Determination of the rate of discount to be used for the new investment.

The cost of debt is as before i.e. 7.8%.

The cost of equity is $12 + 1.5 (16 - 12)$ $=$ $12 + 6$
$=$ 18%

New weighting is 1:3 so weighted average cost is

$$\frac{(7.8 \times 1) + (18 \times 3)}{4} = 15.45\%$$

(c) The chief difficulty in using the capital asset pricing model is that the value for beta is very difficult, in practice, to determine. It may also not be stable over time.

Question 43

Analysis

This is question requiring a miscellaneous collection of knowledge about the workings of markets and the implication for the financial manager. A knowledgeable candidate should easily pick up good marks here. There should be little time pressure as 36 minutes may be allocated.

Model solution

(a) The factors affecting security prices under the efficient market hypothesis in its semi-strong form consist of all the information publicly available concerning the market, the individual companies and the economy in general. The only type of information which is not taken into account by the market is that which is available only privately, i.e. insider information. Many people believe that, particularly since insider trading was made into a criminal offence, the semi-strong form of the efficient market hypothesis best describes the actual working of the market.

(b) The formula is: $E = \dfrac{d}{m} + g$

where   D is the initial dividend per share
           M is the market price of the share
           G is the rate of growth
           E is the ordinary shareholder's cost of capital

(c) Systematic risk in relation to the Capital Asset Pricing Model is that part of the total risk attaching to a particular investment which cannot be diversified away. This is because it is the risk deriving from the market as a whole to which all projects are subject. The systematic elements of all risks are positively correlated with one another.

(d) Arbitrage is that process of trading in shares which will create an appropriate equilibrium between them. Modigliani and Miller assumed it would take place in such a way that the value of a business and hence its cost of capital would be unrelated to the way in which it was financed. In practice transaction costs and the incidence of taxation will inhibit this process.

(e) A Forward Option Contract is one where the prospective purchaser of foreign currency is sold the right to purchase that currency on a specified future date at a rate of exchange determined at the present time. He has the choice of either letting the option lapse if it is better then to purchase the currency at the spot rate or to take it up if this is more favourable. The amount paid for the option is not, in any event, returnable.

Appendix 4: Further Examination Questions

Question 1

CIMA

Three companies, A, B and C are engaged in the same type of business within the United Kingdom. The business is to a certain extent cyclical, and from past experience profits before tax and loan interest are liable to fluctuate up to 25% in either direction from the current level.

Recent information about these companies is given below. Based on this data you are required to discuss, with appropriate calculations, the relative merits of the financing structure of the companies from the points of view of:

(a) equity investors;

(b) the company management.

Existing financing structure
Company A
2,160,000 Ordinary shares of £1 each
Reserves £3,000,000
Company B
4,359,200 Ordinary shares of 25 pence each
Reserves £2,910,000
£1,000,00010% Debentures 1980-2003
Company C
1,428,600 Ordinary shares of 40 pence each
Reserves £1,630,000
£3,000,000 7½% Unsecured Loan Stock 1983-88

Other Statistics

	A	Company B	C
Latest annual dividend per share, pence	4.00	1.25	1.50
Dividend cover	2.2x	2.6x	3.5x
Current market price per share (ex div), pence	80.00	26.00	31.50
Current market price of loan stock	–	£80	£60

The basic rate of corporation tax may be assumed to be 50% and the rate of advance corporation tax (ACT) to be 30%. The P.E. ratio of B Limited is the approximate median for the industry group.

(Total 25 marks)

Question 2 ACCA

The Laser Supply Company Limited produces a specialist lubricant – Lase – which is used in the manufacture of scientific instruments. The Standard Revenue/Cost of 100 gallons of Lase based on an annual output of 2,000,000 gallons is as follows:

	£	£
Standard Selling Price per 100 gallons		200
Standard Cost-		
120 gallons of Lubo at £1 per gallon	120	
10 hours of labour at £2.50 per hour	25	
Variable expenses	15	
Fixed expenses	20	180
Standard profit for 100 gallons		20

Lase requires highly specialist storage equipment and as the equipment available only allows a restricted amount to be kept in store the manufacture of Lase is normally only made to order. The marketing director is very keen that the company extend significantly its storage capacity so that it can accept special orders which would be met immediately from stock. He believes if this facility were available not only would the company sell another 1,000,000 gallons per annum but these special orders would have a significant selling price premium over what is obtained at present. The price premium is difficult to estimate with any certainty but the marketing director believes that it could be as high as 60% with the probability distribution taking the following form:

Selling Price Premium Over Standard %	Probability
0	0.30
10	0.30
20	0.15
30	0.10
40	0.05
50	0.05
60	0.05
70	-
80	-
90	-
100	-

Marketing of this facility would require additional sales promotion over and above that which appears in the standard cost schedule and this is estimated at £25,000 in the first year and £12,000 in the second year.

Fixed expenses in total would increase by 25% over budget if another 1,000,000 gallons were produced and sold.

Working capital required would also increase by £500,000, and in addition for the first three years increased bank overdraft facilities of £250,000 would be required. It is estimated that the average annual interest rate payable on this would be 12%. The marketing director has pointed out also the advantages of longer production runs which should enable the company to achieve some cost economies. The production figures for the most recent month are:

Amount produced	125,000 gallons
Material cost	£165,000 (150,000 gallons)
Labour cost	£37,500 (15,000 hours)
Variable overheads	£18,750

The total cost of the equipment including installation would be £1,500,000 with a nil scrap value and although it has a technical life of 12 years it is felt prudent to assess the project over a life of only two thirds of this.

The company has a target return on the capital of 20% before taxation, and in addition requires that all high risk projects pay for themselves within 5 years. Advise management on the financial implications of approving this project.

Note: Taxation can be ignored.

		15%	20%	24%
The present value of £1 due in	1 year	0.87	0.83	0.81
	2 years	0.76	0.69	0.65
	3 years	0.66	0.58	0.52
	4 years	0.57	0.48	0.42
	5 years	0.50	0.40	0.34
	6 years	0.43	0.34	0.28
	7 years	0.38	0.28	0.22
	8 years	0.33	0.23	0.18
	9 years	0.28	0.19	0.14
	10 years	0.25	0.16	0.12

(Total 25 marks)

Question 3   ACCA

The Biloxi Company is considering investing in a new plant which would enable it to increase its production of Floss, a fertilizer product. If the plant is constructed its operation is expected to increase the net after tax cash flow of Biloxi by £178,500 per annum. There would be no production after the plant's tenth year of life and the plant would have zero salvage value.

The cost of constructing the plant with all its support facilities would be £750,000.

The company is unsure whether to go ahead with the investment. A crucial factor in the decision is the risk associated with the project. In the past the company has not taken risk into account when evaluating an investment proposal, but this is a major project involving a significant capital outlay and the company wishes to be thorough in its analysis. The company seek your advice on the methods of allowing for risk in investment appraisal.

The company has already been given two conflicting pieces of advice. One suggestion is that a single discount rate, reflecting the average cost of capital of the company should be used for all investment decisions within the company. With this approach, the uncertainty can be allowed for in the probability estimates of the cash flow resulting from the project.

The other suggestion involves estimating the risk adjusted discount rate appropriate to the particular project under consideration. This approach has been formalised in the capital asset pricing model which can be used to estimate an appropriate discount rate. According to this suggestion it is the risk adjusted rate, the cost of capital appropriate to each project, that should be used to discount the returns expected to result from the project.

You are giving the following information:

(i) The after tax risk free rate of interest in the economy is 10%.

(ii) The expected rate of return on a market portfolio of investments is 15% .

(iii) The revenues and expenses associated with the sales and production of Floss are expected to be highly dependent on the state of the economy and industry; if the economy grows in a year by 10%, the sales and costs of Floss are expected to rise by 16% if there is a 10% downturn in the economy, the cash flow of Floss is expected to suffer by 16%.

(iv) The after tax weighted average cost of capital of Biloxi Ltd is estimated to be 16%.

(v) The probability distribution of the annual net cash flows arising from the production in the new plant and the sale of Floss is:

Probability	Net Cash Flows
0.30	0 – £149,999
0.50	£150,000 – £249,999
0.20	£250,000 – £300,000

Required:

(a) You are asked to offer specific advice to Biloxi Ltd., on the appropriate discount rate to use in the appraisal of the investment in the Floss plant. Illustrate your answer by using the data given in the question. (12 marks)

(b) Advise the company on alternative methods of allowing for risk in project appraisal. (8 marks)

(Total 20 marks)

Question 4   CIMA

(a) The current market price of the ordinary shares in A plc is £2.50. Earnings per share and dividends per share over the past five years have been as listed below. The directors have forecast that future dividends will increase at a rate of 10% per annum, though the market will not necessarily accept the validity of this forecast.

Year	Earnings per share after tax (pence)	Dividend per share – net (pence)
1	30.0	7.5
2	32.5	8.0
3	35.0	9.0
4	38.0	10.0
5	41.0	11.0

Taxation is to be ignored.

You are required to:

(i) state and explain the derivation of the dividend growth model used in calculating the cost of equity capital;

(ii) calculate and comment on the possible cost of equity capital for the above company;

(iii) comment on possible difficulties and limitations in the use of the dividend growth model, illustrating your answer by reference to the following alternative patterns of earnings and dividends per share:

Year	Alternative 1		Alternative 2	
	Earnings per share pence	Dividend per share pence	Earnings per share pence	Dividend per share pence
1	30.0	7.5	30.0	7.5
2	32.5	8.0	35.0	9.0
3	35.0	7.5	42.0	14.0
4	38.0	9.0	50.0	25.0
5	41.0	10.0	60.0	40.0

The market price of the shares at the end of Year 5 is still assumed to be £2.50 in each case.

(b) (i) State and explain the capital asset pricing model, used in calculating the cost of equity capital for a company.

(ii) Calculate the cost of capital for a company having a beta of 1.60, the estimated risk free rate of return before tax being 10%, and the expected market rate of return 19%.

(iii) Comment briefly on possible problems in applying the capital asset pricing model in practice.

(c) Summarise your own views on the usefulness and adequacy of alternative methods of calculating a company's cost of equity capital.

(Total 25 marks)

Question 5 ACCA

As the financial consultant of the Bourbon Can Company, a medium sized manufacturing business, you have been asked to advise on the current year's investment proposals. The proposed projects, shown below, are not mutually exclusive.

Project A

To replace the existing data processing equipment. Initial cost £250,000. Expected life of new equipment 6 years. Expected annual after tax cash inflow £72,500

Project B

To develop a new type of container. Cost £70,000. All to be incurred in the current year. Expected life of product 5 years. Expected annual after tax cash inflow £30,000, the inflows to commence in one year's time.

Project C

To install safety equipment. Initial cost £90,000. Expected life 3 years. Expected annual after tax cash inflow £45,000.

Project D

To construct a new factory building. Initial cost £210,000. Expected life 8 years. Expected annual after tax cash inflow £57,000.

Project E

To extend the existing loading equipment. Initial cost £170,000. Expected life 4 years. Expected annual after tax cash inflow £70,000.

Project F

To purchase patent rights to a new process. Initial cost £135,000. Expected life 7 years. Expected annual after tax cash inflow £36,000.

You may assume that with the exception of project B, all cash inflows would commence in the current year. For calculation purposes, you may assume that the annual cash inflows are always received on the last day of the year. Tax can be assumed to have been paid in the year in which the profits are earned.

The company's marginal cost of capital for the coming year is estimated at 16%. The company is, however, in a capital rationing situation and it estimates it will only have £600,000 to invest on capital projects in the current year.

Required:

(a) Which projects would you recommend the company to undertake? Give the reasons for your choice. (12 marks)

(b) What factors, if any, other than those given in the question, would you advise the company to consider before making a decision? (8 marks)

(Total 20 marks)

Question 6   ACCA

Oxlake plc has export orders from a company in Singapore for 250,000 china cups, and from a company in Indonesia for 100,000 china cups. The unit variable cost to Oxlake of producing china cups is 55 pence and unit sales price to Singapore is Singapore $2.862 and to Indonesia, 2,246 rupiahs. Both orders are subject to credit terms of 60 days, and are payable in the currency of the importers. Past experience suggests that there is 50% chance of the customer in Singapore paying 30 days late. The Indonesian customer has offered to Oxlake the alternative of being paid US $125,000 in 3 months time instead of payment in the Indonesian currency. The Indonesian currency is forecast by Oxlake's bank to depreciate in value during the next year by 30% (from an Indonesian viewpoint) relative to the $US.

	Foreign Exchange Rates (mid rates)		
	$Singapore/$US	$US/£	Rupiahs/£
Spot	2.1378	1.4875	2,481
1 month forward	2.1132	1.4963	No forward
2 months forward	2.0964	1.5047	market
3 months forward	2.0915	1.5105	exists

Assume that in the United Kingdom any foreign currency holding must be immediately converted into pounds sterling.

	Money Market Rates (% per year)	
	Deposit	*Borrowing*
UK clearing bank	6	11
Singapore bank	4	7
Euro-dollars	7.5	12
Indonesian bank	15	Not available
Euro-sterling	6.5	10.5
US domestic bank	8	12.5

These interest rates are fixed rates for either immediate deposits or borrowing over a period of two or three months, but the rates are subject to future movements according to economic pressures.

Required:

(a) Using what you consider to be the most suitable way of protecting against foreign exchange risk evaluate the sterling receipts that Oxlake can expect from its sales to Singapore and to Indonesia, without taking any risks.

All contracts, including foreign exchange and money market contracts, may be assumed to be free from the risk of default. Transactions costs may be ignored. (13 marks)

(b) If the Indonesian customer offered another form of payment to Oxlake, immediate payment in $US of the full amount owed in return for a 5% discount on the rupiah unit sales price, calculate whether Oxlake is likely to benefit from this form of payment.

(7 marks)

(c) Discuss the advantages and disadvantages to a company of invoicing an export sale in a foreign currency. (5 marks)

(Total 25 marks)

Question 7 CIMA

Certain organisational and policy adjustments may be made internally by a business for the purpose of minimising the effects of transactions in foreign currencies.

(a) A group of companies controlled from the United Kingdom includes subsidiaries in Belgium, France and the USA. It is forecast that at the end of the current month, inter-company indebtedness will be as follows:

The Belgian subsidiary will be owed 144,381,000 Belgian francs by the French subsidiary and will owe the USA subsidiary $1,060,070.

The French subsidiary will be owed 14,438,000 French francs by the USA subsidiary and will owe it $800,000.

It is a function of the central treasury department to net off inter-company balances as far as possible and to issue instructions for settlement of the net balances. For this purpose the relevant exchange rates in terms of £1 are: $1.415; French francs 10.215; Belgian francs 68.10.

You are required to calculate the net payments to be made in respect of the above balances and to state the possible advantages and disadvantages of such multilateral netting. (10 marks)

(b) **You are required to** explain the terms 'leading' and 'lagging' in relation to foreign currency settlements and state the circumstances under which this technique might be used. (5 marks)

(c) **You are required to** explain the procedures for matching foreign currency receipts and payments, having regard to the possibility that these might be on different time scales, and to state their possible advantages. (5 marks)

This question is concerned with internal techniques and does not require reference to methods involving external bodies, such as forward contracts, options or swaps. **(Total 20 marks)**

Question 8 ACCA

Feret Ltd., has ten million shares in issue and has been paying dividends at 10p per share for a number of years and with its existing business is expected to be able to continue to earn sufficient profits to enable it to pay such a dividend for the foreseeable future. The company has been offered a new contract which would take two years to complete and would involve Feret in an investment outlay of £500,000 in each of the next two years. The board plan to finance the investment by a reduction of dividend.

If the project is undertaken, when it is completed it will increase the earnings of the company above their expected level by £350,000 per annum for the foreseeable future.

The current market price of an equity share of Feret Ltd is £0.90. The yield on company debentures is 10%. The management of Feret believes that the market value of shares in the company is based on dividends. Taxation can be ignored.

Required:

(a) Would an announcement of a decision to reduce dividends with an explanation of why this was being done and with details of the proposed investment, lead to an increase or decrease in the current share price? Show calculations to justify your conclusion. (8 marks)

(b) Is it possible for an investor owning 100 shares in Feret Ltd who is dependent on the annual income from investments to increase his spending power during the next two years while still being able to maintain his spending potential in subsequent years? Illustrate your answer with appropriate figures. (6 marks)

(c) What are the implications of your analysis for dividend decision making? On what assumptions does your answer depend, and how might these deviate from what in fact happens in practice? (6 marks)
(Total 20 marks)

Question 9 ACCA

Green, plc operates in only one industry and all its projects are equally risky. An extract from Green's current balance sheet shows:

	£ million
Ordinary Share Capital – Authorised and Issued	
5 million shares at £4	20
Reserves	5
	25
Deferred Taxation	2
Long Term Debt – 9% Irredeemable Debentures	20
	47

Depreciation provisions amounting to £3 million are shown as a deduction from fixed assets.

Green has recently paid both the annual dividend to shareholders and the annual interest payable on the debentures. The ordinary shares each have a current market value of £9 (Ex Div.), whilst the debentures are quoted at £75 (Ex Int.) per cent.

The beta value for Green's equity has a best estimate of 1.4. Green has not changed its gearing ratio for several years.

The expected return on Green's debentures is generally agreed to be risk free and at the currently quoted price the debentures promise a gross (i.e. pre tax) yield to investors which equals the current risk free interest rate. The annual return on the stock market all share index is expected to be 5% above the risk free interest rate.

Green is profitable and subject to tax at a rate of 50%. Interest payments are a tax deductible expense which produce immediate tax relief, i.e. without any tax delay.

Bell, plc is not subject to taxation and has calculated its cost of equity and debt capital as follows:

	Total Amounts		Cost
	Book Values	Market Values	
	(£ million)	(£ million)	%
Equity- 10 million shares issued	50	80	15
Debt- Irredeemable debentures	20	20	10

Bell wishes to invest in a new project which will provide equal expected annual cash flows in perpetuity. Investment in the project can be at several different levels. The project will be financed entirely from the net proceeds of the issue of

3 million shares, issue costs £600,000

£6 million 10% debentures issued at par, issue costs £400,000.

Issue costs will be borne by Bell at the time the issue of securities is carried out.

The price and method of issuing shares are still not determined. Three specific possibilities are under consideration; these are:

(i) shares issued at their current market value;

(ii) shares issued to existing shareholders at a discount of 25% from current market value;

(iii) shares issued to entirely new shareholders at a discount of 25% from current market value.

The Financial Director estimates that, because of the additional risks involved, undertaking the project will increase the cost of all issued equity to 16% but will not alter the cost of debt.

Required:

(a) For Green

  (i) determine the expected weighted average cost of capital for use in appraising the after tax cash flows of Green's expansion projects; (6 marks)

  (ii) estimate, on the assumption that leverage has an effect on firm valuation only via the tax implications of debt interest, the expected cost of Green's equity capital if the firm were to continue its existing operations but become all equity financed. (3 marks)

(b) For each of the three possibilities concerning the issue price and method for Bell's new equity, determine the minimum expected internal rate of return required from the net investment in the proposed project if the wealth of the existing shareholders is not to be reduced. (10 marks)

(c) 'In recent years it has been rare for medium or long term debt to be issued at a fixed interest rate; a floating (or variable) rate of interest, usually a few percentage points different from some variable base interest rate, has become much more common.'

Briefly outline, from the viewpoint of corporate financial management, the main advantages and disadvantages of issuing floating rate debt.

Indicate how a firm which has medium or long term floating rate debt should incorporate the cost of debt in its weighted average cost of capital calculation. (6 marks)

(Total 25 marks)

Question 10 ACCA

Answer any two parts of this question. Each part carries equal marks.

Required:

(a) (i) Prepare a report advising a small company of the criteria that a bank is likely to use when considering a request for a loan. (7 marks)

(ii) The chairman of a company with a turnover of £5 million has stated that it is impossible for a company of this size to raise finance for a period of 15 years or more.

Required:

Briefly discuss how it might be possible for the company to raise funds for the desired period. (5½ marks)

(b) (i) Explain why the adjusted present value technique (APV) is sometimes advocated as being a more appropriate way of evaluating a project than net present value. (4 marks)

(ii) Bigoyte Inc is developing a new personal computer with an expected life of three years. The investment has a total initial cost of $283 million, or which $106 million will be provided from internally generated funds, $90 million from a rights issue and the remainder from a fixed rate term loan at 12% per year. The proportion represented by the term loan reflects the optimum debt capacity of the company.

Issue costs are estimated at 3½% for the rights issue and 1% for the term loan. Corporate taxes are payable at a rate of 40% on net operating cash flows in the year that the cash flows occur. The Treasury Bill yield is 9%, market return 14%, and an appropriate asset beta for the investment is believed to be 1.5.

	Project Net operating cash flows (after tax)		
Year	1	2	3
	$89 million	$198 million	$59 million

Additionally, a residual value of $28 million (after all taxes) is expected at the end of year three.

Required:

Estimate the adjusted present value of the investment and recommend if the investment should be undertaken.

($8\frac{1}{2}$ marks)

(c) (i) Your company wishes to raise new debt capital on the stock market. Your managing director has heard of warrants and traded options and suggests that an issue of debt accompanied by either attached warrants or traded options might be attractive to investors and have benefits for your company.

Required:

Discuss whether you consider your managing director's suggestion to be useful. (5 marks)

(ii) Several years ago Nopen plc issued 15% fifteen year loan stock with warrants attached. The warrants may be exercised at any time during the next four years and each warrant allows the purchase of one ordinary share at a price of 400 pence.

The company has also issued a 9% convertible debenture which is due for redemption at the par value of £100 in 5 years time. Conversion rights which are available at any time up to the redemption date allow the conversion of one debenture into 25 ordinary shares. The current market yield on straight debentures for a company of Nopen's risk class is 12% per year.

Required:

Estimate the minimum market price of a warrant and of a £100 convertible debenture if the current share price of Nopen is

(1) 300 pence;

(2) 420 pence;

(3) 500 pence.

Explain why the market price of a warrant or convertible debenture is likely to be more than the price that you have estimated. Taxation may be ignored. ($7\frac{1}{2}$ marks)

Total (25 marks)

Question 11 ACCA

There is concern within Cantan, plc about the impact of inflation on financial planning as well as its impact on both the availability, and desirability, of long term fixed interest debt finance.

There is also conflict over whether, in an inflationary environment cash flow forecasts for capital budgeting purposes should be expressed in today's money values, or in nominal terms i.e. including an adjustment for expected inflation.

Arguing in favour of using today's money values one non-executive director has stated 'To include estimates of future general inflation, or specific price changes, in the capital budgeting process merely increases the level of uncertainty to be appraised. Forecasts made in terms of today's money values reduce this uncertainty.'

Required:

(a) Describe the impact of inflation on

   (i) financial planning, and

   (ii) both the availability and desirability of long term fixed interest debt finance.

   Outline the advantages and risks of pursuing a policy of meeting all debt finance needs, including those of a long term nature, by borrowing only short term when inflation is high.   (14 marks)

(b) For each of the two stated approaches to the treatment of inflation in capital budgeting, advise Cantan of their

   (i) relative merits and disadvantages, and

   (ii) implications for the determination of the discount rate.

   Comment on the assertion of the non-executive director.

(10 marks)
(Total 24 marks)

Question 12 CIMA

The 1986 annual report of T plc., a company engaged in the leisure industry, states its objectives as: 'to adjust to new circumstances so as to preserve our service to our customers and to provide shareholders with steady capital and dividend growth prospects.'

The five-year financial summary contained in the report includes the following information:

	1986	1985	1984	1983	1982
	£000	£000	£000	£000	£000
Net revenue	12,203	10,433	9,346	7,727	7,055

Profit on ordinary activities	1,515	1,124	1,007	551	482
Less : Taxation	(621)	(511)	(424)	(181)	(225)
Extraordinary items			(385)	36	
	894	613	198	406	257
Dividends	210	176	160	134	114
Retained profits	684	437	38	272	143

Ordinary shareholders' funds:					
Issued share capital	840	840	840	420	420
Revaluation reserve	961	897	790	694	634
Profit and loss account	2,384	1,700	1,264	1,645	1,373
	4,185	3,437	2,894	2,759	2,427

The financial press dated 31 March 1987 provides the following share service information relating to T p.l.c. and seven other companies (A – G) in the same type of industry:

Company	Nominal value	Share price 1986/87 High	Low	Net Today	Div.	Cover Gross	Yield	P/E
T p.l.c.	25p	151	74	124	3.13	3.6	3.5	11.1
A p.l.c.	25p	318	176	318	8.5	2.7	3.8	13.9
B p.l.c.	25p	704	263	689	18.15	2.2	3.7	17.4
C p.l.c.	25p	462	219	459	9.5	1.9	2.9	25.8
D p.l.c.	25p	282	136	279	6.25	2.9	3.2	15.3
E p.l.c.	10p	99	27	97	2.0	3.5	2.9	14.0
F p.l.c.	10p	491.5	175	490	10.5	3.3	3.0	14.1
G p.l.c.	5p	82.5	31	82	2.05	2.6	3.5	15.6

You are required to

(a) appraise the company's objectives as stated;   (7 marks)

(b) relate those objectives to the information provided in the question;   (10 marks)

(c) compare the performance of T p.l.c. with that of its competitors.
                (8 marks)
                (Total 25 marks)

Question 13   CIMA

You are required to list and discuss four possible reasons why companies in the same type of business have different P/E ratios.

A recently published article referred to the P/E ratio as an 'attempt to value a company in terms of its earnings' and suggested that, from the point of view of an individual investor, this attempt involved a basic fallacy. In your answer comment on these views.

(Total 15 marks)

Question 14   CIMA

Whatever advantages were originally expected at the time of a merger or acquisition, circumstances may arise under which some form of demerger or divestment of activities may become desirable.

You are required to:

(a) suggest five possible circumstances under which such action might be taken;

(b) outline three ways in which the required results might be achieved, making reference where appropriate to any relevant provisions of the Companies Acts and to the practical problems involved;

(c) comment on the powers and duties of directors in relation to demerger or divestment decisions.   **(Total 20 marks)**

Question 15   ACCA

Kirkby, plc does not have any overseas projects but appraises all its UK projects by utilising both Accounting Rate of Return and Payback. Kirkby's management explain their preference for the two appraisal methods used by stating 'Accounting Rate of Return, based on average profit to initial investment, will indicate how each project will be reflected in the published accounts and will show its impact on our 'profit to capital employed' ratio; we do not undertake projects which will reduce this ratio. Payback indicates how long our money is at risk by determining the length of time it takes for the initial investment in the project to be repaid by the total of accounting profit plus depreciation'.

Both methods are applied on a pre tax basis as Kirkby's management argue 'A pre and post tax analysis differs only by the effect of the tax rate and this is outside the control of management. Hence tax should be excluded for practical project appraisal'.

Kirkby is subject to tax at a rate of 50% with a delay of 1 year. Kirkby has erratic profit levels and these are frequently insufficient to enable it to utilise in full all first year allowances at the earliest opportunity.

A recent small project appraised by Kirkby was the purchase of industrial equipment, eligible for 100% first year allowances, costing £90,000 which was expected to produce the following results:

	Per Year – Years 1 to 3	
	(£'000s)	(£'000s)
Sales		100
Incremental cash costs	50	
Depreciation	30	80
Annual Profit		20

The life of the project is 3 years and no salvage value is expected. Receipts from sales are 20% in year of sale and 80% in the following year. Cash costs arise in the year to which they relate.

Required:

Using the project whose details are given above as an example, if required, advise Kirkby of the practical and theoretical deficiencies of:

(a) its current appraisal techniques, and

(b) appraising projects on a pre, rather than post, tax basis.

(Total 8 marks)

Question 16 ACCA

The Thornton Company, a small sized manufacturing business, was experiencing a short term liquidity crisis at the end of 1979. Its management estimated that the company would need by the end of February 1980 an extra £100,000 of funds. It would be six months' time after receipt of the funds before it is able to repay. The company is already heavily in debt and its normal banker will not advance any more money. The company has made losses for the last two years and has unused capital allowances. Consequently it is not thought it will have any corporation tax to pay for a number of years. The accountant has suggested three possible short term solutions to the liquidity problem.

They are:

(a) A £100,000 short term loan at an annual interest rate of 18%.

This can be obtained from a local finance company, and no finding charge will need to be paid.

(b) The company could forgo the cash discounts it has been obtaining on its purchases of materials. The company purchases approximately £50,000 of materials each month, and has in the past been paying for these within a month of purchase and obtaining a 2% cash discount. The discounts are only offered for payment within 30 days. If Thornton takes longer than 90 days to pay it could endanger its relationship with suppliers.

(c) The company could factor its trade debtors. A factor has been found who will advance Thornton 75% of the value of the invoices, less the deduction of all factoring charges, immediately upon receipt of the invoices. The factor will take responsibility for collecting the debts, and pay over to the company the balance of the value of the invoices, upon receipt of the cash from customers.

On average Thornton's customers pay at the end of the first month following the month in which the sales took place. The average level of sales of Thornton is £150,000 per month and this level is expected to remain steady over the next year.

The factor's interest charge is 15% per annum on the amount of money advanced, calculated on a day-to-day basis. The factoring fee is a charge of 2% of the turnover of Thornton. Thornton estimate that as a result of the factor's managing the collection of debts, it will save on bad debts and the cost of credit control, an amount of £2,000 per month. Surprisingly the factor would enter into an agreement with Thornton to cover just the first six months of 1980. It would begin with the factoring of January 1980 sales. The company can use any surplus funds available to reduce its overdraft which is costing 1% per month.

Required:

(a) Advise the company as to which of these three alternatives is cheapest. (10 marks)

(b) Assuming Thornton enters into the factoring arrangement, using the information given in the question, show the cash flow position for each of the first nine months of 1980. (6 marks)

(c) What factors other than cost would you advise the company to take into account when deciding between these three alternatives?

(4 marks)
(20 marks)

Question 17 CIMA

X Limited is a family-controlled company formed in 1968 and engaged in the fabrication of metal products. Although its fortunes have fluctuated, it had shown an upward trend in sales and profitability up to the financial year 1977. This was based primarily on the considerable skills of its technical director who is a member of the family.

From that year however its increases in selling prices were greater than those of its main competitors and apparently, in consequence, it lost some of its major customers. In order to keep the plant fully occupied it accepted a number of major long-term contracts for high-quality work at prices which did not cover the full cost of production.

Extracts from the accounts of the business for the past four years, and the managing director's preliminary forecasts for 1980 and for 1981 (the year in which the special contracts will be completed) with explanatory notes are given in the table.

Y Limited is a quoted company which is in the same type of business as that traditionally carried on by X Limited. For a variety of reasons (possibly including a weakness in technical capability) Y Limited could be interested in acquiring X Limited. Its current rate of return on net assets employed is 25% before taxation, which could be regarded as normal for the type of business.

An extract from share information in the financial press relating to this company and to the industry group within which it operates is as follows:

	Price	Net Dividend	Cover	Yield gross	P/E
Y Limited	72	3.5	3.5	6.9	5.9
Industry group					
Median					6.3
Upper quartile					11.4
Lower quartile					3.0

It may be assumed that the notional P/E ratio for a private company would be about half that for a similar quoted company.

X Limited - Profit and Loss Statements

Note:

Trad. work = traditional work
Special = special long-term contracts

| | Extracts from accounts | | | | | | Forecasts | | | |
| | 1976 | 1977 | 1978 | | 1979 | | 1980 | | 1981 | |
	Trad. work	Trad. work	Trad. work	Special	Trad. work	Special	Trad. work	Special	Trad. work	Special
Sales										
Hours sold in thousands	162	160	125	50	115	60	96	80	100	72
Price per hour	£2.90	£3.20	£3.80	£5.00	£4.40	£5.00	£4.40	£5.00	£4.70	£5.00
	£000	£000	£000	£000	£000	£000	£000	£000	£000	£000
Amount	469	512	475	250	506	300	422	400	470	360
Direct Material	147	173	156	141	161	160	153	232	176	216
Direct Wages	93	96	85	35	81	42	72	66	85	61
Gross Margin	229	243	234	74	264	98	197	102	209	83
Overhead			308		362		299		292	
Factory general	114	125	140		160		180		190	
Special contract	--	--	30		50		50		30	
Depreciation general	16	19	17		17		20		22	
Other expenses	62	66	72		76		80		80	
Sub total	192	210	259		303		330		322	
Operating profit	37	33	49		59		(31)		(30)	
Interest payable	8	22	32		27		22		22	
Profit before tax	29	11	17		32		(53)		(52)	
Taxation	14	5	8		16		--		--	
Profit after tax	15	6	9		16		(53)		(52)	
Dividends	6	6	6		6		6		6	
Retained profit	9	--	3		10		(59)		(58)	

X Limited
Summary Balance Sheet as at 31st December, 1979

	£000's	£000's
Current assets		
Stock and work-in-progress:		
General	67	
Special contract	161	228
Debtors:		
General	44	
Special contract	50	94
Total		322
Current liabilities		
Trade creditors:		
General	27	
Special contract	26	
Taxation	16	
Dividends	3	
Bank overdraft	33	105
Net current assets		217
Fixed assets		
General plant and machinery, at cost	450	
Less : Depreciation	331	119
Net assets employed		336
Share capital: 40,000 Ordinary shares of £1 each		40
Reserves		146
		186
Loan capital		150
		336

Notes on X Limited

(i) Fixed assets are depreciated on a straight line basis at an average of 10% per annum, based on year-end values. During 1980 and 1981, fully depreciated assets to a value of £25,000 will be withdrawn from service.

Additional expenditure on fixed assets is forecast at £30,000 in 1980, and £20,000 in 1981.

(ii) The ratios from the 1979 accounts of:

   ❑ stocks, work-in-progress and trade creditors to direct material usage;

   ❑ debtors to invoices sales:

are expected to be maintained during 1980 and 1981 subject to the final completion of and payment for special contract work.

(iii) On a current cost basis the following figures in the 1976-1979 accounts would appear as follows:

	1976	1977	1978	1979
Fixed assets, at cost *less* depreciation				190
Depreciation charge for year	19	24	22	24
Stocks and work-in-progress				262
Direct material usage for year	154	182	315	347

(iv) There is no intention at present to raise further long term loans.

You are required:

(a) to set out the courses of action which might be open to X Limited, other than take-over by another company, bearing in mind its likely balance sheet position by the end of 1981;

(b) to suggest and comment on the several values which might be placed on the business of X Limited, as a basis for a take-over approach by Y Limited, stating clearly in each case the assumptions you have made;

(c) assuming that an agreed acquisition price was to be satisfied in part by an exchange of shares, to calculate the share for share ratio on which this might be effected;

(d) assuming that Y Limited decided to issue 15% loan stock in order to finance the acquisition for cash, to comment on any effect this approach could have on the price Y Limited would be willing to pay.

(Total 45 marks)

Question 18 ACCA

Summarised financial accounts for Skett plc are shown below:

Group consolidated profit and loss accounts

£m

	1982	1983	1984	1985	1986
Turnover	440	528	588	628	653
Operating profit	59	63	68	78	86
Net interest	14	15	20	24	31
Profit before tax	45	48	48	54	55
Taxation	14	15	18	19	21
	31	33	30	35	34
Extraordinary items	2	-	2	-	1
	29	33	28	35	33

	1982	1983	1984	1985	1986
Dividends	10	11	12	14	15
Retained earnings	19	22	16	21	18

Group consolidated balance sheets

	1982	1983	1984	1985	1986
Capital employed					
Ordinary shares					
(par value 50 pence)	95	95	95	95	95
Reserves	148	170	186	207	225
	243	265	281	302	320
Loan capital	66	81	99	113	145
	309	346	380	415	465
Use of capital					
Land, buildings,					
plant and					
equipment (net of					
depreciation)	194	212	223	223	231
Long-term investments	13	11	14	13	13
Fixed assets	207	223	237	236	244
Stock	160	186	198	218	248
Debtors	118	113	148	182	222
Cash	18	46	32	3	17
	296	345	378	403	487
Short-term loans[1]	62	66	71	44	71
Creditors	107	132	138	149	162
Taxation payable	16	14	15	18	19
Dividends	9	10	11	13	14
	194	222	235	224	266
Net current assets	102	123	143	179	221
	1982	1983	1984	1985	1986
Assets employed	309	346	380	415	465

[1]Loan capital as at the end of 1986	£m
Unsecured 16% loan 1989/91	49
14½% Debenture 1988	52
Secured variable rate term loan 1994	44
Bank overdraft	71

	1982	1983	1984	1985	1986
Average share price of					
Skett (pence)	184	167	195	220	235
Average PE ratio for					
Skett's industry	10	9	14	15	18

Additional notes:

(i) 85% of Skett's sales in 1986 were in the United Kingdom.

(ii) The company's long-term investments yield negligible returns.

(iii) The company is committed to a major capital expenditure in Spain during the next year, costing a total of £75 million. The investment is expected to have a life of at least 10 years.

(iv) The FT Ordinary Share Index has fallen by 75 points during the last month and the downward trend is expected to continue.

Required:

(a) Prepare a report detailing and commenting upon, the main features of the recent financial performance and current financial position of Skett plc. (15 marks)

State clearly any assumptions that you make.

(b) Discuss what strategy you would recommend for the company's future financing. (10 marks)

(Total 25 marks)

Question 19 CIMA

(a) At a time of historically high interest rates, the treasurer of W p.l.c. explains to you that any acquisitions or other new investments by the company are required to yield a rate of return at least as high as that from any alternative uses to which the money could be put.

You are required to explain the implications of this policy.

(5 marks)

(b) X plc has large liquid resources, currently invested at an average interest rate of $10\frac{1}{2}\%$.

The company's latest annual accounts have just been published, showing pre-tax earnings of £120 million on 470 million ordinary shares. Immediately following publication, the Stock Exchange price of the shares stands at 213 pence. The company decides to repurchase 37.5 million of its own shares for cash at that price. You are required to comment on the likely financial implications of this decision. (8 marks)

(c) Y p.l.c., in its annual report, has announced the following financial policies:

(i) to increase earnings per share by 5% per annum;

(ii) to achieve an annual return on assets of 25%;

(iii) dividend cover to be not more than three times;

557

(iv) the ratio of debt to equity not to exceed 50%;

(v) interest charges to be covered six times by trading profit.

During the year covered by the report, assets totalling £1,200,000 were financed by debt £400,000 and ordinary shareholders' funds £800,000. There were 500,000 ordinary shares in issue. Profit before interest was £300,000 and dividends were covered exactly three times.

You are required to review the operation of policies (i) to (v) above from the points of view of their desirability, practicability and internal consistency, illustrating your answer with reference to the data given, where appropriate. (12 marks)

Note: Where appropriate, the rate of corporation tax may be assumed to be 35%. **(Total 25 marks)**

Question 20 CIMA

(a) The table below shows representative figures for the FT-Actuaries Industrial Group share index for the years 1975 – 1983, together with estimated P/E ratios (net) and the earnings index corresponding to those ratios. Movements each year in the London Clearing Banks Base Rate (or previous equivalent) are also given.

Year	FT-Actuaries industrial share index	PE ratio	Earnings index	Base interest rate
1975	152	10.1	15.0	Year end: 11.25%
1976	143	8.2	17.4	Declined to 9% (March) then rose to 14.25%
1977	209	8.9	23.5	Declined to 5% (October) November: 7%
1978	217	8.0	27.1	Increased to 12.5% (November)
1979	207	6.5	31.8	Around 13%, then 17% (November)
1980	255	7.7	33.1	Fell in July (16%), November: 14%
1981	292	10.5	27.8	12% until September, then around 15%
1982	396	11.9	33.3	Declined to 9% (November), then 10%
1983	462	13.1	35.3	Declined to 9% (October)

(a) **You are required to** comment on any relationships that might exist between earnings and share prices, both for the stock market as a whole and for individual companies, and on the factors that might influence such relationships. Use the data in the above table to illustrate your answer. (12 marks)

(b) **You are required to** explain and exemplify how the P/E ratio can be used to determine whether a company's shares appear to be under- or over-valued for the purposes of long-term or short term decisions to invest in the company. (7 marks)

(c) **You are required to** explain two ways in which the cost-of equity capital for a particular company might be calculated on the basis of earnings, and to comment on the theoretical soundness of this approach to share valuation. (6 marks)

(Total 25 marks)

Question 21 ACCA

(a) Discuss the factors that might influence a company's choice of dividend policy. (10 marks)

(b) The managing directors of three profitable listed companies discussed their companies' dividend policies at a business lunch.

Company A has deliberately paid no dividends for the last five years.

Company B always pays a dividend of 50% of earnings after taxation.

Company C maintains a low but constant dividend per share (after adjusting for the general price index), and offers regular scrip issues and shareholder concessions.

Each managing director is convinced that his company's policy is maximising shareholder wealth.

Required:

What are the advantages and disadvantages of the alternative dividend policies of the three companies? Discuss the circumstances under which each managing director might be correct in his belief that his company's dividend policy is maximising shareholder wealth. State clearly any assumptions that you make. (15 marks)

(Total 25 marks)

Question 22 CIMA

You are required to discuss the extent to which the concept of maximisation of wealth is relevant to the formulation of company financial objectives. In doing this, you should make reference to a valuation formula based on dividend growth and to the importance of statistics of earnings per share. **(Total 25 marks)**

Question 23 CIMA

The following data are based on an extract from the 'share service' pages of the financial press:

Stock	Price	Dividend net	Cover	Yield gross	P/E
ABC 25p	260	7.2	2.8	3.8	12.7

(a) **You are required to**

   (i) explain how 'Yield gross' has been calculated;

   (ii) calculate (to the nearest £10,000) the figure of earnings that would have been disclosed in the company's latest published financial statements, on the assumption that this company has 12,165,000 shares in issue;

   (iii) explain why statistics of earnings per share could be important to investors and also to the company. (12 marks)

(b) In view of the world-wide collapse of share prices in October 1987, you are required to discuss the significance of P/E ratios as a basis for business valuation. (7 marks)

(c) You are required to suggest possible reasons why some public limited companies have recently decided to convert into private companies. (6 marks)

(Total 25 marks)

Question 24 CIMA

It has been stated that one of the objectives of financial management should be to obtain a steady rate of increase in earnings per share.

The achievement of such a trend will obviously be affected by factors external to the business, by the structure of its operating costs and by its capital gearing having regard to the cost of its debt capital.

You are required to:

(a) exemplify these various factors, making use of the data given on the previous page relating to A Limited and B Limited.

(A Limited is a relatively small company engaged in the erection of structural steel work, while B Limited is a manufacturer of ladies' footwear.)

(b) discuss the financial management of the companies so far as possible from the figures provided.

Question 25 **CIMA**

(a) You are required to state what you understand by the term 'convertible bond'; and explain in detail four circumstances under which a convertible bond issue might be made. (13 marks)

(b) You are required to explain:

(i) the difference between national and international capital markets;

(ii) the nature of Euromarkets, and the reasons for their popularity;

(iii) the terms used in the following extract from the financial press: 'X Ltd, a New Zealand company, made a successful foray into the Eurobond markets with a $100m 10-year convertible bond. The lead manager indicated a 12.5% coupon and a 94.5 price. Investors were attracted by put options after three, four and five years.' (12 marks)

(Total 25 marks)

Question 26 **ACCA**

The board of directors of Oxclose, plc is considering making an offer to purchase Satac Ltd, a private limited company in the same industry. If Satac is purchased it is proposed to continue operating the company as a going concern in the same line of business.

Summarised details from the most recent financial accounts of Oxclose and Satac are shown below:

	Oxclose plc Balance Sheet as at 31 March (£ millions)		Satac Ltd Balance Sheet as at 31 March (£000s)	
Freehold property		33		460
Plant and equipment (net)		58		1,310
Stock	29		330	
Debtors	24		290	
Cash	3		30	
Less : Current liabilities	(31)	25	(518)	122
		116		1,892
Financed by				
Ordinary shares[1]		35		160
Reserves		43		964
Shareholders' equity		78		1,124
Medium term bank loans		38		768
		116		1,892

[1]Oxclose plc 50 pence ordinary shares, Satac Ltd 25 pence ordinary shares.

Year[2]	Oxclose plc (£millions)		Satac Ltd (£000s)	
	Profit after tax	Dividend	Profit after tax	Dividend
t – 5	14.30	9.01	143	85
t – 4	15.56	9.80	162	93.5
t – 3	16.93	10.67	151	93.5
t – 2	18.42	11.60	175	102.8
t – 1	20.04	12.62	183	113.1

[2]t – 5 is five years ago, t – 1 the most recent year etc.

Satac's shares are owned by a small number of private individuals. The company is dominated by its managing director who receives an annual salary of £80,000, double the average salary received by managing directors of similar companies. The managing director would be replaced if the company is purchased by Oxclose.

The freehold property of Satac has not been revalued for several years and is believed to have a market value of £800,000.

The balance sheet value of plant and equipment is thought to fairly reflect its replacement cost, but its value if sold is not likely to exceed £800,000. Approximately £55,000 of stock is obsolete and could only be sold as scrap for £5,000.

The ordinary shares of Oxclose are currently trading at 430 pence ex-div. It is estimate that because of difference in size, risk and other factors the required return on equity by shareholders of Satac is approximately 15% higher than the required return on equity of Oxclose's shareholders (i.e. 115% of Oxclose's required return). Both companies are subject to corporate taxation at a rate of 40%

Required:

(a) Prepare estimates of the value of Satac using three different methods of valuation, and advise the board of Oxclose plc as to the price or possible range of prices, that it should be prepared to offer to purchase Satac's shares. (12 marks)

(b) Briefly discuss the theoretical and practical problems of the valuation methods that you have chosen. (6 marks)

(c) Discuss the advantages and disadvantages of the various terms that might be offered to the shareholders of a potential 'victim' company in a takeover situation. (7 marks)

(Total 25 marks)

Appendix 5: Glossary

Abandonment value The value which a project would have if it were abandoned. It will include any proceeds from the sale of fixed assets or stocks and any savings of costs which can be avoided by abandoning the project.

Arbitrage That process whereby market forces will restore equilibrium should investment in one security be temporarily more attractive than investment in another. The existence of arbitrage is an important component in the Modigliani/Miller theory of capital structure.

Beta or β factor A measure of the portfolio effect of a proposed investment. It is helpful in determining the extent to which the addition of the investment to the portfolio will affect overall portfolio risk. A low value for β implies that overall portfolio risk will be lowered by its addition. This may occur even if the project has a high individual risk attaching to it.

Break-even chart A diagram exhibiting a schedule of possible relationships between revenues and costs. From it can be deduced the profit expected at any given level of output and also the break-even point – that level of output at which neither profit nor loss is made.

Budget A plan stated in financial terms. A budget is established in advance of a financial period in a form which enables actual results to be compared with the plan on a regular basis. This facilitates the monitoring of progress and the correction of divergences from the plan.

Capital allowance The amount which a business is permitted to charge against revenues in respect of capital expenditure when calculating its taxable profit. It appears in place of depreciation.

Capital asset pricing model This is a model of diversification in investment which seeks to evaluate additions to a portfolio of investment projects in terms of the effect they will have on overall portfolio risk. Thus risk reducing (i.e. inversely correlated) projects are favoured, other things being equal, over others.

Capital budgeting The process whereby decisions are taken on how capital funds shall be deployed. It includes the appraisal of proposed investment projects by reference to their expected returns and to the cost of capital.

Capital rationing This exists where some artificial constraint is placed on the investment of funds. It implies that some profitable projects are forgone because the constraint prevents funds from being allocated to them.

Capital structure The term refers to the particular combination of components of financing which a business uses. Share capital, reserves and loan capital all form part of the capital structure although the basic division is that between equity and debt. The importance of capital structure is the effect it may have on the overall cost of capital and its relevance to the risks borne by equity holders.

Contribution The surplus which revenues show over directly attributable costs. The contribution must first be applied in meeting unattributable fixed cost after which it becomes available as profit.

Corporation tax A tax on the profits of incorporated businesses and other organisations. The rate is varied from time to time by the government but stands at around 35% of the taxable profit. Its importance to the financial manager is that the tax rules have a substantial influence on the pattern of cash flows from a project as well as on their size.

Cost of capital The rate of return which a company must offer in order to attract funds. This will vary between one company and another and between one source of funds and another. The overall cost of capital is the weighted average of the costs of capital from individual sources.

Current cost accounting A system of accounting in which valuations (of assets and of inputs to the profit and loss account) are based on current cost rather than on historic cost. It is widely advocated as a system which overcomes many of the distortions caused to conventional accounting statements by inflation. Its principles underlay SSAP 16 now, however, withdrawn.

Current purchasing power A system of accounting for inflation in which indices are used to restate historic cost valuation in terms of a currency unit having a purchasing power equal to that which it has at the accounting date. Its principles underlie the now withdrawn SSAP7

Current ratio The relationship between current assets and current liabilities. It is a measure of a business's short term solvency.

Debt A term referring to borrowed funds used as a source of finance. It is a characteristic of debt that there is a contractual obligation to pay interest and to repay principal which is not related to profits earned.

Discounted cash flow This is the cash flow expected to arise from a project as discounted to allow for the time which has to elapse before the flow is received. The sum of the components of a discounted cash flow make up the total present value.

Diversification The spreading of a business's activities into numerous unrelated fields. When used scientifically (as in the capital asset pricing model) diversification is a method of reducing overall risk.

Dividend That part of the profit of a company which is distributed to its shareholders. It is common for a company regularly to retain some proportion of its profits to finance expansion.

Earnings per share The total earnings, net of tax, attributable to equity divided by the number of shares. It is the subject of an accounting standard, SSAP 3.

Economic order quantity The size of regular order required for an item of stock in order to minimise the combined cost of holding the stock and of processing orders.

Efficient market A market which responds instantly and fully to all information as it becomes available. In an efficient market, such as the stock exchange, prices follow a 'random walk' and their future course cannot be predicted.

Equity The risk bearing capital of a business. The equity holder is entitled to a share in the outcomes of the venture both as regards his income and as regards his capital (on a winding up).

Expected return The average, weighted by their probabilities, of the possible returns from a project. The calculation of expected return is one way in which the risk inherent in a project can be allowed for.

Financial risk That risk borne by equity holders over and above commercial risk and arising from the existence of debt. Debt holders have a prior fixed charge over profits in respect of their interest and this magnifies the variations in the amount attributable to equity holders.

Fixed cost A cost which does not vary with the level of output.

Gearing A measure of the extent to which a business relies on debt finance. In a highly geared company (relatively high debt) fluctuations in profits attributable to equity holders are magnified. This makes the return to equity more risky.

Gross profit rate The proportion which gross profit bears to sales. It is regarded as an important measure of the effectiveness of the basic profit earning process of the business.

Inflation The phenomenon of generally rising prices, i.e. a general decline in the purchasing power of money. It is basically an economic problem but has an impact on financial management and accounting because these are based on measurements made in terms of money.

Internal rate of return The rate of return on invested capital given by a project. It is determined as the rate of discount required to give a net present value of nil.

Leasing A method of financing fixed assets coming from that group of sources known as off balance sheet. The asset, instead of being acquired by its user, is purchased by an investment company which then leases (rents) the asset to its ultimate user. The user thus substitutes a flow of lease payments for a lump sum payment of capital.

Mutually exclusive projects Projects such that investment in one precludes investment in another regardless of its profitability or of the availability of funds. Alternative uses for the same plot of land would be an example of a set of mutually exclusive projects.

Off balance sheet finance Finance provided in such a way that its source does not appear as a liability on the balance sheet. Leasing and debt factoring are examples of such sources of finance.

Pay back method A method of appraising a proposed capital project which concerns itself with the period of time over which the initial capital investment will be recovered. It is a rough and ready method of project selection which takes no account of ultimate profitability.

Present value The value attached at the present time to the expectation of a stream of future cash flows. It is determined by discounting the cash flows at some appropriate rate to allow for the period of waiting until they are received.

Price/Earnings ratio The relationship between the market price of a share in a company and the earnings attributable to that share. It is calculated to aid decisions on whether or not to purchase or sell shares in a company.

Relevant cost A cost which will be affected by a decision and which is thus relevant to it. Broadly speaking it is variable and other directs costs which are relevant to a decision.

Sensitivity analysis This is used to identify those components in projected cash flows in which variations have the most profound effect on ultimate profit. These sensitive elements may then be given special attention in the formulation of forecasts.

Synergy The extra value attaching to a summation of parts which did not exist in the individual components. When two companies merge the hope is that synergy will make the group more valuable than the total value of its members before merger.

Variable cost A cost which varies proportionately with the level of output.

Appendix 6: Discounted cash flow tables

The figures in the body of the table give the discount factor to three places of decimals (decimal point omitted) for cash receivable at the indicated future times and at the indicated rate of discount.

Years	Rate of discount (%)									
	1	2	3	4	5	6	7	8	9	10
1	990	980	971	962	952	943	935	926	917	909
2	980	961	943	925	907	890	873	857	842	826
3	971	942	915	889	864	840	816	794	772	751
4	961	924	888	855	823	792	763	735	708	683
5	951	906	863	822	784	747	713	681	650	621
6	942	888	837	790	746	705	666	630	596	564
7	933	871	813	760	711	665	623	583	547	513
8	923	853	789	731	677	627	582	540	502	467
9	914	837	766	703	645	592	544	500	460	424
10	905	820	744	676	614	558	508	463	422	386
11	896	804	722	650	585	527	475	429	388	350
12	887	788	701	625	557	497	444	397	356	319
13	879	773	681	601	530	469	415	368	326	290
14	870	758	661	577	505	442	388	340	299	263
15	861	743	642	555	481	417	362	315	275	239
16	853	728	623	534	458	394	339	292	252	218
17	844	714	605	513	436	371	317	270	231	198
18	836	700	587	494	416	350	296	250	212	180
19	828	686	570	475	396	331	277	232	194	164
20	820	673	554	456	377	312	258	215	178	149
21	811	660	538	439	359	294	242	199	164	135
22	803	647	522	422	342	278	226	184	150	123
23	795	634	507	406	326	262	211	170	138	112
24	788	622	492	390	310	247	197	158	126	102
25	780	610	478	375	295	233	184	146	116	092

Years	Rate of discount (%)									
	11	12	13	14	15	16	17	18	19	20
1	901	893	885	877	870	862	855	847	840	833
2	812	797	783	769	756	743	731	718	706	694
3	731	712	693	675	658	641	624	609	593	579
4	659	636	613	592	572	552	534	516	499	482
5	593	567	543	519	497	476	456	437	419	402
6	535	507	480	456	432	410	390	370	352	335
7	482	452	425	400	376	354	333	314	296	279
8	434	404	376	351	327	305	285	266	249	233
9	391	361	333	308	284	263	243	225	209	194
10	352	322	295	270	247	227	208	191	176	162
11	317	287	261	237	215	195	178	162	148	135
12	286	257	231	208	187	168	152	137	124	112
13	258	229	204	182	163	145	130	116	104	093
14	232	205	181	160	141	125	111	099	088	078
15	209	183	160	140	123	108	095	084	074	065
16	188	163	141	123	107	093	081	071	062	054
17	170	146	125	108	093	080	069	060	052	045
18	153	130	111	095	081	069	059	051	044	038
19	138	116	098	083	070	060	051	043	037	031
20	124	104	087	073	061	051	043	037	031	026
21	112	093	077	064	053	044	037	031	026	022
22	101	083	068	056	046	038	032	026	022	018
23	091	074	060	049	040	033	027	022	018	015
24	082	066	053	043	035	028	023	019	015	013
25	074	059	047	038	030	024	020	016	013	010

Years	Rate of discount (%)									
	21	22	23	24	25	26	27	28	29	30
1	826	820	813	806	800	794	787	781	775	769
2	683	672	661	650	640	630	620	610	601	592
3	564	551	537	524	512	500	488	477	466	455
4	467	451	437	423	410	397	384	373	361	350
5	386	370	355	341	328	315	303	291	280	269
6	319	303	289	275	262	250	238	227	217	207
7	263	249	235	222	210	198	188	178	168	159
8	218	204	191	179	168	157	148	139	130	123
9	180	167	155	144	134	125	116	108	101	094
10	149	137	126	116	107	099	092	085	078	073
11	123	112	103	094	086	079	072	066	061	056
12	102	092	083	076	069	062	057	052	047	043
13	084	075	068	061	055	050	045	040	037	033
14	069	062	055	049	044	039	035	032	028	025
15	057	051	045	040	035	031	028	025	022	020
16	047	042	036	032	028	025	022	019	017	015
17	039	034	030	026	023	020	017	015	013	012
18	032	028	024	021	018	016	014	012	010	009
19	027	023	020	017	014	012	011	009	008	007
20	022	019	016	014	012	010	008	007	006	005
21	018	015	013	011	009	008	007	006	005	004
22	015	013	011	009	007	006	005	004	004	003
23	012	010	009	007	006	005	004	003	003	002
24	010	008	007	006	005	004	003	003	002	002
25	009	007	006	005	004	003	003	002	002	001

Index